NEW HEAVEN AND NEW EARTH
PROPHECY AND THE MILLENNIUM

SUPPLEMENTS

TO

VETUS TESTAMENTUM

EDITED BY
THE BOARD OF THE QUARTERLY

VOLUME LXXVII

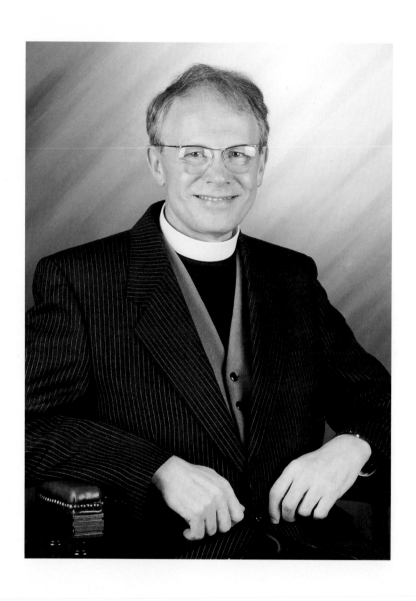

NEW HEAVEN AND NEW EARTH PROPHECY AND THE MILLENNIUM

ESSAYS IN HONOUR OF ANTHONY GELSTON

EDITED BY

P.J. HARLAND

AND

C.T.R. HAYWARD

BRILL
LEIDEN · BOSTON · KÖLN
1999

This book is printed on acid-free paper.

Library of Congress Cataloging-in-Publication Data

New heaven and new earth-prophecy and the millennium : essays in
honour of Anthony Gelston / edited by P.J. Harland and C.T.R.
Hayward.
     p.   cm. — (Supplements to Vetus Testamentum, ISSN 0083–5889 ;
v. 77)
   "Publications of Anthony Gelston" : p.
   Includes bibliographical references and index.
   ISBN 9004108416 (cl. : alk. paper)
   1. Bible—Prophecies. 2. Millennialism.   I. Gelston, A.
II. Harland, P.J.   III. Hayward, Robert, 1948-   .   IV. Series.
BS410.V452   vol. 77
[BS647.2]
210.1'5—dc21
                                  99-30452
                                            CIP

Die Deutsche Bibliothek - CIP-Einheitsaufnahme

New heaven and new earth - prophecy and the millennium:
essays in honour of Anthony Gelston / ed. by P.J. Harland and C.T.R.
Hayward. – Leiden ; Boston ; Köln : Brill, 1999
   (Supplements to Vetus testamentum ; Vol. 77)
   ISBN 90-04-10841-6
[Vetus testamentum / Supplements]
  Supplements to Vetus testamentum. - Leiden ; Boston ; Köln :
Brill
   Früher Schriftenreihe
   Reihe Supplements zu: Vetus Testamentum
   ISSN 0083-5889
Vol. 77. New heaven and new earth - prophecy and the millennium.-
1999

Photograph by David Antony, Sunderland

ISSN   0083-5889
ISBN   90 04 10841 6

CONTENTS

FOREWORD

This collection of essays is offered to Tony Gelston with the respect, affection, and gratitude of his many friends, who have appreciated and benefited both from his gifts as a fine tutor and supervisor, as well as from his many meticulous scholarly writings, which span a period of some forty years. He will celebrate his sixty-fifth birthday in the year 2000, and this *Festschrift* therefore represents a birthday tribute to a fine scholar. That same year, however, has been designated by British, European, and North American governments as the beginning of the third Millennium, despite protests from mathematicians and purists that the new century properly begins with the year 2001. The editors of this volume have bowed to the apparently inevitable: the year 2000 will celebrate the new Millennium, purists notwithstanding; and the *Festschrift* for Tony Gelston should, they felt, in some measure share public concern with the future, the new century, and the ultimate destiny of the planet. It soon became clear that the themes of the future and "the end", which have long occupied students of the Hebrew Bible, were entirely appropriate for a book honouring Tony Gelston, and for a number of different reasons.

First, Tony's scholarly work is perhaps best known for its scrupulous accuracy and attention to detail. Such accuracy in and of itself is the mark of the true scholar down the ages. It is of some particular interest for this volume, however, since in years gone by it was often the hallmark of those who searched the Bible for detailed information about God's plan for the future of the world, for weal or woe. A number of the essays in this collection remind the reader that both ancient and early modern interpreters of the Hebrew Bible have found therein a code which (so they understood) might be accurately deciphered to yield hard facts about the future of the cosmos. This is a matter of enduring significance touched upon in the essays by Graham Davies, David Lane, Loren Stuckenbruck, Linda Munk, and finally by Sheridan Gilley, who offers a serious yet gently humorous critique of this old, yet seemingly ever new tendency on the part of certain exegetes to find the future written down to the smallest details in the pages of the Hebrew Scriptures.

Secondly, precise knowledge of the exact words of the Biblical text is a prerequisite for those who would elucidate its message about the future and the end. Textual criticism of the Hebrew Bible has ever been one of Tony Gelston's enthusiasms. It is only right that it should be represented here with an essay by Hugh Williamson, as well as featuring in contributions from John Healey, Peter Harland, and John Rogerson, all of whom seek in addition to elucidate aspects of hopes for the future expressed by the Hebrew prophets Deutero-Isaiah (so Hugh Williamson), Hosea (John Healey), Ezekiel (Peter Harland), and Malachi (John Rogerson), and thereby pay tribute to Tony Gelston's long-standing interest in the study of prophecy in general and the "writing prophets" in particular. Ronald Clements continues the theme of prophetic concern for the future with an essay on First Isaiah's oracles which addresses the modern pre-occupation with ecology: he strikes a contemporary note which is taken up in other essays, and to which we shall return at the end of this introduction.

Lest it be thought, however, that concern for the future, or indeed Tony Gelston's scholarly endeavours, were restricted to the prophetic literature, treatments of our theme in other writings of the Hebrew Bible are not overlooked in this book. Thus Walter Moberly's essay takes us to the Pentateuch, and analyses the character of Balaam as he came to predict Israel's destiny; Piet Dirksen provides an essay on the Chronicler's hopes for the future of Israel; John Gibson expounds Job's famous utterance about his 'redeemer'; and Mark Vincent asks whether the present form of the Psalter betrays an eschatological interest on the part of the redactors. Since some of the most significant writings in the Hebrew Bible which relate to the future are transmitted to us under the pen-names of great worthies of the past, the problem of pseudonymous authorship is ever present: it is addressed here in a challenging essay by Stuart Weeks. Margaret Barker brings forward the discussion of the future into the period of the New Testament, exploring the interpretation of the Bible assumed by the author of the Johannine Apocalypse.

Finally, from the beginning of his scholarly career, Tony Gelston has been well known as one of a relatively small band of English enthusiasts who have devoted themselves to the study of the Syriac version of the Bible and Syriac ecclesiastical literature. Celebrating his impressive contributions to this area of research are essays by David Lane and Loren Stuckenbruck, both of whom treat of post-biblical Syriac writers and their hopes for future times arising from their studies of the Scriptures. To underline the importance which Tony Gelston granted to studies of post-biblical themes, his learning in the Wisdom literature, the Aramaic Targum, and the so-called Apocrypha is celebrated further in the essays by James Aitken, Robert Hayward, and Alan Millard. Not least do these essays bear witness to Tony's wide range of interests and academic expertise.

It has already been suggested that some of the essays in this book address topics which exercise the thoughts of modern men and women who rarely, if ever, read the Bible. Three examples will have to suffice. The essay of Ronald Clements should challenge ecologists (a powerful group in modern Western society) to consider the Hebrew Bible seriously as they plan for the future, whatever their political or religious convictions. John Rogerson's essay, however, speaks to the professional scholar, stressing the value of the relatively 'new' discipline of sociology in study of the Bible, a value which is sure to increase with the coming century. Finally, Linda Munk's paper is a timely reminder that the Hebrew Bible remains what it always has been: the sacred Scripture of the Jewish people, whose use by Christians demands respect and reverence as well as responsibility. These, and other weighty matters addressed in this book, reach out to a world beyond the academy, and thereby serve also to celebrate Tony Gelston's life as an Anglican priest-scholar, for whom study and learning, worship and everyday life make up one inseparable whole.

There are a number of people whom the editors wish to thank for their assistance in the production of this volume. We are grateful to Professor Linda Munk for the advice which she gave when we were planning the book. Staff at the Cambridge University Computing Service gave valuable assistance with converting material on disk, and Cambridge University Library and the Libraries of the Faculties of Divinity and Oriental Languages provided ideal environments for checking references etc. We should like to thank those in the Department of Theology at the University of Durham who helped with typing. Above all we are grateful to Brill for publishing this book.

Peter Harland   Robert Hayward
Cambridge   Durham

ABBREVIATIONS

ANET	J.B. Pritchard, (ed.), *Ancient Near Eastern Texts Relating to the Old Testament*, (3rd edition, Princeton, 1969)
AOAT	Alter Orient und Alten Testament
ATD	Das Alte Testament Deutsch
AV	Authorised Version
BASOR	*Bulletin of the American Schools of Oriental Research*
BCAT	Biblischer Commentar über das Alte Testament
BCE	Before the Common Era
BDB	F. Brown, S.R. Driver and C.A. Briggs, *A Hebrew and English Lexicon of the Old Testament* (Oxford, 1906)
BHS	Biblica Hebraica Stuttgartensia
Bib	*Biblica*
BN	*Biblische Notizen*
BZAW	Beihefte zur Zeitschrift für die alttestamentliche Wissenschaft
CBQ	*Catholic Biblical Quarterly*
CD	Damascus Document from Qumran
CE	Common Era
CSCO	Corpus Scriptorum Christianorum Orientalium
DJD	*Discoveries in the Judean Desert*
DSD	*Dead Sea Discoveries*
ET	English Translation
ET	*Expository Times*
ETS	*Ephemerides theologicae lovanienses*
FOTL	The Forms of Old Testament Literature
FTP	Fragment Targum according to Ms. Paris Bibliothèque nationale Héb. 110
FTV	Fragment Targum according to Ms. Vatican Ebr. 440
GK	*Gesenius' Hebrew Grammar as Edited and Enlarged by the Late E. Kautzsch* (2nd edition, Oxford, 1910)
GNB	Good News Bible
HAL	Hebräisches und Aramäisches Lexikon zum Alten Testament
HAT	Handbuch zum Alten Testament
HTR	*Harvard Theological Review*
ICC	International Critical Commentary
JAOS	*Journal of the American Oriental Society*
JB	Jerusalem Bible
JBL	*Journal of Biblical Literature*
JEA	*Journal of Egyptian Archaeology*

JJS	*Journal of Jewish Studies*
JM	P. Jouön and T. Muraoka, *A Grammar of Biblical Hebrew* (Rome, 1991)
JPS	Jewish Publication Society
JSJ	*Journal for the Study of Judaism*
JSOT	*Journal for the Study of the Old Testament*
JSOTSS	Journal for the Study of the Old Testament Supplement Series
JSP	*Journal for the Study of the Pseudepigrapha*
JSPSS	Journal for the Study of the Pseudepigrapha Supplement Series
JSS	*Journal of Semitic Studies*
JTS	*Journal of Theological Studies* (New Series)
KTU	Keilalphabetischen Texte aus Ugarit, M. Dietrich (ed.), (Neukirchen-Vluyn, 1996)
LXX	Septuagint
MT	Masoretic Text
NEB	New English Bible
NIV	New International Version
NRSV	New Revised Standard Version
NTS	*New Testament Studies*
OBO	*Orbis Biblicus et Orientalis*
OCA	*Orientalia Christiana Analecta*
OCP	*Orientalia Christiana Periodica*
Or	*Orientalia*
OSB	*Oriental Studies Bulletin*
OT	Old Testament
PJ	Pseudo-Jonathan
RB	*Revue Biblique*
REB	Revised English Bible
RH	*Revue Historique*
RQ	*Revue de Qumran*
RSR	*Recherches de Science Religieuse*
RSV	Revised Standard Version (2nd edition, London, 1971)
RThPH	*Revue de Theologie et de Philosophie*
SBL	Society of Biblical Literature
SBLDS	Society of Biblical Literature Dissertation Series
SBS	Stuttgarter Bibelstudien
SJOT	*Scandinavian Journal of the Old Testament*
SJT	*Scottish Journal of Theology*

ST	*Studia Theologica*
SVT	Supplements to *Vetus Testamentum*
TB	*Tyndale Bulletin*
TJ	Targum Jonathan of the Prophets
TN	Targum Neofiti
TO	Targum Onqelos
TWAT	G.J. Botterweck and H. Ringgren, (eds.), *Theologisches Wörterbuch zum Alten Testament* (Stuttgart 1970–)
TDOT	*Theological Dictionary of the Old Testament* (Grand Rapids, 1974–)
VT	*Vetus Testamentum*
WMANT	Wissenschaftliche Monographien zum Alten und Neuen Testament
WUNT	Wissenschaftliche Untersuchungen zum Neuen Testament
ZA	*Zeitschrift für Assyriologie*
ZAW	*Zeitschrift für die alttestamentliche Wissenschaft*

ON LEARNING TO BE A TRUE PROPHET: THE STORY OF BALAAM AND HIS ASS

BY

R.W.L. MOBERLY

Durham

It is with a sense of pleasure and gratitude that I write this essay in honour of Tony Gelston. When I was appointed at Durham in 1985, Tony was a model of kindness and thoughtfulness in helping me as a novice scholar to settle in and learn the ropes. And when I showed him my early research writings I could be confident that, whatever the other deficiencies of content might be, my discussion of the Hebrew language of the Old Testament would not be inaccurate if it survived his meticulous scrutiny.

A prime reason for choosing the topic of this essay for this *Festschrift* is that the Balaam story of Numbers 22–24 in general, and the logic of the narrative dynamics of Numbers 22 in particular, was the subject of our Durham postgraduate seminar in Old Testament on 16 February 1993. Some of the content of this essay was sketched out in our discussion, to which Tony was a significant contributor. I hope, therefore, that in the context of honouring Tony as a scholar, this essay may also stand as a memorial to our many enjoyable and fruitful seminar discussions in St. Chad's College and in Abbey House.

The story of Balaam and his ass is one of the well known stories of the Old Testament. But it is not, I think, one of the best understood. I would like in this essay to revisit this famous story and suggest that there are dimensions of its meaning which are often missed, yet which make good sense not only in relation to the specific details of the Hebrew text but also in relation to a wider Hebrew conception of the phenomenon of prophecy and in relation to the reception and appropriation of that Hebrew conception in Jewish and Christian faiths. As such the text may inform and engage with a contemporary faith that is rooted in scripture in more interesting ways than is sometimes supposed.

The overall story of Balaam in Numbers 22–24 stands as a self-contained unit within the book of Numbers. The summoning of Balaam and his journey prior to his encounter with Balak (22:1–35) is a natural subdivision within the larger story, and this will be our focus here. Although there are many questions which might be addressed as preliminaries to an exposition of the text, in this present essay I will concentrate solely upon an analytical exposition.

The presuppositions of the story are deftly set out in the opening sentences (Num. 22:1–6). The people of Israel are encamped east of the Jordan in the general region of Moab. Balak, king of Moab, knows of other peoples east of the Jordan whom Israel has already defeated and dispossessed, and is fearful lest a similar fate befall himself and his people. He therefore summons assistance in the form of Balaam, the power of whose curse may enable Balak to overcome the otherwise superior numbers and strength of Israel; for blessings and curses pronounced by Balaam are, in Balak's view, definitive and determinative. In terms of the narrator's overall perspective and purpose, Balak foolishly supposes Balaam to possess the kind of power of speech which the narrator knows (and as Balak will discover the hard way) belongs only to God.[1]

Senior officials[2] travel on Balak's behalf, to carry out the necessary negotiations to secure Balaam's assistance. Balaam responds as one who speaks for God should, in the Old Testament's view of things, respond. He says that he must respond as directed by God – and so, implicitly, does not decide in terms of his own priorities and interests insofar as these might differ from those of God. He also speaks of God with the proper name, YHWH, as known by Israel and characteristic of true spokesmen for God (22:8,13; even though the narrator uses the generic term, 'God', 22:9,10,12). That night God speaks to Balaam in familiar terms – this is no first meeting or giving of vocation, but a dialogue between those who already know each other.[3] When Balaam explains the situation in response

---

[1] For some of the necessary presuppositions of pronouncements of blessing and curse – their dependence not on word magic but on appropriate and recognised linguistic and social conventions – see A.C. Thiselton, "The Supposed Power of Words in the Biblical Writings", *JTS* 25 (1974), pp. 283–99 (with special reference to Balak and Balaam, p. 296).

[2] 'Elders', זְקֵנִים v. 7; 'princes', שָׂרִים, vv. 8, 13, 14, 15; 'servants', עֲבָדִים, v. 18 (with variants in the Versions); and, on the lips of God, simply "the men", הָאֲנָשִׁים, vv. 20, 35. The variations in terminology seem natural in context.

[3] The rhetorical logic of God's opening question, which seeks to engage Balaam,

to God's question, God's directive is crisp and clear. In an emphatic negative (לֹא rather than אַל), Balaam is not to accompany Balak's officials; he is not to curse the people "for they are blessed" (כִּי בָרוּךְ הוּא). So next day, Balaam dismisses Balak's officials, and they return to their master to report their failure (Num. 22:7–14).

Within this context, one point of detail deserves further comment. The officials bring with them 'divinations' (קְסָמִים, 22:7), the precise meaning of which is disputed. Probably the most common interpretation, predominant in modern translations,[4] and at least as old as the Vulgate,[5] is that of 'fees' for divination. Such a meaning is perfectly plausible, because payment of Balaam is explicitly an issue in the second embassy, at least as Balaam, no doubt correctly, interprets Balak's offer (22:17–18); such payment may also be considered intrinsically likely in the situation. The Hebrew language, however, has a common word for 'fee' – שָׂכָר – which one might expect to be used here were that the intended meaning.[6] Also, the regular Hebrew terms for 'money' (שָׂכָר, זָהָב, כֶּסֶף) are grammatically singular forms whose plural is uncommon; so the plural form of קְסָמִים suggests a plurality of objects which are not readily comprehended by a generic singular. Moreover, the fact that payment is an issue in the second embassy need not imply that it is an issue in the first embassy: Balak's homage to Balaam's supposed powers could be considered by Balak as reason for Balaam to come. Finally, when Balak makes the offer which Balaam interprets in terms of money, the envoys do not bring the money with them, for the offer is of payment after the job is done (a crucial point in the development of the story).

More likely, therefore, is that קְסָמִים means something intrinsic to the practice of divining, i.e. either people who themselves are diviners (קֹסֵם),[7] or objects wherewith divination (קֶסֶם) is carried out. The

---

is similar to that of God's question to Adam in Genesis 3:9, a point of similarity noted (in this latter context) by Rashi, among others (M. Rosenbaum & A.M. Silbermann (eds.), *The Pentateuch with the Commentary of Rashi: Genesis* (Jerusalem, 5733/1973), p. 14).

[4] For example, RSV, NRSV, NEB, REB, JB.

[5] *Habentes divinationis pretium in manibus.* LXX τὰ μαντεῖα closely follows the Hebrew, but in a way that specifies objects rather than people.

[6] The verbal form שָׂכַר is used with reference to Balaam in Deut. 23:5. This is fully explicable in terms of the fact that it is Balak's second offer, which Balaam interprets in terms of money, which leads to Balaam's acceding to Balak's request. It supports the contention that שָׂכָר would be the appropriate term in v. 7, if fees for hiring were the issue.

[7] This is the understanding of the MT in the New JPS Translation: "The

former would presumably require a small repointing of the text
(קֹסְמִים); however, it makes no sense of בְיָדָם, "in their hands", which
in other comparable Hebrew usage implies something portable and
is never an equivalent of "in their midst" (בְּתֹכָם).[8] Thus קְסָמִים probably means "tools of divination", and envisages the kinds of object
depicted in Ezekiel's vignette of the king of Babylon, i.e. arrows,
תְּרָפִים, liver (Ezek. 21:26–28 [ET 21–23]). Whether Balaam would
really want or need such objects is beside the point,[9] for the point
is that this is what Balak thinks is appropriate. Balak's eager provision of tools of divination is part of the wider contrast in the narrative between the uncomprehending Moabite view of how the divine
realm is accessed and the dynamics of prophecy as understood by
Israel and as practised by Balaam[10] (who, later in the story, cate-
gorically pronounces the futility of divination against Israel, Num.
23:23).[11]

---

elders . . . , versed in divination, set out". It is adopted by J. Milgrom, who follows
a suggestion of Ehrlich that Balaam's "colleagues were present for the purpose of
honouring him" (*The JPS Torah Commentary: Numbers/Bamidbar* (Philadelphia & New
York, 5750/1990), pp. 187, 319).

[8] For the carrying of money or an offering בְיָד, see Gen. 43:15, Jdg. 16:18, Jer.
41:5; for other portable objects בְיָד, see Gen. 35:4, Exod. 5:21. Sometimes בְיָד
refers to human instrumentality, 1 Kgs. 10:29, 2 Chron. 24:13. The other regular
idiomatic use of בְיָד is with reference to the giving of enemies by God into Israel's
hands, Josh. 21:44, Jdg. 7:2, Neh. 9:24. The one possible exception is 1 Sam. 21:14
(ET 13), but here the most natural sense is that David acted madly "in their hands"
in putting himself at the mercy of their physical power, i.e. an extension of the
usage of Israel's enemies being given "into their hands".

[9] Thus Milgrom's objection for this reason to קְסָמִים as divinatory objects misses
the irony of the text (1990, p. 187).

[10] Neither Num. 22–24, nor the Old Testament more generally, ever offers a
definition or account of קֶסֶם 'divination', whose meaning must be inferred from its
particular context. Here, Balak's ascription of power to Balaam, together with his
provision of divinatory tools, suggests a view of human ability in some way to be
in control of the spiritual realm, which lacks both the moral accountability and the
sense of contingency of human life before divine transcendence which generally
characterise Old Testament prophecy (which I do not equate with prophecy as a
phenomenon of Israelite history). Of course, a clear general distinction between divination and prophecy is not incompatible with recognition that often in practice
the distinction may become more or less blurred. Both the Old Testament and subsequent Jewish and Christian faiths provide plenty of evidence for such blurrings.

[11] The precise sense of Balaam's words in 23:23, וְלֹא־קֶסֶם בְּיִשְׂרָאֵל is open to
debate. The futility of divination, rather than its non-occurrence – which might be
better expressed by אַיִן rather than לֹא – is probably the prime thrust. It is unclear
whether the preposition בְּ means 'within' or 'against', but both senses are appropriate: the latter in the immediate context of Num. 22–24, the former as a general axiom of Old Testament prophecy.

Thus far Balaam is a model 'prophet',[12] for he is accountable and responsive to God, faithfully speaking God's words. If that were all, it could be the end of the story, at least this particular story of Balak's desire that Balaam should curse Israel. It is not, however, for reasons both simple and complex. Balak thinks that Balaam's refusal to come is not a genuine refusal but a negotiating stance; the real meaning of Balaam's words is not 'no' but "you must offer me more". So Balak acts accordingly with a more prestigious embassy and an offer that, he supposes, one could hardly refuse, i.e. "name your price, as long as you do what I ask" (Num. 22:15–17).

This provides the first turning point in the story. How will Balaam respond? In the terms of the story Balak sees Balaam as an astute negotiator. One might, however, stand back for a moment and recast the issue in terms related to Balaam's role as one who speaks with God and for God, i.e. as a prophet. In various parts of Hebrew scripture – parts highlighted and affirmed by Jewish and Christian faiths – the responsibility to speak and act for God is construed as a morally demanding vocation, whose full dimensions may sometimes be engendered by an act of divine testing.[13] That is, the person

---

[12] In classic Hebrew parlance the term for 'prophet' is נביא. An alternative term, ראה ('seer') might well be appropriate to the context of the Balaam story. For 'seeing' is one of the story's prime thematic concerns, and not only is the verb ראה used repeatedly, particularly in the ass episode, but the related root חזה and the idiom of "having eyes opened" introduce Balaam's two climactic oracles (24:4,16). Within Num. 22–24 itself, ראה would seem a natural term for Balaam.
However, the interesting terminological note in 1 Samuel 9:9 indicates that although popular parlance once preferred ראה when speaking of 'prophets' the standard Hebrew term has become נביא. Because Num. 22–24 depicts Balaam for the most part in categories familiar from Hebrew prophecy elsewhere, to call him a 'seer' rather than a 'prophet' would, I suggest, distract from, more than illuminate, the working assumptions of the Balaam narrative. The wide-ranging generic term 'prophet' (נביא) is the least misleading, as long as it is used with appropriate nuance.

[13] In this context it is interesting to note that the portrayal of Joseph in Genesis, whose possible linkages with wisdom literature have often been discussed, shows striking similarities to concerns of prophetic literature. To be sure, Joseph's vocation is to be a "civil servant" rather than a specifically religious figure (נביא or whatever), but at the climactic encounter with the pharaoh his speech is similar to that of a prophet (Gen. 41:25ff.). He definitively interprets the mind of God with a message as demanding of practical response (and not just discussion) as any prophetic call to Israel to turn to God (שוב); and the positive response to Joseph's message averts disaster (רעה). Joseph himself is prepared for this vocation through his resisting of temptation and enduring of malice and disappointment (Gen. 39,40). The psalmist's interpretation of Joseph's story in terms of a divine vocation which involves hard testing (Ps. 105:16–22, esp. 18–19) makes explicit what is consistently implicit in the Genesis narratives.

accountable to God finds himself[14] in a situation – in divine terms, a situation initiated by God – in which costly demands or difficulties confront him, and in which he must make a renewed, and more searching, affirmative response to his vocation. In terms of our story, what Balak intends as financial negotiation could also be intended by God as a test of the integrity of Balaam's vocation.

How then should one understand Balaam's response to Balak's renewed embassy? The wording of v. 18 is impeccably correct: obedience to God is completely non-negotiable, no matter what the inducement to gain. Thus should a true prophet speak. Then in v. 19, Balaam proposes to repeat his nocturnal encounter with the will of God. At first sight, this may seem unproblematic, for it is apparently a repetition of the good practice displayed earlier, seeking God's will rather than following his own preferences. But within this context there are factors which arouse suspicion as to Balaam's motives. First and foremost is the fact that Balaam does not simply dismiss the men. If the words of accountability to God in v. 18 are genuine, then they should suffice, for Balaam already knows God's mind with regard to Balak's request and he could dismiss the men without more ado. In particular, the reason given for God's previous refusal to let Balaam go with the initial embassy is not a particular issue of time or circumstance, which might readily change, but a fundamental principle – "they are blessed" (v. 12).

Whatever the precise nature of Balaam's ability to grasp this principle at this stage in the story (he enunciates the principle of God's blessing of Israel with strong, and increasing, emphasis as the basis of his oracles to Balak when he gets to that point, 23:7–8, 18–20), it remains the kind of axiom that a prophet ought to be able to recognise as such. Moreover, response to such a principle shares the logic of response to divine commandments and prohibitions generally (something which in other contexts is often handled in terms of conscience). If such is the will of God, then obedience is the correct response. The recognition that what counts as obedience may sometimes be problematic, and that sometimes divine command-

---

[14] The use of the masculine pronoun is to conform with the fact that the majority of prophets in Hebrew scripture are men, and that in those stories where women are prophets (Deborah, Huldah) the dynamics of testing are not present. It is not intended to discount or preclude recognition that within the contexts of post-biblical faith the dynamics of prophetic vocation and testing may be as applicable to women as to men.

ments may point in conflicting directions, makes no difference here. For offers of public honour and financial gain are not the kind of factors that make problematic what counts as obedience.[15] Rather, they specify the cost of what such obedience might entail. They create a problem not for the understanding but for the will and for the imagination which fuels the will.

Thus the fact that Balaam goes again to consult God suggests that he does not mean what he says in v. 18. In other words, Balaam is acceding to Balak's construal of his earlier refusal, that it was not a genuine refusal but a negotiating ploy. He now wants to come with the envoys, because Balak's offer is one that he 'cannot' refuse. So he wants God to speak again and say something more,[16] so that he may have the opportunity to accede to Balak's invitation. The language of religious vocation, which is preserved unchanged, is becoming a tool of self-interested financial negotiation. It is becoming, in a word, corrupt; or, in the terminology of ancient Jewish and Christian interpretation of the story, Balaam is succumbing to greed.[17]

Balaam's acceptance here of Balak's understanding of his earlier refusal does of course raise the possibility that that earlier refusal is

---

[15] Similarly, for example, if adultery is wrong, it remains wrong however great the material inducement. The 1993 Paramount film *Indecent Proposal*, starring Robert Redford, Demi Moore and Woody Harrelson, is an interesting recent exploration of this issue; although, characteristically of the time and place of the film, the nature and significance of 'adultery' (a term not used) is redefined in individualistic and personalist terms with diminished moral content and no familial or social content.

[16] The Hebrew idiom of יסף with דבר indicates not simply that God will speak again but that God will say something more than was said previously. For the general idiomatic usage of שׁוב and יסף to express the adverbial sense of 'again', see Joüon/Muraoka #177 b,c. They observe that "יסף expresses continuation ... or augmentation". In the context of Num. 22:19, for God to continue is for God to augment what has already been said.

In a pentateuchal context there are strong resonances with the Mosaic prohibition on "adding to (יסף, Hiph) the word which I am commanding you" (Deut. 4:2). In the deuteronomic context, the point of the prohibition on adding (or subtracting) seems to be a moral one about not seeking expedients to avoid the cost of obedience, rather than a quantitative point that all possibly desirable laws are contained within Deuteronomy, which would make no practical sense. Balaam's desire that God should say something more seems a good narrative example of the kind of evasiveness with regard to the demands of obedience which Deuteronomy 4:2 envisages.

[17] In the interpretation incorporated in the New Testament, the keyword for Balaam's failing is μισθός, 'profit' (Jude 11; 2 Pet. 2:15 is fuller, μισθὸν ἀδικίας ἠγάπησεν, "he set his heart on profit gained wrongly"). In St. Augustine's interpretation, the keyword is *cupiditas* (*Quaest. in Hept: Num.*, XLVIII; for example, "*se victum cupiditate monstravit*").

also to be understood thus by the reader. Such a suspicion, once raised, cannot easily be confirmed or rebutted, for the text of vv. 7–14 is open to either construal. My judgement of the story as a whole, however, is that the reader should resist any facile or moralistic tendency to assume that a person who becomes corrupt must always have been so (a moralistic tendency is a weakness in much traditional Jewish and Christian interpretation of the story).[18] Rather, the text is portraying the more complex situation of the person who is genuinely a prophet (in that he knows and can practise the responsibilities of such a vocation) but who yet may go astray. When a serious divine test, serious because of its genuine allure, confronts Balaam, he wavers from his initial faithfulness to his vocation and succumbs to temptation.

If the construal of Balaam as succumbing to temptation is correct, God's initial response in v. 20 may seem puzzling. Why should God direct Balaam to go with the envoys? Would one not rather expect reference to God's anger, of the kind specified in v. 22, and that divine anger would be accompanied at least by a prohibition on going and possibly also by some act of judgement? But the puzzle

---

[18] So, for example, Rashi, characteristic of predominant Jewish tradition, sees Balaam negatively from the outset. Already in v. 9 Balaam is seeking to get round God, whose knowledge he mistakenly infers is limited; and in v. 11 Balaam wants to drive out Israel not just "from the land" but "from the world", thereby showing hatred of Israel even greater than that of Balak (R. Rosenbaum & A.M. Silbermann (eds.), *The Pentateuch with the Commentary of Rashi: Numbers* (Jerusalem, 5733/1973), p. 108). For convenient introductions to traditional Jewish interpretation of the Balaam story, see Milgrom (1990), pp. 185ff.; and, more fully, G. Vermes, *Scripture and Tradition in Judaism* (2nd ed., Leiden, 1973), chapter 6.

A characteristic Christian voice is that of Charles Simeon: "Who that had heard all the fine speeches which he made respecting his determination to adhere to the will of God. . . . would not have conceived him to be a pious character? Yet from beginning to the end his conduct was a continued course of horrible impiety" ("Sermon 170", *Horae Homileticae*, vol. 2 (London, 1832), pp. 132f.).

The classic commentators of course read the story of Num. 22–24 in the light of the negative references to Balaam in Num. 31:8,16. Modern commentators have properly insisted that the story of Num. 22–24 be interpreted in its own right; and that if Num. 31:16 does presuppose a substantive Balaam tradition, then it is a tradition other than that in Num. 22–24. Nonetheless, the logic of rereading a text, and finding it to have a significance other than that which one may have initially supposed in terms of its *prima facie* meaning, is clearly implicit within Num. 22:15–21. So the move of the classic commentators is not without warrant within the biblical text. A clear recent restatement of the logic of the classic position is offered by Gordon Wenham, who argues that, in the light of Numbers 31, "the deeds of Balaam which many commentators construe so positively might have a more sinister meaning . . ." (*Numbers* (Leicester, 1981), pp. 167f.).

is clarified by the wider context of the narrative (and it might also be eased through consideration of other Old Testament portrayals of divine testing, in which extended probing is common).[19]

First, the whole episode with the ass which follows (vv. 22–35) ends with the same divine command to go but say only what God says (v. 35a) with which God responds to Balaam's nocturnal enquiry in v. 20.[20] At the very point of Balaam's submissiveness to God, where Balaam offers to turn back (שׁוב, v. 34), God does not, as one might perhaps have expected, say "go back" (שׁוב) but rather "go on" (לך). This must mean that whatever the nature of the divine anger and the angelic adversary to Balaam in vv. 22–35, God is not simply, *tout court*, opposed to Balaam going to Balak. Balaam's going must in some way represent God's will (the nature of which will become clear in chapters 23–24).

Secondly, when the divine anger is specified and represented in the episode with the ass, the anger takes an unusual and surprising form. One might expect that divine anger would take the form of direct action against the offender, in some such form as afflicting with disease, blinding the eyes, or even striking dead (all actions of divine judgement attested elsewhere in the Old Testament). In whatever such form it would be immediate and inescapable for the one afflicted, in this case Balaam. Yet the angel with the sword is not like this, for the angel can be, initially at least, avoided. Instead of the angel coming to and at Balaam, the angel is a stationary object which can be circumvented. What this might signify is a matter to which we will return. At present, the important point is the surprising and complex form which the divine anger with Balaam takes in vv. 22–35.

In the light of these two factors in vv. 22–35, both of which indicate subtlety and complexity in God's anger with Balaam, it becomes appropriate to find some similar complexity in God's initial words in v. 20. That is, God's words are not just to be taken at face value as straightforward permission to go, any more than Balaam's pious-sounding words in vv. 18–19 are to be taken at their face value as expressing obedience to God (and just as Balak did not take Balaam's

---

[19] See, for example, Deuteronomy 8:2–3 with its pivotal construal of Israel's 40 years in the desert, which arose through unfaithfulness, as a demanding and positive time of divine teaching through testing.

[20] The minor verbal differences between v. 20b and v. 35a make no difference to the meaning of each divine command, whose sense is identical.

initial words at their face value). God tells Balaam the very thing he wants to hear, but it will not mean for Balaam what he may think it will mean[21] – and this is made clear to the reader by the interpretation of God's attitude as one of anger in v. 22. In rhetorical terms, God's words in v. 20 are ironic. In substantive terms, God's response to the prophet's seeking to corrupt his vocation is to seek to teach him a lesson.

What this lesson involves is the subject of the episode which follows. Recognition of the episode's crafted and dryly humorous quality – the highly esteemed and expensive prophet can see less than a proverbially dull animal – and its patterned structure – the threefold encounter with the angel, the two balancing dialogues – should enhance appreciation of its specific meaning, a meaning which is specified through conventions characteristic of Hebrew narrative.

First, at the outset the angel is said to stand in Balaam's way as an 'adversary' (שָׂטָן, v. 22). The most illuminating parallel to this is in the story of Solomon in 1 Kings. Here, specifically in the context of divine anger with Solomon for unfaithfulness (11:9), God raises up two particular people, Hadad and Rezon, each to be an 'adversary' (שָׂטָן, 11:14,23) to Solomon. Neither of them defeat or displace Solomon, but each is seen to be an obstacle and irritant to Solomon, and indeed to Israel (11:25), thereby removing the preceding divinely bestowed rest which was characterized by the absence of such hostile irritant (שָׂטָן, 5:18 [ET 5:14]). In significant respects, as Hadad and Rezon are to Solomon, so is the angel with the sword to Balaam: a figure who opposes, dangerous yet without instant or overwhelming implementation of that danger, a figure whose opposing presence symbolises divine disfavour with the failure in faithfulness of someone who once did, and still should, know better.

Secondly, there is the sequence of threefold confrontation with the angel (vv. 23–27). The fact that the angel has a drawn sword means that encounter with the angel will be deadly. So when the ass sees the angel, she[22] naturally takes appropriate evasive action, going

---

[21] This general point – that the divine permission is morally charged and complex – is well represented in traditional Jewish interpretation, which Milgrom summarises thus: "The rabbis . . . see in this tale the source of the doctrine of human responsibility and free will: 'From this you learn that a man is led in the way he desires to go' [Mak. 10b, Num.R. 20:18]; 'If one comes to defile himself, he is given an opening", that is, he is given the opportunity [Shab. 104a, Yoma 38b]'", (1990, p. 189). An obvious scriptural analogue would be Psalm 106:15, "He gave them what they asked for, and sent a wasting disease among them".
[22] The Hebrew noun, and related verbs, are all feminine.

around the angel rather as one might go around anything hostile or dangerous which is blocking the way in which one is going. This detour irritates Balaam, who expresses his irritation by hitting the ass in such a way as to redirect her. Unfortunately for the ass, the angel reappears, this time in a narrower place where going around is more difficult. Detour is only possible by squeezing through a narrow gap which involves pressing against a wall. This detour not only irritates Balaam but also hurts him, and again he takes this out on his ass. The angel then reappears a third time, in such a narrow place that evasive action is no longer possible. So the ass does the only thing she can, ceasing to move and adopting a posture in which she no longer can move. Balaam is now not merely irritated but positively angry, and hits the ass accordingly.

The ass's attempts to avoid a deadly danger which keeps reappearing in an ever more compelling way evoke solely incomprehension, anger and violence on the part of the prophet. The scene is set for two dialogues which reveal all – for each dialogue is initiated by a divine action (opening the ass's mouth, opening Balaam's eyes) which enables the truth of the situation first to be expressed and then to be grasped (22:28–30,31–35).

The ass's first question is a protest at the injustice of Balaam's repeated hitting his ass. The "what have I done?" means "what have I done to deserve this?" The ass has thrice saved her master's life, and so should be thanked rather than maltreated. But to Balaam this is not the case. Because he has seen nothing of what the ass has seen, he sees the ass's behaviour not as saving him but as humiliating him, making him look foolish.[23] To crown his incomprehension, he ironically threatens the ass with the very fate of a deadly sword from which she was trying to save them. The first exchange thus underlines the unjust, because ignorant and mistaken, behaviour of the prophet.

The ass's second question pinpoints the failure of the prophet in the very area in which he should excel: discernment, that is seeing and understanding what is going on, especially in relation to God. Specifically, how can the man who cannot interpret the obvious actions of his ass interpret the more difficult actions of God?[24] The

---

[23] A comparable sense of the verb התעלל is found with reference to YHWH's humiliation of Egypt (Exod. 10:2, 1 Sam. 6:6).

[24] The implicit logic is similar to what in subsequent rabbinic interpretation would be called *Qal wahomer*, which is that what applies in a less important case applies also in a more important case.

ass points to the wholly unprecedented nature of her behaviour. Balaam has had the ass and ridden on her for as long as he can remember with no break up to the present time (מעודך עד היום הזה), and so his familiarity with her patterns of behaviour is as extensive as it could possibly be. So when he is asked whether there is any precedent whatever for her present behaviour (the Hebrew is emphatic, ההסכן הסכנתי, "have I ever been in the habit of behaving thus?"), he knows full well that the answer is negative and has to say so. The point is that unusual behaviour should have caught his attention and signified to him that all was not well, particularly when repeated twice more even in the face of his immediate and pain-inflicting expression of displeasure. Such unusual behaviour was obvious both to see and interpret in terms of its general tenor – "something must be wrong". Balaam's failure to carry out even the simplest exercise of discernment is manifest.[25] His greed has made him blind and foolish.[26]

But now that the ass has pointed out his inability to see the obvious implications of her behaviour, there remains a further necessary step. It is one thing to infer from the animal's visible behaviour that all is not well, it is another to see the specific cause and meaning of this behaviour. The ass, having taught Balaam the first part of his lesson, now gives way to the angel to complete it.

When YHWH opens Balaam's eyes, he is able to see what was in front of his eyes, which the ass could already see, the angel standing before him in his way with a drawn, and so deadly, sword (what Balaam sees, v. 31a, is depicted identically with what the ass sees, v. 23a). Balaam responds in correct manner, with reverent prostration; though whether this action is other than that of a guilty person who recognises that he is caught by the proper authority is not specified. In any case, what matters is the dialogue, which gives content to, and brings out the meaning of, the encounter.

---

[25] Milgrom's comment, drawing on an article by R. Largement, that "as a Mesopotamian diviner, Balaam should have recognised that his animal's bizarre actions may have held a divine portent" (1990, p. 190), while consistent with his own larger interpretation of Balaam as a diviner, misses the primary point of the ass's words which are about the discernment of something that is accessible to *anyone*.

[26] Calvin's comments are characteristically apt: "To the great disgrace of the prophet, the glory of the angel was first of all apparent to the ass . . . Whence came this blindness, but from the avarice by which he had been so stupefied, that he preferred filthy lucre to the holy calling of God?" (cited in C.F. Keil & F. Delitzsch, *Commentary on the Old Testament: I: The Pentateuch* (reprinted, Grand Rapids, 1980), Pt. 3, pp. 169f.).

The angel draws together the two complaints voiced by the ass, Balaam's blindness and injustice, and interprets the meaning of her unprecedented behaviour (vv. 32–33). The angel had come as an 'adversary' to Balaam, because there was something unacceptable about the journey he was making.[27] The angel underlines that the ass's actions were not only appropriate but were for Balaam's benefit, for it is only he, not the ass (whether or not the ass realised this), whose life is in peril, for the divine judgement would, significantly, have left the ass unscathed. The angel does not spell out the precise reason why Balaam's course is unacceptable, for in context the reason is obvious as soon as the challenge is made: Balaam is allowing his prophetic vocation to be corrupted by greed, a greed which has made him blind to the presence of the God in whose name he speaks.

These words of the angel, to which we will return, achieve their purpose.[28] They touch Balaam's heart, they bring him to his senses (or, in traditional evangelical terminology, they convict him of sin). Balaam's response (v. 34) is one of true turning to God (i.e. he repents, שׁוב).[29] First, he unconditionally acknowledges his wrongdoing: "I have sinned" (חטאתי). Secondly, he acknowledges his uncomprehending inability to see what he should have seen.[30] Thirdly, he expresses

---

[27] The precise meaning of the verb ירט (v. 32) is difficult to determine, and there is the related question of whether ירט הדרך is the correct text. BHS, with some support from the Versions, proposes emending the text to ירע דרכך, "your way is wrong". However, to introduce such unproblematic Hebrew here is surely to offend against the basic text-critical principle of *lectio difficilior potior*. The MT is intelligible as saying something about the actual route which Balaam is following, that route in which the angel has stood (cf. the repeated prior use of הדרך and בדרך, vv. 22, 23, 31). By older commentators ירט "is alternately rendered 'twisted' (Ibn Ezra, Ramban, Abravanel) or 'blocked' (Mid. Lek. Tov, Meyuhas), interpreting דרך as 'road'" (Milgrom (1990), p. 320, n. 77), while modern scholars regularly appeal to an Arabic root which has the sense of 'throw', "cast headlong". Thus ירט הדרך probably means "the way is precipitate/headlong". This would be an idiom similar to the modern idiom of a "slippery slope", and it makes good sense of MT.

[28] Recent commentators regularly see the ass episode solely as satirizing or vilifying Balaam. So, for example, John Van Seters says that "the talking ass story is the final degradation of the faithful prophet into a buffoon who must be instructed by his own humble donkey" ("From Faithful Prophet to Villain: Observations on the Tradition History of the Balaam Story" in E.E. Carpenter (ed.), *A Biblical Itinerary: In Search of Method, Form and Content: Essays in Honor of George W. Coats* JSOTS 240 (Sheffield, 1997), pp. 126–132, quotation p. 132). Such a judgement is exegetically superficial in terms of the actual content of the story, where the humbling of Balaam is not an end in itself but has a didactic and restorative purpose.

[29] Traditional interpreters, who see Balaam as consistently perverted, construe this repentance as superficial and/or momentary.

[30] The first כי in Balaam's words is generally taken as causative, i.e. "I have

willingness to abandon the enterprise that is causing offence; he will relinquish the hoped-for honour and wealth.

Now, however, because Balaam has turned from that which was corrupting his vocation, the angel says that he should indeed continue to go with Balak's envoys. What was a deadly error when undertaken in greed becomes a fruitful course to pursue if done in obedience to God (v. 35). The reason for God's direction to Balaam to continue becomes abundantly clear as the story continues in chapters 23–24, and has already been hinted at in Balak's initial summons to Balaam: Balaam's ability to bless as well as curse. So Balaam's prophetic responsibility to speak the message of God is repeated, now with the prospect that he will genuinely fulfil his mandate, even though it will not be what Balak wants or expects.

As the story unfolds, thrice an unseeing and obstinate Balak urges on a seeing Balaam, just as Balaam had urged on his ass.[31] Thrice Balaam pronounces blessing on Israel, each blessing with greater length and emphasis. Finally, an angry Balak loses his temper and dismisses Balaam, warning him to leave quickly, and telling him that the God of Israel has deprived him of all he could have expected to receive. Balaam simply replies that obedience to God is more

---

sinned for (כִּי) I did not know . . .". Although this makes sense, the sense may be better if כִּי is taken as asseverative, and the preceding הַטָאתִי is taken as an independent exclamation; i.e. "I have sinned. Truly (כִּי) I did not know that it was you . . .". The massoretic punctuation of הַטָאתִי with pausal *zaqef qaton* also suggests an understanding of the word as an exclamation distinct from the words which follow. Directly comparable in terms of context and text (and punctuation) is Saul's confession to Samuel in 1 Sam. 15:24, where also I suggest that the first כִּי is asseverative, and only the second כִּי is causative; i.e. "I have sinned. Truly (כִּי) I have transgressed the commandment of YHWH and your words because (כִּי) I feared the people . . .". A good preliminary guide to the complexities of asseverative כִּי is Joüon/Muraoka #164b, 165b,e.

[31] Credit for recognising the linkage between the ass episode and the wider structure of the story belongs, at least in recent times, I believe, to two Jewish scholars with a strong feel for Hebrew narrative: D. Daube, *Ancient Hebrew Fables* (Oxford, 1973), pp. 14–16, and R. Alter, *The Art of Biblical Narrative* (London & Sydney, 1981), pp. 104–107. The point, so obvious once seen, has been missed by many modern commentators who have usually assumed the non-integral nature of the ass episode and have sometimes been so prepossessed with questions of tradition-history and composition (usually ascribing two oracles each to J and E), that the actual pattern of three plus one, and the correlation with the ass episode, has remained effectively unnoticed; thus standard commentaries such as G.B. Gray, *Numbers* (Edinburgh, 1903), pp. 307ff.; M. Noth, *Numbers* (London, 1968; ET of German of 1966), pp. 171ff.; P.J. Budd, *Numbers* (Waco, 1984), pp. 248ff.; E.W. Davies, *Numbers* (London, 1995), pp. 236ff.

important than unlimited riches (24:10–13).[32] Before departing he offers unsolicited oracles: a long oracle, which climaxes in a victorious leader for Israel who will defeat many, Moab first of all (24:17b), and some brief visions of glory and disaster for other peoples near to Israel – the kind of visions appropriate to one who has learned to discern God's will as Balaam has.

To conclude, it may be helpful briefly to stand back from the story and to reflect further on the peculiar nature of the angel's opposition to Balaam – the potentially deadly adversary who can initially be circumvented (for he only takes his stand within the road that Balaam is taking), but with whom an encounter is ultimately inescapable. What is the significance of this particular expression of divine anger?

An analogy may perhaps prove helpful.[33] Consider an active man (or woman) who begins to have health problems. Where previously he had been able to push his body to do more or less what he wanted, his body starts to function differently and to display symptoms that it had never displayed before – breathlessness, vertigo, sharp pains, or whatever. The man knows his body and its previous capabilities, so how should he interpret these unprecedented symptoms? He might decide (no doubt with appropriate medical advice) that his bodily symptoms are warning signs of potentially dangerous overload and that he can no longer do what he did before, and so he begins to modify his activities so that his body returns to normal. But he might decide to ignore the bodily symptoms, dismissing them as a mere passing irritant of no real significance. Suppose he is in

---

[32] The tone of Balaam's words in 24:12,13 is elusive. For Balaam can easily sound complacent, as though his grasp of the basic moral and spiritual principle was consistent, when in fact it had not been. He is economical with the truth in omitting any reference to what had happened to him en route. Perhaps the narrator was content with the simple statement of a basic principle through a sense of what is dramatically appropriate at this moment of departure (for if Balaam was going to explain to Balak what he had learned en route, the beginning of their encounter would have been the time for it, yet in that context also he simply reiterates the basic prophetic principle, 22:38). However, the way Balaam extends his earlier "I cannot go beyond the word of YHWH" (24:13a, cf. 22:18b) with "to do anything, good or bad, of my own will" (לעשות טובה או רעה מלבי) may suggest at least to the reader, even if not to Balak, that Balaam had had to learn a hard way that an obedient renunciation of self-will may be unexpectedly demanding.

[33] My analogy has obvious resonances with the famous designation, ascribed to St. Francis of Assisi, of one's body as "Brother Ass". The analogy is intended, however, as a genuine analogy and not a covert allegory – even though in some contexts the distinction between analogy and allegory may become blurred.

the middle of an important project, which needs his full energies. So he makes the latter decision, and continues to push himself
as previously. After a while, the symptoms recur, in more acute and
prolonged form. He faces the same choice as before. His important
project is still his first priority, and so he continues to ignore the
symptoms and pushes on. A few days later he has a major heart
attack and drops dead.

The analogy suggests a possible situation where there are warning signals which, while clear on one level, are such that they can
be misunderstood and ignored if their obvious *prima facie* significance
conflicts with other priorities. What is needed in such a situation is
careful discernment to find out what the symptoms signify. On the
one hand, one must attend to the precise nature of the symptoms.
On the other hand, one needs a wider knowledge of the body and
health such that the symptoms can be rightly understood.

So too, I suggest, Balaam's predicament with the angel requires
not only attention to the ass's unusual behaviour but also a wider
knowledge, a frame of reference, rightly to locate and understand
that behaviour. Within the context of the story that frame of reference is not some form of ancient Israelite zoology but rather Old
Testament prophecy. The story is a story of a prophet who succumbs to temptation by corrupting his prophetic vocation through
ambitious greed. Balaam's problem is at heart a moral and spiritual
failure. God's anger, and the adversarial appearance of the angel,
are the counterpart to that failure, to be understood in the moral
and spiritual categories of prophecy.

Specifically, the angel with the deadly sword represents the moral
and spiritual responsiveness of God to Balaam's self-seeking, with
all the two-edged nature of divine encounter, whose outcome is not
determinable apart from the human response to that encounter. On
the one hand, the angel means death if Balaam persists in the way
he is going, for the corruption of prophetic vocation is a course that
leads to death. The deadly nature of Balaam's corrupting is not
instant and obvious, for the angel may initially be circumvented and
the angel does not pursue Balaam. However, the angel reappears
always in the very way in which Balaam is going, and the initial
possibility of detouring while still remaining on course is progres-
sively removed. Ultimately, there is no avoiding death on that particular road – though death would only strike the one who is choosing
to go that way, and the innocent animal would remain unscathed.

On the other hand, there is the possibility of repentance and a trans-formation of Balaam's mission, a possibility initiated by actions of divine mercy (opening the ass's mouth, opening Balaam's eyes). This mercy humbles Balaam by confronting him with his utter incompe-tence and showing him how close to disaster his quest had brought him. But this mercy also teaches him the necessary lesson when he acknowledges his sin, and so enables him to go and speak as a prophet should speak.

BALAAM'S PROPHECIES AS INTERPRETED BY PHILO AND THE ARAMAIC TARGUMS OF THE PENTATEUCH

BY

C.T.R. HAYWARD

Durham

Discussing Philo's eschatological views, Peder Borgen has argued that a future universal dominion of the Hebrews, bound up with the kingly role of Moses as promulgator of God's cosmic law given to the Jews at Sinai, is fundamental to the sage's thinking. Philo believed that the Jewish people would eventually realize their divinely promised destiny through the agency of a 'man', a commander of the Hebrew army who would appear as world emperor. Balaam, a Gentile seer imbued with true prophecy, had foretold the advent of the 'man' and the future eating up of Israel's enemies: in short, Philo had discerned the ultimate goal of Israel's existence as the subjection of the human race to God's universal law, the law which He gave to Moses.[1] This essay attempts to show that Borgen's thesis finds support not only in Philo's own writings, but also in traditional Jewish exegesis of the Balaam oracles. It will note how apt is Borgen's description as imperial of the 'man' destined to arise from Israel; and it will suggest that the evidence allows for further definition of the man's

---

[1] See P. Borgen, "'There shall come forth a Man': Reflections on Messianic Ideas in Philo", in J.H. Charlesworth (ed.), *The Messiah: Developments in Earliest Judaism and Christianity* (Minneapolis, 1992), pp. 341–361. For Philo's eschatological views, see H.A. Wolfson, *Philo: Foundations of Religious Philosophy in Judaism, Christianity and Islam*, 2 vols., (Cambridge Mass., 2nd ed. 1948), vol. 2, pp. 395–426; Borgen (1992), pp. 341–342 and literature there cited; R.D. Hecht, "Philo and Messiah", in J. Neusner, W.S. Green, and E. Frerichs (eds.), *Judaisms and Their Messiahs at the Turn of the Christian Era* (Cambridge, 1987), pp. 139–148. Students disagree (*inter alia*) whether messianism was central or tangential in Philo's thought; whether he understated kingly messianic elements out of political expediency; and whether his eschatological hopes stress messiah less than transformation of individual souls by the Logos. Conclusions of this essay suggest that messianism was important to Philo; that he predicted a royal messianic figure, but somewhat obliquely; and that both a messiah and enlightenment of the individual soul characterize the last days.

identity. It begins, however, with necessary preliminary observations about Philo's treatment of the Balaam oracles.[2]

1. *Balaam's Oracles in Philo: General Remarks*

Three points must be emphasized. First, the Bible records four separate oracles of Balaam concerning Israel (Num. 23:7–10, 18–24; 24:3–9, 15–19): Philo reduced these to three (*Vit. Mos.* I. 278–279, 283–284, 289–291). His love of arithmology may explain this change. For Philo, the number three is "an image of a solid body, since a solid can be divided according to a three-fold division" (*Leg. All.* I.3); it is "full and perfect, consisting of beginning, middle, and end" (*Qu. Gen.* III.3); and the triad is complete, "having beginning, middle, and end, which are equal" (*Qu. Gen.* II.5). Thus Philo refers the oracles to Israel's beginnings in the past (*Vit. Mos.* I. 279), on Israel's γένεσις, her present status as divinely blessed (*e.g.*, *Vit. Mos.* I. 284, 289), and her future victorious destiny (*Vit. Mos.* I. 290–291). Signifying completeness, the number three used to formulate Balaam's oracles invites the reader to regard the seer's words as a full expression of Israel's significance.

Secondly, Philo and the Rabbis insist that Balaam was a villain.[3] Despite this, Philo contends that his words about Israel were genuinely prophetic. Balaam spoke his first oracle as one possessed by the prophetic spirit (προφητικοῦ πνεύματος ἐπιφοιτήσαντος) which had ridded him of his soothsayer's craft, since it was not right for magical sophistry to dwell alongside most holy possession (*Vit. Mos.* I. 277); the second oracle he *prophesied* in words not his own (*Vit. Mos.* I. 283, 286); and the third he spoke ἔνθους, inspired by God (*Vit. Mos.* I. 288). Balaam contributed nothing to the oracles: he spoke as God's instrument, expounding another's words, without employing his own reason (*Vit. Mos.* I. 277, 283). Even as a Gentile sooth-

---

[2] On the related text *De Praem.* 91–97, 163–172, see Borgen (1992), pp. 342–343, 348–351, 354–360.

[3] See G. Vermes, "The Story of Balaam: The Scriptural Origin of Haggadah", in G. Vermes, *Scripture and Tradition in Judaism* (Leiden, 2nd ed. 1973), pp. 127–177; J.R. Baskin, *Pharaoh's Counsellors: Job, Jethro, and Balaam in Rabbinic and Patristic Tradition* (Chico, 1983), pp. 94–96; M.S. Moore, *The Balaam Traditions: Their Character and Development* (Atlanta, 1990), pp. 66–67, 103; J.T. Greene, *Balaam and His Interpreters* (Atlanta, 1992), pp. 145–147; and M. McNamara, "Early Exegesis in the Palestinian Targum (Neofiti 1) Numbers 24", *Proc. of the Irish Bib. Ass.* 16 (1993), pp. 57–79.

sayer, Balaam accurately predicted the future (*Vit. Mos.* I. 264–265). Inspired by God, therefore, his prophecy was to be of exceptional quality.[4] So much is evident when Philo's words are juxtaposed with LXX's account of Balaam: never do the latter refer to him as προφήτης or say that he spoke in προφητεία, saying only that the Spirit of God came upon him.[5] Rather, it is the Targums which most closely reflect Philo's belief that Balaam's oracles about Israel were those of a remarkable prophet.

Where MT records that Balaam "took up his parable", the Targums specify that he "took up the parable of his prophecy" (Num. 23:7; 24:3, 15 in TN, PJ, FTV, FTP; Num. 23:18 TN, PJ). The spirit of God which came upon him (MT of Num. 24:2) was, for TO and PJ, "the spirit of prophecy from before the Lord". Balaam calls himself שְׁתֻם הָעָיִן (Num. 24:3,15), the one "with the penetrating eye".[6] TN, FTP, and FTP took this to mean that "what had been concealed from all the prophets is revealed to him"; PJ put "for hidden mysteries [דרזיא סתימיא] which had been concealed from the prophets were revealed to him".[7] These Targums elevate the revelation to Balaam above that granted to other prophets, further stressing his status in their versions of Num. 24:4 with the note (TN, FTP, FTV) that "mysteries of prophecy were revealed to him": PJ of this verse calls these "hidden mysteries". How these Targums

---

[4] For Philo's theory of prophecy, see Baskin (1983), pp. 93–94; J.R. Levison, "Inspiration and the Divine Spirit in the Writings of Philo Judaeus", *JSJ* 26 (1995), pp. 271–323. J.R. Levison, *The Spirit in First Century Judaism* (Leiden, 1997), pp. 29–33, 47–55, 229–233 examines Philo's Balaam story, comparing it with that of Josephus: both writers, in his view, distance God's direct power from Balaam, by making an angelic spirit possess him. He argues that both have been influenced by (*inter alia*) Hellenistic treatises on oracular inspiration, including Plutarch's essay *De Defectu Oraculorum*. He says little, however, about the content of the oracles, and does not discuss Philo's emphasis on Balaam's seeing rather than hearing them. See further below.

[5] So MT and LXX of Num. 24:2; cf. LXX Num. 23:6. See further Vermes (1973), pp. 144–145, and G. Dorival, *La Bible d'Alexandrie*, vol. 4 *Les Nombres* (Paris, 1994), pp. 434, 444–445.

[6] So rendered by M. Rosenbaum and A.M. Silbermann, *Pentateuch with Targum Onkelos, Haphtaroth and Rashi's Commentary*, Numbers (New York, 1946), pp. 118, 120.

[7] These Targums expound the first Hebrew word twice, first as from root שתם "to close" implying something concealed, and then as from root שתם "to open" as it occurs in some Rabbinic texts: see also *b. Sanh.* 105a; *Nid.* 31a, and B. Grossfeld, *The Targum Onqelos to Leviticus and Numbers* (Edinburgh, 1988), p. 136; H. Rouillard, *La Péricope de Balaam (Nombres 22–24) La Prose et les 'Oracles'* (Paris, 1985), pp. 347–350; Dorival (1994), p. 138; A. Salvesen, *Symmachus in the Pentateuch* (Manchester, 1991), p. 133; M. McNamara, *Targum Neofiti 1: Numbers* (Edinburgh, 1995), p. 136.

relate to Philo's description of Balaam constitutes the final general point.

LXX translated Balaam's self-description "the man with the penetrating eye" (Num. 24:3,15) as ὁ ἄνθρωπος ὁ ἀληθινῶς ὁρῶν, "the man who truly sees". This Philo retained as introduction to his third and final Balaam oracle. LXX of Num. 24:4 and 16 describe Balaam as "hearing the utterances of God"; 24:16 says that he "knows the knowledge of the Most High"; and both verses state that "he saw the vision of God in sleep, his eyes being uncovered". Philo radically altered these words, to make Balaam speak of himself as ὅστις καθ᾽ ὕπνον ἐναργῆ φαντασίαν εἶδε θεοῦ τοῖς τῆς ψυχῆς ἀκοιμήτοις ὄμμασιν, "the one who saw in sleep a clear presentation of God with the unsleeping eyes of the soul" (*Vit. Mos.* I. 289). He suppressed the references to Balaam's hearing God, and his knowledge of the Most High. His emphasis is wholly on *sight*. Most tellingly, Balaam's "uncovered eyes" of LXX become "the unsleeping eyes of the soul".

Something extraordinary has happened. By so speaking of Balaam, Philo has invested him with the character of Israel, whose name at first was Jacob. Philo insists that 'Israel' means "the one who sees God", as distinct from Jacob, which means 'practiser' and who receives instruction by hearing.[8] The object of Israel's sight is knowledge of the divine, as the following passage from *De Mig. Abr.* 39 makes plain: it should be carefully compared with Philo's words about Balaam. Here Philo comments on Jacob's change of name to Israel, indicating vision through the eyes of the soul which is superior to hearing:

> For the coin of learning and teaching from which Jacob took his surname is engraved anew into Israel, "the one who sees". Now through this comes about the seeing of the divine light, which does not differ from knowledge, which opens the eye of the soul and leads it to perceptions more luminous and clear than those which come by hearing.[9]

---

[8] Of numerous examples, see especially *Leg. All.* II.34; III.172,186; *De Conf.* 56, 72; *De Praem.* 27; *De. Ebr.* 82; *De Mig.* 125, 200, 224. For etymologies of Hebrew names, Philo possibly used Jewish tradition: see G.J. Brooke, *Exegesis at Qumran: 4QFlorilegium in its Jewish Context* (Sheffield, 1985), pp. 17–25. L.L. Grabbe, *Etymology in Early Jewish Interpretation: The Hebrew Names in Philo* (Atlanta, 1988), argues (pp. 102–113) that Philo may have used an onomasticon: for discussion of Israel, see pp. 172–173.

[9] See also *De Somn.* I.129. For Philo's interpretation of Jacob's encounter at the Jabbok, when his name was changed to Israel, see A. Butterweck, *Jakobs Ringkampf am Jabbok: Gen. 32, 4ff. in der jüdischen Tradition bis zum Frühmittelatler* (Frankfurt-am-Main, 1981), pp. 62–71.

Why should Balaam be presented as prophesying *in persona Israel*, about the past, present and future of the Jewish people? Undoubtedly his self-designation as "the man who truly sees" (LXX Num. 24:3,15; cf. 23:9) gave Philo reason to link the prophet with Israel; but Jewish tradition encouraged him to go further. For according to TN, PJ, FTV, and a Tosefta Targum of Gen. 49:1, the dying Jacob-Israel had summoned his twelve sons to announce to them "the hidden mysteries", including the secret of Israel's redemption; but these mysteries, when revealed, were immediately concealed from him.[10] The Targums, however, declare that Balaam knew "hidden mysteries" in his prophecy, the very things hidden from Jacob-Israel. Thus the Targums, like Philo, made of Balaam a latter-day mouthpiece of Jacob-Israel. This is not surprising. The Targumists could not fail to notice strong similarities in wording between Jacob-Israel's blessings in Gen. 49 and Balaam's oracles. Most striking among these are the lion imagery applied by Jacob to the tribe of Judah in Gen. 49:9, reflected closely in Num. 23:24 and 24:9; and mysterious reference to a שֵׁבֶט, 'sceptre', in both Gen. 49:10 and Num. 24:17. These, and other verbal similarities, allowed the Targumists to interpret Balaam's oracles with an eye to Jacob's blessings.[11] That Philo followed a similar procedure is indicated by a small but significant detail. In paraphrasing Balaam's lion imagery he twice (*Vit. Mos.* I. 284, 291) uses forms of the verb ἐγείρειν to refer to the rousing or rising up of the lion alluded to in Num. 23:24; 24:9. LXX used this same verb at Gen. 49:9, where Jacob asks who shall rouse (τίς ἐγερεῖ) the lion's whelp which is Judah? Strikingly, LXX used a compound form of this verb in their translation of Num. 24:19, speaking of the famous 'star' which Balaam predicted as destined to arise from Jacob: the Hebrew states that this star shall "exercise dominion" (וירד), but LXX rendered the verb as "he shall awake" or "rise up"

---

[10] For the Tosefta Targum, see M.L. Klein, *Genizah Manuscripts of Palestinian Targum to the Pentateuch*, vol. 1 (Cincinnati, 1986), pp. 162–163, which speaks of רזייה טמירה (cf. FTV). TN and PJ speak of the mysteries as סתמייא, as in their version of Num. 24:3. On the Targums of Gen. 49:1 and the Balaam oracles, see also A.N. Chester, *Divine Revelation and Divine Titles in the Pentateuchal Targumim* (Tübingen, 1986), pp. 199–203.

[11] Note references to טרף, 'prey', in Num. 23:24 and Gen. 49:9; the verb כרע, "bow down" in Num. 24:9 and Gen. 49:9, and the 'lioness' with the lion in Num. 24:9 and Gen. 49:9; and cf. B.B. Levy, *Targum Neophyti 1: A Textual Study*, vol. 1 (Lanham, 1986), pp. 281–282; R. Syrén, *The Blessings in the Targums* (Åbo, 1986), pp. 54, 102, 196; and J.L.W. Schaper, "The Unicorn in the Messianic Imagery of the Greek Bible", *JTS* 45 (1994), pp. 130–131.

(ἐξεγερθήσεται). It seems likely that LXX had already established a lexical connection between the fourth Balaam oracle and Jacob's blessing of Judah, which later interpreters might exploit.[12]

In fine, Philo portrayed Balaam's oracles as prophecy of the highest order, uttered in the person of Jacob-Israel. This prophecy he presented as three oracles, thereby signifying its completeness and perfection as it speaks of Israel's past, present, and future. Although he evidently knew the LXX version of the Balaam narrative, Philo makes use of exegetical details found also in the Targums. These clarify his purpose in re-writing Balaam's oracles, and must now be addressed.

2. Philo's version of the oracles and the Aramaic Targums

Examination of the substance of Balaam's three oracles shows that Philo is familiar with traditions of Jewish exegesis preserved in the Aramaic Targums. Here we can discuss only a selection of those germane to the task in hand. Thus in the first oracle Balaam declares of Israel:

> Behold, the people shall dwell alone, and shall not be reckoned among the nations. (Num. 23:9)

Philo recasts this as follows to speak of

> ... a people which shall dwell on its own, not numbered with other nations – not because they dwell at random, nor because of the segregation of their lands (from those of others), but because of the distinctive character of their special customs – not being mixed with others so as to change the customs of their forefathers. (*Vit. Mos.* I. 278)

This owes little to LXX, who remained close to the original Hebrew; but it recalls FTP and FTV (cf. also TN):

> Behold, these people encamp on their own, and do not mix themselves with the laws (*or:* customs, Aramaic נימוסי) of the nations.

More complex is what follows. Having made Balaam proclaim Israel's fidelity to ancestral custom, Philo uses his first of the three prophetic utterances to describe Israel's origins in *Vit. Mos.* I. 279:

---

[12] In LXX of the Pentateuch, ἐγείρειν occurs at Gen. 41:4, 7; 49:9; Exod. 5:8; 23:5 (some Mss.); Num. 10:35 (some Mss.), and ἐξεγείρειν at Gen. 28:16; 41:21; Num. 10:35; 24:19. For its rendering of Hebrew "have dominion" in this last verse, see Dorival (1994), p. 140.

Who has found accurately the first foundation of the beginning (γενέσεως) of these people? Their bodies are formed of human seed, but their souls are sprung from divine seed; therefore, they are near of kin to God.[13]

Philo seems to be expounding LXX Num. 23:10, where Balaam asks who has calculated accurately the seed of Jacob, and who shall number the peoples of Israel? Yet on closer inspection LXX seem not to provide Philo with a springboard for such specific comments about Israel's beginning and character. The Hebrew of Num. 23:9 and its Targums offered him much more. In the Hebrew of this verse, Balaam sees Israel "from the top of the rocks", צֻרִים מֵרֹאשׁ, words which may equally be rendered "from the *beginning* of the rocks". The Targums understood them thus, with reference to the spiritual character of Israel's great founding ancestors, making Balaam say:

> For I see this people being led and walking in the merit of the right-
> eous fathers who are likened to mountains, Abraham, Isaac, and Jacob;
> and through the merit of the righteous mothers who are likened to
> the hills, Sarah, Rebeccah, Rachel and Leah.[14]

Like Philo's exegesis, this takes account both of Israel's ancestry and spiritual affinity. On the latter, Philo is forceful: Israel's souls are of divine origin, being near of kin to God, ἀγχίσποροι θεοῦ. The word ἀγχίσπορος is rare in Philo's writings; and its use here relates the Israel of Balaam's prophecy both with their righteous ancestors, and with all those whose reason leads them to practise virtue in accord with God's law.[15] Thus in *De Op. Mundi* 144 Philo speaks of rational natures like the *stars* in whose company dwells man, who is "near of kin to God": the stars are divine, unblemished souls in purest form (*De Plant.* 12; *De Gig.* 7–8) and especially represent the Patriarchs (*Quis Rerum* 86ff.) to whom God promised that their seed

---

[13] See Colson's note in *Philo* VI, p. 420, where he renders καταβολή as 'sowing' rather than 'foundation': he gains support from Philo's use of the word in *De Op. Mundi* 132; *Quis Rerum* 115; *Spec. Leg.* III.36; *Leg. ad Gaium* 54.

[14] TN of Num. 23:9; see also PJ, FTP, and FTV. On LXX of Num. 23:9–10, see Dorival (1994), pp. 435–436. For 'rocks' as Patriarchs and 'hills' as Matriarchs, see TN, PJ, FTP of Gen. 49:26; Deut. 33:15; FTP of Exod. 17:12; *Exod. Rab.* 16:8; *Numb. Rab.* 20:19; *b. RH* 11a; *Tanh. Balak* 12; *Mekh. de R. Ishmael Amalek* 1:116–118; N.A. van Uchelen, "The Targumic Versions of Deuteronomy 33:15: Some Remarks on the Origin of a Traditional Exegesis", *JJS* 31 (1980), pp. 199–209; Syrén (1986), p. 59; McNamara (1995), p. 131.

[15] For Philo's other uses of ἀγχίσπορος, see *De Op. Mundi* 144; *Spec. Leg.* IV.14, 236; *De Virt.* 80. In what follows, Philo applies Balaam's words about Israel to prac-tisers of virtue: see further Borgen (1992), pp. 346–351.

should be like the stars (Gen. 15:5). The Patriarchs and their right-eous children are privileged, like all who obey God's law: they will live for ever as stars (*De Dec.* 49), realizing the destiny intended by God for people who are "near of kin" to Him (*Spec. Leg.* IV.14). Neither the Hebrew nor LXX of Balaam's first oracle refer to stars, and the association of them with those "near of kin" to God may seem removed from the words of Scripture; but the Targums refer to the stars in Num. 23:10, which asks who has counted the dust of Jacob? FTP and FTV translate the question:

> Who can number the young men of the house of Jacob, of whom it was said that they should be as numerous as the stars of heaven?[16]

Here the Targums introduce *stars*, significant elsewhere in Philo's writings and directly related to his views on souls "near of kin" to God. In brief, the Targums of Num. 23:9–10 catalogue Israel's phys-ical origins, spiritual character, and her numbers like the stars. These elements lay the foundation for Philo's exegesis, not easily derived from LXX, but entirely comprehensible in the light of the Targum.

Philo's second Balaam oracle paraphrases Num. 23:19, the Hebrew of which may be rendered as

> God is not man, that he should lie, nor a son of man, that he should repent. Has he said, and shall he not perform it? Or has he spoken, and shall he not establish it?

LXX altered Balaam's opening words, saying that God is not like man to waver, nor like a son of man to be threatened; but retained the following questions of the original.[17] Philo (*Vit. Mos.* I. 283), how-ever, follows the opening Hebrew of the verse, before continuing with an expanded interpretation:

> He will utter absolutely nothing at all which shall not be steadfastly completed, since his word is his deed.

---

[16] The Hebrew of 23:10 begins: "Who has counted the dust of Jacob, and the number of the fourth part of Israel?" This recalls God's promises to Abraham and Jacob that their descendants should be like the dust of the earth: see Gen. 13:16 (where the same verb 'count', מנה, is used) and 28:14, neither of which, however, has any reference to 'stars'. These are introduced by the Targums: cf. TN, "Who can number the young men of the house of Jacob, of whom it was said that they should be blessed like the dust of the earth? Or who can number one of the four orders of the camps of Israel, of whom it was said, they shall be as numerous as the stars?"

[17] See further Dorival (1994), pp. 438–439.

TN, FTP, FTV and TO eliminate the questions of the second half of the verse, turning them into statements. TO of Num. 23:19 recalls Philo's paraphrase:

> The word of God is not like the words of the sons of man. Sons of man say, and tell lies. Also it is not like the deeds of the sons of flesh, who decree that action be taken, but repent of it. He says and performs, and all his word he establishes.

Again in the second oracle, Philo makes Balaam describe Israel's present status by saying that God, who scattered the Egyptians and brought them up from their land, conspicuously covers them with a shield (*Vit. Mos.* I. 284). He is expounding Num. 23:21, where the Hebrew reports that Israel's God is with him, and the shout of a king is in his midst. Nothing in the Hebrew or LXX of this verse prepares us for mention of a shield; but TN (cf. FTP and FTV) explain that

> The word of the Lord their God is with them; and the trumpet-blast of the glorious splendour of their king is a shield over them.

Philo's correspondence with Targumic exegesis shown here could be illustrated further. He uses LXX's vocabulary, only to depart from its sense to incorporate notions attested in the Targum. Josephus, too, in recounting Balaam's prophecy, shows knowledge of traditions found in Targum, demonstrating their currency in his day and strengthening the case for Philo's knowledge of them: Geza Vermes has presented the evidence for this, which need not be repeated.[18] With due care, therefore, Targumic material may be used to illuminate Philo's re-written Balaam oracles.

3. *Imperial victory and the triumphal hymn*

Borgen has perceived that Philo fastened upon Israel's victory over Egypt at the Exodus as a guarantee of future victories.[19] This is corroborated by his retaining Balaam's two almost identical utterances of Num. 23:22; 24:8 at *Vit. Mos.* I. 284, 290 within his second and third Balaam oracles respectively. Since he has condensed four biblical oracles into three, this is of moment: he uses one verse in his second oracle, speaking mostly of Israel's present, and the other in

---

[18] See Vermes (1973) *passim*.
[19] See Borgen (1992), pp. 352–354.

the third oracle, dealing with Israel's future. A translation of the Hebrew
of the verses yields:

> God brings them (Num. 24:8 has 'him') out from Egypt: he has as it
> were the horns (or: strength) of a wild ox.

Interpreters could not ignore two such verses, loosely phrased and
slightly differing from each other, separated only by a brief intervening text. Both LXX and Targum shed light on what Philo made
of them. First, the majority of LXX witnesses to Num. 23:22 took
the verse to mean:

> God is the One who brings *them* out from Egypt: He has as it were
> the glory of an unicorn (δόξα μονοκέρωτος).

Here the unicorn's glory can belong only to God, and what Schaper
calls a "spiritualizing translation" has been adopted.[20] This has no
bearing on Philo's second and third Balaam oracles, where he takes
the beast with one horn as a description of Israel: God brought
Israel from Egypt "as one man" (*Vit. Mos.* I. 284) and is led by God
from Egypt "as a single army wing" (Vit. Mos. I. 290).[21] The ambiguous LXX of Num. 24:8, however, allows such an exposition: God
brought *him* out of Egypt and *he* (understood as meaning Israel) has
an unicorn's glory.[22]

The Targums of Num. 23:22; 24:8, however, took the 'horns' or
"strength of a wild ox" as attributes of God, who had redeemed
Israel at the Exodus. FTP and FTV of both verses read:

> God who redeemed and brought them out redeemed from Egypt,
> strength and praise and exaltation belong to him.

PJ is similar, adding 'power' to the list. TN and TO omit references
to redemption, TO listing only "strength and exaltation" as belong-
ing to God; otherwise, they agree with the Fragment Targums. The
language of the Targums of Num. 23:22; 24:8 recalls Targums of
the hymn sung after the Exodus. It is called "the hymn of this praise"
(TN Exod. 15:1) or "the praise of this hymn" (FTP, FTV, PJ, and
glosses of TN Exod. 15:1). In it, God is styled "the strength and
mighty One of our praises" (PJ; cf. TN, TO, FTP Exod. 15:2). Israel
must 'exalt' God (PJ, FTP, FTV Exod. 15:2). God's 'power' and

---

[20] See Schaper (1994), pp. 120–121, and Dorival (1994), p. 138.
[21] See further Borgen (1992), p. 352.
[22] See also LXX in Codex Alexandrinus of Num. 23:22; but the unicorn as such
has no place in Philo's work.

'strength' are acclaimed (PJ, FTP, FTV Exod. 15:3; TO, TN Exod. 15:7; TN, FTP Exod. 15:13; TN, PJ Exod. 15:18). God is the one "feared in praises" (PJ, FTP, FTV Exod. 15:11), whose 'strength' and 'power' destroyed the Egyptians (TN, PJ, FTV Exod. 15:16).

The Targums took Balaam's words about the wild ox to mean attributes of God revealed in the Exodus, later celebrated in the hymn honouring his triumph. Philo understood this hymn as addressed to "God the giver of victory and the gloriously victorious" (*De Agr.* 79) and sung by all the men of Israel, "not with blind intention, but seeing keenly" (*De Agr.* 81). Now the Targumic interpretation of the phrase "horns of a wild ox" helps to explain the otherwise baffling mention of a hymn at the end of Philo's second Balaam oracle, paraphrasing LXX Num. 23:24,

> Behold, the people shall rise up like a lion's cub, and like a lion it shall exult: it shall not sleep until it eat prey and drink the blood of the wounded.

Philo retains some LXX vocabulary, but gives the verse a different sense:

> I see the people rising like a lion's cub, and like a lion exulting: he shall eat his fill of prey and take for drink the blood of the wounded; and when he is satiated he will not turn to sleep, but unsleeping he will sing the hymn of victory, ἐγρηγορὼς τὸν ἐπινίκιον ᾄσεται ὕμνον. (*Vit. Mos.* I. 284)

Nothing in the Bible suggests this climax of Philo's second Balaam oracle. The Targumic evidence is thus especially valuable, and is best appreciated in light of Philo's overall train of thought. First (*Vit. Mos.* I. 282) he tells how Balak sent Balaam to get good auspicies (αἰσίους) by means of birds and voices (οἰωνοὺς καὶ φήμας). Balaam, however, prophesied that God would be a shield for the Hebrews: he had scattered the evils of the Egyptians and brought up Israel as one man. Therefore Hebrews disregard omens of birds (οἰωνῶν) and oracle-mongering, trusting in the One Ruler of the world (*Vit. Mos.* I. 283–284). Then Balaam sees the people rising like a lion to sing the victory hymn.

All this smacks of the Roman triumph. The words ἐπινίκιον ὕμνον in particular suggest chants sung during the triumphal procession of a victorious *imperator*.[23] To qualify for a triumph, the victor must

---

[23] This very phrase is found in Plutarch's *Life of Romulus* 16 describing one of the archetypical triumphs of a Roman leader.

have been a magistrate possessing his own *auspicia*, that is, the right
to consult the omens, especially those of birds: at least five thousand
of a foreign enemy must have been killed, with outright victory ensuing. The victor must have been acclaimed *imperator*, and have been
granted the right to retain his *imperium* within the boundaries of
Rome. Such was the custom in the last days of the Roman republic.
As an adult, however, Philo would have known the custom of the
Empire established by Augustus, when triumphs became the prerogative of the emperor himself or members of his family.[24] On one
level, the message is plain. Philo makes Balaam prophesy the triumph of the One God, the "emperor of the world", celebrated by
his unique people (*Vit. Mos.* I. 278–279) in their triumphal hymn at
the Exodus.[25] This emperor's triumph requires no *auspicia*: Balaam,
prophesying *in persona Israel*, does without them – like the people he
represents, who 'unsleeping', "wide awake" (ἐγρηγορὼς) sing the triumphal ode in honour of God the victor.

There is, however, another sense of the words about the triumphal
hymn, which use future tenses about it and hint at victories yet to be
won. Furthermore, the role of Moses as Israel's (earthly) *imperator*
in the defeat of the Egyptians, although not explicitly acknowledged,
would be evident to any Jew reading Philo's words. A resounding
victory achieved without the taking of auspicies may be construed
as a victory over *auspicia* themselves, and over the polytheistic religion which they represent. Philo's words imply future victories (however understood) for Jewish monotheism over pagan polytheism, as
his treatise *De Vita Contemplativa* shows.

There, Balaam's prophecy of the triumphal hymn chanted by the
unsleeping is fulfilled among the Therapeutae.[26] They truly represent

---

[24] Philo's emphasis on the bird omens (again at *Vit. Mos.* I. 287) confirms that
he here speaks in terms of a triumph and its necessary *auspicia*: see details in H.S.
Versnel, *Triumphus: An Inquiry into the Origin, Development and Meaning of the Roman
Triumph* (Leiden, 1970), pp. 174–193, and (for the relationship of *auspicia* to *imperium*)
pp. 304–355. For bird omens, see also Moore (1990), pp. 66–67. Space forbids discussion of religious aspects of the Roman triumph, which may illuminate further
what Philo makes Balaam say in this second oracle.

[25] See above and PJ of Num. 23:24 where Israel's likeness to a lioness is interpreted to mean that she is unique, יחידאה.

[26] For this group, see Philo's *De Vita Contemplativa*, relevant passages of which are
given in G. Vermes and M. Goodman (ed.), *The Essenes according to the Classical Sources*
(Sheffield, 1989), pp. 75–99; and see E. Schürer, *The History of the Jewish People in
the Age of Jesus Christ*, vol. 2, G. Vermes, F. Millar, and M. Black (eds.) (Edinburgh,
1979), pp. 591–597.

Israel, "the one who sees God", since they are constantly taught to use sight and to aspire to the vision of the One who exists (*Vit. Con.* 10–13). They mind only the pursuit of virtue and contemplation of God, which they celebrate each year in a great festival (most likely Pentecost). This celebration culminates in hymns, dancing, and hymns of thanksgiving (εὐχαριστηρίους ὕμνους) throughout the night in imitation of the victory song which Moses and Miriam led after the Exodus (*Vit. Con.* 84–88). The participants celebrate without sleep until dawn; then, more wide awake (διεγηγερμένοι) than when the feast began, they greet sunrise with a prayer for truth and sharp-sighted reasoning (*Vit. Con.* 89). These people, says Philo, live for the contemplation of nature, and in soul alone; they are citizens of heaven and of the world, presented to the Father and maker of all by vitue (*Vit. Con.* 90).

This description marks the Therapeutae as supreme examples of those who have fought and obtained spiritual victory over the passions. Thus in *De Sob.* 13 Philo remarks that Moses' hymn is sung by "the one who sees" after defeating Egypt, the enemy of the soul; and in *De Ebr.* 104–121, speaking of the war waged in each human body between virtue and the passions, he contrasts the person who has vision of the One with the thoughtless man who fails to discern the cause of things and ends up fashioning 'gods'. Such polytheism produces atheism in the souls of the senseless, whom Abraham rebuked in his hymn of thanks (Gen. 14:22).[27] Moses led the song at the Exodus and the song of the well (Num. 21:16–18): both he and Abraham are leaders of the hymn of triumph and thanksgiving, τὸν ἐπινίκιον καὶ εὐχαριστικὸν ὕμνον, celebrating the triumph of virtue in the soul. Simply expressed, everyone who overcomes the passions, embraces virtue, and arrives at the vision of God (and thus shares Israel's character) may chant the imperial triumph hymn, now and in the future. In this sense, there are yet victories for Jews to win, the most important of which will bring all mankind into submission to the universal cosmic Law, the Law given to Moses. As Borgen has perceived, Philo believed that this last victory would come about through the 'man' of Balaam's prophecy.[28]

---

[27] For affinities between Philo's depiction of Abraham and his description of the Therapeutae, see R. Martin-Achard, *Actualité d'Abraham* (Neuchâtel, 1969), pp. 132–137.

[28] Borgen (1992), pp. 353–360. From what has been said here about the Therapeutae, it should be evident that there is truth in Hecht's comment (1987),

4. The "man who shall come forth" and his antecedents

The Hebrew text of Balaam's third oracle (Num. 24:7) cryptically declares of Israel that

> Water shall flow from his buckets, and his seed shall be on many waters; and his king shall be higher than Agag, and his kingdom shall be exalted.

LXX 'decoded' this metaphorical language to yield:

> A man shall come forth from his seed and shall exercise lordship over many nations; and his kingdom shall be exalted higher than Gog, and his kingdom shall be increased.[29]

Philo represents this in his third oracle, dealing with Israel's future, working changes to LXX which are italicized in the translation below. He makes Balaam say (*Vit. Mos.* I. 290):

> *At some time* a man shall come forth from *you* and he shall *get the mastery* over many nations: and *the* kingdom *of this man, advancing day by day* shall be *exalted to the height.*

Balaam, speaking in the person of Israel, predicts his coming from 'you', Israel's children here addressed. He will get mastery (ἐπικρατήσει) rather than exercise lordship (κυριεύσει), suggesting an extension of his power through struggle, confirmed by the note that his kingdom will advance daily. The imagery suggests a military commander like a Roman general exercising *imperium*, inexorably overcoming opposition. The goal of his kingdom is "the height", that is, heaven.

The exegesis shows affinities with both LXX and interpretation preserved in Targum. Philo compressed Balaam's four biblical oracles into three, encouraged no doubt by verbal similarities between the third and fourth oracles. Noteworthy is Num. 24:17, the prophecy in the fourth oracle that "a star shall march forth from Jacob, and a sceptre arise out of Israel", which LXX took to mean that a star should come from Jacob, and a *man* rise up out of Israel, thus inviting a direct link with LXX Num. 24:7's prediction of a *man* com-

---

p. 162 that for Philo "the first line of meaning for Messiah and Messianic Era was the inner experience in which the soul was transformed. The Logos turns man from the chaos of the senses and pleasure toward the intelligible world". But that is not the whole story as regards the Balaam oracles.

[29] On this exegesis, see Dorival (1994), pp. 139, 446.

ing forth.[30] This last verse could then be read in the light of 24:17, which Hebrew and LXX amplify (in Num. 24:18–19) by predicting the man's destruction of Moabites, the sons of Seth, Edomites, and an unnamed city: here we have a ready-made list of "many nations" which the man will subdue one by one. Philo says nothing of the *star* predicted in Num. 24:17; but stars featured in his interpretation of these oracles, as he intimates that the whole Jewish people may be regarded as stars insofar as they are "near of kin to God".[31] In this last oracle, he appears deliberately to focus on the 'man' as single leader and representative of the multitudinous 'stars' who are "near of kin to God".

Philo has links with traditions preserved in Targum. We give TO, then TN, of Num. 24:7.

> The king who shall be anointed from among his sons shall increase and have dominion over many nations; and his king shall be stronger than Agag, and his kingship shall be exalted.
>
> Their king shall arise from among them, and their redeemer shall be from among them. He shall gather for them their exiles from the provinces of their enemies; and his sons shall have dominion over many peoples. He shall be stronger than Saul [who] sp[ared] Agag, king of the Amalekites; and the kingship of King Messiah shall be exalted.

In certain details, LXX and Targum share the same essential exegesis. The 'water' of the Hebrew text becomes a person, 'man' who has a 'kingdom' in LXX and 'king' in Targum; both versions take its 'flowing' from the 'buckets' to indicate the origin of this person from Israel; and the "many waters" become "many nations" ruled by this individual.[32] LXX, however, speak of Gog rather than Agag of the Hebrew text: this is followed neither by Targums nor by Philo.[33] Finally, the Targums refer this verse and its companion Num. 24:17 to an anointed king or Messiah. LXX are more reticent, speak-

---

[30] For a succinct account of messianic interpretation of this verse, see Dorival (1994), pp. 451–453; for its use in eschatological prayer at Qumran, see B. Nitzan, *Qumran Prayer and Religious Poetry* (Leiden, 1994), pp. 216–217. On the Balaam oracles and Qumran in general, see McNamara (1993), pp. 61–62 and the literature there cited.

[31] See above pp. 25–26.

[32] See further Dorival (1994), p. 139, and R. le Déaut, *Targum du Pentateuque III Nombres* (Paris, 1979), pp. 230–233.

[33] Mention of Gog may allow LXX to avoid reference to a Davidic monarch: so Dorival (1994), pp. 139–140; but see Schaper (1994), pp. 127–131 for a different view.

ing of the 'man' and "his kingdom". While at first glance Philo seems
to reflect the reserve of LXX, closer inspection suggests that he has
in mind a figure arising from the tribe of Judah, as a summary of
the rest of his third oracle (*Vit. Mos.* I. 290–291) will help to show.
For mention of the 'man' is followed by the second exposition of the
"horns of the wild ox": God has acted as Israel's guide from Egypt,
leading them as a single army-wing consuming its enemies and eating
their fatness to the marrow and destroying them with his archery
(cf. Num. 24:8). The oracle ends with Philo's version of Num. 24:9,
a prediction that the people, after the appearing of the 'man',

> shall rest lying down like a lion or a lion's cub, entirely disdainful,
> fearing no-one, producing fear in others. Wretched is he who disturbs
> and rouses him. Those who bless you are worthy of blessing, but those
> who curse you are worthy of curses.

Philo has so restructured the oracle as to place the 'man' and his
kingdom in the same network of ideas as the single army-wing led
by divine guidance under Moses from Egypt. As Borgen has shown,
this past activity of God's provides the guarantee for what will happen in the future.[34] The final outcome is the lying down of Israel
to rest in the manner of a lion, elaborated on the basis of Num.
24:9, which concludes the oracles. Philo has yet retained the two
separate biblical mentions of the lion (Num. 23:24 in *Vit. Mos.* I.
284; Num. 24:9 in *Vit. Mos.* I. 291). Evidently, he regards them as
significant as the two Biblical verses with their 'unicorn' imagery.
They somehow encapsulate Israel's destiny as she is led by the 'man',
whose kingdom advances and is exalted to the height. LXX of Num.
24:9 alone cannot account for Philo's words. It reads:

> He lay down, he rested like a lion and like a lion's cub: who shall
> raise him up? Those who bless you are blessed, and those who curse
> you are cursed.

Philo made the first part of this utterance refer to the future, elim-
inated the question, and added remarks about the lion's lack of fear
and his inculcation of terror in others. In certain respects, his exegesis recalls TN of Num. 24:9, reading

> They rest and encamp (Ngl adds: in the midst of war) like a lion and
> like a lioness, and there is no nation or kingdom which shall stand
> bef(ore them) . . .

---

[34] Borgen (1992), pp. 353–357.

The repetition of the lion imagery recalls Israel's praise of Judah in Gen. 49:8ff.; and given that Balaam prophesies *in the person of Israel*, this emphasis on the lion and its cub compels us to return to the words of Jacob-Israel in blessing his sons, and their interpretation amongst Philo's fellow Jews. Here is TN's version of Jacob-Israel's blessing of Judah in Gen. 49:9, so similar to TN of Num. 24:9.

> I liken you, O Judah, to a lion's cub. You rescued my son Joseph from his killers. In the matter of Tamar, my son, you were innocent. You rest and encamp in the midst of war like a lion and like a lioness; and there is no kingdom or people that shall stand against you.[35]

TN and other Targums have undoubtedly associated Jacob's blessing with Balaam's prophecy. Philo has done much the same, linking the 'man' and the lion imagery to an army encamping; for as he remarks before embarking on Balaam's final oracle, the Hebrews were encamped (ἐστρατοπεδευκότας) in order, resembling a city rather than a camp (*Vit. Mos.* I. 288). Philo's language is allusive rather than direct; but its sustained use of lion imagery, of terms associated with the imperial triumph, and of themes shared with Targumic tradition, combine to suggest that the 'man' whom he expected as the Jews' representative and final leader would emerge from the tribe of Judah, a lion of a man to represent a lion-like people.

5. *Conclusion*

The content of Balaam's oracles as re-written by Philo supports several elements of Peder Borgen's interpretation of the sage's eschatological opinions. By making Balaam speak *in persona Israel*, and by representing him as uttering *three* oracles (thus signalling their comprehensive character), Philo invests the prophecies with massive authority. This authority he reinforces with frequent allusions to traditional Jewish exegesis of these difficult utterances. Underlying his explanation of them is his awareness of their affinities with Jacob's blessing of his royal son Judah in Gen. 49:8–12, an awareness he shares with the Targums. He makes Balaam predict that Israel, after battle, will sing a victory hymn: this is without precedent in the Biblical text of the oracles, but may be explained with the help of the Targums and

---

[35] See also TO, and B. Grossfeld, *The Targum Onqelos to Genesis* (Edinburgh, 1988), pp. 162–163.

their exposition of Balaam's words. Philo has in mind a hymn of the sort sung at a Roman triumph, although the One to whom it is sung has no truck (unlike an earthly Roman *imperator*) with ominous birds. Mention of the hymn, nonetheless, emphasises the imperial character of Israel's leader, be it God throughout the ages, or the 'man' who shall come in future to get mastery over nations. This leader will eventually rule the world. And given Philo's strong affinities with the Targums throughout his exposition of Balaam's words, and his awareness of the links between those words and Gen. 49:8–12, it is likely that the 'man' will belong to the royal tribe of Judah.[36]

Philo acts primarily as a Biblical exegete in re-writing the Balaam oracles. He takes and moulds LXX to his needs by careful substitution of a word or phrase to bring it into conformity with tradition. Space prevents full comparison of Philo's exegetical work in these oracles with the Targums; but enough has been said to show beyond reasonable doubt that he knew of, and used, traditional material surviving today in those texts.[37] This evidence not only confirms Borgen's emphasis on Philo as a Biblical exegete, but also gives some support to Wolfson's view that Philo's notions of the messianic age agree in some measure with contemporary ideas in the Land of Israel.[38] In supporting conclusions advanced by these two scholars, this study has (it is hoped) underlined the importance of the *content* of Balaam's prophecies as represented by Philo. He evidently regarded them as having great authority. While much has been written about Philo's messianism in his writings as a whole, his re-structuring of Balaam's words and his motives for that re-writing have been comparatively neglected. This essay represents a modest attempt to address that neglect.

---

[36] *Pace* S. Sandmel, *Philo of Alexandria: An Introduction* (Oxford, 1979), pp. 109–110 and Hecht (1987), pp. 139–168, the latter seeing Philo's messianism as at best "a "realized eschatology" in which exegetical elements that might be nationalized and identified with specific mythical or historical figures in other systems of Jewish thought . . . became allegorical designators for the Logos . . ." (p. 162).

[37] See Vermes, (1973).

[38] See P. Borgen, "Philo of Alexandria", in M.E. Stone (ed.), *Jewish Writings of the Second Temple Period*, CRINT Section 2 (Assen, 1984), pp. 259–264; article "Philo of Alexandria", in *The Anchor Bible Dictionary*, D.N. Freedman (ed.), vol. 5 (New York, 1992), pp. 337–339. Wolfson (1948), vol. 2, pp. 395–426, advances some Targumic evidence in support of his case. Hecht's strictures on this (1987), pp. 143, 164, n. 12) should be reconsidered, given that Wolfson did not have access to Targum Neofiti.

THE FUTURE IN THE BOOK OF CHRONICLES

BY

P.B. DIRKSEN[1]
Leiden

Did the Chronicler[2] intend to convey to his readers a specific expectation concerning the future, be it 'eschatological', 'messianic', 'royalistic', or otherwise? This question has been a point of debate at least since G. Von Rad argued that there is a strong messianic expectation in Chronicles (*Geschichtsbild*; see below).[3]

This debate has not led to a consensus. On the contrary: there is still a wide spectrum of opinion. In general there are two diametrically opposed views, one assuming a specific expectation, the other refuting this assumption and arguing that the Chronicler was basically satisfied with the situation as it was.

The first view is advanced by the majority of scholars, but among them there is again a great variety of views with respect to both the arguments and the conclusions. There are, generally speaking, two lines of argumentation: (1) the idealized portrayal of (certain aspects of) the past implicitly refers to its realization in the future, understood either in a historical or in an eschatological sense; (2) the dynastic promise (1 Chron. 17), also in view of the references to it

---

[1] Full details of works referred to by author's name and date of publication can be found in the bibliography at the end of the article. I am indebted to my former missionary colleague, Mr. Richard G. Gibson, Lakeland, Fl., for correcting the English of this article at a number of points.

[2] In the past it was assumed by most scholars that Chronicles and Ezra-Nehemiah formed a single work, "the Chronistic History", from the hand of "the Chronicler". This consensus was challenged by S. Japhet, "The Supposed Common Authorship of Chronicles and Ezra-Nehemiah Investigated Anew", *VT* 18 (1968), pp. 330–71, and H.G.M. Williamson, *Israel in the Books of Chronicles* (Cambridge, 1977), pp. 5–70. Most scholars now no longer adopt this unity. In this article "the Chronicler" is the author of 1/2 Chronicles only.

[3] Von Rad (1930) made this messianic expectation an important aspect of the Chronicler's message, but, as Williamson (1983), pp. 306–7, has noted, the messianic interpretation of the Nathan passage in 1 Chron. 17, which plays a central role in Von Rad's argument, was defended as early as 1870 by C.F. Keil, *Biblischer Commentar über die nachexilischen Geschichtsbücher: Chronik, Esra, Nehemia und Esther*, BCAT (Leipzig, 1870), p. 164.

elsewhere in Chronicles, remains valid and awaits its fulfilment. In the latter case a distinction can again be made between a 'messianic' and a 'royalist' expectation, the latter being the expectation of a Davidic restoration in the course of history.

Within the confines of this article it is not possible to give a survey, let alone a discussion, of the various views and their underlying arguments. A useful survey is presented by H.G.M. Williamson, in his article "Eschatology in Chronicles" of 1977, in which special attention is paid, among others, to Mosis and Plöger, mentioned below.[4]

As an orientation it may suffice here to mention briefly some major views, including those of some authors who have expressed themselves on the subject more recently.

A prominent representative of the eschatological view is R. Mosis in his important monograph of 1973. Mosis bases his view on the overall structure of Chronicles. The past consists of three periods: that of Saul, which typifies the exilic situation (1 Chron. 10), that of David, which is the period of preparation, and that of Solomon, which is the era of completion. With the first period corresponds the exile, whereas the period of David finds its correspondence in the post-exilic period, in which the writer himself lives and which is still the time of preparation. This will be followed by a future Solomonic era, which will be one of final fulfilment.[5]

Apart from other reservations one may have, a major objection, as Williamson (1977, p. 132) has rightly pointed out, is that in these views David and Solomon are separated from each other, whereas the Chronicler consciously presents them as a unity. Moreover, although we must be cautious in attributing to a writer of almost two and a half millennia ago our sense of what constitutes literary clarity, one may wonder whether it is probable that a writing is directed toward such great expectations, yet keeps these implicit if not hidden in the overall structure. This holds good also for the following studies.

As indicated in the subtitle of his 1985 monograph, T.-S. Im defends the view that the Chronicler's idealized portrayal of David implicitly expresses the expectation of a Davidic messiah. This messianic expectation is, however, not eschatological but theocratic: the

---

[4] Another extensive survey is to be found in Kelly (1996), pp. 135–55. See for literature on the subject also I. Kalimi, *The Book of Chronicles – A Classified Bibliography* (Jerusalem, 1990), pp. 104–5 (Eschatology and Messianism).

[5] Mosis (1973), e.g. pp. 164–167.

future Davidic ruler of Israel will appear in the course of history
and his rule will be the realization of God's rule over his people.[6]

Another view has been advanced by E.M. Dörrfuss in his 1994
monograph. He argues that the Moses passages in Chronicles are
additions by a later redactor who was critical of the dominant role
attributed to David/Solomon and the Jerusalem temple with its cultic establishment based on royal authority. He tried to redress this
by emphasising the role of Moses and the early cultic order based
on his God-given authority. The Moses redaction, and with it the
Book of Chronicles in its final form (pp. 17, 282), stands over against
both viewing the present cultic practice as an ideal situation, and
expecting a restoration of the Davidic dynasty. It presents a "theokrati-
sche Zukunftserwartung" (p. 282), that is the expectation of a future
in which God's rule over his people will be unimpeded (pp. 115–18).

The major advocate of the view that the dynastic promise points
to a messianic expectation in Chronicles was Von Rad in his 1930
monograph (but see note 3). Von Rad argues on the basis of the
Chronicler's changes in the Nathan passage (2 Sam. 7 // 1 Chron. 17,
esp. vs. 11) and the allusions to the Nathan prophecy elsewhere in
Chronicles that the dynastic promise refers to "etwas Grundneues"
("something basically new"), and to an 'Enderwartung' ("eschatological expectation"; p. 123); the Davidic throne is no longer just
something 'innerweltlich' ('inner-worldly'), but "die Schwerpunkt dieser
Institution wird in die Transzendenz verlegt" ("the point of gravity
of this institution is relocated into the transcendental sphere"; p. 126).
Although this expectation does not take a central place (p. 128) there
is "ein starker Zug messianischer Erwartung" ("a strong trait of messianic expectation" p. 135).[7]

In two articles, the first mentioned above, the second published
in 1983, Williamson argues that there is no eschatological or messianic expectation in Chronicles, but a 'royalist' expectation: in the
future, within the course of history, YHWH will restore the rule of
the Davidic dynasty. Williamson's view is based on a study of the
dynastic promise in 1 Chron. 17 and the allusions to it elsewhere
(1 Chron. 22:9–10; 28:6–7; 2 Chron. 6:16,42; 7:17–18; 13:5–8; 21:7;

---

[6] Im (1985), pp. 164–179.
[7] In his *Theologie des Alten Testaments* I (München, 1961³), p. 349 = *Old Testament Theology 1 The Theology of Israel's Historical Traditions* (London, 1975), p. 352 Von Rad only remarks that the Chronicler is a representative of the messianic tradition.

23:3). Central to his argument is the much debated question whether the dynastic promise in Chronicles is conditional or unconditional. Williamson takes a middle road: the promise is conditional with respect to Solomon but unconditional with respect to the dynasty after Solomon once the latter has fulfilled the condition of obedience. "With the completion of the period of Davidic-Solomonic rule . . . the Chronicler intends his readers to understand that the dynasty has been eternally established" (1983, p. 318), which means a royalist expectation, "the perpetuation into the post-exilic period of a continuing expectation of the re-emergence of a ruling Davidic household" (*ibid.*).

Williamson's detailed exegesis is plausible in itself, but in my view not compelling. The difficulty is that many details in the passages involved are ambiguous, as is clear from the history of their exegesis, and also from Williamson's own discussion. Much depends on the overall perspective from which these passages are approached, and it would seem that when on other grounds this happens from an attitude of doubt concerning a messianic or royalist expectation, an alternative interpretation is also possible. With respect to this perspective, Williamson's contribution leaves me with the following general reservation. The real great future is yet to begin. The restoration of the Davidic dynasty may be in the course of our history, but it remains, in Williamson's own words, "a dramatic transformation in the future" (1983, p. 153), which renders the present, including the temple service, a provisional situation, with the real thing yet to come. Aware of the subjective aspect of this reservation, I wonder whether it is probable that so great an expectation is to be inferred by the readers from just a few allusions to the dynastic promise. A few examples of an alternative interpretation may suffice.

In 2 Chron. 13 we have the well-known speech by King Abiah of Judah to King Jeroboam of Israel. In vs. 5 Abiah begins his speech with an allusion to the dynastic promise: "Do you not know that the Lord God of Israel gave the kingship over Israel forever to David and his sons by a covenant of salt?" There is no hint of a condition, but could there possibly be? The Chronicler has Abiah declare Jeroboam's kingship to be illegitimate. Over against this rebellious kingship he defends the legitimacy of the Davidic dynasty, which is grounded in nothing less than God's choice and commitment to it: there is no way for Jeroboam to claim divine legitimacy for his kingship. The conditional or unconditional character of the promise is not at issue. It is in keeping with the context that it is stressed (vs. 8) that what is at stake is "the kingdom of YHWH". The Chronicler can hardly have meant to say that the Davidic dynasty as its expression was "therefore permanent and indestructible" (Williamson, 1977, p. 147). If that were the case, one wonders how, from the Chronicler's perspective, the kingdom of God had been expressed since 586. The expression "a covenant of salt" in vs. 5 may well indicate the stability of the covenant but I think it is going too far to say that this "points clearly to its eternal significance" (Williamson (1977), p. 147). The narrative context of a competing claim gave the Chronicler an excellent opportunity to emphasize God's choice of and faithfulness to the Davidic dynasty, which were basic to his theological position.

More or less the same reasoning applies to 2 Chron. 23:3. Again the legitimacy of the Davidic dynasty is at stake, this time over against the usurper Athaliah. Jehoiadah says to the assembly of Israel, referring to Joash, the only Davidide left: "Here is the king's son! Let him reign, as the Lord promised concerning the sons of David". Again, in my view, what is relevant in this situation is God's choice of the Davidic dynasty, not the conditional/unconditional character of the dynastic promise.

Another allusion is found in 2 Chron. 21:7: "Yet the Lord would not destroy the house of David, because of the covenant which he had made with David, and since he had promised to give a lamp to him and to his descendants for ever" (RSV). Williamson (1977, pp. 145, 153) argues that by means of the two divergences from his *Vorlage*, 2 Kgs. 8:19, ("the house of David" instead of 'Judah', and the reference to the covenant with David) the Chronicler emphasizes the unconditional character of the promise. With respect to the first change, however, another interpretation is also possible. In 2 Kgs. 8:19 there is a very close relation between the dynasty and Judah: the failure of the dynasty might well entail the destruction of Judah, but Judah is saved for the sake of the dynasty. For the Chronicler, history has proved this wrong and he severs this lifeline connection. At stake is only the dynasty, not – and not possibly so – Judah. In this connection it is noteworthy that in 2 Kgs. 24:18–20 it is at least suggested that the fate of Jerusalem and Judah is bound up with that of the king. In 2 Chron. 36:11–14, however, it is made unambiguously clear that what had caused the catastrophe of 586 was the disobedience of the people.

With respect to the second change, the reference to the covenant with David, if it is more than a stylistic change, may emphasize God's faithfulness, but that does not necessarily imply unconditionality. The Chronicler uses this opportunity to emphasize the exclusive legitimacy of the Davidic dynasty. On God's choice of this dynasty hinged the legitimacy and efficacy of the Jerusalem temple and its cultus. The (un)conditionality is, in my assessment, not at issue.

Williamson's approach is adopted and amplified by B.E. Kelly (1996). According to Kelly, "The cultus reflects not a satisfaction with the status quo . . . but a longing for and hopeful expectation of salvation . . ., which embraces land, people and Davidic line" (p. 185).

The 'royalist' position is also shared by M. Oeming in his 1990 monograph, on the basis of the great interest in David's family in the genealogical section, 1 Chron. 1–9 (p. 209).

The approach of I. Gabriel in her monograph of 1990 is between the 'royalist' and the 'messianic' position. She attributes to Chronicles a "restaurativer Messianismus" (p. 202). It is 'restaurativ' in as far as Israel's past greatness will be restored, 'messianisch' because this restoration will coincide with the re-establishment of Davidic rule. Part of this basically 'royalist' attitude are eschatological traits which are beyond the historically possible (p. 203). Her main argument is the Chronicler's portrayal of the Solomonic era as a golden age of peace, which points to his expectation of a future life for Israel in freedom and peace under the rule of a *Salomo redivivus* (pp. 107f.).

The opposite view, that there is no specific expectation of the future, has been defended by W. Rudolph in his commentary and his 1954 article. He holds that the Chronicler's purpose was to present the realized theocracy in the post-exilic temple community. He admits that there are "eschatological undertones in the stress upon the everlasting nature of the Davidic dynasty . . .", but "The fact that in the whole of the Chronicler's work only these few hints of a Messianic expectation are to be found, shows how little real significance they had for the author" (1954, p. 408). Rudolph's view was adopted and developed by O. Plöger in his influential work *Theokratie und Eschatologie* of 1959, 1962². According to Plöger there were in post-exilic Judah two main currents of theological thought, one eschatological and one theocratic. For the Chronicler the post-exilic Jewish community represented the realized theocracy. Not only does the

Chronicler not preach any form of eschatological expectation, he even polemizes against such expectations which existed in the Jerusalem community of his time (p. 54).

In this approach the function of the Davidic dynasty, especially of David and Solomon, within the divine economy is primarily and mainly the building of the temple and the establishment of its cultus. After that its role is basically finished.

A recent defence of this position is W. Riley's monograph of 1993. Riley opines that the Davidic covenant was not bound up with the dynasty, but remained in force in the temple cultus after the dynasty had ended. In the establishment of temple and cultus the dynasty had finished its cultic task. It could now be disposed of without the covenant being affected (1993, e.g. p. 201).

There seems to be some ambiguity in the approach of S. Japhet. I fully agree when she writes: "The book of Chronicles cannot be defined as eschatological in any sense of the word" (1989, p. 501), and, "Continuity, not change, characterizes the Chronistic way of thinking on every subject" (1989, p. 502). I also agree when a little further on she states that the Chronistic elements such as trust in God, his power, divine retribution are directed toward the future (1989, p. 503), but I find it difficult to follow her when she continues, "They are concrete hopes that the land will be redeemed and Israel's greatness and glory will be restored", to end her discussion of the issue with "The Chronicler . . . awaited the restoration of Israel's fortunes" (1989, p. 504). It may not happen as a sudden change, but it does constitute a radical change, which, in my view, is nowhere suggested by the Chronicler, unless one assumes by inference this to be implicitly meant by the Chronicler, a method, however, Japhet herself strongly rejects.

To close this survey, mention may be made of D.F. Murray's article of 1993. On the basis of a detailed discussion of three passages, 2 Chron. 36:10–21; 7:12–22; 29:5–11 and 30:6–12, Murray comes to the conclusion that the Chronicler did not expect any form of a Davidic restoration, but rather was concerned about the restoration of the people. This had been brought about by the advent of Persian sovereignty. In this new situation the kingdom of God among his people has assumed a different form. The future of the people depends upon their present relationship to God, and this is bound up with the faithful adherence to the temple and its cultus.

From this very general survey it may be clear that the answer to the question at the beginning of this article does not depend on a few specific passages, but is bound up with one's view of what the book of Chronicles is all about. This in its turn depends upon one's assessment of the many variables at stake and the way these may be combined in a cohesive overall view. There is unavoidably a subjective element in this, as also in the present article.

In my own assessment the view that the Chronicler does not intend to convey any specific hope for the future best accounts for the evidence. It is not possible now to go over the evidence and the arguments which have been advanced in its support or against it. I only intend to offer another pointer in this direction, viz. the observation that the Chronicler recognizably portrays a development which culminates in the dedication of the temple, without this being paralleled by anything comparable in the way of future bliss. This development is not just a historical one, but consists of a series of divine interventions which should make clear that the institution of the temple and the temple service is, from beginning to end, totally and solely God's work and not subject to any historical contingency. This process begins with God's choice of David as king and culminates in his acceptance of the temple as his sanctuary. This development is built up as follows: (1) God turns over the kingship from Saul to David; (2) God indicates to David the place of the future temple; (3) God chooses Solomon as David's successor; (4a) God chooses Solomon as the temple builder; (4b) for this God himself has to disqualify David; (5) God reveals to David the design of the temple; (6) God accepts the temple as his sanctuary. In this order these points will be worked out in more detail.

(1) The Chronicler's narrative begins in chapter 10 with the death of Saul in his battle against the Philistines. The question has often been asked why the Chronicler did this. According to Mosis this chapter is paradigmatic in that it portrays the exilic situation (see p. 38 above). A number of scholars hold that this chapter functions as the backdrop of David's kingship. Von Rad, for example, states: "Saul ist nur noch die dunkle Folie von der sich die Lichtgestalt seines Nachfolgers um so strahlender abhebt" ("Saul is only the dark foil against which the shining figure of his successor is the more sharply contrasted"; (1930), p. 79). K. Galling (1954, p. 41) and Rudolph (1955, p. 96), among others, write in the same vein. This view may be true to some extent. Saul was a legitimate king, chosen by God. His rejection by God is the consequence of his disobedience.

This chapter thus makes clear that a king (which means: David), albeit chosen by God, has to be obedient to be successful. Failure remains a possibility. In contrast to Saul's disobedience, David's obedience comes better to the fore (cf. 1 Chron. 13:3). But this is not the main function. Verses 13 and 14 make clear what this chapter is all about: God turns over the kingship from Saul to David. For this to be possible Saul's death itself was not sufficient. From the Chronicler's perspective, God himself had to reject him, which necessitated the portrayal of Saul's death as the consequence of his disobedience. Of course, both for Saul's rejection and God's choice of David, the Chronicler could find support in the Deuteronomist's narrative (1 Sam. 13,15,16), but in 1 Sam. 21–2 Sam. 5 the story of the battle on Gilboa and the ensuing development have nothing to do with either: Saul is killed, succeeded by his son, while David seizes the opportunity to have himself acclaimed king of Judah, and only two years later he becomes king also of northern Israel. Nothing of all this is alluded to in Chronicles. In one divine move God turns aside Saul and puts David in his place. There is no historical contingency in the rise to power of the king who would prepare the building of the temple and whose son would complete the project. Incidentally, in a number of translations the title of this chapter refers to the story told; so, for example, *New American Bible*: His [Saul's] death and burial; *Traduction Oecuménique de la Bible*: Mort du roi Saül; *New International Version*: Saul takes his life; *Revised English Bible* comes a bit closer with "David succeeds Saul". If the title is supposed to reflect the purpose of a passage, then the above means that the title should be "God turns over the kingship from Saul to David". In 1 Sam. 31, of course, a title such as the first three mentioned above is fully applicable.

(2) In 1 Chron. 21 we have the report of David's census. This is the only case in Chronicles where David transgresses against God. There is virtual unanimity as to why the Chonicler gave this report a place in his book: it leads up to God indicating the place of the future temple in vs. 26; 22:1; compare 2 Chron. 3:1 and 7:3,16 (בחר). For this the Chronicler had to edit the story as told in 2 Sam. 24, where this is not at issue at all. Neither is there in 1 Kgs. 5 any hint that the temple is to be built at a place assigned by God, and, presumably, Solomon himself decides where the temple will be built. For the Chronicler this could not be. The story of the census provided him with an opportunity to have God assign the place of the temple.

(3) In 1 Kgs. 1 Solomon becomes king after a history of court intrigues. The Chronicler, of course, omits all this. Solomon is the unchallenged successor of David, installed by the latter himself. But this is not enough; the succession would still be a matter of historical contingency, and therefore, in 1 Chron. 28:5 God himself chooses Solomon as David's successor. As many scholars have noted, this is the only instance of the use of בחר for a king after David. This is, moreover, emphasized in the previous verse, which makes clear that God's choice of Solomon stands in a line of divine choices: Judah > David's father's house > David.

(4a) But even his status as David's successor does not automatically qualify Solomon for being the temple builder. It is rather the other way round: Solomon was chosen as king because he was to build the temple instead of vice versa. God's direct choice (again בחר) of him as temple builder is mentioned in 1 Chron. 28:10: "Take heed now, for the Lord has chosen you to build a house as the sanctuary"; compare 22:11, and 29:1.

(4b) Still, even with God's choice of Solomon as David's successor, there remains the difficult question why the temple was not built by David, but by his son, or to be more precise, why God chose Solomon instead of David for the task. The course of history could, as a matter of principle, not suffice as an explanation. This problem is solved in 1 Chron. 22:8 // 28:3.[8] David is denied the building project because of his wars and his shedding much blood, and therefore the task is turned over to his son. The argument with respect to David's wars is remarkable since it was with God's blessing that these wars were carried out (1 Chron. 14:10–17; 18:6,13). The argument is a theological adaptation of 1 Kgs. 5:17 (English verse 3), where it is said that David could not build the temple because of his being engaged in warfare. This was an impossible line of thought for the Chronicler. This theological adaptation already makes clear that the argument is an *ad hoc* one, not based on a negative view of David's wars or wars in general. This is confirmed by the argument of David having shed much blood. This cannot refer to the wars, since nowhere in the Old Testament is warfare equated with shedding blood. The latter is always a guilty taking of the life of innocent people. In the Chronicler's view God's choice of Solo-

---

[8] For a detailed treatment of this verse see my article "Why was David disqualified as a temple builder?" *JSOT* 70 (1976), pp. 51–6.

mon implied that David as the person first in line was disqualified
by God, just as God's choice of David as king entailed God's rejection of Saul. David's warfare and shedding of blood are purely theological and do not refer to any details of David's life as told by
the Chronicler, or for that matter by the Deuteronomist. That the
argument is an *ad hoc* one, only to explain the fact of history that
it was Solomon who built the temple, is also apparent from the fact
that it did not prevent the Chronicler from making David do everything possible in the way of preparations. Another pointer in the
same direction, at least with regard to warfare, is that the Chronicler
saw no problem in having David dedicate part of the spoils of war
to YHWH (1 Chron. 18:11) and in having Solomon use them for
the manufacturing of the bronze sea, the pillars of the temple and
temple vessels (1 Chron. 18:8).

The difference with the other case of David's sin occasioning
God's intervention, that of the census, is, that in the latter case the
Chronicler could make use of the story of 2 Sam. 24, whereas in
this case he had to rely solely on his own theological creativity.

(5) One thing still remains: the design of the temple. This is dealt
with in 1 Chron. 28:11–19: David hands over to Solomon the design
(תבנית) of the temple building, the courts, and the cherubs covering
the ark.[9] This design has been revealed to him by God (vs. 19). It
recalls the design which had been revealed to Moses for the manufacturing of the tabernacle and its furniture (Exod. 25:9,40), but
there is no allusion to any divinely inspired design with respect to
the temple in the book of Kings, in which rather the Phoenician
participation in the project is highlighted (1 Kgs. 5:21–26 [English
verses 7–12]; 7:13–47). With this God-given design, nothing has been
left to chance. The whole project of the building of the temple has
been God's affair, from choosing David till his handing over the
design to the chosen temple builder.

(6) After the temple has been built the ark is put in its place.
Both 1 Kgs. 8:11–12 and 2 Chron. 5:13,14 relate that at that occasion the glory of YHWH fills the temple. After that Solomon offers
his prayer of dedication, which in 1 Kings closes the ceremony. In
2 Chron. 7:1–3, however, there is an interesting addition: fire from
heaven consumes the offerings and the glory of YHWH fills the

---

[9] In my article "1 Chronicles xxviii 11–18: its textual development", *VT* 47 (1997),
pp. 429–38, I have argued that 1 Chron. 28:12b–18a is a later addition.

house. In other words: after Solomon's prayer God indicates his acceptance of the temple as his sanctuary. For heavenly fire consuming the offering as a sign of God's acceptance there is a parallel in 1 Chron. 21:26; cp. Judg. 6:21.

Williamson (1977, p. 146) takes this verse to point to God's underlining the unconditionality of the divine promise to the Davidic dynasty (2 Chron. 6:42). There seems, however, to be no reason to apply 2 Chron. 7:1–3 only to the last verse of the long prayer, instead of to the whole prayer of dedication. The latter is clearly suggested by verse 1, which begins with "When Solomon had finished praying . . .". These words have been taken over from 1 Kgs. 8:54, but are directly related to the signs of God's acceptance by the Chronicler.

The above interpretation is confirmed by 2 Chron. 7:12 and 16. In verse 12, after "I have heard your prayer", taken over from Kings, the Chronicler added "and chosen (ובחרתי) this place as a house of offering". Verse 16 adds "I have chosen (בחרתי)" before "(and) sanctified this house", which was taken over from 1 Kgs. 9:3. This way the Chronicler makes abundantly clear that Solomon's dedication ceremony by itself does not guarantee anything. It is answered by God by his own acceptance of it as his sanctuary.

There is one more noteworthy case of divine intervention which concerns the temple, though indirectly. 1 Chron. 13 and 15 recount the transfer of the ark to Jerusalem. There is an interesting and telling difference with 2 Sam. 6. In the latter chapter Uzza is killed because of his touching the ark. David is frightened and discontinues the undertaking, leaving the ark in the care of Obed-Edom. Only when he hears about the blessing bestowed on Obed-Edom does he decide to continue. The Chronicler mentions the blessing (13:14), but not in relation to David's decision to continue the transfer. David has had this intention all along. He prepares a place for the ark in Jerusalem (15:1). The important change is that the incident of Uzza is interpreted by David as an expression of God's displeasure because the ark had not been carried by Levites (15:13).[10] That only Levites should carry the ark was an ancient rule (Deut.

---

[10] Although the purport of this verse is clear, its text has probably not been preserved intact. In my article "The Development of the Text of I Chronicles 15:1–24", *Henoch* 17 (1995), pp. 267–77 (reference on p. 271, n. 6), I have suggested that נשאתם may have been dropped by homoioteleuton after אתם "because it was not you who carried (it)".

10:8), and David could not be presented as inaugurating this, but he is prompted by God to reinforce it. There can be no doubt as to what motivated the Chronicler to have God intervene at this point. The real issue was not how the ark was to be transported but the role of the Levites as temple singers. They formed an important aspect of the Chronicler's contemporary temple cultus, which he held in high esteem. In emphasizing their exclusive task with respect to the ark he found a possibility to introduce them into the cultus: "These are the men whom David put in charge of the service of song in the house of the Lord, after the ark came to rest there" (1 Chron. 6:16 [English verse 31]; compare 16:4–7,37). This way he created a theological basis for their function in the cultus.[11] The Chronicler uses here the same story technique as in the cases just mentioned: although David's negligence with respect to the ark is not presented as a sin, rather as an oversight, it does open the way for God's intervention to introduce (indirectly) an important aspect of the Jerusalem temple cultus.

The contention of this article is that 1 Chron. 10–2 Chron. 6 is wholly and recognizably directed toward the building and inauguration of the temple, and along with it toward the installation of the Levites as singers. The inauguration of the temple is the culmination of God's guidance which began with his choice of David. God's interventions at the decisive points of the development form the axis around which the whole development evolves. There is nothing comparable which points to a drastic change which lies yet in the future. It is unlikely that the Chronicler structured the greater part of his work so as to make it point to the building of the temple as the culmination of God's intervention on behalf of his people, and yet intended his readers to understand that the great future, in which the final consummation of God's purposes for Israel will take place, is yet to come. Rather, the Chronicler's stress on God's choice of the Davidic dynasty and his faithfulness toward it serve to emphasize the sole legitimacy of the temple. 'Legitimacy', of course, is a rather formal notion. The Chronicler's purpose goes beyond this.

---

[11] For the connection between Levites and the ark as the bridge for their later cultic role, see Von Rad (1930), pp. 98–115, and J.W. Kleinig, *The Lord's Song: The Basis, Function and Significance of Choral Music in Chronicles*, JSOTS 156 (Sheffield, 1993), pp. 91–5.

His real purpose is to emphasize that the temple is not a human institution but God's gift to his people. They are called upon to adhere faithfully to its cultus to be assured of God's faithfulness and his guidance with respect to the future.

This brings me to a final point. In the discussion of this issue, the alternative to an eschatological or messianic expectation is usually taken to be the view of the post-exilic Jewish community as a theocracy. Prominent proponents of this position were Rudolph and Plöger, according to whom the Chronicler considered this community a "realized theocracy". Other scholars, such as J. Becker, (1977, pp. 43–8, 74–7), just use 'theocracy' or "theocratic community". Sometimes this is specified as 'hierocracy', e.g. by A. Caquot, (1966, p. 120). These terms, however, are not unambiguous and especially 'theocracy' can be understood in many different ways.[12] At any rate, however, it easily suggests a contentment with the present situation, or the idea of "die statische, gegenwartszufriedene Gottesherrschaft im Gegensatz zur dynamischen, in die Zukunft gerichteten eschatologischen Strömung" ("the static contentment with the present situation of God's rule, over against the dynamic current which is directed toward the future").[13] This, however, need not be the case. The absence of a specific eschatological/messianic expectation does not mean that people look to the future as closed. Faith in God's guidance and his involvement in our history leaves the future in God's hands, and therefore open. The Chronicler preaches no attitude of acquiescence with respect to the present, but faith in God, and perseverance in participating in the cultic experience of the believing community, in the place God has given for that purpose: the Jerusalem temple.[14]

---

[12] See Dörrfuss (1994), pp. 18–118, which deals with the way 'theocracy' has been understood by a great number of authors.

[13] Becker (1977), p. 43. With these words Becker characterizes the way many scholars view the two opposite possibilities.

[14] In this respect I agree with Murray (1993), and, apart from the reservation expressed above, with Japhet (1989), pp. 499–504.

BIBLIOGRAPHY

J. Becker, *Messiaserwartung im Alten Testament*, SBS 83 (Stuttgart, 1977)

A. Caquot, "Peut-on parler de messianisme dans l'oeuvre du Chroniste?", *RThPh* 99 (= 3/16; 1966)

E.M. Dörrfuss, *Mose in den Chronikbüchern: Garant theokratischer Zukunftserwartung*, BZAW 219 (Berlin, 1994)

I. Gabriel, *Friede über Israel: Eine Untersuchung zur Friedenstheologie in Chronik I 10–II 36* OSB 10 (Klosterneuburg, 1990)

K. Galling, *Die Bücher der Chronik, Esra, Nehemia*, ATD (Göttingen, 1954)

T.-S. Im, *Das Davidbild in den Chronikbüchern: David als Idealbild des theokratischen Messianismus für den Chronisten*, Europäische Hochschulschriften 23/vol. 263 (Frankfurt am Main, 1985)

S. Japhet, *The Ideology of the Book of Chronicles and its Place in Biblical Thought*, BEAT 9 (Frankfurt am Main, 1989)

——, *I & II Chronicles: A Commentary* (London, 1993)

B.E. Kelly, *Retribution and Eschatology in Chronicles*, JSOTSS 211 (Sheffield, 1996)

R. Mosis, *Untersuchungen zur Theologie des chronistischen Geschichtswerkes*, Freiburger Theologische Studien 29 (Freiburg, 1973)

D.F. Murray, "Dynasty, People, and the Future: The Message of Chronicles", *JSOT* 58 (1993), pp. 71–92

M. Oeming, *Das wahre Israel: "Die genealogische Vorhalle" 1 Chronik 1–9*, BWANT 128 (= 7/8; Stuttgart, 1990)

O. Plöger, *Theokratie und Eschatologie*, WMANT 2 (Neukirchen, 1959, 1962²)

G. Von Rad, *Das Geschichtsbild des chronistischen Werkes*, BWANT, 54 (Stuttgart, 1930)

W. Riley, *King and Cultus in Chronicles: Worship and the Interpretation of History*, JSOTSS 160 (Sheffield, 1993)

W. Rudolph, "Problems of the Book of Chronicles", *VT* 4 (1954), pp. 401–409

——, *Chronikbücher*, HAT (Tübingen, 1955)

H.G.M. Williamson, "Eschatology in Chronicles", *Tyndale Bulletin* 28 (1977), pp. 115–54

——, "The Dynastic Oracle in the Books of Chronicles", A. Rofé and Y. Zakovitch, (eds.), *Essays on the Bible and the Ancient World*, Fs. I.L. Seeligmann (Jerusalem, 1983), vol. 3, pp. 305–18

I KNOW THAT MY REDEEMER LIVETH

BY

J. GIBSON

Edinburgh

There are not many hopeful passages in the speeches of Job, but they play a crucial role in his slow recovery of faith. The first to surface is Job's poignant wish of 9:32ff. for an arbiter to stand between him and God, who would see to it that the cards were not always stacked against him. The next is the famous passage in 13:15ff., translated in the AV "Though he slay me, yet will I trust in him" but more accurately in the RV, "Yet will I wait for him". This is followed in the same speech by 14:13ff., where Job asks God to hide him in Sheol, and goes on "All the days of my service I would wait, till my release should come". Finally, there are the two visions in 16:18ff. and, the celebrated passage with which we are concerned, in 19:25ff., in which Job calls God his witness and his redeemer.

There are, of course, many authorities who deny that these passages are hopeful. In particular, considering the subject of this paper, they deny that the witness of chapter 16 and the redeemer of chapter 19 are to be equated with God or some heavenly advocate; rather they represent metaphorically Job's own stated case; his own words alone can speak for him until (if ever) God deigns to respond. Such views, namely that Job cannot be allowed to express hope in the God whom elsewhere he so remorselessly attacks, seem to me too modernistic for an Old Testament book. I mean, if given the opportunity, to engage more fully with them at another time. Meanwhile, I cite as chief evidence for my own view an archetypal Old Testament source.

It is probable that for these hopeful passages, which for a moment here and there pierce through the darkness of Job's despair and anger, we should look to the model of the Lamentation Psalms, upon which Job draws so richly for the language of complaint and protest which otherwise dominates his rhetoric. There are in most, if not quite all of the Lamentation Psalms little warm sections called declarations of trust where the Psalmist, having made his attacks on God and being about to appeal to him for help, states his confidence that the God in whom he had lost faith is, as he ought to have realised, fully able to answer his appeal and supply the remedy for his affliction. We cannot but feel the sudden infusion of warmth. A good example is Psalm 102, a prayer of one afflicted, as the heading tells us. In the first part of the psalm the Psalmist's days are passing away like smoke, he is like a vulture in the wilderness or a lonely bird on the housetop (AV, probably wrongly, but much more poetically, has **a pelican** and **a sparrow**), he is taunted and derided by his enemies, and he knows that this is all due to God's indignation, who has taken him up and thrown him away. But then at verse 12 there is an abrupt change of gear: "But thou, O Lord, art enthroned for ever . . . (16) For the Lord will build up Zion, . . . and he will regard the prayer of the destitute, and will not despise their supplication" (RSV). Thereafter comes the appeal: "'O my God', I say, 'take me not hence in the midst of my days, thou whose years endure throughout all generations'" (24) (RSV), and the psalm closes with praise to him, who is always the same and whose years have no end. The Lamentation Psalms have been well defined as "strategies for consolation", they provide the words whereby the suffering and perplexed worshipper may edge himself gradually into the frame of mind, in which he can be sure in his God again and begin again to praise him; and the sections of trust and confidence are a vital component in such strategies. So it is, I believe, in the speeches of Job; the hopeful passages I mentioned show him resiling momentarily from his continuous onslaughts on God and winning through to the conviction that only God can – and will – restore his reputation and lead him to faith in the divine providence once more; their importance is out of all proportion to their numbers.

To fill in the background to the redeemer passage it is salutary to take a brief look at the witness passage in chapter 16. It is just when in both speeches Job is at his lowest that the light of hope breaks through. In chapter 16 it is of his anguished cries reaching at last to heaven, where they are taken up by a witness who will argue his case for him before God. If you read carefully (RSV), you will see that the witness too can only be God.

> O earth, cover not my blood,
>   and let my cry find no resting place.
> Even now, behold, my witness is in heaven,
>   and he that vouches for me is on high.
> My friends scorn me;

> my eye pours out tears to God,
> that he would maintain the right of a man with God,
> like a man with his neighbour.
> For when a few years have passed,
> I shall go the way whence I shall not return.
> My spirit is broken, my days are extinct,
> the grave is ready for me. (16.18–17.1)

Job, as he looks around him, sees the open derision of his friends, and he knows that his days are numbered. He is about to set out on a journey from which there can be no way back. There will be no reward for him in this life. His spirit is broken and only the grave awaits (Coverdale here has the splendid rendering "I am harde at deathes dore"). Yet in his mind's eye he also sees a future court in heaven, at which he himself will not – alas! – be present. But his spilt blood will speak for him, as the murdered Abel's blood cried out from the ground in Genesis 4; and there will be another speaker too. As God his enemy sits on the bench, God his witness will be present to say on Job's behalf what he himself will never now have the opportunity to say, and to wrest from that other God the verdict that is his due. The vision does not last, and in chapter 17 Job is back with his vanished hopes again: they will descend with him to the bars of Sheol and die with him in the dust; but how brightly it shines the little while it does last!

Which brings us to the redeemer of chapter 19. Both textually and interpretatively the passage is one of the most difficult in the whole Old Testament. Surely part of the reason must be that Job's emotions are so taughtly stretched that his language veers, despite its magnificence, on the incoherent. He is at the frontier of what human words are capable of expressing; it therefore behoves us to proceed warily, for we are treading on theological eggshells. I discuss three renderings. The first is the King James version, better known perhaps from the ravishing soprano aria from Handel's *Messiah*, where it is juxtaposed with a verse from the New Testament (1 Cor. 15:20, "But now is Christ risen from the dead"), and thus given a thoroughly Christianized meaning which is quite illegitimate. The second and third are my own translations, representing what I consider to be the two possible ways of understanding the passage in its context in the pre-Christian Book of Job. The third is the one I would claim to be the right interpretation.

What are we meant to understand by the AV's translation:

> I know *that* my redeemer liveth, and *that* he shall stand at the latter
> *day* upon the earth; and *though* after my skin *worms* destroy this *body*,
> yet in my flesh shall I see God: whom I shall see for myself, and mine
> eyes shall behold, and not another,

especially if we read it (and who now does not?) with the sound of
Handel's music in our ears? *At the latter day* takes us forward to the
Last Judgement and the resurrection of the dead at the end of the
age, when Christ will return to earth to inaugurate God's final kingdom; and we, escaping through the merits of our Redeemer, the
threat of an adverse verdict on our sins, shall rise from our graves,
leaving behind us the earthly bodies which the *worms* have devoured,
and shall live for ever in God's nearer presence, enjoying in *body*,
that is in our new resurrection bodies, the beatific vision. You will
notice that I have underlined some words; these words do not appear
in the Hebrew text but have been added by the translators of 1611
(they are italicised in the AV). Remove them, and we get an entirely
different meaning. This passage cannot be referring to the last times,
nor can it be referring to resurrection, far less immortality, for Job,
who lived in a period when there was no real belief in a life after
death. And the Redeemer he glimpses is God, not yet God's son
and, in conformity with what Job is pleading for, he is clearing Job's
name, not clearing him from guilt.

It is very revealing that only once in the whole OT does redeem
or redeemer, applied to God, refer to forgiving sins (in Ps. 130:8).
The contrast with the New Testament could hardly be greater, the
equivalent Greek nouns and verbs, though not so common, nearly
always denoting salvation through Christ from sin or some alien
spiritual power (e.g., Gal. 3:13; Eph. 1:7; Titus 2:14; 1 Pet. 1:18). Elsewhere in the Old Testament the words are used of God as deliverer
of his people from bondage in Egypt (Exod. 6:6; 15:13; Ps. 77:15;
106:10) or from slavery in exile (Isa. 43:1; 44:22–23; 51:10–11; 52:9),
including pleading their cause against Babylon (Isa. 52:3–4), or indeed from general trouble (Ps. 25:22), though just before the Psalmist
is complaining of the calumnies of enemies. God also redeems individuals, often from mortal illness (Ps. 49:15, Hos. 13:14), but also
from the reproach of widowhood (Isa. 54:5), from the unjust treatment meted out to orphans (Prov. 23:11), from the malice of per-
secutors (Ps. 119:154), from imprisonment in a pit (Lam. 3:58).
Sentences with God as redeemer or redeeming are of course metaphorical; but they derive from a secular source, from old Israelite clan
law, where the redeemer (in Hebrew *goel*) is the technical term for

a near relative who is obliged to buy back property so that it may
be kept within the family (Lev. 25:25–34), or to ransom a kinsman
from slavery (Lev. 25:47–55), or to marry a widow so that an heir
may be provided for her dead husband (Ruth 4:1–6), or to avenge
the blood of a murdered relative (Deut. 19:11–13; 2 Sam. 14:4–11).
There is no case recorded where a human *goel* takes part in a law-
suit, though the metaphorical legal language adopted in several of
the examples at the beginning of this paragraph makes it likely that
such did exist.[1] But whether or not they did exist in the secular
sphere, the passages containing Ps. 119:154 or Lam. 3:58 describe
situations sufficiently akin to Job's of slander and false accusation
from all around as to make it not altogether unique, even where
God himself is, in Job's view, the chief slanderer and accuser. Above
all, in contexts human or divine, *goel* is a word redolent of clan sol-
idarity and family affection and duty, which is no doubt why the
author puts it on Job's lips here. God, Job is tantamount to implying, owes him one.

The only two viable interpretations of Job 19:25ff., that is, interpretations that will have a relevant meaning in the book of Job, are:
Either (with the NEB and GNB among modern versions), Job is
expecting to have his vision before he dies, in which case we may
translate:

> I know that my kinsman is now living
>   and that he will be the last to stand up on the earth;
> and after my skin has [all but] peeled away – [I know] this,
>   that while still in my flesh I shall see God.
> I shall see him to be on my side;
>   my very own eyes shall see him and not another's.

Everything in this book so far, however, even his previous vision of
the witness in chapter 16, has Job accepting that he is going to die,
even welcoming the prospect of death; and all he is hoping for at
this point is that his reputation for integrity will survive him.

Or therefore, Job does not expect to have his vision until after he
dies; rather, in a moment of exceptional daring for an Old Testament
believer, he expects God to appear to him in Sheol. He is convinced
at this moment that his sufferings are caused, not by anything he
has done, but by God himself: "Have pity on me, have pity on me,
O ye my friends, for the hand of God hath touched me". He rails

---

[1] See J.C.L. Gibson, *Language and Imagery in the Old Testament* (London, 1998),
p. 137.

at the surrounding company; but they are only the monkey, not the organ-grinder. He longs for a memorial to be cut in the rock, but realizes this will not be enough. Only God can undo what God has done and give him justice. So he cries out in an interpretation, which is in essentials if not in its details that of the RSV and several other modern translations:

> I know that my kinsman does not die,
>   and that as the one who will come after me
> he will take his stand over my grave;
> and after my skin has [wholly] peeled away- [I know] this,
>   that even without my flesh I shall see God.
> I shall see him to be on my side;
>   my own eyes shall see him, and [he will] no [longer be a] stranger.

In visionary flight Job sees his erstwhile enemy become his kinsman and standing over his grave to pronounce his innocence. He will himself be dead, but somehow he will know, for God will appear to him in Sheol to tell him, and he, a bodiless shade, will see him there. The passage is both sublime and disjointed; it does not fore-see resurrection for Job, but it does break through the barrier of death in much the same way as that other exceptional Old Testament passage, Ps. 139, "though I make my bed in Sheol, thou art there". That we should not read too much into Ps. 139 is shown by the previous line, giving rise to an equally impossible scenario: "If I ascend up into heaven, thou art there". Neither Job nor the Psalmist is giving us a doctrine of resurrection, but both are piercing through to the other side of death and asserting that whatever may happen there, God will be present.

Alas! the vision soon fades, as the earlier one in chapter 16 faded, but while it lasts, it surely marks the zenith of the book. Job cries out, "My heart sinks within me", as though saying "This cannot be"; and in the succeeding chapters he gives way once more to pes-simism and despair, though significantly not again to sarcasm and blasphemy. He is now sincerely and indeed desperately searching for God and, when the moment is right, God will speak to him out of the whirlwind. The encounter will happen in this life, as will Job's restoration to prosperity afterward; for the time in which the Book of Job was written this was inevitable, and in no way detracts from the force of the short and unique vision of chapter 19. In it a sad and angry man having, by extrapolation from his own experience, reproached God for his mismanagement of the universe, finds the faith to see beyond a bleak present and catch sight of the kind God behind the cruel and call him redeemer, because one day, be it after his death, he will spell out his vindication; and he will meet him face to face. A leap of faith can momentarily shatter reality even in a book which is only too well acquainted with reality's pain.

There are two lessons to be learned from this glorious vision. One is theological, for it invites us to stretch our ideas of salvation to include not only those like St. Paul, weighed down with a hopeless sense of sin and guilt and shame, but those millions of innocent victims in our world who are hopeless in another way and in their agony cry out for relief and recognition. We must all bow before God's majesty and power, but not everyone needs to confess his sins in order to be saved; his distress may be enough to draw down heaven's compassion. That is the pattern we meet in the Book of Exodus where the people need only to cry out because of their bondage to have God coming down to rescue them from Pharaoh's clutches. And it is the pattern we meet in Jesus' first sermon at Nazareth where, citing Isaiah, he says:

> The Spirit of the Lord *is* upon me, because he hath anointed me to preach the gospel to the poor; he hath sent me to heal the broken hearted, to preach deliverance to the captives, and the recovering of sight to the blind, to set at liberty them that are bruised (Luke 4:18, AV)

Where there do you find anything about forgiveness of sins? It is simply, is it not, Jesus being compassionate to those in need? This pattern of salvation is as thoroughly biblical as the Pauline, and should get more of a hearing than it often does.

The second lesson has more to do with the inner life. It is that the vision of the living God is granted, not to the pious, but to the desperate; not to the well-meaning, but the drowning man; not to those who set themselves doughtily to defend the faith once delivered to the saints, but to the man who has thought himself to a standstill and is, like Job, at the end of his tether. The vision will not be the self-indulgent vision of the mystic but a sudden glimpse of God engaging with evil and, though he finds it hard, carrying his purpose out.

This little study is presented to Tony Gelston, whom I first met in Sir Godfrey Driver's classes so long ago at Oxford, with my warmest wishes for a long and healthy retirement.

THE SHAPE OF THE PSALTER:
AN ESCHATOLOGICAL DIMENSION?

BY

M.A. VINCENT
Durham

Tony Gelston has written several interesting articles on the Psalter, one of which is a sober review of the debate surrounding the expression יהוה מלך which recurs among a group of psalms in book 4 of the Psalter.[1] It was the cultic approach of Mowinckel and his proposals of an autumn enthronement festival which began the scholarly focus on these psalms which has continued ever since.[2] Even if Mowinckel's reading "YHWH has become king" is unwarranted (as Gelston argues), the theory of an autumn festival does not hang on it, and Mowinckel's work has left an indelible stamp on psalms study.

Recently a number of scholars have focused on the יהוה מלך expression and the associated psalms in book 4 from a quite different perspective. Pursuing the question of the organisation of the Psalter and the process of editorial shaping which produced it,[3] some scholars have seen in the assertion יהוה מלך and in the other distinguishing features of book 4[4] the 'answer' to a crisis perceived to be addressed in book 3. This has led to the description of book 4 as the "editorial

---

[1] A. Gelston, "A Note on יהוה מלך," *VT* 16 (1966), pp. 507–512. For other bibliography, see for example, J. Day, *God's Conflict with the Dragon and the Sea* University of Cambridge Oriental Publications 35 (Cambridge, 1985), p. 36.

[2] S. Mowinckel, *Psalmenstudien* 2 (Oslo, 1922), pp. 6ff. = *The Psalms in Israel's Worship* 2 (Oxford, 1962), pp. 222–224.

[3] The pioneering work (and still the best) is G.H. Wilson, *The Editing of the Hebrew Psalter* SBLDS 76; (Chico, 1985). The most up-to-date survey of the literature and bibliography is in D.M. Howard, *The Structure of Psalms 93–100* Biblical and Judaic Studies from the University of California, San Diego 5 (Winona Lake, 1997). Other treatments include J.C. McCann (ed.), *The Shape and Shaping of the Psalter* JSOTSS 150 (Sheffield, 1993), N. deClaisse-Walfoord, *Reading from the Beginning* (Mercer, 1998), and other works in the following footnotes. For a more critical assessment see R.N. Whybray, *Reading the Psalms as a Book* JSOTSS 222 (Sheffield, 1996), especially pp. 118–124.

[4] There can be little doubt that the יהוה מלך psalms form a crucial group (if not the dominant one) among the psalms of Book 4. Other themes will be introduced later in this essay.

centre of the Psalter".[5] Such suggestions will be amplified and examined later.

This is a volume about eschatology, and it is worth pointing out that the expression יהוה מלך can be read as an affirmation of the validity of eschatological hope. Indeed, to assert that "The Lord is king" *and* that one's enemies will perish and one day be no more (as does 92:10–13, for example) implies a divine intervention that may well be eschatological. A related psalm,[6] 94, asserts that there will one day be an answer to the apparent triumph of the wicked (94:14,15,23). Such statements echo the assertions of Pss. 1 and 2 which, as I shall argue below, are organisationally significant. To continue in book 4, the picture of the whole creation (including even the nations!) rejoicing before the Lord is more clearly still a vision of the future (96, 97, 98, 100), and there is also the twice repeated assertion that "he is coming; he is coming to judge the earth!" (96:13 and 98:9).

Given, then, that some scholars have suggested book 4 and the יהוה מלך expression to be theologically and organisationally central to the Psalter, *and* that there are elements associated with the יהוה מלך psalms and their neighbours which suggest an eschatological hope, it seemed worthwhile to explore the possibility that the shape of the Psalter as a whole might betray an eschatological interest.

Searching for eschatology in the psalms is no new enterprise; both Jews and Christians have long pursued the quest. There are many psalms which *can* be so read, even though they may not require it. David Mitchell's recent work[7] demonstrates clearly some of the possibilities here. Norman Whybray's *Reading the Psalms as a Book*[8] is rather less positive, but also contains important material on the topic. Whybray examines evidence that certain psalms may show traces of a process of eschatological redaction. He concludes that such was not a stage of major significance in the history of the Psalter, even

---

[5] The expression is Wilson's (1985), p. 215. Witness, too, the title of J.L. Mays's book: *The Lord Reigns – A Theological Handbook to the Psalms* (Louisville, 1994).

[6] The interconnectedness of Pss. 93–100 and the importance of considering them as a group is demonstrated convincingly in Howard (1997). See also his shorter summary article "A Contextual Reading of Psalms 90–94" in McCann (1993), pp. 108–123.

[7] D.C. Mitchell, *An Eschatological Programme in the Book of Psalms* JSOTSS 252 (Sheffield: Sheffield, 1997). Unfortunately Mitchell's work was not available to me when this study was researched. See, however, the review in L.L. Grabbe (ed.), *SOTS Booklist 1998* (Sheffield, 1998), p. 87.

[8] Whybray (1996), pp. 88–99.

though certain psalms may contain accretions which manifest an eschatological interest.

My aim here is not to inquire to what extent eschatology may be found in the Psalter as a whole. Rather I am concerned with the question of the Psalter's shape and organisation: does the final form of the Psalter contain clear organisational patterns – and if so, can an interest in eschatology be discerned among them?

To do this I shall present a synthesis of the work done so far by various scholars on the organisational shaping of the Psalter, supplemented by some suggestions of my own. Much of this will not focus specifically on eschatology, since this is not the predominant direction in which scholars have gone. Nevertheless, I shall at every stage be asking whether the alleged patterning or shaping may have an eschatological aspect to it. Perhaps the most significant element of this study, however, will be the attempt to evaluate and critique the suggestions which have been put forward, something which has been all too rare in the literature. Just how much evidence is there concerning the shaping and organisation of the Psalter, and how much weight can be attached to the suggestions of scholars working in this fashionable field?

1. *The beginning and ending of the Psalter*

All books have a beginning, middle and end, and most authors (and editors) pay particular attention to the first and last of these. The beginning helps form vital first impressions; the ending can strongly colour the overall effect of a work. In line with this it makes sense to begin the search for structure and organisation in the Psalter in these very places. What do the choices made by the final compilers of the Psalter betray about their interests?

i) *The introduction to the Psalter: Psalms 1&2*

Whatever the historical processes according to which the Psalter obtained its present opening, there are a number of pieces of evidence which suggest that *both* psalms 1 and 2 are intended to constitute the introduction to the Psalter in its present form. These are as follows:

1. Neither psalm has a title. This sets them apart from the other psalms in books 1–3, the vast majority of which do have titles.

Indeed, the two psalms stand out even more strikingly from the other psalms in book 1 – only Pss. 10 and 33 do not contain titles and a Davidic ascription in MT.[9] Furthermore, in LXX Pss. 1 and 2 are the only psalms in the entire Psalter which do not have a title. This suggests these two psalms are to be considered independently of the others.

2. There are a number of key word-links between psalms 1 and 2 which disappear in subsequent psalms: the occurrence of הגה, *meditate, devise* in 1:2 and 2:1; the use of אבד, *perish*, at the end of both psalms: 1:6; 2:12. This suggests that 1 and 2 are to be considered together.

3. There is an inclusio around the two psalms: "Blessed is the man that . . .," 1:1; "Blessed are all they that put their trust in him", 2:12. Although Ps. 3 also concludes with an expression of blessing, a different root, ברך, is used on that occasion.

4. Whilst most commentators have recognised the introductory function of Ps. 1, some have questioned it for Ps. 2. However, its themes as a royal psalm (with clear eschatological overtones) are repeated as a motif throughout the Psalter, often in places which are organisationally significant (as I shall show below). This suggests that Ps. 2 may also be deliberately positioned and intended to carry an introductory function.

5. On a more subjective note, both psalms 1 and 2 are distinctive and unique psalms. Whilst it is quite possible to find other psalms which make basically the same points as, say, Pss. 3, 4, 5, 6, 7 (and so forth, though not 8), the content and mode of expression of Pss. 1 and 2 is more distinctive. This is reflected in the fact that, along with certain other psalms (18, 19, 45, 72, 110, 119, etc.) both have held the attention of scholars (despite Ps. 1's apparent simplicity). This again suggests a deliberate editorial placement of these psalms, and the likelihood of an introductory function.

What, then, is the introductory function performed by Pss. 1 and 2?

---

[9] The absence of titles for these two psalms can be accounted for. Either, they were originally unified compositions with the following psalm (witness the corrupted alphabetic pattern across 9–10, and compare the usual assumption for 42–43); or, the absence of a title is an editorial strategy to indicate that in this otherwise Davidic book these psalms are to be considered as linked to (and considered in conjunction with) the Davidic psalms which preceded them.

ii) *Psalm 1: individual obedience*

Psalm 1 begins by emphasising the importance of individual responsibility and obedience. It depicts a righteous and 'blessed' man in relation to the ungodly (1:1–3) and then inverts this by depicting the wicked in relation to the righteous (1:4–5). Only the righteous man will be fruitful and thus 'stand' in God's judgement; the wicked will be blown away like chaff and perish. The psalm thus contains an unambiguous statement both of man's duty and of a reward/penalty system.

A further crucial theme is that of God's law (Torah). The righteous man is one who "meditates day and night" upon it. Through the positioning of this psalm as the first in the Psalter, pride of place is given to God's Torah (which I take to be a reference both to the Pentateuch, to God's instruction and teaching elsewhere, and to the teaching which is to follow in the remainder of the Psalter).[10] It seems to be beyond coincidence that a book with a clear five-fold structure (like the Pentateuch) should begin with a psalm which extols the virtues of one who meditates day and night in God's Torah. The word Torah and the topic of man's meditating upon it will recur later in the Psalter (e.g. 19, 37, 119), and it is thus significant that it should be introduced at the very start.[11]

It is important also to notice the eschatological dimension to Ps. 1. It asserts that there will be a future day of reckoning and judgement in which the righteous will survive but the wicked will not. Thus one's behaviour and one's alignment towards God's Torah do

---

[10] In this sense the use of the word torah at the beginning claims for the Psalter a continuity between God's revelation in the Pentateuch and the material contained in the psalms which are to follow (interestingly, the Psalter begins the third section of the Hebrew canon, so the point may be extended). A particular status as 'torah' is thus obliquely claimed for the Psalter by the use of this term in the opening psalm.

[11] J.L. Mays, "The Place of the Torah-Psalms in the Psalter," *JBL* 106 (1987), pp. 3–12; and (1994), places considerable emphasis on these 'torah' psalms, suggesting that they are one of the keys to the Psalter and that their positioning is organisationally significant. While his demonstration of the importance of the motif is helpful, I cannot accept that there is convincing evidence for seeing any except psalm 1 to occur in places of structural prominence within the Psalter. Claus Westermann, "Zur Sammlung des Psalters," *Theologia Viatorum* 8 (1962), pp. 278–284 = "The Formation of the Psalter," in *Praise and Lament in the Psalms* (Atlanta, 1981), pp. 250–258 attempts a case for 119, suggesting that an earlier form of the Psalter originally concluded with that psalm, but there is scant evidence for his proposal. It seems better to recognise that while the motif of the importance of God's torah is an important one in the Psalter, it is not one of the central organising concerns.

matter. This was a theme we noted in book 4, and it is repeated
throughout the Psalter. I suggest that its occurrence in this first psalm
is important; anyone with an eschatology would find support for it
in these assertions of Ps. 1.

iii) *Psalm 2: international responsibility*

Psalm 2 also emphasises responsibility before God, but this time it
is *national* not individual. Whereas psalm 1 called for personal righteousness, psalm 2 is international in scope, addressing the nations
and summoning them to submit to God and his 'Messiah' and 'son.'
There are other important motifs also which will recur throughout
the Psalter (the choice of Zion, the purpose with the nations), but
these cannot be developed here.

It is important to stress that this psalm was chosen (or at the very
least allowed to remain) as an introductory psalm for the Psalter
when it was finally compiled after the Exile. Victory for God and
his son/king is promised and asserted, *at a time when there was no king*,
and when the nation had little political significance. To this king
God promises the nations and the uttermost parts of the world as
his inheritance. He will subdue them and reign over them as king
from God's holy hill of Zion. Reading the Psalter from the perspective of its final form and taking into account the editorial decision made in placing this psalm in this position we are forced into
understanding it eschatologically, whatever its origins may have been.

Let me emphasise this point. It is remarkable that this psalm
should front a collection which includes a substantial number of
psalms which deal with God's *rejection* of Zion and the *failure* of the
kingship and kingdom. That this psalm should assert God's rule
(when we know what is coming in the rest of the Psalter) makes it
almost certain that this Psalm is to be given an eschatological interpretation. All has not been lost despite the captivity and the loss of
the kingdom; God will still be vindicated, and will vindicate his people; Zion will still be the centre of the world! So the Psalm asserts.
The Davidic promise of 2 Samuel 7 is reasserted here, even though
other parts of the Psalter recognise that it was not historically fulfilled.
That fulfilment (following a clash between God and the nations,
v1–5,8,9) is yet to come.

The final stanza of the Psalm brings the reader back to the present, and effectively admits that the situation described previously
has not happened yet. The kings and princes are addressed and

exhorted to be wise while they still have opportunity – before it is too late. The moment of decision and judgement has not yet come, and the nations are encouraged to make the right choice now while they still have chance. This is a powerful lead-in to the Psalter.

Putting these points from Pss. 1 and 2 together, we have found emphasis on both individual and national responsibility, along with an explanation of the implications of this in view of what is yet to come. The judgement of God is proclaimed as applying to both the individual and to the world. As readers of the first two psalms of the Psalter we already know what *we* have to do, and we know what *God* is planning to do.

This programmatic beginning contrasts sharply with the following psalms (3ff.) which form the heart of book 1. Those psalms are all about troubles and difficulties, anxiety and suffering. They are psalms which arise out of the personal experience of crisis in life. We shall consider the significance of these later, but for the present Pss. 1 and 2 can be seen as the programmatic foundation that can hold one steady through such crisis.

iv) *The ending of the Psalter: psalm 150 or psalms 146–150?*

Psalm 150 is generally thought to constitute the conclusion to the Psalter, the whole psalm serving as a doxology rather than a single sentence (as is the case for the other books). This is an attractive option: though only one of a number of psalms in book 5 framed by the expression 'Hallelujah,' the psalm stands out because of its total concentration on praising God – to such an extent that the personality of the psalmist and his community is entirely forgotten. God is brought totally to the fore as the object of man's praise; man is completely in the background. Contrary to the usual practice, no justification is given here as to *why* God is to be praised. The psalm is so totally God-focused that to specify one's motivation would be out of place.[12]

I believe that a closer look at the closure of book 5 brings to light an analysis superior to the above, however.[13] Since there is good evidence that the Psalter has an introduction which is not part of the

---

[12] A point made in W. Brueggemann, "Bounded by Obedience and Praise: The Psalms as Canon," *JSOT* 50 (1991), pp. 63–92; reprinted in P.D. Miller (ed.), *The Psalms and the Life of Faith*, (Minneapolis, 1995), here pp. 192–193.

[13] Wilson (1985), pp. 225–226, gives a similar analysis, although I came to the conclusion independently.

five-fold structure of the Psalter but rather stands outside that structure (book 1 really consisting of psalms 3–41), this suggests that we look for a similarly independent conclusion. Furthermore, Ps. 150 is the finale of a sequence of the five Hallelujah Pss. 146–150. It is thus part of a larger structure; it does not stand alone. I suggest therefore that Ps. 145 is the concluding psalm of book 5, and that the Hallelujah sequence 146–150 forms the conclusion of the Psalter as a whole (of which 150 is the "grand finale").

But what of a concluding doxology for book 5? I suggest that it may be identified as the last verse of Ps. 145: "My mouth shall speak the praise of the LORD: And let all flesh bless his holy name for ever and ever." (145:21, RSV). This requires comparison with the doxologies of the other books:

1. Blessed be the LORD the God of Israel, from everlasting, and to everlasting. Amen, and Amen. (41:14, RSV).
2. Blessed be the LORD, the God of Israel, who alone does wondrous things. Blessed be his glorious name for ever; and may his glory fill the whole earth; Amen, and Amen. (72:18–19, RSV).
3. Blessed be the LORD for ever. Amen, and Amen. (89:53, RSV).
4. Blessed be the LORD, the God of Israel, from everlasting to everlasting. And let all the people say, 'Amen'. (106:48, RSV).

There are, admittedly, big differences between these and 145:21. Ps. 145 does not use the phrases "God of Israel" or "Amen and Amen" which are characteristic elsewhere (although "God of Israel" is not found in Ps. 89 either). Nevertheless, the parallels are equally striking: the reference to blessing the holy name of the Lord and the expression "for ever and ever" are to be found in all the other doxologies. This seems to me to be convincing evidence that this psalm does indeed function as the last psalm in the group that make up Book 5. Also (given the proposal to be presented below that royal psalms occur at the end of books or important divisions in the Psalter), it is significant that the theme of Ps. 145 is the *kingdom* or *reign* of God. The concluding doxology of the psalm not only blesses God's holy name as do the other doxologies, but it also stresses the international dimension of the kingdom: "and let *all flesh* bless his holy name for ever and ever" (RSV). An eschatological vision once more?

This leaves us with Pss. 146–150 as the conclusion to the Psalter. With their crescendo of praise to God culminating in 150 they are eminently suitable for this function. There is also a contrast with the introduction to the Psalter. The introduction focused on the responsibility of *man* (whether individual or national) to acknowledge and serve God. The Psalter concludes by focusing on *God* and on the joys of praising him. Man is now thoroughly wrapped up in this work of praise (or in enforcing it, Ps. 149!). At the end of the Psalter the whole creation is united in praising God (Pss. 148 and 150 in particular, picking up on themes from the יהוה מלך psalms). Anyone who read those psalms and believed that the picture they present would come about (as the psalmists certainly seem to have believed) must have had an eschatology. Ps. 149 describes the judgements of God, spoken of in Pss. 1 and 2[14] and reiterated again and again (compare the יהוה מלך psalms), at last being carried out on the earth by the saints. The vengeance promised is at last being performed, and God's praise will thus ascend unhindered by the deeds of those wicked enemies the Psalter so frequently described. Such is the goal towards which the Psalter moves.

2. *Keynotes of the Psalter: what happens in between?*

Having established that the psalms at the beginning and ending of the Psalter appear to have been deliberately chosen to function as the introduction and conclusion to the collection – that the Psalter has a definite "starting place" and 'ending' – the next question is "what happens in between?" Is there a progression as the reader passes from start to finish?

i) *Progressions*

We can begin simply by "joining the dots", as it were. The Psalter begins with obedience and ends with praise: the two can easily be linked up in the suggestion that the Psalter charts a progression, a path or a journey, whether in the life of the faithful individual or in the experiences of Israel, from *obedience* to *praise*. This suggestion is the basis of Brueggeman's justly famous essay "Bounded by Obedience and Praise."[15] The Psalter begins with one and ends with the other; in between it will explore and expand on the problems of

---

[14] Perhaps an inclusio is to be seen here between Pss. 2 and 149? It is also worth exploring the possibility that one is to be discerned between 1 and 150 also.

[15] Brueggemann (1991), pp. 63–92; reprinted in Miller (1995), pp. 189–213.

obedience and faith which arise through the circumstances and hardship of life. It will show that through obedience in times of crisis and distress the believer will learn how to praise God, to be less focused on 'I' and more centred on praising God.

The progression may be expressed differently as a progression from *lament* to *praise*. The Psalter is like a pendulum constantly alternating between the two extremes of lament and praise; in form-critical terms these are the most common genres of psalm. But it is significant that numerically laments are in the ascendancy in the first half of the Psalter (books 1–3) and in decline thereafter. In contrast, we find an increasing number of hymns and praises as we progress towards the conclusion, with a particularly high proportion in books 4 and 5.[16]

Consonant with this observation, it is also true that there is less imprecation to be found as we move through the Psalter. Although it depends on one's definition of imprecation (this is not the place to discuss it), on a rough estimate the ratio of psalms containing imprecatory passages across Pss. 1–50, 51–100, 101–150 is approximately 3:2:1. There is less focus on *me* and *my* enemies, and more focus on God as we progress through the Psalter (the 'I' of the psalms fades into the background). All these facts lend support to the suggestion that reading through the Psalter represents a journey from lament to praise, from focus on self to focus on God.

In another context Walter Brueggemann has suggested a "typology of function" to categorise the psalms as an alternative to the standard form-critical distinctions.[17] He has discerned three types of psalm: psalms of orientation (statements of theoretical and untried faith), disorientation ('lament' psalms in which faith hits crisis), and reorientation (in which crisis is worked through, responded to, and a deeper and wiser faith reaffirmed). Although this terminology was developed to categorise individual psalms and not the Psalter as a whole, it is perhaps worth observing that although the 'body' of the Psalter contains a mixture of the three types, Pss. 1 and 2 are definitely psalms of orientation and Pss. 146–150 make sense as psalms

---

[16] It is in books 4 and 5 and in the conclusion of the Psalter that the Hallelujah and "bless the Lord" psalms are found. It is here too that there are more 'straightforward' compositions transparently suited to every age (that is, not requiring a strategy of interpretation in the way that imprecatory psalms and laments seem to require for modern readers).

[17] W. Brueggemann, *The Message of the Psalms – A Theological Commentary* Augsburg OT Studies (Minneapolis, 1984); also Miller (1995), pp. 3–32.

of reorientation. What happens in between is the transition between the two: largely psalms of disorientation (coming to a head in book 3), but with a new orientation emerging ever stronger in books 4 and 5.

The progression can be seen in eschatological terms also (albeit less convincingly). The Psalter begins with the responsibilities *now* to show obedience to God, coupled with the promise that one day there will be a reward for this, and that God and his 'son' will reign over the earth. We then move through a series of lament/crisis psalms which reflect the trials of faith and harsh experience of life as it is *now*. But as we continue the vision of the whole world praising God in the eschaton grows stronger.

In outlining this progression we are of course in the realm of sweeping generalisation. Characterising the Psalter as a progression from lament to praise, from obedience to praise, from 'me' to 'Him' is an attempt to characterise a large, diverse and complex work in the bounds of a sentence. The question is, how useful is the generalisation? For the present two points are worth making. First, there are many counterexamples that spoil the pattern: hymns and praises in book 1, laments and imprecation in book 5. The Psalter constantly alternates between lament and praise; there is not a smooth transition from one to the other. Second, and in tension with the foregoing, the generalisation is nevertheless based on facts. It is undeniably true that the *frequency* of laments, imprecation and 'I'-centredness decreases through the Psalter. To be able to account for this through a proposal of an overall framework for the Psalter is a very attractive option.

ii) *The book divisions*

The five-fold division of the Psalter is central to its organisational structure. The five 'books' of psalms reflect important differences, not only in the usage of psalm titles and other technical terms but also in genre of psalm, subject matter, and even vocabulary and style.[18] On the lookout for editorial shaping, some scholars have paid particular attention to the psalms which open and conclude the five

---

[18] M.A. Vincent, "The Organisation of the Psalter: What can Lexical Evidence Contribute?" unpublished paper read at the Psalms Group of the 1998 SBL Meeting in Orlando, Florida.

books, the psalms at the 'seams' of the Psalter, as Gerald Wilson has termed them.[19]

Wilson found an examination of the concluding psalms of the five books to be particularly fruitful. He claimed that the final psalm was usually a royal psalm, and saw organisational activity lying behind this. This is certainly true in the case of Pss. 72 and 89, and it is interesting that 145 is also a psalm about the kingdom/reign of God (see above). The problem with Wilson's observation is that the pattern fails at Pss. 41 and 106 (although Wilson claims that 41 contains elements of the royal genre, the attempt has been found unconvincing by others, including myself). Wilson's proposal cannot be sustained without modification, since it only works in three out of five cases.

As will be suggested below, books 1 and 2 and books 4 and 5 should in some respects be considered together, and from this point of view Wilson's point still has merit (since Pss. 72, 89 and 145 mark the end of the books 1+2, 3, 4+5);[20] furthermore, the introduction to the Psalter (Pss. 1+2) also contains a royal psalm in final place. Each of these psalms is important not only from the point of view of tracing the Davidic king, but also because they have an important bearing on the questions of Messianic and eschatological hope in the Psalter. We shall withhold a final judgement until later.

Another option is to look at the opening psalm of each of the five books. This has been the strategy of Clinton McCann.[21] He rightly points out that Pss. 3, 42, 73 and 90 are all laments. This is true, but two observations serve to limit the power of the observation. First, Ps. 107, the opening psalm of book 5, is not a lament, so the pattern only works in four out of five cases. Second, the observation that Pss. 3, 42 and 73 are laments is *uninteresting*, since most of the other psalms in those books are laments also. Psalm 3 does

---

[19] Wilson (1985), pp. 207–208, but compare also pp. 207–228. deClaisse-Walford (1998) is an example of this approach being taken too far. In a short monograph she dedicates most of her space to a treatment of the opening and closing psalms of each of the five books without arguing that these psalms are typical or representative of the books as a whole.

[20] From the point of view of structural symmetry this suggests that book 3, not book 4 as is claimed by Wilson, McCann and others, is the editorial heart of the Psalter. Further evidence for this will be brought forward when each of the books is considered below.

[21] J.C. McCann, "Books 1–3 and the Editorial Purpose of the Hebrew Psalter," in McCann (1993), pp. 93–107.

not stand out from any of the psalms which follow it as a lament; neither does Ps. 42. In no way can these psalms be said to betray a clue about the organisational shaping of the Psalter; they are merely typical of the psalms that are to follow later in the respective book.

Other strategies for determining the organisational shape of the Psalter have been to pay less attention to the book divisions and instead to look for signs of editorial redaction. Attempts have been made to discern a wisdom redaction, a sacrificial redaction and an eschatological redaction. Each of these avenues is explored in Whybray's work, and his conclusion is that each is ultimately unconvincing.[22]

3. Do the five books have a story to tell?

I shall now discuss each of the five books in turn, outlining the distinctive themes and emphases of each in an endeavour to determine if or how they can be seen as contributing to a 'story' or 'message' for the Psalter as a whole, and whether or not eschatology has a part to play in such a scheme.

i) Books 1&2

It is difficult to distinguish between books 1 and 2 on anything other than stylistic grounds,[23] although it is true that communal psalms are more frequent in book 2. In the final editorial shaping of the Psalter the two books are to be connected because according to the psalm titles[24] they are both predominantly Davidic.[25] It is noteworthy that the colophon to book 2, "The prayers of David the son of Jesse are ended," provides a fitting conclusion not just to book 2, but to both books 1 and 2. Furthermore, common themes and moods (predominantly individual laments) are developed in the two books.

---

[22] Whybray (1996).

[23] Particularly the use of אלהים in book 2, a feature which continues into Ps. 83 of book 3. See Vincent, (1998).

[24] See note 9, above.

[25] The exception is the Korah cycle 42–49. An explanation of this and other stylistic facts connecting books 2 and 3 may be that book 2 and most of book 3 (the so-called 'elohistic' Psalter, 42–83) originally constituted a collection, that 84–89 (a second Korah group) was then added to create a symmetry with the opening of the collection (an inclusio of Korah psalms: 42–49 and 84–88/89). The colophon of 72 may have been left intact from such a collection, and, in the final form of the Psalter, it would serve a double function when book 1 was put in front – it concluded the whole group of predominantly Davidic psalms, 1–72.

The figure of David is thus the key to the function of books 1 and 2 as part of the overall structure of the Psalter. Not only do 55 psalms have Davidic superscriptions; all but one of the psalms containing historical titles relating to incidents in David's life occur in these two books. Although there are psalms about David as king (18, 20, 21, 61, 63), it is significant that most of these Davidic psalms portray David as a suffering and victimised figure, rather than as a mighty swashbuckling king. Childs suggests that David is to be seen as a representative individual, whose sufferings are typical of those experienced by everyone.[26] It was to this suffering figure (as a representative of each individual Israelite, and in all probability as a symbol of the nation as well) that the promises were made. David, like Israel and like the Israelite he epitomises, had to cling on to this belief in the face of the crises which he suffered.

The proposal to be developed below is that one of the themes being traced through the Psalter is the story of the Davidic monarchy from the times of David in which the promises were received, through to its collapse in the exilic period (and the associated question "what happened to the promises, then?!"). In this schema books 1 and 2 deal with the historical David himself. The two psalms at the close of book 2 appear particularly pertinent here as David passes off the scene. Psalm 71 is about old age; at last the great king is coming to the end of his life – God, who has been with him throughout his life from his youth, is pleaded with not to desert him now that he is old. But what will follow the passing of the great king? Is this the end of the Davidic dynasty? Of course not! – a point made very clearly in Ps. 72, the final psalm of the Davidic Psalter (note: a royal psalm at the conclusion of an important division in the Psalter). This final psalm is about the Davidic king – but not about David himself. The promises made to David in 2 Samuel 7 are echoed here (as well as the promises to Abraham) as David hands over the reins to Solomon (the psalm title reads "to/for Solomon"), asking God to give his judgements to *his (David's)* son. The hope and future of the Davidic monarchy is now being placed in the hands of Solomon and his successors. Even though David is dying, his kingship will be immortalised in his children.

---

[26] B.S. Childs, *Introduction to the Old Testament as Scripture* (London, 1979), p. 522. I like this interpretation, although it must be said that the function of the historical titles appears to do the very opposite: to situate them specifically in the life of David, and to insist that these are not 'generalised' or 'stylised' sufferings.

ii) *Book 3*

The kingship was indeed passed on, but the nation's fortunes soon went downhill (according to the historical narratives), a degeneration which culminated in the captivity. Book 3 wastes no time in informing us that all has gone badly awry, and in taking us forward to the trauma of the exile: the short book is dominated by psalms of crisis which tell God in the most direct terms of suffering, doubt, unfairness, and of *God's* apparent failure to do anything about it. God is questioned and criticised more forcefully here than elsewhere in the Psalter.

There are two types of crisis psalm in the book, reflecting two different levels in which crisis was experienced. First there are psalms which record individual crises of faith: in particular the theodicy question (especially psalms 73 and 77). Then there are national or communal laments which complain that God has rejected his people and is doing nothing about their national dilemma (which I take to be the captivity). God is not being a proper shepherd;[27] rather he is destroying his people and their expectation. God seems to have completely rejected the Davidic monarchy and the promises he made (74, 79, 80). All this comes to a head in the final two psalms of the book, 88 and 89. 88 is significant for its totally bleak outlook,[28] 89 because it is a rehearsal of God's promises to David – with the deliberate intention of throwing them back in God's face in the second half of the psalm to ask what has become of them. Once again a psalm about the king/kingdom is placed at a turning point in the Psalter, this time a psalm challenging the truth of these hopes and promises.

It is surely significant that the problem being dealt with in the psalms of individual lament in book 3 is the apparent falsity of the assertion of Ps. 1 – that the righteous are blessed and the wicked suffer – in the light of the psalmist's experience of life. The problem being dealt with in the communal laments is the apparent failure of Ps. 2, the other psalm which forms the introduction to the Psalter. Where is God's 'Messiah'? Where is the king sitting on God's holy hill of Zion? Why are the other nations triumphing over God's monarchy instead of being subdued by it? The crises of book 3 are a direct

---

[27] The use of shepherd language appears to be dominant in the Asaph Pss. 73–83. It is usually invoked in order to criticise God (contrast Ps. 23, whose words are in effect thrown back at God in Ps. 80).

[28] Brueggemann (1984), pp. 78–81; (1995), pp. 56, 57.

challenge to the assertions of psalms 1 and 2. Although hinting at answers here and there, book 3 does not attempt to answer this crisis of faith directly, particularly the national crisis and the failure of the monarchy. This is left hanging, in most dramatic fashion, by the bitter complaint of psalms 88 and 89.[29]

iv) *Book 4*

Book 4 plays a very important role in the structure developing so far since it presents the 'answer' to the crisis of book 3. So much so that, as noted earlier, it has been termed the theological 'heart' of the Psalter. Some scholars have seen great significance in the appearance of Moses in the first psalm of the book, suggesting that he is the representative intercessor who pleads with God to turn again to his people and heal the breach of captivity (contrast this with the arguing that has occupied so much of book 3).[30] It is certainly true that there is a sustained Mosaic/wilderness theme in book 4 which must be accounted for (90:1 (title); 99:6; 103:7; 105:26; 106:16,23,32; also note the wilderness theme in 81 and 95). Even if the idea of Moses as an intercessor be dismissed as fanciful, it is nevertheless possible that a parallel is being drawn between Israel's experience in the wilderness (many dying, *not* inheriting the land God promised – and yet a subsequent generation seeing the fulfilment of those promises by God's mercy) and Israel's experience in captivity (many dying/being taken captive, the Davidic monarchy lying in tatters – and yet the hope that God will nevertheless keep his promises and that there will be a return). In the wake of the experience of captivity, Israel have to learn their lesson, reform, and be patient – just like the wilderness generation. The theme of God's repeated mercy is nowhere more clear than in the last psalm of the book, 106, a point which may be significant (notice Moses' particular significance in the first and last psalms of the book, 90 and 106).

There are two further themes which are central to an appreciation of book 4. The first is the emphasis on praising God; God is

---

[29] *Pace* McCann, (1993), pp. 95–100, especially p. 97. McCann's table gives a misleading impression about the extent of positive material in book 3; furthermore, the alternation between positive and negative moods that he describes is characteristic of the Psalter as a whole and is not a noteworthy feature of book 3.

[30] C.R. Seitz, "Royal Promises in the Canonical Books of Isaiah and the Psalms," in *Word Without End: The Old Testament as Abiding Theological Witness* (Grand Rapids, 1998), pp. 162–165.

still to be praised despite all that has been endured, and in whatever situation one finds oneself (the יהוה מלך psalms, and others like 100, 103, 104, 106 all emphasise this). This note of praise continues into book 5,[31] and builds up towards a crescendo at the conclusion of the Psalter. The second theme central to book 4 is the יהוה מלך motif itself, the assertion that he is king despite it all (despite the individual doubt and national/historical crisis of book 3). In the face of all appearances to the contrary these psalms press the notion that God is king (even if he doesn't have an earthly ruler on his throne!), and that he is in control.

In the light of the crisis of captivity the יהוה מלך phrase can on one level be understood as an assertion that *God* is still king, even if the human Davidic king has long since disappeared. The human king may have been taken away because of the repeated sinfulness of both him and his people, but God remains enthroned in heaven. Thus he is still to be praised, as the יהוה מלך psalms encourage, as the lord of all creation. However, as we noted at the outset, this is not the only way of looking at the יהוה מלך psalms. It is also possible to interpret them in an eschatological sense: since God is king his promises will yet be fulfilled and either he himself, or his representative (the future Messianic king) will come. This very assertion forms the climax of two of the יהוה מלך psalms, 96 and 98. Through the body of these psalms there is not a *pronounced* emphasis on this eschatological solution, but there is no doubt that it is discernible.

v) *Book 5*

Book 5 is the most difficult of the five books to categorise, and it is here that the progression that we have been developing appears at its weakest. The book ends in an appropriate way, with psalm 145 dealing extensively with the topic of God's kingdom and his lordship over the earth. This psalm can easily be interpreted in an eschatological manner. Further, the emphasis on praise in the book (with the 'hallelujah' and "bless the Lord" psalms, along with the Songs

---

[31] In this sense, books 4 and 5 are best seen together (book 4 is not closed with a royal psalm, unlike the Davidic Psalter and unlike book 3). Furthermore, the two books have many stylistic similarities: Vincent, (1998). However, in other respects book 4 stands apart with its Mosaic emphasis and the yhwh mlk motif. Thus it is not clear whether the superior analysis would be to group books 4 and 5 together or to consider them separately. As will become apparent, book 5 is difficult whichever strategy is adopted, though less so if the two books are linked.

of Ascents) also chimes with the general movement in the Psalter from lament to praise (trusting and rejoicing in God whatever the circumstance). Nevertheless, the book does not appear to have a specific message or story to tell in the way that can be claimed for the other four books. Instead we find a chiastic pattern in terms of authorship ascription:

107	no author		
108–110		David	
111–119			no author
120–134				Songs of Ascents
135–137			no author
138–144		David	
145	no author		

Most of the psalms in book 5 are content to get on with the job of praising God in a simple and direct manner without tirades against enemies, or, indeed, against God himself. The incessant lament and imprecation of earlier books have largely disappeared (though there appears to be a deliberate reminder of it right at the end of the book: 140, 143, 144).

More difficult is the apparent lack of interest in the Davidic king, in Messiah, and in eschatology. Given that the Davidic monarchy has failed in book 3 and that this failure has been dealt with in book 4, we would expect messianic and eschatological interest to be at a height in book 5. Yet this is the place where (with the odd exception, such as psalm 110) it is conspicuously absent. There appears to be no conscious attempt to project the hopes for the Davidic monarchy forward to the future, to say "yes, it did fail in the past, but all is going to be put right in the future!" Instead, we have a sequence of psalms which are straightforward hymns of praise to God. It is only towards the end of book 5, particularly in psalms 144 and 145, that eschatological interests are revived.

vi) *An eschatological interest?*

The twin themes of both individual faith and the Davidic monarchy in crisis that have been sketched for books 1–3 might be expected to lead to a clear expression of eschatological hope in books 4 and 5. However, although it is possible to see such at certain points in book 4 (as outlined in the beginning of this essay), it does not seem that this is a dominating emphasis in that book, let alone book 5.

Thus, although from a consideration of the introduction and conclusion to the Psalter it appeared probable that there may be an eschatological emphasis in its shaping, it appears on closer examination of the individual books themselves that this is not a dominant concern. Even if the concluding psalms of book 5 and the emphases of book 4 are accorded extra weight, the bulk of the Psalter shows little trace of having been subjected to a systematic editorial process intended to highlight eschatological solutions. The absence of such material in the body of book 5 counts strongly against this.

Even if one of the key organisational concerns of the Psalter is to chart the rise and fall of the monarchy and of how faith in God is meant to cope with those experiences, the solutions implicitly suggested by the Psalter's organisation (if they are not imaginary!) are not predominantly eschatological. They are rather to keep trusting and to keep praising. To this message one can add "until one day everything will be put right", a message which can indeed be seen at various points in the Psalter (among others: 2, 72, יהוה מלך Pss. 144, 145), particularly if one is looking for it. But it is a theme which has to be searched for, rather than being deliberately put in the reader's way to encourage him or her to think eschatologically. One *can* read the Psalter eschatologically, even to the extent of finding an eschatological 'programme' within it; but the final editors' organisational scheme is a far cry from *making* one or even *encouraging* one to read the Psalter in that way. Even someone who was keen to emphasise the importance of eschatology would be able to claim only that such themes were dominant at the boundaries of major collections of the Psalter (perhaps in the יהוה מלך psalms too, and haphazardly elsewhere). Such a person would not be able to claim a systematic scheme through the body of the Psalter as a whole.

4. *Evaluation and Conclusion*

I turn now from the specific question of eschatology to an evaluation of the thesis of an organisational plan and message from the Psalter as developed in this essay and by other scholars in the secondary literature. At least the following critique should be made.

1. More consideration needs to be given to the possible artificiality of looking for an organisational master-plan for the Psalter in the first place. Why should the Psalter be thought to have such a

plan? Is some such comparable scheme to be found in other ancient collections?[32] One could perhaps take any hymn-book or poetry collection (to use a modern analogy), look at the pieces which begin and end it and likewise construct an interpretation of the editorial plan. But in all likelihood this would be to read something into the editorial work far beyond anything the editors themselves ever intended. Hymn books would not normally seem to be constructed according to elaborate theological schemes containing hidden 'messages' even in their very organisational structures. This becomes all the more pertinent in the light of the following points.

2. There are an uncomfortable number of exceptions to the generalisations. It is *generally true* to say that there is less imprecation in book 5, for example, yet psalms 109 and 137 from that book are generally thought to be the most violent examples within the Psalter! Likewise, in books 1 and 2 there are many examples of psalms which are not individual laments and which do not conform to the generalisations made earlier. Although book 3 does *mainly* contain psalms of crisis, the book also contains Pss. 76 and 82. How are all these exceptions to be explained, and do they make the generalisations put forward above too weak to be interesting?

3. The so-called 'message' concerning the Davidic monarchy and promises – developing from books 1 and 2, to the crisis in book 3, to its resolution in books 4 and 5 – may reflect nothing more than the chronological order in which the Psalter was put together. Books 1 and 2 may be the earliest (containing many pieces from pre-exilic times), book 3 may contain psalms from the exilic period, and books 4–5 may consist predominantly of post-exilic psalms. Trying to detect an "editorial message" may be an example of overreading a simple chronological fact.

4. Book 5, often assumed to be the latest book of the Psalter (correctly, in my view) and thus most accessible to a process of editorial adjustment, bears the least evidence of thematic shaping of any of the books, and conforms in only the most weak way to the thematic development put forward for books 1–4. Thus, in

---

[32] Wilson tries to tackle this point by an investigation of collections of Sumerian temple hymns. He does indeed find clear organisational criteria, but they are not of the thematic and even theological kind that is here being put forward for the Psalter. Wilson (1985), pp. 13–61.

the very place where one would most like to see confirmation of a developing message within the Psalter (the final book), one is most clearly aware of its absence.

One of the mediating factors which may partially account for point two above is an editorial conservatism concerning already established groupings of psalms. It is abundantly evident that the compilers of the Psalter have kept intact previously existing collections (witness the duplication of psalms, the colophon at the end of 72, and the statistical distribution of stylistic features). Thus, while deeming the Asaph collection of book 3, for example, to be particularly appropriate as an expression of the crisis at the dissolution of the monarchy (amongst other things), the editors may have been reluctant to select only those psalms that *precisely* suited their theme and detach them from other psalms (such as 76) which may have existed as part of a sequence in a pre-existing collection. A study of the organisation of the Psalter very quickly reveals the tension between conservatism to pre-existing collections on one hand, and innovation in the placing of psalms and groupings on the other. It is not enough merely to cite such conservatism as a potential reason why the perceived organisational pattern might not be quite as clear as we may like, however. More work needs to be done to illustrate in detail how such editorial principles might be traced in the Psalter, and how they have interacted with one another in specific instances. Up to now the work carried out has been primarily to identify overall themes. This has been done with very broad brush strokes, but the time is now ripe to produce detailed evidence (if it exists) to corroborate what has been proposed. This must be done both at a lexical level (indicating the interconnectedness of sequences of psalms to show that deliberate organisation has taken place), and at a thematic level (the themes need to be identified and established more precisely than has hitherto been the case).

Therefore, at the current state of research it seems questionable whether we can speak with any certainty about editorial intentionality – that we can discern an editorial master-plan for the Psalter such that we can state that the editors were deliberately giving us a particular message in the very way in which they ordered their materials. There is not enough evidence to assert confidently a deliberate theological shaping to the Psalter, even though certain tendencies do seem to be clear.

These considerations do not require the abandonment of what has been put forward in this essay, however. Although it remains to be seen whether the general patterns and shapes that have been proposed can be borne out by closer study, the generalisations that have been made are sound *as far as they go*, and they are susceptible to the kind of interpretation being offered here, even if they may not require it. What has been put forward is one useful way of saying *something* about the Psalter as a whole within a very short compass; it is a valid way of characterising some of the themes of the Psalter – *whether or not the editors originally intended it that way*. It can scarcely be disputed that the Psalter does indeed begin in one place (with a particular set of themes), and that it ends in another. Nor can the generalisations about the general movement from lament to praise be questioned. What can be questioned is whether or not one should read significance into these facts – whether the start and finish of the Psalter should be linked in such a conscious manner, whether the "lament to praise" generalisation has too many exceptions to be interesting or not, whether it is fair to assign to the five books a 'message' and link them all together (even if it be granted that they do each have dominant themes). These are of course all matters of interpretation, how the data contained in the Psalter are understood. They are not sufficiently weighty, it seems to me, to speak with certainty about what the editors planned – but they are data capable of (and, in my view, worthy of) being assigned the sort of interpretation being put forward here, *of being read in that way*.

It thus emerges that what has been produced here should be regarded as a *reading* of the Psalter. It is a reading which some people will accept, and others will not. At the present stage of research it seems to me that this is how we should look at proposals regarding the organisation of the Psalter. Talking about authorial intentionality is a suspicious enterprise at the best of times; with the present amount of evidence it would seem unwise to attempt to specify precisely the editorial intentionality of the compilers.

In conclusion, then, to see the Psalter as a whole in the structural and thematic terms outlined in this essay can be a genuinely helpful way of comprehending it, of saying *something* meaningful about the Psalter within a brief compass. It provides a way for readers to approach the work and enables them to take home a message from it as a whole. But whether it is any more than that is a matter which requires more detailed further investigation than that which appears to have been carried out thus far.

THE WOLF SHALL LIVE WITH THE LAMB:
READING ISAIAH 11:6–9 TODAY

BY

R.E. CLEMENTS
Cambridge

Isa. 11:6–9 is widely used in Christian churches as an Advent reading anticipating the coming of Israel's messiah in the days of the Old Testament and thereby encouraging us to look forward in the present to an era of world peace. In this not only will human aspirations and expectations for harmony between nations be realised, but a new order in the natural world will come into being. It belongs closely alongside the more overtly political assurance of Isa. 2:4 and for modern readers it possesses a poetic quality which enables us to see in it an element of hyperbole, and so to limit its literal implications. Nevertheless its content raises serious questions for the modern mind.

The general reader is probably better informed in the present concerning patterns of animal behaviour than any previous generation has been through modern ecological researches and the remarkable visual expression that these have enjoyed on television. The well-merited success of studies of the natural world in David Attenborough's *The Trials of Life, Life in the Freezer* and other similar programmes have served to bring home to even the most unphilosophical of observers a knowledge that the natural world is full of violence and predation. "Is it suitable for the children?" is a question that is quickly forced upon us. The reality of this pattern of animal behaviour is not easily intelligible to those brought up on the stories of Beatrix Potter and Kenneth Grahame. Moreover such predatory violence is a necessary feature, and any concern with protecting the habitat of endangered species draws attention to it. Vital links in the chain of species survival are formed by the availability to predatory animals of their natural food supply. To soften the impact of this behaviour by arguing that it is never for play or sport, but solely for essential food, is itself open to serious questioning.

Acquaintance with a recognition of the extent to which one species relies upon its exploitation of other weaker species in the natural order of life reveals to us the positive contribution for survival that the impulse to aggression makes. These behavioural traits appear everywhere throughout the natural world and have rightly become the subject of close study.[1] Moreover we can see clearly that such violence plays an important role in the natural order of animal and human survival. From the plains of Serengeti to the ice-floes of Antarctica the fact that survival of many species rests on their ability to hunt and consume other species highlights a feature of Darwin's argumentation for the survival of the fittest which has persistently aroused ethical debate. Stylised and conventional portrayals of a primitive paradisal state which were once popular as a mythical and idealised picture of the world's beginnings run counter to our knowledge of the actual origins of life on earth. Not surprisingly Jurassic Park has become to the contemporary world a more meaningful portrayal of the primeval past than the Garden of Eden!

However it is not only the strong popular awareness of the essential role that predatory behaviour plays in ensuring the survival of the variety of animal life in the natural world that makes Isa. 11:6–9 a rather uncertain expression of future hope. Such a state threatens our environmental concerns since it would clearly mean the abolition of "the wild" in the form in which we have come to know it. It is not only the growing numbers of enthusiastic conservationists who are aware that much of immense aesthetic and scientific worth would then be lost to future ages. To a significant degree we can hardly desire a literal fulfilment of the Isaianic prophecy.

The challenging neo-Darwinist portrayals of the evolution of life on earth have served to show how sharply the biblical portrayals of a future state of non-violence within the animal realm differ from modern scientific understanding of the reasons why things are the way they are. The aggression and predatory instincts which abound in the natural order of animal life belong to the reality and continuance of its existence. They cannot simply be cast aside to enable the wolf to live with the lamb without the wolf ceasing to be what it is, and quite evidently ceasing to survive.

These may appear to be rather speculative and hypothetical issues, generated by wresting from poetry an excessively formal and literal

---

[1] Compare R. Dawkins, *The Selfish Gene* (Oxford, 1989), pp. 66–87 "Aggression: stability and the selfish machine".

sense. The new relationships between animal and human species which are foretold in the prophetic vision of Isa. 11:6–9 are clearly intended to illustrate the coming of an entirely new, and different, world order.

It is the ending of violence in all its forms which establishes the primary focus of the future promise. Nonetheless its presence in the Bible draws attention to questions regarding the relationship between prophetic vision, Christian theology and modern ecological science. In the past the chief theological impact of the Isaianic promise has been in relation to what it infers about the present order of the natural world and its origins. It projects into the future a portrayal of a very distinctive divine pattern of life on earth, which implies that something is seriously wrong with the present shape of things. By making this contrast, and foretelling a new, completely re-ordered and re-created world, it builds on a recognition that the present order is not in accord with the divine will but has somehow become disordered and "cursed". So this Isaianic picture fits in with the belief that the natural world has itself been subjected to the effects of a divine "curse" which distorts its conformity to the original divine intention (compare 4 Ezra 7:10–12; Rom. 8:20–22). Our concern in the present essay, however, lies in what it has to say regarding the nature of evil, of human responsibility for the created order of life and for the kind of new world order for which the Christian may strive.

The issue of what kind of vision for the future of the world may be set before us as a genuinely biblical and Christian goal remains an important feature of the drawing of theological parameters to the conception of hope.[2] Only so can theology address basic questions concerning ecology, and the role of the environment in upholding a Christian quality of life. All too often the claim that Christian thought and commitment should be indifferent to matters regarding the hunting, farming and general use (and abuse) of animals, has been allowed to prevail.[3]

From the perspective of the text of Isa. 11:6–9 the primary focus is upon an eschatological new world order in which the problems

---

[2] Compare B.W. Anderson, "Creation and Ecology", *Creation in the Old Testament*, Issues in Religion and Theology 6 (London, 1984), pp. 152–171.

[3] Compare especially A. Linzey, *Christianity and the Rights of Animals* (London: SPCK, 1987); *idem, Animal Theology* (London, 1994).

of violence and aggression will be overcome and a new relationship established between human beings and the animals with which they share their planet. Such a hope has sometimes been taken in a negative fashion as a strong disincentive to dealing with problems of ecological significance. If the order of creation in a future end-time is to be wholly different from that which exists in the present, then there is little point in seeking to preserve this or in doing anything other than exploiting it to the point of its destruction.[4]

Yet this is not how the passage has been understood in Christian tradition. Rather it serves as a recognition that we live in a world of potential which displays life-enhancing and life-enriching possibilities of immense range. At the same time it also carries great risks and dangers which place heavy responsibilities upon human decision-making. These reach far beyond merely deciding to do nothing and leaving things alone to take their natural course. They call for action and restraints in order to move towards the ideal of a "Kingdom of Peace" which the Isaianic prophecy holds out as a future hope. This offers an envisioned portrayal of a new richness in the quality of life which will become possible through an ordered, and peaceable, universe. A new order of relationships between man and the animal realm will be realised and the Kingdom of Christ will embrace more than a just human society. It will extend across the entire spectrum of the living world.

A second issue that derives from this Isaianic vision of a Kingdom of Peace which will be radically different from the present is that concerning the nature of evil.[5] Since we know that aggression and violence are necessary for survival in an evolutionary world, the question of how far it is evil must be reopened. To what extent do aggressive and violent behavioural strategies represent a manifestation of natural evil? From a human ethical perspective, can we make recognisable distinctions between necessary, and therefore justifiable, forms of aggression, and illegitimate and immoral forms of it? It is the age-old debate concerning a "just war" brought into a new, and wider, perspective.

---

[4] Compare P. Boyer, *When Time Shall Be no More: Prophecy Belief in Modern American Culture* (Cambridge, Mass, 1992), especially pp. 301–2, 331–337. The citation from Billy Graham (p. 442, note 18) is most revealing of prevalent attitudes.

[5] Compare M. Midgely, *Beast and Man: The Roots of Human Nature* (London, 1980), especially pp. 25–49 "Animals and the Problem of Evil". *Idem, Wickedness: A Philosophical Essay* (London & New York, 1986), especially pp. 1–16.

Traditional Christian understanding of a primordial Fall has tended towards defining evil within an imaginative and instructive frame of reference, but has done little to relate this mythological imagery to concepts amenable to science, biology and social anthropology. All too often the emphasis has been upon contrast and contradiction, rather than complementarity. How do patterns of human and animal behaviour relate to each other and how far can the idea of "what is natural" provide an ethical value-judgement? Is evil a part of the order of nature, or are human beings responsible for "the way things are"? The traditional Christian belief that evil in the natural world is the consequence of human evil calls for considerable modification.

It is not difficult to see that the complex, and richly instructive, history of exegesis of the stories of the Fall in Genesis 2–3 serves to highlight the differences between a traditional Jewish and Christian understanding of them and modern scientific interpretations of the origin of life. Darwin posed an ethical, and not simply a historical, dilemma for the Jewish-Christian tradition to address.[6] There would not appear to be any great profit in ignoring these differences by seeking to construct a theological approach which fails to address the problems and issues raised by these traditional interpretations. Simply labelling the biblical material as mythological gets nowhere until what is implied by such a term is dealt with. To a significant degree therefore the vision of a kingdom of peace set out in Isa. 11:6–9 involves questions relating to the biblical understanding of the natural world and the possibility of a divine revelation in it.[7]

It is appropriate at this stage to note that the element of future promise set out in Isa. 11:6–9 requires first of all to be understood against its own biblical, and more narrowly prophetic, background. Only then can its place in any larger theological scene be usefully evaluated. We must therefore start by examining its place in its Isaianic context.

---

[6] Compare G. Himmelfarb, *Darwin and the Darwinian Revolution* (New York, 1968), pp. 380–411, "Darwinism, Religion and Morality".

[7] The whole subject is most usefully raised by James Barr in *Biblical Faith and Natural Theology* (Oxford, 1993), especially pp. 59–75, and also the same author's *The Garden of Eden and the Hope of Immortality* (London, 1992), pp. 21–56.

1. *Isaiah 11 and the Origin of Verses 6–9*

The passage that we are primarily concerned with in Isa. 11:6–9 reads straightforwardly and has frequently been taken to form a unit with the five verses which precede it. Its message is clear and unequivocal:

> The wolf shall live with the lamb,
>   the leopard shall lie down with the kid,
> the calf and the lion and the fatling together,
>   and a little child shall lead them.
> The cow and the bear shall graze,
>   their young shall lie down together;
> and the lion shall eat straw like the ox.
> The nursing child shall play over the hole of the asp,
>   and the weaned child shall put its hand on the adder's den.
> They will not hurt or destroy
>   on all my holy mountain;
> for the land will be full of the knowledge of the LORD
>   as the waters cover the sea.
>
> Isa. 11:6–9

So far as its literary setting is concerned, we may note that the larger unit of Isa. 11:1–9 occupies a central place in what is undoubtedly the extended structural unit of Isa. 10:5–12.6.[8] In looking closely at the four verses, 6–9, the first question that needs to be addressed concerns their own integral unity. Verse 9 presents a broad and general summary of the message concerning the new relationship which is to arise between wild and domestic animals and between all wild creatures and human beings. These latter are typified by the references in verses 6 and 8 to the dangers posed by snakes to unwary, and unsuspecting, children. The concluding refrain of v. 9 reappears in Hab. 2:14. Whether this can be taken as an indication that it has been drawn from a widely known motif current in Hebrew psalmody remains an uncertain point, but appears quite possible. J. Vermeylen

---

[8] For a structural analysis of Isa. 11 in its literary setting see now especially M.A. Sweeney, *Isaiah 1–39: With an Introduction to Prophetic Literature*, FOTL XVI (Grand Rapids, 1996), pp. 196–211. I find myself in disagreement with Sweeney's conclusions regarding the date of the material in chapter 11, but his comments and insights regarding its structure serve to clarify the way in which the material has been developed around central themes. See also his study referred to in note 12 below. The material in R.E. Clements *Isaiah 1–39*, New Century Bible (London, 1980) is now in need of some revision in the light of recent studies of the use and development of the Davidic tradition in the book of Isaiah.

follows a number of other scholars in arguing that v. 9 should certainly be regarded as a late post-exilic addition to verses 6–8.[9] Such
a conclusion appears quite probable, in spite of my earlier reluctance to countenance it.[10]

More important than the separate origin of verse 9, however, is
Vermeylen's recognition that verses 6–8 have been directly influenced
from Ps. 91:13:

> You will tread on the lion and the adder,
>   the young lion and the serpent
>   you will trample under foot.

Such a recognition reinforces the conclusion that the high level
of divine protection that is assured in Ps. 91 was primarily a royal
motif which is here related to the promise in Isa. 11:1–5 concerning the restoration of the dynasty founded by Jesse's son. This both
indicates the post-exilic 'messianic' interpretation of Psalm 91 and
reinforces the claim that vv.6–8(9) were intended to be taken along
with vv.1–5. They form an addition to the promise concerning the new
scion of Judah's royal dynastic line set out in these verses and significantly reinterpret them. Our next question therefore concerns their
time of origin.

Vermeylen,[11] is followed by Marvin A. Sweeney[12] in claiming that
Isa. 11:1–5 probably dates to the time of Josiah's reign, and forms
a part of the extensive reworking of the royal Zion traditions in the
wake of the collapse of Assyrian control over Judah at that time.
Yet this conclusion regarding the time of origin must be questioned,
especially if the prophecy of Isa. 9:2–7 (Heb. 1–6) belongs to this
Josianic period. Isa. 11:1–5 seems most plausibly to have been intended
to update the promise of 9:2–7 after events had transpired to render its hope questionable. Even if the intention in this celebrated
coronation oracle was intended to refer to Hezekiah's accession in

---

[9] J. Vermeylen, *Du Prophète Isaïe à l'apocalyptique: Isaïe, i–xxxv miroir d'un demi-
millénaire d'expérience religieuse en Israël*, 2 vols. Études bibliques (Paris: Gabalda, 1978),
I, p. 276.
[10] Clements (1980), p. 124.
[11] J. Vermeylen (1978), pp. 269–275.
[12] Sweeney (1996), pp. 203–210; *idem*, "Jesse's New Shoot in Isaiah 11: A Josianic
Reading of the Prophet Isaiah", R.D. Weis & D.M. Carr (eds.), *A Gift of God in
Due Season: Essays on Scripture and Community in Honor of James A. Sanders*, JSOTSS 225
(Sheffield, 1996), pp. 103–118.

replacing the hated Ahaz, its Josianic time of origin appears the most likely.[13]

A primary feature regarding the origin and setting of Isa. 11:6–8(9) concerns its relationship to the preceding promise of a shoot "from the stump of Jesse" which is to be found in Isa. 11:1–5.[14]

First, as regards Isa. 11:1–5, the reference to "the stump of Jesse" (Isa. 11:1) reflects the fact that the political situation of the royal house of David had been very seriously weakened, but not completely destroyed. The metaphor is more fully explicable if it refers to the post-587 B.C.E. situation, than if it arose earlier. The interpretation placed upon the hopes surrounding Josiah appear to have been more akin to a vindication of the Davidic tradition, *vis à vis* the seceding northern tribes, rather than a warning concerning its weakness and vulnerability. With the exiling of Jehoiachin in 598 and the deposition of Zedekiah in 587 the image of a tree stump is wholly appropriate. The survival of the royal dynasty descended from Jesse's son was far from certain and its restoration to Jerusalem's throne was a bold assurance which was certainly not uniformly supported or desired.

However, some circles clearly did nurture such a hope and looked for its fulfilment, either through Jehoiachin himself, or his descendants who had survived in Babylon (compare 2 Kgs. 25:27–30). This must be the original intended reference of Isa. 11:1–5 which can then be dated to sometime around 550 B.C.E. This is the period in which we must also place much of the editorial activity which revised the story of the monarchy (Joshua – 2 Kings). Probably from as early as the 590's a royalist circle attached to the exiled Davidic dynasty contended that Jehoiachin remained the legitimate king in exile. This developed into the hope that he, and his descendants, would eventually be restored to the throne in Judah. So it makes sense for some to have claimed at this time that there was hope for the 'tree' of Jesse, even when reduced to a stump (cp. Isa. 6:13)! Conflicts of interest relating to Judah's political future between roy-

---

[13] Compare R.E. Clements, "The Immanuel Prophecy of Isa. 7:10–17 and Its Messianic Interpretation", in E. Blum, C. Macholz and E.W. Stegemann (eds.), *Die Hebräische Bibel und ihre zweifache Nachgeschichte*. Festschrift R. Rendtorff (Neukirchen-Vluyn, 1990), pp. 225–240 [= R.E. Clements, *Old Testament Prophecy. From Oracles to Canon* (Louisville, 1996), pp. 65–77].

[14] The significance of the use of the metaphor of the stump of a tree for a royal family is dealt with extensively in K. Nielsen, *There is Hope for a Tree: The Tree as Metaphor in Isaiah*, JSOTSS 65 (Sheffield, 1989), pp. 123–144.

alist factions located in Judah and Babylon echo through many of the prophecies of both Jeremiah and Ezekiel.

The remainder of Isa. 11 addresses a different theme – that of the eventual return of Judah's citizens to their homeland from their places of dispersion and exile (11:12–16). Verses 10 and 11 turn the direction of interest outwards to address the fate of those many survivors from the disasters of 598 and 587 B.C.E. and a hope of their return is summed up in verses 12–16. The theme has now become that of the ending of the time of Israel's division and dispersion. The gathering-in of these survivors to a reborn nation from the many places to which they had been scattered has become a basic component of the hope of Israel's renewal. So verses 10–16 represent a post-538 B.C.E. expression of hope. In all probability this expectation of a great world-wide return of Jews from among the nations derives from a considerably later period probably in the fourth century B.C.E.

Such a hope forms a primary structural element for the final shaping of the book (compare Isa. 60:1–22). We conclude therefore that verses 10–16 were the latest additions to have been made to the chapter and belong to the final phase of the composition of the Isaiah scroll. So the sequence of growth in Isa. 11 still shows through, with an early prophecy from soon after 587 B.C.E. (vv. 1–5) having received supplementation at varying stages. Whether vv. 6–8 (9) were added before (10)11–16 is not wholly certain. After vv. 1–5 the separateness of the units, viz. 6–8, 9, 10, 11, 12–16 is quite noteworthy as are the many allusions back to earlier scriptural passages, not only from Isaiah.

2. *The Wolf and the Lamb in the Context of the Isaiah Scroll*

An explicit allusion back to Isa. 11:6–9 and a summarising citation of it, is then to be found later in Isa. 65:25:[15]

> The wolf and the lamb shall feed together,
>   the lion shall eat straw like the ox;
>   but the serpent – its food shall be dust!
> They shall not hurt or destroy
>   on all my holy mountain,
>   says the LORD.

---

[15] For the role of Isa. 11:6–9 in the emergence of the Jewish eschatological tradition compare now especially the studies by O.H. Steck, "... ein kleiner Knabe

This assurance comes as the conclusion (65:17–25) to a pronounce-
ment of coming judgement upon wrongdoers within the restored
nation (65:11–16).[16] An important mediating text between the earlier hope of the restoration of the Davidic dynasty to a position of
power and the expectation of a transformed world order is to be
found in Isa. 43:18–21:

> Do not remember the former things,
>   or consider the things of old.
> I am about to do a new thing;
>   now it springs forth, do you not perceive it?
> I will make a way in the wilderness
>   and rivers in the desert.
> The wild animals will honor me,
>   the jackals and the ostriches;
> for I give water in the wilderness,
>   rivers in the desert
> to give drink to my chosen people,
>   the people whom I formed for myself
> so that they might declare my praise.
>
>   Isa. 43:18–21

The contrast between "the former things" and "the new things"
of v. 18 has a bearing on the interpretation of 11:6–9 through to its
further connection with 65:17. The reference to the role of the wild
animals in 43:20 in bringing honour to the LORD God has almost
certainly given rise to the elaboration of this in Isa. 11:6–8. In a
further development of this the sentencing in Isa. 65:25 of the serpent to the limitation of "eating dust" makes an allusion back to the
curse of Gen. 3:14. So, in a process of verbal allusion and interplay,
we can see how Isa. 43:18; 11:6–9 and 65:17 form a sequential development. This phenomenon of intertextuality, by which the interpretation of one text takes on a greater range in the light of others,
indicates a fundamental technique, both of the formation of prophetic
scrolls and also of the process of Jewish doctrinal development. In
these three passages we are faced with more than mere chance similarities of language and ideas. A conscious process of scribal allusion

---

kann sie leiten", Beobachtungen zum Tierfrieden in Jesaja 11,6–8 und 65,25", in
J. Hausmann & H.J. Zobel (eds.), *Alttestamentliche Glaube und Biblische Theologie: Festschrift
H.D. Preuss* (Stuttgart-Berlin-Cologne, 1992), pp. 104–113; *idem*, "Die neue Himmel
und die neue Erde. Beobachtungen zur Rezeption von Gen. 1–3 in Jes. 65, 16b–25",
J. Van Ruiten & M. Vervenne (eds.), *Studies in the Book of Isaiah: Festschrift W.A.M.
Beuken* (Leuven, 1997), pp. 349–365.
    [16] Compare Steck (1997), pp. 349–50.

has been employed in order to construct a thematic outline of God's plan for the created orders of life.

Besides Isa. 43:18 a further step in the rise of a radical prophetic eschatology is to be seen in Isa. 54:9–17. The ravaged and desolate condition of Jerusalem in the present is contrasted with the wholly transformed portrayal of the splendour and wealth which the rebuilt city will enjoy in the future. Language that, in its original context could be understood as poetic hyperbole, has become a vehicle for a new understanding of universal world history. The rhetorical impetus to exhort and encourage a dispirited and despondent community has ultimately led to a world-encompassing hope of a transformed future for all creation. Expectations which were initially anchored in definable and recognisable events have been enlarged to the point of embracing a radically different conception of divine providence from that which originally shaped the prophetic preaching. Prophecy has given way to apocalyptic. In no small measure the written preservation of prophecy, with the possibility which it offers for revised readings of earlier sayings, names and themes, has become the instrument for constructing this radical message of hope.[17]

3. *Wild Animals as Seen in the Context of the Hebrew Bible*

When we look more widely across the doctrine of creation presented in the Hebrew scriptures it is evident that Isa. 11:6–9 stands out on account of its implicit assumption that something is seriously wrong with the present order of the world. Only in the new age promised by the prophet will the violence which permeates the present animal kingdom be removed. Currently aggression is taken to be the order of the day, and this affects the relationship between wild animals and humans as well as between one species and another. In the age to come this order will give way to one of peace and harmony. Such a doctrine is echoed in the celebrated Pauline understanding that the present world order has been subjected to curse and corruption on account of human wickedness (Rom. 8:18–39).[18]

---

[17] Compare B.D. Sommer, "Allusions and Illusions: The Unity of the Book of Isaiah in Light of Deutero-Isaiah's Use of Prophetic Tradition", R.F. Melugin & M.A. Sweeney (eds.), *New Visions of Isaiah*, JSOTSS 214 (Sheffield, 1996), pp. 156–186.

[18] Compare J.D.G. Dunn, *Romans 1–8*, Word Biblical Commentary 38 (Dallas, 1988), pp. 470–1.

Such a view, however, is not that which prevails more generally throughout the Old Testament. That predatory animals obtain their food by the taking of other animal life is not only taken to be normal, but is quite openly presented as the designed purpose of God:

> The young lions roar for their prey,
>   seeking their food from God.
>
> Ps. 104:21 (cp. Job 38:39–41) (RSV)

Elsewhere it is taken for granted that for lions and bears to kill young lambs is normal, although God could intervene to protect a shepherd from becoming a victim of the predatory instincts of such creatures (compare 1 Sam. 17:34–37). Yet even for a person who has angered God to be killed by a lion could be construed as a divinely willed act of retribution (1 Kgs. 13:24–25). Overall the experience of violence throughout the natural world, including sometimes the killing of humans by animals, is understood as a feature of life which is to be accepted as a feature of the way the world has been created, but which may call for special theological explanation when circumstances warrant it (compare 2 Kgs. 17:25–28). The instinctive human fear and dislike of snakes forms the readily intelligible background to the curse of Gen. 3:14–15). That the serpent is simply the representative of a larger segment of the animal kingdom is not spelt out, although this could later be inferred. In general it is accepted that there are forms of animal behaviour which involve the killing of one species by another. The human dominion over the animal kingdom (Gen. 1:28) is presented as a paramount human prerogative which is not defined by any clearly prescribed limitations. Yet these were undoubtedly felt to exist, as the ruling regarding the protection of birds in Deut. 22:6–7 shows. Within and between the various living orders of the world a pattern of proper relationships was assumed to exist, but which could get out of hand when excessive, or needless, violence arose. Because this living world was the product of an act of divine creation it required to be respected and its essential features maintained.

When suitable reasons for such deeds can be presented by a prophet, then violence in the animal kingdom could even be regarded as serving a religious purpose in the enforcement of divine honour and justice (so especially 2 Kgs. 17:26). Such perceptions indicate that there were assumed to be recognisable boundaries which belonged to the hierarchy of life on earth. In certain circumstances these boundaries could be crossed, either wilfully, or accidentally.[19] It is this crossing of the boundaries of normal conduct which indicated the presence of חמס violence, or disorder, which disrupted the שלום – the peace and harmony – of the world.

This attitude to the world can lead at one moment to praise of God for the generous provision of prey for the lion to hunt, and then at another time to implicit condemnation of the taking of one species of animal for food by another, as in Isa. 11:6–9. This inconsistency and diversity of attitudes undoubtedly reflects the uncertain and partial perceptions that surround the idea of a divinely given order to the natural world. It is a feature of the Old Testament world-view that such an order exists. It is taken for granted that it was an order created by God according to a grand design so that the biblical understanding of biological and zoological features of the world is essentially theological in character. The question "What does God mean by this or that?" is a primary matter of concern when observing animal behaviour, or venturing to encroach on animal territory.

It is because this divine order to life was believed to exist and control relationships that recognisable distinctions were upheld between various kinds of animals which were allowed to be killed and eaten.[20] Yet this perception of order does not appear to have been extended to the point of forming a complete system, leaving open contrasts and contradictions which might then call for further explanation. Even the apparent carelessness of the female ostrich regarding her motherly duty of protecting her future young could be construed moralistically as a failure to observe the intended divine order (Job 39:13–18).

Much the same may be held to be the case in regard to the taking of animal life by human beings for food.[21] Although Gen. 1:29–30 clearly portrays an understanding that the original human beings were vegetarian, this is carefully modified after the Great Flood so

---

[19] In Exod. 21:28–32 the question of culpability when an ox gores a man or woman to death raises several significant issues concerning the way in which the natural tendency of fierce animals was perceived and the extent to which ownership imposed acceptance of the risks which these tendencies brought.

[20] So especially Deut. 14:1–21. Compare W.J. Houston, *Purity and Monotheism: Clean and Unclean Animals in Biblical Law*, JSOTSS 140 (Sheffield, 1996).

[21] For the following see especially S.A. Reed, "Meat Eating and the Hebrew Bible", H.T.C. Sun & K.L. Eades (eds.), *Problems in Biblical Theology: Essays in Honor of Rolf Knierim* (Grand Rapids, 1997), pp. 281–294.

that the killing of animals for food is allowed, subject to certain restrictions (Gen. 9:2–3). It is noteworthy that the careful provisos in regard to the disposal of the blood, even in the most extreme cases, recognise the sanctity of all life, both of humans and animals. Since life is the unique gift and creation of God it is sacred.

Yet, because God's order regarding the protection and preservation of life in the world is not wholly defined and fully classified, its ambiguities and inconsistencies are regarded as tolerable. For cities to be returned to ruins where wild animals roam can be seen as a justified punishment ordained by God (compare Isa. 13:21–22). For domestic animals to be slaughtered soon after birth as a necessary sacrifice to God is not only permitted, but demanded (Exod. 22:30; Deut. 15:19–20). This is apparently because such an offering was believed ultimately to promote the greater vitality and fertility of flocks and herds. Nevertheless life was never to be confused with death, which appears to be the reasoning that underlies the prohibition of boiling a kid in its mother's milk (Exod. 23:19; Deut. 14:21).

There is no doubt that many of these contrasting, and often seemingly contradictory, rules and perceptions regarding death and slaughter in the animal kingdom were the consequence of the drawing together of a mixture of responses to the phenomenon of life. This was a gift which was shrouded in mystery and which could ultimately only be understood within a religious frame of reference.

The natural world was itself seen to display incongruities and tensions. Creatures which, at one moment could be praised for their awesome beauty, could, in other contexts, be regarded as a threat deliberately used by God to serve as warnings and punishment (2 Kgs. 2:23–24; 17:25–28). For God to stop the mouths of lions was a singularly unique divine intervention in the natural order of the wild (Dan. 6:16–24; compare Heb. 11:33).

It is not inappropriate to claim that similar contradictions prevail in regard to the biblical perceptions of human warfare.[22] These stretch between accepting it as a means of accomplishing the divine purpose to regarding it as a regrettable, but inevitable, human tragedy. Only its ultimate abolition could truly fulfil the divine plan for humankind (Isa. 2:4; but compare Joel 3:9–10). The attitude to war-

---

[22] Compare. S. Niditch, *War in the Hebrew Bible: A Study in the Ethics of Violence* (New York-Oxford, 1993). The comment of p. 154 is a helpful summary: "In fact, the history of attitudes to war in ancient Israel is a complex one involving multiplicity, overlap, and self-contradiction".

fare presented in the scroll of Isaiah displays similar ambiguities to those which may be seen in regard to behaviour among the wild beasts. Peace is the ultimate goal, but warfare may be inevitable in order that such a goal may be attained. The experience of conflict between nations threatens a return to chaos, yet may be regarded as a necessary prelude to the coming of world peace.

Probably the Old Testament promise which comes closest to sharing the same expectation of an ultimate ending of violence throughout the animal kingdom as that of Isa. 11:6–9 is to be found in a late passage in the book of Hosea:[23]

> I will make for you a covenant on that day with the wild animals, the birds of the air, and the creeping things of the ground; and I will abolish the bow, the sword, and war in the land; and I will make you lie down in safety.
>
> Hos. 2:20 (English translation 18)

Robert Murray has described this promise as that of a "cosmic covenant"[24] and it is noteworthy that, as with the context of the Isaiah references, the primary emphasis is upon the abolition of human warfare. The ending of violence and the removal of the threat of premature death from the animal kingdom is essentially regarded as an illustration of this. The longed-for removal of any possibility of further military threat to the peace and prosperity of Jerusalem in future years (Isa. 54:14–17) has called for a comprehensive and radical interpretation of all that is implied in the description of Jerusalem as "the city of peace" (compare also Lev. 26:6).

4. Animal Violence in the Context of Christian Ethics

In Beatrix Potter's stories of Jemima Puddleduck, Mrs. Tiggywinkle and other creatures, the radical divide between the status of human beings and other creatures of the natural world is crossed. Not only is the animal world portrayed in terms of the human world, but the creatures which inhabit it are assumed to be subject to basic moral restraints and obligations. The wolf can indeed dwell with the lamb, since they have acquired the moral understanding which enables them to relate to each other in a responsible manner. Much of the

---

[23] A.A. Macintosh, *Hosea*, ICC (Edinburgh, 1997), pp. 81–2.
[24] R. Murray, *The Cosmic Covenant: Biblical Themes of Justice, Peace and the Integrity of Creation* (London, 1992).

fun of the Beatrix Potter stories lies in their genteel humanising of the animal world and converting it into a pale, but comforting, reflection of human society.

It is, however, a matter of maximum importance to the biblical doctrine of creation that the moral responsibility of human beings is regarded as a feature which separates them from the rest of creation, as is emphasised in the story of the Fall in Gen. 3. Morality is a human phenomenon and the varied patterns of behaviour which are to be found in the animal world are not regarded as reflecting upon the uniqueness of this human privilege. Human beings have a responsibility towards the animal realm which has been conferred upon them as a consequence of the design of creation (Gen. 1:28).

It is arguable that there are exceptions to this in the biblical wisdom tradition where the apparent exemplary forms of conduct displayed by even seemingly unimportant insects and despised forms of animal life are held up for serious moral reflection (so especially in Prov. 30:24–31). Birds may become God's agents to serve moral ends (Prov. 30:17). Yet it is far from clear that such use of specific examples to serve a didactic purpose was seriously intended to imply a moral order prevailing throughout all animal life. Rather it is more plausibly the desire to exploit the possibilities of incongruity and humour in order to draw attention to important moral duties which has occasioned the composition of such sayings. At most it is the desire of the sages to discern the presence of a planned, and morally resonant, order to all life which has given rise to such sayings. They cannot be taken to imply too much regarding the sharp distinction between the moral responsibilities of human beings and the conduct of the animal kingdom.

When we return therefore to the primary question of the significance of the eschatological promise of Isa. 11:6–9 for an understanding of the Christian doctrine of creation we can find in it a number of points that concern the relationship between a doctrine of creation and a Christian ethic of non-violence. In the first instance its assumption that the present order of the living world, with its dangers and violence, demands submission to wider ethical restraints, is important. There is assumed to be a degree of neutrality regarding the experienced order of the natural world, which regards it as neither innately evil, nor yet naturally good. The necessity for the imposition of human care and restraints is frankly recognised. The envisioning of a re-ordered and consistently non-violent pattern of life throughout the universe accepts that currently imperfections exist.

We do not live in a finished and rigidly ordered world, but one in which many distortions and incongruities are to be found. It is a world that is becoming, and not simply a world in being. We are not therefore committed to rigid preservation of the *status quo*, nor yet are we bound to endorse as natural, and therefore desirable, all that happens in the wild. The need to control aggression in establishing and securing human life does not outlaw all violence, nor yet endorse it as the necessary law of life. To look for any wholly uniform rules of conduct, modelled on "the survival of the fittest" is to make one facet of the natural world into an unjustifiable moral imperative, regardless of the many other factors which relate to human social life. As with a whole cluster of instinctive and natural aspects of behaviour, both in animals and humans, aggression is seen to be part of a more complex whole. The balancing and controlling of the competing claims which these innate forces promote is a vital part of what it means to be human.

So an important legacy of the promise of Isa. 11:6–9 towards a Christian doctrine of creation is its highlighting of the complexity of the ethic of aggression in its biblical context. Biblical perceptions of the natural world accept that aggression may serve goals that are ultimately beneficial to the needs of specific animals, among whom the lion is the chief example. Yet there are many indications also of concerns to limit violence to specified areas so as to make it conform to an understanding of natural order.

Perhaps the most important legacy of Isa. 11:6–9 and its use in Christian liturgy is its drawing attention to the presence of "the wild" as a facet of creation. Its role in the ecological and ethical scheme of things can then be placed in perspective against the larger biblical insights into the nature of creation and the presence of life on earth in its great variety of forms. There is undoubtedly an element of hyperbole in Isa. 11:6–9, as also in Hos. 2:20 (English translation 18), which appears to have arisen out of a concern to outlaw human warfare. The aggression shown in the natural world was not to be used to excuse the predatory and violent behaviour which appears to prevail so extensively on earth. In these passages it is human violence which is the primary target, and the examples of animal conduct are excluded from the picture so that they can no longer serve as an excuse for human aggression. Even the age-old example of the lion – so widely employed as a symbol of military might and power throughout the ancient Near East – is brought into the shelter of peaceful domesticity.

GNATS, GLOSSES AND ETERNITY: ISAIAH 51:6 RECONSIDERED

BY

H.G.M. WILLIAMSON
Oxford

Over the course of many years, Dr. Gelston has published an extensive series of articles on textual and theological problems in Isaiah 40–55. Some have been on matters of major importance, others on relatively minor issues. The present study falls firmly in the latter category, but it is offered on the understanding which Gelston has himself exemplified so well that sometimes scholarship advances by the accumulation of details.

By comparison with what may be called a traditional English version of the Old Testament such as the *Revised Version*, the *New English Bible* rendering of Isaiah 51:6 differs in several respects. The two translations are as follows, with the significant differences highlighted in italics:

> Lift up your eyes to the heavens, and look upon the earth beneath: for the heavens shall vanish away like smoke, and the earth shall wax old like a garment, and they that dwell therein shall die in like manner: but my salvation shall be for ever, and my righteousness shall not be abolished.

> Lift up your eyes to the heavens,
> look at the earth beneath:
> the heavens *grow murky* as smoke;
> the earth wears into tatters like a garment,
> and those who live on it die *like maggots*;
> but my deliverance is everlasting
> and my *saving power* shall never *wane*.

None of these differences is to be explained on the basis of text-critical judgements – the Masoretic Text is presupposed in both cases;[1] rather, the changes are due to supposed improvements in our understanding of the meaning of Classical Hebrew words.

---

[1] For the *NEB*, see the lack of any entry under this verse in L.H. Brockington,

As is well known, many such improvements were proposed during the middle decades of the present century, often on the basis of
comparison with cognate semitic languages. This procedure was subjected to a searching critical analysis by Barr,[2] who of course did
not reject the method in principle, but who urged caution and suggested guidelines for its proper application. On the whole, his strictures have been accepted, and the appearance of *The Revised English
Bible* (1989) reflects this changed atmosphere; its rendering may be
appropriately compared:

> Raise your eyes heavenwards;
> look on the earth beneath:
> though the heavens be dispersed as smoke
> and the earth wear out like a garment
> and its inhabitants die like flies,
> my deliverance will be everlasting
> and my saving power will remain unbroken.

This rendering accepts two of the changes which the *NEB* entered
by comparison with the *RV* and rejects the other two. Concerning
"saving power" as an equivalent in certain contexts for Hebrew צדקה,
this is a matter of semantics internal to the corpus of classical Hebrew,
and would be widely accepted today.[3] It is unnecessary to discuss it
further here.

The translation of תחת by 'wane' in the *NEB* goes back to a suggestion of G.R. Driver in 1935.[4] He maintained that the usual explanation of the word as an imperfect qal of חתת, "was shattered,
dismayed" (hence "be abolished" in *RV*, "be ended" in *RSV* and
NRSV), "yields no satisfactory sense in the context" and proposed
instead that the word should be analysed as an imperfect qal of נחת,

---

*The Hebrew Text of the Old Testament: The Readings Adopted by the Translators of the New
English Bible* (Oxford and Cambridge, 1973), p. 194.
    [2] J. Barr, *Comparative Philology and the Text of the Old Testament* (Oxford, 1968). See
too the discussion by J.A. Emerton in his review of the first fascicule of the third
edition of *HAL* in *VT* 22 (1972), pp. 502–11, and L.L. Grabbe, *Comparative Philology
and the Text of Job: A Study in Methodology* SBLDS 34 (Missoula, 1977).
    [3] See most fully F.V. Reiterer, *Gerechtigkeit als Heil:* צדק *bei Deuterojesaja. Aussage
und Vergleich mit der alttestamentlichen Tradition* (Graz, 1976), and most recently J.N.
Oswalt, "Righteousness in Isaiah: A Study of the Function of Chapters 56–66 in
the Present Structure of the Book", in C.C. Broyles and C.A. Evans (eds.), *Writing
and Reading the Scroll of Isaiah: Studies of an Interpretive Tradition* SVT 70 (Leiden, 1997),
1, pp. 177–91.
    [4] G.R. Driver, "Linguistic and Textual Problems: Isaiah xl–lxvi", *JTS* 36 (1935),
pp. 396–406, p. 402.

'descend', with the metaphorically developed sense of "to set, abate". He observed in support of this that in Syriac nouns derived from the cognate verb demonstrate a comparable semantic development, and that the meaning proposed produced a satisfactory parallelism.

On the other hand, it should be observed that in the very next verse we find the form תחתו, and here the context leaves us in no doubt that the meaning must be "be dismayed", as the *NEB* itself accepts. We should normally suppose that the singular form of the same word in the previous verse would be likely to come from the same verb. This, indeed, was one of the examples which Torrey adduced in support of his view that playing on the different meanings of Hebrew words was a characteristic stylistic device of Deutero-Isaiah,[5] and Payne, who is generally critical of this suggestion (as of Driver's development of it in terms of play on homonymous roots)[6] agrees that "this would seem to be one of the weightiest examples in Torrey's list".[7]

More seriously, however, it must be observed that nowhere else in the Hebrew Bible does the verb נחח show the metaphorical development in meaning to which Driver appeals.[8] While that does not rule out the possibility absolutely, it nevertheless falls foul of the generally accepted point of method that one should not import new meanings to Hebrew words from the cognate languages if an attested meaning elsewhere in Hebrew itself is satisfactory.

Thus, although Driver's suggestion, and the *NEB* rendering which is based upon it, are attractive in their immediate context, it is more probable that the usual understanding "be shattered", and hence 'ended', as included in the more recent *REB* ("remain unbroken") and *NRSV* ("be ended"), is correct. It is not clear why Driver should have thought that this makes no sense.

---

[5] C.C. Torrey, *The Second Isaiah: A New Interpretation* (Edinburgh, 1928), esp. pp. 199–203 and 398–9.

[6] It is somewhat surprising that Driver did not, in fact, include this verse in the list of passages at the end of his article (1935, p. 406) where he appeals to Torrey's observation in support of a number of the other solutions which he proposes for textual difficulties in these chapters. Whether or not the evidence is sufficiently strong to sustain Torrey's view, I certainly agree with Payne (see next note) that the evidence cannot justify Driver's development of the view to cover plays on homonymous roots or forms.

[7] D.F. Payne, "Characteristic Word-Play in 'Second Isaiah': A Reappraisal", *JSS* 12 (1967), pp. 207–29, p. 221. Payne himself is inclined to favour emendation of verse 6 to avoid conceding even this example to Torrey.

[8] His reference to the use of the verb in Isaiah 7:8 does not help his case here.

The second proposal in *NEB* which is changed in the *REB* relates to the translation of נמלחו in the middle line of the verse. To set the scene, let it be remembered that the conventional renderings in English (*RV*: "shall vanish away"; *RSV*: "will vanish") presuppose a *hapax legomenon*, listed as מלח I in BDB and KB. These lexicographers cited Arabic and Ethiopic cognates to support the meaning "tear away, fig. dissipate", and hence for the niphʻal "be dispersed in fragments, dissipated", "zerissen werden". It is probable, however, that they were quite as much influenced by the occurrence of the plural noun מלחים (Jer. 38:11,12), where the context and close association with סחבות point unmistakably to the meaning 'rags'. Though poorly attested in classical Hebrew, the verb and noun will have seemed to be mutually self-supporting.

While not disputing the comparative evidence, and without further attention to the cognate noun מלחים, Driver nevertheless objected to this rendering on the ground that it "does not agree with כעשן" ("like smoke").[9] He urged instead that the word was a denominative from the familiar noun מלח 'salt',[10] and that its meaning was to be compared with a similar development in Arabic of *maliḥa*, I, "become salt, was greyish, dust-coloured", and IX (*imlaḥḥa*), "was mixed black and white". The explanation for this semantic development was, of course, that unpurified salt in ancient times was "of a dirty grey colour". Hence for our verse he proposed "are murky" (cf. *NEB*: "grow murky"), with the explanation "in other words, darkness spreading over the heavens will be a portent of the end".

In evaluating Driver's proposal, several points deserve mention. First, it should be noted that the parallel half-line states that "the earth shall wear out as a garment". While it is true that parallelism

---

[9] Driver (1935), pp. 401–2. He later repeated his argument, if anything with a more vehement objection to the traditional view – "une conjecture dépourvue de tout appui scientifique", which, in the light of the evidence already available to him, must be charitably regarded as a rhetorical exaggeration; cf. "L'Interprétation du texte masorétique à la lumière de la lexicographie hébraïque", *ETL* 26 (1950), pp. 337–53 (349–50).

[10] For a discussion of why Aquila and Symmachus associate the verb with 'salt', and a conjectural emendation of the LXX (ηρεωθη = ἠραιώθη for ἐστερεώθη, originally proposed by de Lagarde) which would conform the LXX closely with MT as traditionally understood, see P. Katz, "Two Kindred Corruptions in the Septuagint", *VT* 1 (1951), pp. 261–6 (262–5). Alternatively, and without reference to Katz, H. Jacobson, "A Note on Isaiah 51:6", *JBL* 114 (1995), p. 291, suggests that both the LXX and Jerome's comments on Aquila and Symmachus, together with his own translation (*liquescent*), can be explained on the basis that their text read נמוגו.

is not necessarily a decisive clue as to meaning, it is striking that no one has challenged the meaning of 'rags' for the noun מלחים, and that a verbal equivalent of this would be highly suitable in context. Secondly, and against Driver's opinion that the comparison "like smoke" is inappropriate, it may be said that observation of the dissipation of smoke as it rises into the air is not at all unsuitable as an image of cloth turning into rags. And as this is postulated precisely of the sky, it is further possible that the image was suggested by the similar manner in which cloud formations, which resemble smoke in many ways, can sometimes tend to break apart like cloth into rags. Putting these first two points together, it appears that Driver rather missed the force of the analogy. The poet is not so much claiming that smoke can be "torn asunder" as that the action of tearing cloth into rags is comparable in effect to the breaking up of a column of smoke.[11]

Thirdly, it must be questioned whether, conversely, Driver's proposal is itself appropriate to the context. The point of the verse as a whole is to contrast the transitory nature of the created order with the durability of God's salvation/deliverance and righteousness/ saving power. It is difficult to see how a change of colour in the sky (even as "a portent of the end") can contribute to this contrast. As with the wearing out of the earth, so a reference to the ending or destruction of the sky is clearly demanded. Fourthly, and in extension of this point, smoke occurs elsewhere too as an image for transitoriness, for instance at Hos. 13:3; Ps. 37:20; 68:3; 102:4. To the extent that it may be regarded as a stereotypical image, its use in Isa. 51:6 helps to reinforce the main point of the verse. For these reasons, I conclude that the *REB* was justified in rejecting the rendering of this line in the *NEB* (which clearly follows Driver) and in returning to the more traditional understanding, though a translation which specifically included a reference to rags might be less open to misunderstanding and would make clearer the intended parallelism: "though the sky be torn to rags like smoke" may be tentatively proposed. Finally in this connection, it is worth observing in passing that the comparative evidence on which the older rendering was based can now be strengthened by reference to Akkadian *malaḫu*.[12]

---

[11] For the so-called pregnant use of the preposition ב, see, for instance, JM §133h.
[12] Cf. *CAD* 10, pp. 152–3, which includes "tear apart" and IV "be torn out". *The Concise Dictionary of Akkadian* (in preparation) suggests for its *malāḫu* IV "to tear

Thus far, then, we have seen that of the four differences in translation between *NEB* and *RV, REB* accepts one and rejects two. Clearly, the revisers were thinking independently, and furthermore we have noted reasons to approve their decisions in each case. This suggests that they must have been strongly impressed by the evidence for the fourth change, "like maggots" (*REB*, "like flies"), by comparison with the *RV*'s "in like manner". And in this, of course, they have the support of the majority of modern commentators.

The translation of כְּמוֹ כֵן by "in like manner", though supported by all the ancient authorities, has long been regarded as weak; the first part of the line leads us to expect some more specific point of comparison. Because of this, it was already common in the last century[13] to associate כֵּן rather with the כִּנִּים of Exod. 8:12–14 and Ps. 105:31, hence "like gnats".[14] However, there are two difficulties with this view. First, it is unlikely that the singular of כִּנִּים is כֵּן,[15] for the only evidence which we have, namely, post-Biblical Hebrew, points to a singular כִּנָּה. And secondly, even if there were a singular form כֵּן, it would be necessary to understand it as a collective, "swarm of gnats". There is no evidence to support this, and one widely-adopted explanation of the variant form כִּנָּם (Exod. 8:12, 13) as just such a collective[16] rather tells against it. To avoid such problems, a number of older commentators therefore emended כֵּן to כִּנִּים in Isa. 51:6.[17] This is admittedly only a small textual change, and the corruption

---

out", D "reduce to fibres, shred", N "be torn out". *HAL*, p. 556, also adduces Ugaritic *mlḥ*, but the meaning of this word is still disputed.

[13] F. Delitzsch, *Commentar über das Buch Jesaia* (Leipzig, 1889⁴), p. 500 = *Biblical Commentary on the Prophecies of Isaiah* (Edinburgh, 1894), II, p. 262, cites Hitzig, Meier, Ewald, Knobel, Umbreit, Stier, Hahn and Orelli among those who adopted this solution. R. Lowth too, we may add, offered the translation "like the vilest insect", but without making any comment upon it; see *Isaiah: A New Translation; with Preliminary Dissertation, and Notes, Critical, Philological, and Explanatory* (2 vols.; London, 1824), p. 164.

[14] The precise identification of the insects in question is inevitably uncertain. Among the main suggestions are 'gnats' (LXX, V and Philo), 'lice' (Pesh. and TO), 'mosquitoes', "sand flies", 'fleas', and 'maggots' (so various modern versions). For discussion, see, for instance, J.P. Hyatt, *Commentary on Exodus* (London, 1971), p. 110, and B.S. Childs, *Exodus: A Commentary* (London, 1974), p. 129, who observes that "the evidence is indecisive".

[15] Despite Duhm's proposal to find this form in Num. 13:33; see B. Duhm, *Das Buch Jesaia* (Göttingen, 1892), p. 356. It is noteworthy that Duhm himself later dropped this proposal; see p. 384 of the 4th edition of the commentary (1922).

[16] So A. Dillmann, *Die Bücher Exodus und Leviticus* (Leipzig, 1880), pp. 77–8; cf. GK §85t.

[17] E.g. K. Marti, *Das Buch Jesaja* (Tübingen, 1900), p. 338; Duhm (1922, 4th edn.), p. 384.

could easily be explained as a haplography before (וֹחתוֹן)יְמַ, but it remains a purely conjectural emendation nonetheless.

In 1935 Reider suggested an alternative way of achieving the same result without the need to change the consonantal text. He took the phrase as a single word, כְּמֹזְכֶ, and by comparison with the Arabic root *m-k-n* arrived at a translation "like locusts".[18] The subsequent discovery that 1QIsa[b], which is remarkably close to the MT for the most part, writes the consonants as a single word[19] has been thought to give this proposal additional and weighty support.[20]

One way or another, therefore, virtually all modern translations and commentaries[21] agree that the point of comparison in our clause is with some kind of insect, and a cross-reference to Isa. 40:22, where the earth's inhabitants (יֹשְׁבֵי again) are said to be "like grasshoppers", is thought to furnish an adequate comment. Taking each phrase of the verse one by one, and given the attraction of solving textual problems by the comparative philological method which prevailed in the middle decades of this century, it is not difficult to understand how such a consensus could have emerged. In this climate of opinion, it is perhaps not surprising that the *REB* should have seen no reason to dissent.

Despite such strength of opinion, however, several important considerations necessary for the understanding of the verse as a whole seem to have been completely overlooked. Ironically, the *REB* itself shows awareness of one of these, but appears not to have followed it through to its logical consequence.

The first point concerns syntax, and in particular the function of

---

[18] J. Reider, "Contributions to the Hebrew Lexicon", *ZAW* 53 (1935), pp. 270–77 (270–1). C.R. North, *The Second Isaiah: Introduction, Translation and Commentary to Chapters xl–lv* (Oxford, 1964), p. 207, reports that the same suggestion was made to him by G.R. Driver "in a private communication". There is no way of knowing whether Driver derived this from Reider or whether he hit upon the idea independently.

[19] See E.L. Sukenik, *'wsr hmgylwt hgnwzwt šbydy h'wnybrsyth h'bryt* (Jerusalem, 1954), pl. 9, line 17. 1QIsa[a] attests the division into two words. The passage is not preserved in any of the other fragments of Isaiah from Qumran; cf. E. Ulrich, "An Index to the Contents of the Isaiah Manuscripts from the Judean Desert", in Broyles and Evans (1997), pp. 477–80. For the substantial, but secondary, deviation of 1QIsa[a] earlier in the line, see J. Koenig, *L'Herméneutique analogique du Judaïsme antique d'après les témoins textuels d'Isaïe* (Leiden, 1982), pp. 261–2.

[20] See *BHS*, and R.N. Whybray, *Isaiah 40–66* (London, 1975), p. 157.

[21] Among the very few who still explicitly prefer the older rendering, I have noted only Torrey (1928), p. 398; I. Knabenbauer-F. Zorrell, *Commentarius in Isaiam Prophetam*, 2 (Paris, 1923), p. 288, and A. Motyer, *The Prophecy of Isaiah* (Leicester, 1993), p. 406.

כִּי at the start of the second line. The commonest, causal sense of כִּי, "for, because", is clearly inappropriate here, despite the fact that it is conventional in older translations: it makes no sense to adduce the dispersal and wearing out of the heavens and earth as a ground for looking at them. Rather, כִּי here should be regarded as introducing a concessive sentence, with its apodosis introduced by the *waw* at the start of the following line: "Even if . . . yet".[22] Indeed, a well-recognized example of this very construction comes a little later within Deutero-Isaiah itself, at 54:10, to give expression to a sentiment which is strikingly similar to 51:6: "Though (כִּי) the mountains depart and the hills be removed, yet (ו) my steadfast love shall not depart from you, and my covenant of peace shall not be removed". We may thus readily agree that the *REB* is correct in translating כִּי as 'though' in 51:6.

Secondly and in consequence of this, we need to inquire after the force of this concession. The point is obvious: the prophet takes what he regards as the most durable things known to his audience[23] in order to make the rhetorical point that even if they should pass away, God's salvation will not. Just as at 54:10, the prophet is stressing that God's salvation is utterly secure and enduring.

It follows, thirdly, that in this setting precisely what the earth's inhabitants are compared with is much less important than the fact that a reference to them is out of place altogether. In the Hebrew Bible generally, but in Deutero-Isaiah especially, humanity is characterised by weakness and transitoriness. At 40:6, for instance, one of the dialogue partners in the heavenly court laments that "all flesh is grass, and all the goodliness thereof (חַסְדּוֹ) is as the flower of the field: the grass withereth, the flower fadeth; because the breath of

---

[22] For this construction, see JM §171, and, more cautiously, A. Aejmelaeus, "Function and Interpretation of כִּי in Biblical Hebrew", *JBL* 105 (1986), pp. 193–209. Her condition that the concessive force of כִּי is impossible where the clause it introduces follows the main clause is fully satisfied here, of course. On p. 199, n. 18, she proposes a different analysis of our verse, but for the reasons given above it seems improbable to me. Th. C. Vriezen, "Einige Notizen zur Übersetzung des Bindewortes *kî*," in J. Hempel and L. Rost (eds.), *Von Ugarit nach Qumran: Beiträge zur alttestamentlichen und altorientalischen Forschung* (*Festschrift* Otto Eissfeldt; Berlin, 1958), pp. 266–73, also discusses the concessive use of כִּי at length, with particular reference to Isa. 51:6 by comparison with 54:10 on p. 268.

[23] The enduring nature of heaven and earth is found in a number of passages in the Hebrew Bible; for discussion, see C. Houtman, *Der Himmel im Alten Testament: Israels Weltbild und Weltanschauung* (Leiden, 1993), pp. 177–81. His discussion of the syntax of Isa. 51:6 on p. 179 with its consequence for the main point of the verse coincides with mine.

the Lord bloweth upon it" (*RV*);[24] at 40:15 and 17 the nations are said to be "like a drop from a bucket" and "as nothing"; at 40:22–3, as we have already noted, the earth's inhabitants are "like grasshoppers" and their rulers "as nothing", while in 40:30 even young people "will faint and be weary" and "fall exhausted". This theme, so emphatically introduced in chapter 40, recurs time and again in different forms throughout Deutero-Isaiah, including very clearly in chapter 51 itself: "who art thou, that thou art afraid of man that shall die, and of the son of man which shall be made as grass?" (51:12). In view of this, a reference to the earth's mortal inhabitants alongside the heavens and the earth within the rhetoric of 51:6 ruins the positive emphasis which the prophet is concerned to convey. Only those elements which may be thought of as completely durable serve the purpose of underlining the even greater permanence and reliability of God's salvation. The conclusion must be that the whole clause "and they that dwell therein shall die in like manner" is a gloss.[25]

Two other arguments further support this conclusion. The first line of the verse encourages the reader to look at the heavens and the earth, and these two elements are then picked up in the protasis of the concessive sentence following. Had humanity been an original part of the latter, we should have expected it also to be an object of the opening exhortation to look and consider.

Secondly, it is clear that the second line of the verse has an extra, third stich, which raises the suspicion that something has been added. Volz[26] was evidently aware that a case might be made for deleting the clause on this ground, but rejected the argument because Deutero-Isaiah "den dreifachen Parallelismus liebt". While it is true that this argument is not decisive in itself, it is noteworthy that this particular passage (51:1–8) is mostly, if not entirely,[27] made up of balanced lines of two stichs, so that the point adds some further support to a conclusion based primarily on other arguments.

---

[24] There are well-known textual and philological problems here, but they do not affect the main point at issue. For some preliminary discussion, see my *The Book Called Isaiah: Deutero-Isaiah's Role in Composition and Redaction* (Oxford, 1994), pp. 254–6.

[25] This conclusion has occasionally been maintained previously, but it has never been taken seriously to the extent of warranting mention in any of the major commentaries; cf. A.B. Ehrlich, *Randglossen zur hebräischen Bibel*, 4 (Leipzig, 1912), p. 184, and J. Skinner, *The Book of the Prophet Isaiah Chapters xl–lxvi* (Cambridge, 1917), p. 120.

[26] P. Volz, *Jesaia II* (Leipzig, 1932), p. 109. Duhm's attempt (1892, p. 356) to avoid the problem by conjecturally lengthening the line has not found favour.

[27] The only exception may be the end of v. 4 and the first line of v. 5. There

The identification of the last clause of 51:6*b* as a gloss suggests that the traditional understanding of כמו־כן as "in like manner" may, after all, be correct. Commenting on the possibility that the heavens and earth might come to an end in the light of (Deutero-) Isaiah's view of humanity generally (and 40:22 perhaps in particular), the glossator felt moved to add the remark that the earth's inhabitants would similarly pass away – a gloomy observation were it not for the fact that God's deliverance and saving power, which are directed primarily towards people, would endure. The gloss is thus ultimately not pessimistic, but an attempt explicitly to incorporate the destiny of the human race within God's ultimate purposes for good.

The book of Isaiah as a whole, and chapters 40–55 in particular, makes frequent use of the word-pair heaven and earth. In Deutero-Isaiah, its predominant focus is to emphasise God's power as creator (e.g. 40:12; 42:5; 45:18; 48:13), which on the one hand draws attention to the insignificance of humanity (e.g. 40:21–4; 45:12) while on the other it stresses that there is a sure ground for confidence by Israel in God's ability to reverse their fortunes (e.g. 51:13, 16). Further afield in the book, and in those parts which are certainly post-exilic in date, we find that God's judgement, which had earlier been directed towards particular individuals, groups or nations, now also acquires cosmic dimensions (e.g. 24:4, 21), so that a reader might wonder to what extent the cosmos really gives grounds for such confidence. The answer, it seems, comes at the close of the book, where the tension is resolved by the promise that God will create new heavens and earth (65:17) and that they will truly endure (66:22). This, then, becomes the basis for the book's concluding ground of confidence that the righteous too will endure: "For as the new heavens and the new earth, which I will make, shall remain before me, saith the Lord, so shall your seed and your name remain".[28]

It may be suggested in conclusion, therefore, that the glossator at 51:6 read his text in the light of these wider considerations. Whereas Deutero-Isaiah probably pointed to heaven and earth in order to use his readers' understanding of them as permanent and enduring

---

are textual problems here, however, as shown by the proposal in *BHS* to alter the Masoretic verse division. In view of this uncertainty, it would be unwise to allow it to override a conclusion based upon what is so clear everywhere else.

[28] For an approach to these texts from a very different critical perspective, see P.D. Miscall, "Isaiah: New Heavens, New Earth, New Book", in D.N. Fewell (ed.), *Reading Between Texts: Intertextuality and the Hebrew Bible* (Louisville, 1992), pp. 41–56.

as a means of emphasising the utter durability and reliability of God's salvation, the later glossator lived at a time when even these elements were regarded as subject to judgement and so liable themselves to pass away. Earth's inhabitants could therefore now be legitimately included alongside them as being equally ephemeral, and then be pointed forward to God's saving work in establishing a new heaven and a new earth where true and lasting salvation was to be found.

It remains a ground of confidence too at the start of a new millennium where the pace of change in nature and in society, though differently conceived and understood, gives many equal cause to fear. Identifying our clause as a gloss, therefore, does not in any way diminish its value or significance. On the contrary, it points the way forward in its own small way towards an integrative reading of the book as a whole, so that what started as a historically-bound proclamation became in due course a literary work of timeless relevance.

A LAND FULL OF VIOLENCE:
THE VALUE OF HUMAN LIFE IN THE BOOK OF THE PROPHET EZEKIEL

BY

P.J. HARLAND

Cambridge

The twentieth century has seen more violence than any other. Perhaps as many as 100 million people have died as a result of warfare or persecution since 1900. As the century draws to a close, it would seem appropriate to turn to the prophet Ezekiel who more than his contemporaries devotes special attention to the crimes of murder which were committed by the people of Judah (Ezek. 7:23, 9:9, 22:1ff., 24:6ff., 33:25ff. and 36:18).[1] This essay will examine how Ezekiel confronts the bloodshed perpetrated by the people and how he understands the ethical question of the value of human life.

1. *The Sin of the People*

The book of Ezekiel has two foci: the inevitability of judgement and the hope for future restoration.[2] The book is an attempt to make sense of the exile; to explain why the people had lost everything, been sent to a foreign land, and yet at the same time to offer hope for the future to those who were in Babylon. The reason for this punishment was the people's persistent wickedness. Israel's sins were many, including idolatry, robbery, and sexual immorality, but Ezekiel, perhaps more than other prophets, particularly draws attention to the murder which had been committed by the people. This can be seen by comparing Zeph. 3:3ff. "Her officials within her are roaring lions; her judges are evening wolves that leave nothing till the morning. Her prophets are wanton, faithless men; her priests profane

---

[1] Y. Kaufmann, *The Religion of Israel: From its Beginnings to the Babylonian Exile* (London, 1961), p. 433.
[2] H. McKeating, *Ezekiel* (Sheffield, 1993), pp. 74–77.

what is sacred, they do violence to the law" (RSV), and Ezek. 22:26ff.,
"Her priests have done violence to my law and have profaned my
holy things; they have made no distinction between the holy and
the common, neither have they taught the difference between the
unclean and the clean, and they have disregarded my Sabbaths, so
that I am profaned among them. Her princes in the midst of her
are like wolves tearing the prey, shedding blood, destroying lives to
get dishonest gain" (RSV).[3] By adapting the text from Zephaniah
and adding that the princes shed blood, Ezekiel emphasises that the
people were especially culpable for disregarding human life.

In Ezek. 7:23–27 the reason for the punishment of the exile is
specifically attributed to bloody crimes and violence: "Because the
land is full of bloody crimes and the city is full of violence, I will
bring the worst of the nations to take possession of their houses; I
will put an end to their proud might, and their holy places shall be
profaned. When anguish comes, they will seek peace, but there shall
be none. . . . According to their way I will do to them, and according to their own judgements I will judge them; and they shall know
that I am the LORD" (RSV). Similarly in 8:17ff. the punishment
which is inflicted by God is a direct result of filling the land with
violence, "Have you seen this, O son of man? Is it too slight a thing
for the house of Judah to commit the abominations which they commit here, that they should fill the land with violence, and provoke
me further to anger? Lo, they put the branch to their nose. Therefore
I will deal in wrath; my eye will not spare, nor will I have pity; and
though they cry in my ears with a loud voice, I will not hear them"
(RSV).[4] In 9:9 Ezekiel writes, "The guilt of the house of Israel and
Judah is exceedingly great; the land is full of blood, and the city full

---

[3] See M. Fishbane, *Biblical Interpretation in Ancient Israel* (Oxford, 1985), pp. 461–463.
For a discussion of Ezek. 22:26 see P.J. Harland, "What Kind of Violence in Ezekiel
22", *ET* 108 (1997), pp. 111–114.

[4] The phrase את הזמורה אל אפם is unclear. N.M. Sarna has suggested that זמורה
be translated as "band of strong men". He argues that the Semitic root *dmr* meaning 'strong' has been used in its Hebrew form of זמר. This would mean that the
rich are attacking the poor through the use of strong men (cf. Hos. 6:9, Jer. 18:21ff.):
N. Sarna, "Ezekiel 8:17: a Fresh Examination", *HTR* 57 (1964), pp. 347–352.
Naturally this interpretation fits in well with the violence referred to in 8:17, 22:2,
24:6, 9, but it cannot be proved, and comparative philology is not always a suitable
way of interpreting words in the Hebrew context. זמורה is usually rendered 'branch',
as in its only other occurrence in Ezekiel in 15:2 where it cannot refer to strong
men (see with the same meaning for the word Num. 13:23 and Isa. 17:10, BDB
p. 274) and here in 8:17 it could refer to a form of idolatrous worship.

of injustice" (RSV). Clearly the taking of life was a central concern of Ezekiel.[5]

It is important to note that Ezekiel uses the word חמס to describe the sin of the people: 7:11,23, 8:17, 12:19, 28:16, 45:9. The most suitable translation of this word is 'violence', but this is not an exact rendering because the word refers to violence to people rather than to objects, in particular bloodshed and oppression (e.g. Gen. 49:5, Judg. 9:24, Ps. 140:1,4 (2, 5 Hebrew), Isa. 59:6, Joel 3:19 (4:19 Hebrew) and Hab. 1:2,3). Hebrew has a separate word for violence to property שד (e.g. Isa. 13:6, 22:4).[6] What Ezekiel is therefore condemning was not violence in general but the taking of human life in particular. The people of Judah had shown a callous disregard for the worth of other people and this had brought the wrath of God upon them. The taking of human life was no trivial matter; the widespread, persistent violence to people could only result in the drastic punishment of the exile and the death and destruction which that entailed.

Ezekiel emphasises his concern for the taking of life by frequently referring to the spilling of blood in the land (e.g. 22:3ff., 23:45, 33:25). The people who use the sword to spill blood (33:26) will themselves fall by the same weapon (33:27), so that the land becomes a desolation (33:28). In Ezek. 22:2 Jerusalem is described as a bloody city and the people have become guilty through the shedding of blood, a central theme of the chapter.

The parable of the pot in Ezek. 24 is a good illustration of this aspect of Ezekiel's thought. In these verses Jerusalem is likened to a boiling pot which has rusted (24:6). The pot depicts a city where the deliberate corruption and violence have made God's judgement inevitable and the people are doomed by the blood which they have shed there.[7] The people were so unashamed when they took life, that they did not even cover up the blood, so God left it on the bare rock for all to see (24:7ff.). Such blood cried out to God for vengeance (24:8, cf. Gen. 4:10, 9:5–6, Job 16:18, Isa. 26:21).[8] As it

---

[5] Sarna (1964), p. 348.

[6] For a discussion of חמס see P.J. Harland, *The Value of Human Life: A Study of the Story of the Flood (Genesis 6–9)* SVT 64 (Leiden, 1996), pp. 32–40 and H. Haag, "חמס", *TWAT* 2 (1977), pp. 1050–1061 = *TDOT* 4 (1980), pp. 478–487.

[7] E.F. Davis, *Swallowing the Scroll: Textuality and the Dynamics of Discourse in Ezekiel's Prophecy*, JSOTSS 78 (Sheffield, 1989), pp. 91–2.

[8] W. Zimmerli, *Ezekiel 1–24* (Neukirchen-Vluyn, 1969), p. 565 = *A Commentary on the Book of the Prophet Ezekiel, Chapters 1–24* (Philadelphia, 1979), p. 500.

is exposed, it will arouse God's anger and bring suitable reprisal. The spilling of blood should have induced a sense of fear (compare the ritual of atonement in Deut. 21:1–9), at the terrible consequences which ensue, but instead the people displayed an unabashed attitude which could only provoke God to intervene and punish. Indeed so evil were they that they may even have indulged in cannibalism (5:10; cf. 36:13). The rust-ridden cauldron which represents the city can only receive the full wrath of God, and when the blaze starts, not only are the rust and the corruption destroyed but the cauldron as well (24:11). Wholesale corruption leads to total destruction; that is the only way in which the city can be treated. The stubbornness of the people led to God coming as judge to bring ruthless punishment (24:13–14).[9] The only way in which this blemish of shed blood could be removed was by the purifying wrath of God. The corruption of the people had led to their own demise.[10]

There is another aspect of this shedding of blood which is worth noting. In Lev. 17:4 we read: דם יחשב לאיש ההוא דם שפך, since non-cultic slaughter is considered as shedding of blood. Not only was the shedding of human blood wrong, but also the blood of animals had to be disposed of correctly (compare Gen. 9:4, Lev. 17:10–16). Although Ezekiel is primarily thinking of the spilling of human blood because he speaks of הדמם, he might also be referring to the incorrect slaughter of animals for sacrifice which could likewise have a polluting effect.[11]

This disregard for the value of human life was shown in another striking way. The people were so wicked that they even sacrificed children (16:20–21, 20:26). The most vulnerable in society were cruelly killed. Even though Exod. 34:19ff. says that all the firstborn were to belong to God, it was only animals, not humans, who were to be sacrificed. Nowhere does the Old Testament approve of human sacrifice, and its practice is seen as a sign of depravity (see 2 Kgs. 16:3, 21:6). It was stamped out by Josiah (2 Kgs. 23:10) and was forbidden by Lev. 18:21 and Deut. 12:31 and 18:10.

What may seem horrific to us is that Ezekiel says that God made the people sacrifice children so that he could execute punishment

---

[9] W. Eichrodt, *Der Prophet Hezekiel Kapitel 19–48 übersetzt und erklärt* (Gottingen, 1966), pp. 226–228 = *Ezekiel: A Commentary* (London, 1970), pp. 337–339.

[10] L.C. Allen, *Ezekiel 20–48* (Dallas, 1990), pp. 59–60, and "Ezekiel 24:3–14: a Rhetorical Perspective", *CBQ* 49 (1987), pp. 404–414.

[11] Zimmerli (1969), p. 409 = (1979), p. 383.

(20:26). How could God be so cruel? It is important to notice that Ezekiel does not claim that sacrificing first born children was ordered by God, because he always condemns the sacrifice of children (16:20–21, 20:31). Rather, Ezek. 20 is about the infidelity of Israel and their punishment. The laws of God were good, but the people had profaned them (20:11–13, 21), and God punishes them by laws which were not good, i.e. sacrifice of children (20:25–26). The law of Exod. 22:28–29 (29–30) was good but the people have made it bad.[12]

Yet the action of God here recalls the hardening of Pharaoh's heart in Exod. 9:7, 10:1 (cf. the placing of a lying spirit in the heart of Ahab in 1 Kgs. 22:22ff., and Isa. 6:10 where the people's heart is hardened). Ezekiel speaks of God setting a stumbling block (3:20) before sinners and the people's refusal to listen to God (2:5,7, 3:7, 20:8) is the same for them as it was for Pharaoh and the death of the firstborn. "As Yahweh's hardening of Pharaoh's heart once caused his failure to listen to Moses and Aaron, which in turn eventually brought on the final plague (Exod. 7:3–5), so his "not-good/not-life-giving" laws confirmed Israel in their rebellion and led again to the death of the firstborn- only this time at the willing hands of the rebels".[13] What has happened in Ezek. 20 is that the law has become a stumbling block so that it can be perverted into child sacrifice. In order for Israel to become aware of the holiness of God, she had to find out how wrong she had been in her over-confident attitude.[14] As the people have made themselves unclean by idolatry (20:30, 31), so God adds to their uncleanness by making them sacrifice children. God is prepared to bring evil as well as good so that the nation would perish for their sins and that they would know that he was the Lord.[15] What Ezekiel is stressing is that the people are so thoroughly wicked that God adds to their wickedness to demonstrate their evil, thereby bringing punishment. The point of 20:26 is not that God is cruel or that he shows contempt for human life. Rather, the purpose of the verse is to demonstrate the deep wickedness of the people who have become so hardened to sin that they

---

[12] R. de Vaux, *Les Sacrifices de l'Ancien Testament* (Paris, 1964), pp. 65ff. = *Studies in Old Testament Sacrifice* (Cardiff, 1964), pp. 71ff.

[13] G.C. Heider, "A Further Turn on Ezekiel's Baroque Twist in Ezek. 20:25–26", *JBL* 107 (1988), pp. 721–724, p. 724.

[14] Eichrodt (1966), pp. 175–178 = (1970), pp. 270–272.

[15] G.A. Cooke, *A Critical and Exegetical Commentary on the Book of Ezekiel* (Edinburgh, 1936), pp. 218–219.

commit atrocious acts without any shame or resistance, and only after further sin and punishment, can they repent and know God. When people no longer know God, he does not come with blessing, but with calamity. Causing the people to sin in this way was part of the punishment. By causing sin God shows the depravity of human wrong. One is reminded of Ps. 18:26, "With the pure thou dost show thyself pure; and with the crooked thou dost show thyself perverse" (RSV).[16]

2. *Murder and Impurity*

Having noted that Ezekiel attacks the people for the crime of murder, it is now appropriate to explore why he is particularly concerned about the question of the value of human life. For Ezekiel crimes of the cult and the social order were closely linked; the law was an integral whole. God's will and judgement entered every part of life. Crimes like murder had cultic as well as social implications. In Gen. 9:4 the consumption of blood is prohibited alongside the prohibition of murder (9:5–6). The cultic banning of the eating of blood was linked to the crime of murder thereby viewing life as a totality and not separating social and cultic wrong.[17] In Ezek. 22:3 the perversion of the cult and the taking of life are closely linked; idolatry and bloodshed affect each other. Where a proper fear of God is lost, reverence for life disappears.[18] When God is no longer worshipped or given due respect, his creatures are open to abuse. Human life is undermined when the relationship with God is broken. The community which loses its hold on God, the source of all life, downgrades the life of its fellow humans.[19]

Given this connection between ritual and social crimes, it can come as no surprise that Ezekiel, who viewed everything from the perspective of a priest (1:3), should be particularly concerned with pollution and impurity. He was preoccupied with the holiness of God which required obedience to the law. God's holiness was not just the will of God, but concerned his essence, his splendour. It was that holiness which found the uncleanness caused by the taking of

---

[16] Eichrodt (1966), p. 177 = (1970), p. 272.
[17] See Harland (1996), pp. 154–167.
[18] Zimmerli (1969), pp. 507ff. = (1979), p. 456.
[19] Eichrodt (1966), pp. 203ff. = (1970), pp. 308–9.

life intolerable. Such holiness cannot tolerate ritual defilement which jeopardises the relationship between man and God. Consequently God cannot abide the corruption caused by the shedding of blood.[20] Hence Ezekiel gives special emphasis to the sin of defilement which the people had committed, and which offended the Priestly view of the sacral order. Central to his ministry was faithfulness to the law and the maintenance of purity.

Many examples of sins in Ezekiel were transgressions against the sacred order; Israel had failed in this area by defiling (טמא) the sanctuary (e.g. 5:11).[21] The people's offences are referred to as abominations תועבות, a word which occurs forty times in the book. The people were condemned for profaning the Sabbath (חלל 22:8), the sanctuary (23:39), and thereby profaning the name of God (36:20–23). All this demanded ritual cleansing because of the pollution (36:25, 33).[22] The land which should have shown purity was unclean and this was caused in a large part by the shedding of blood (33:25). The land should have been treated with reverence because that was where God had chosen to dwell. Instead the place had become an object of loathing because of the sin of the people. Such concepts of purity were fundamental to the life of Israel, and the priesthood, of which Ezekiel was a member, was entrusted with the task of maintaining the cleanliness of the land. The pollution and corruption was so bad that the people had to be destroyed and sent into exile. It was this uncleanness which was the cause of the exile (e.g. 36:17ff.).[23] The profanation of the sanctuary was an insult to God, a detachment from the reverence due to him.[24]

Given this emphasis on the defilement of the holy by the people of Judah, it can be seen why Ezekiel is so concerned with the crime of murder. Time and again he stresses that shedding blood is a

---

[20] W. Brueggemann, *Hopeful Imagination: Prophetic Voices in Exile* (Philadelphia, 1986), pp. 71–72.

[21] G. von Rad, *Theologie des Alten Testaments Band 2 Die Theologie der prophetischen Überlieferungen Israels* (Munich, 1961), p. 237 = *Old Testament Theology 2 The Theology of Israel's Prophetic Traditions* (London, 1975), p. 224.

[22] McKeating (1993), pp. 86ff.

[23] T. Frymer-Kensky, "Pollution, Purification and Purgation in Biblical Israel", in C. Meyers and M. O'Connor (eds.), *The Word of the Lord Shall Go Forth: Essays in Honor of D.N. Freedman Celebrating his Sixtieth Birthday* (Winona Lake, 1983), pp. 399–414, esp. pp. 409–412.

[24] W. Eichrodt, *Der Prophet Hezekiel Kapitel 1–18 übersetzt und erklärt* (Gottingen, 1959), pp. 62–63 = (1970), p. 128.

crime, not just because of the taking of life, but because the spilled blood pollutes and defiles (טמא) the land (36:17,18; cf. Num. 35:33), and the sanctuary in particular (23:39). Jerusalem had become a bloody city (22:2) which instead of being clean was full of violence (7:23, 8:17). No one who had shed blood could be allowed to partake of the worship of the Temple since even spilling blood unintentionally defiled a man (cf. Num. 35 where there is provision for a killer to flee to a city of refuge).[25] What Ezekiel stresses is that murder was not just a social crime but that it separated people from God. Those who had shed blood could have no relationship with God because of their impurity.

3. Punishment

The punishment which God brings is in due measure for the sin which had been committed. God pours out his wrath for the blood which had been shed in the land. Those who commit violent deeds have violence brought upon them; the punishment is therefore just. The penalty seems to be related to the Priestly legislation where the murderer is to be executed. Violent deeds had to be requited life for life (Gen. 9:5ff.). In the Priestly law only the blood of the murderer could atone for the taking of life. This was not just because murder defiled, since that was true also of sexual offences which only led to excommunication (Lev. 18:24–30). Murder deprived God of what was rightfully his property: the blood of the dead which had gone to the control of the murderer. Hence the death penalty was the only means of making expiation for the crime (Num. 35:33), and this was the sole way the control of the blood could go back to God (Gen. 9:5ff.). God seeks the blood of the slain (cf. Gen. 42:22, Ps. 9:12 (13)). There was no way that a murderer could ransom his own life.[26]

Given this background in Priestly thought, it can be seen that the punishment which God brings on Israel is appropriate. The punishment of the exile and the death, destruction, war and siege which preceded it were entirely appropriate for a nation which had become full of violence. The punishment was in a large part caused by Israel's

---

[25] A. Phillips, *Ancient Israel's Criminal Law: A New Approach to the Decalogue* (Oxford, 1970), pp. 107–9.
[26] Phillips (1970), pp. 86, 95ff.

disregard for life. Although idolatry, sexual immorality and cultic wrong were widespread, Ezekiel does give special emphasis to the crime of murder. 7:10ff. explicitly connects the forthcoming punishment to the violence which had been perpetrated. Doom comes because חמס has sprouted into a rod of wickedness. The punishment is directly linked to violence and the filling of the land with bloody crimes (7:23). 7:27 speaks of God doing to the people according to their own way which suggests that as they have taken life, so God will remove their life in accord with the principles of Gen. 9:5ff. and Num. 35:30–34, life for life. God seeks the blood of the slain (Ezek. 3:18,20, 33:6,8). Similarly in 22:31 punishment is seen as a direct outworking of the blood shed in Jerusalem in 22:27. Those who take up the sword will perish by the sword: 33:26–29. The sword, plague and wild animals evoke Lev. 26:21,22,25.[27] As the people have taken life so God destroys them by the exile as a means of making expiation for the crimes and returning the control of the blood back to God. In Ezek. 9 executioners are summoned to kill all those in the city of Jerusalem who do not sigh or groan over the abominations. It was not just those who committed the crimes who were to be punished but, also those who acquiesced without complaint at these terrible deeds. There was to be no pity or mercy; even little children were to die. The house of God was to be filled with the blood of the slain (9:7). Those who take life are destroyed as a just, fair punishment.

The punishment of the exile is also seen as a means of cleansing the land from the bloodshed. In Ezek. 22 where the city is described as being full of bloodshed (22:2), and has become defiled by the blood of the slain (22:4), Judah is to be scattered so that her filthiness can be consumed from out of her (22:15, cf. 24:11,12). God would rather make the land a clean desert than see it become impure by bloodshed and idolatry (33:23–29). Because of the abominations the land will be a desolation (33:28).

This punishment should not be seen as an automatic cause and effect which works according to its own autonomous rules, like the laws of Lev. 18:25,28, 20:22, where the land vomits out its inhabitants or refuses to yield its produce (Deut. 28:38ff.). In Ezekiel there is a much more personal reaction from God in place of this impersonal process. God himself brings the punishment because the crime

---

[27] Allen (1990), p. 153.

is directed against him. Wrath is poured out and Israel is scattered among the nations (36:18–19), thereby causing God's name to be put to shame among the heathen (36:20ff.). Israel's knowledge of God should have been a witness to the rest of the world, but profanation had taken the place of sanctification. God is not going to indulge Israel.[28]

What must be remembered is that the crimes committed by the people were not just wrongs against humanity, but involved profaning the name of God. Killing showed contempt for God's sovereignty over human life. Israel's immorality had led to God's name being profaned and put to contempt in the world (36:22–3). Israel's sin caused God embarrassment and he destroyed Jerusalem to restore the holiness of his name.[29]

The punishment which the people bring on themselves disrupts the world order. In Gen. 1:26ff. man is given authority in creation to rule it.[30] Where that authority is abused by sin such as the taking of life, there are consequences for the created order. Man was created to rule over the animals, but by exercising oppression over his fellows, that dominion can go badly wrong. In Ezek. 5:17 and 33:27 instead of humans ruling over the animal world, they are attacked by beasts who have the upper hand (cf. Lev. 26:22). When people have polluted the land by the shedding of blood, the created order is so disturbed that animals overpower humans. Sin upsets the balance of creation. As the people of Judah abused the sovereignty of God given to humans, so their authority in creation is eroded.

By this stage the sin of the people had become so serious that there could be no chance of forgiveness. It was too late to repent. The tone of urgency in Ezekiel's prophecy is lacking; punishment is announced in a cool matter of fact way. God will not spare nor have pity. There is no hope for Judah to avoid the exile as they have rejected all preaching (2:7, 3:7, 12:2, 24:13–14). Consequently destruction is proclaimed in uncompromising terms.[31] In chapters 1–24 there is an absence of calls to repentance. Ezekiel proclaims that God will not be merciful (5:10–12, 7:4, 8:18). The primary con-

---

[28] Eichrodt (1966), pp. 345–347 = (1970), pp. 494–7.
[29] Brueggemann (1986), pp. 76ff.
[30] Harland (1996), pp. 177–209 and see also D. Clines, "The Image of God in Man", *TB* 19 (1968), pp. 53–103.
[31] T.M. Raitt, *A Theology of the Exile: Judgement/Deliverance in Jeremiah and Ezekiel* (Philadelphia, 1977), p. 47.

cern of Ezekiel was not to call people to repentance, but to explain God's justice to the exiles. Their fate was sealed. Ezekiel has no doubts about the justice of God's decision.[32] This is similar to the story of the flood in Gen. 6–9 where the wicked generation are given no opportunity to repent; they are irredeemably wicked. Like Noah, Ezekiel can only prepare for the coming punishment.

The only small possibility of hope is found in the calling of Ezekiel to be a watchman (3:16–21, 33:1–9). If the watchman fails to warn the guilty, the blood will be required at his hands (3:18), and God will act as the avenger of blood (33:7–9). The prohibition of murder is extended to include not just the taking life, but general responsibility for another person's death. To fail to warn someone of doom was equivalent to taking his life, and would have the same consequences for the prophet. Any indirect act which could lead to the harm of another is ruled out.

33:12–16 emphasises that the righteous and the wicked are not locked into a simple determinism. How people behave affects how God reacts to them. The people are not to be confined to a false sense of security or moral indifference.[33] By employing the watchman God leaves open the possibility of frustrating his own judgement; his will is for life, for the relationship between man and God to continue. A new call to repentance is offered in the midst of judgement. This is not just a call to life but is a summons to God himself.[34] God's judgement will depend on human response. God takes no pleasure in killing people; he prefers to see sinners repenting and living rather than dying (33:10–20). That life which is offered is not just physical existence, but life lived in the presence of God as a faithful member of his covenant people.[35] While the punishment of the exile had already been decided before Ezekiel began his preaching and was therefore not going to be reversed, what the parable of the watchman tells us is that this destruction was not God's

---

[32] M. Fishbane, "Sin and Judgement in the Prophecies of Ezekiel", *Interpretation* 38 (1984), pp. 131–150, 147ff., and see B. Uffenheimer, "Theodicy and Ethics in the Prophecy of Ezekiel", in H.G. Reventlow and Y. Hoffman, *Justice and Righteousness: Biblical Themes and their Influence*, JSOTSS 137 (Sheffield, 1992), pp. 200–227, esp. 201.

[33] Allen (1990), pp. 145–146.

[34] W. Zimmerli, *Ezekiel 25–48* (Neukirchen-Vluyn, 1969), pp. 800ff., 808ff. = *A Commentary on the Book of the Prophet Ezekiel Chapters 25–48* (Philadelphia, 1983), pp. 185, 190.

[35] W.E. Lemche, "Life in the Present and Hope for the Future", *Interpretation* 38 (1984), pp. 165–180, 168ff.

desire for Israel but the consequence of the people's own folly. The small opportunity for repentance which is offered in Ezek. 3 soon vanishes; the end has come (7:2).

The sin of the people was so severe that there was wholesale destruction of both the righteous and the wicked (21:3,4 (Hebrew 21:8–9)). This seems to contradict other areas of Ezekiel's teaching (9:4–6, 14:12–20, 18) where only the guilty are punished but the righteous are spared. Indeed in Ezek. 14:14, 20 the prophet adapts the tradition of Noah and the flood to emphasise that only Noah, not his sons would be saved by his righteousness, in contrast to Gen. 6–9 where Noah saves his family as well as himself by being righteous.[36] For Ezekiel the problem could not be straightforward, as he preserves the freedom of God's retribution which cannot be restricted by any simple system. All human pretensions will be silenced in the face of God's wrath.[37] The point is that the whole people is in jeopardy. Ezekiel was seeking to rule out any chance of reprieve in 21:3ff. (Hebrew 21:8ff.) or optimism. It was too late for the exiles to barter with God; the disaster of 587 was inevitable and the wicked had pulled the righteous into catastrophe.[38] The sin of the people was so severe and widespread that even those who were innocent were caught up in the horror of the punishment. The whole nation is under judgement, both the righteous and the wicked in 21:3–4 (Hebrew 21:8–9). Ezekiel is concerned to declare the impending judgement on Israel and her responsibility for it (24:13–14).[39] The people who committed murder deserved to die for their sin, and because the land was full of bloodshed the whole nation had to suffer.

Above all Ezekiel teaches that God is sovereign over human life and he wills a relationship with people. He has the right to give and take life. God's will was to have a blessed people of his own, who would lead the other nations to approach God with awe. Israel should have sanctified God's name by obedience, but instead profanation had come. Israel had to learn that she could not go her own way but had to acknowledge God as Lord.[40] Life was not just

---

[36] For a discussion of Noah's righteousness, see Harland (1996), pp. 45–69.
[37] Eichrodt (1966), pp. 189ff. = (1970), p. 289.
[38] Allen (1990), pp. 25ff.
[39] P. Joyce, *Divine Initiative and Human Response in Ezekiel*, JSOTSS 51 (Sheffield, 1989), pp. 76–77.
[40] Eichrodt (1966), p. 346 = (1970), pp. 495ff.

bare existence, but it involved communion with God (18:9), obeying him and doing his will.[41] The promise of life which is given in Ezek. 18 is much more than the promise of material existence. It includes communion with God, forgiveness and obedience. The new life which is promised is one where sins are forgiven. The punishment of exile means that God can turn to his people once more, and give them a fresh start in his service.[42] The value of human life for Ezekiel is not found in mere existence but in personal fellowship with God.

The book of Ezekiel does not end with judgement. Hope is given for a better future after the exile. Ezekiel prophesied that there would be a new ceremonial system which would prevent the pollution which had been caused by the sins of the people, especially by the taking of life. Ezek. 40–48 seeks to provide a new order whereby the earlier pollution would be prevented,[43] to create a temple which would be suitable for God's glory (43:4,7). Any place fit for God had to be cleansed from impurity caused by the shedding of blood. Yet a change to buildings or land was not enough; the people needed to be transformed. This cleansing involved giving the people a new heart whereby they had obedience and ritual purity given to them (36:25–27, 37:21–23). Forgiveness of sins is set out in terms of ritual purity; once the people are cleansed they can be forgiven: 36:25 "I will sprinkle clean water upon you, and you shall be clean from all your uncleannesses . . ." (RSV). To rectify the land which had become full of violence, God fundamentally alters human nature by giving a new heart, a new outlook to the people. By giving this spirit to the people they will walk in his statutes, obey his ordinances and be cleansed from all uncleanness, even the spilling of blood (36:26–29). Such a change will bring prosperity (36:29b, 30).

Again this makes an interesting contrast to the story of the flood in Genesis 6–9. There in both the Jahwistic and Priestly accounts, as well as in the canonical form of the text, there is no post-diluvian change in human nature. Gen. 8:21 assumes that man is as wicked after as before the flood, and the commands of Gen. 9 are given to curb a humanity which is still prone to evil. There is no talk there

---

[41] J.W. Wevers, *Ezekiel* (London, 1969), p. 143.
[42] Eichrodt (1959), p. 153 = (1970), pp. 243–4.
[43] S.R. Driver, *An Introduction to the Literature of the Old Testament* (Edinburgh, 9th edition 1913), pp. 292, 295ff.

of a change of heart.[44] Ezekiel appears to be more hopeful.

It is worth noting that there seems to be a difference between a pre- and post-Sinai context in the Old Testament. In Gen. 6–9 there is no explicit reference to ritual purity despite the writer's concern about the taking of human life (Gen. 6:11–13, 9:5–6). The author of the story of the flood might have implied that the חמס of Gen. 6 made the earth impure, but he does not emphasise this because there was no cult before Sinai and hence no ritual impurity.[45] In contrast Ezekiel lays great emphasis on the impurity which is caused by the people's sin, especially by pollution through blood. The same principle may be found in embryo in Gen. 6–9 but it is not made explicit. Ezekiel stresses the need for purity and cleanliness in a way which is not found in the Primeval History because he is writing from the perspective of a priest after the founding of the cult at Sinai.

4. Conclusion

Ezekiel tackles the question of the value of human life from the perspective of a priest. He condemns the land which is full of bloodshed and violence because that results in impurity and uncleanness. For him murder defiled the land and the people. In this and other respects he is profoundly influenced by Priestly thought. Yet there are not only important parallels to the law, but also to the story of the flood in Gen. 6–9. There are similarities in the way in which the two stories confront a world or a land full of חמס. Of course the perspective is different because of the pre- and post- Sinai contexts. Ezekiel is more preoccupied with purity and cultic matters than the Primeval History. Nevertheless both confront the same sin of violence (Gen. 6:11–13), see a link between wicked or upright behaviour and punishment or deliverance (Gen. 6:9), emphasise the sacredness of blood (Gen. 9:4), and endorse the principle of life for life as punishment (Gen. 9:5–6). Given the reference to Noah in Ezek. 14:14–20, is it too much to say that the story of Gen. 6–9 at least in its Priestly form has influenced Ezekiel?

---

[44] See Harland (1996), pp. 114–124, 136, 170 and R.W.L. Moberly, *At the Mountain of God: Story and Theology in Exodus 32–34*, JSOTSS 22 (Sheffield, 1983), pp. 113–115.

[45] Harland (1996), pp. 39–40.

As we approach the millennium, Ezekiel's message seems as appropriate as ever. We look back on a century of unprecedented violence and wonder what the next 100 years will bring. For the people of Judah there was only hope if they received a new heart. As we enter the next century, the only hope for humanity is God's offer of a new heart and spirit (Ezek. 36:26).

It is with great pleasure that I dedicate this essay with thanks to the Reverend Dr. A. Gelston who taught me in my years at Durham, 1985–1992.

THREE CHRISTIAN COMMENTATORS ON HOSEA

BY

GRAHAM DAVIES
Cambridge

The interpretation of the prophets underwent a massive change in the late nineteenth and early twentieth centuries.[1] The most important aspect of this change was not the literary-critical approach – although it was over questions of authorship and date that some of the biggest battles were fought – but the shift in theological evaluation of the prophets. The change is above all one from seeing the importance of the prophets for Christian faith and theology as lying primarily in their predictions of the coming of Christ and the establishment of the Church to a more historical view which emphasises their religious ideas, the ethical element in their teaching and their critique of their contemporaries for failing to match the demand of God. This change was not reversed, but only softened, by the fact that subsequent studies of the prophets represent something of a swing back towards the traditional pre-critical viewpoint. A Christian understanding of the prophets in the first decade of the new millennium will quite rightly be shaped by developments in biblical scholarship at the present time. But it will also benefit from a discriminating study of earlier interpretation, for many of the old issues remain with us. This essay is a small contribution to that task which I hope will bring pleasure to an Old Testament scholar who has long counted the Christian literature of the past among his interests.

The primary purpose of this essay is to gain a more detailed perspective on this change in theological interpretation by examining three major figures in Christian interpretation of the book of Hosea: John Calvin, Edward Bouverie Pusey and George Adam Smith. They are of course a small sample from the much larger number of commentators who wrote on Hosea, and even the study of them could have benefited from more comparison with their predecessors,

---

[1] See, e.g., R.E. Clements, *A Century of Old Testament Study* (Guildford and London, 1976), pp. 51–75.

contemporaries and successors. But they have the merit of representing a variety of approaches to biblical interpretation and each of them can fairly be described as an important and influential commentator, as the reprinting (and in Calvin's case the translation) of their works indicates. Calvin is an obvious choice for an interpreter who lived long before the period of change that is in question here, while yet being, through his setting in the world of the Renaissance and the Reformation, closer to the modern world even than some of his near-contemporaries. His inclusion has additional relevance because of the fact that it was in the mid nineteenth century that most of his biblical commentaries were translated into English for the first time and annotated by those who believed that his interpretation still had much to say to the Church. Pusey and Smith, while separated in time by only a few decades, stand on either side of the "great divide" and as such provide a particularly revealing insight into the changes that were taking place. With them, however, it will become apparent (and in some ways the same is even more strikingly the case with Calvin) that by no means everything changed in the late nineteenth century. To illustrate the character of the three commentaries I have chosen most of my examples from two less well-known chapters of Hosea, chapters 9 and 10.[2] It will, of course, in the space available be possible to present only a little of what might be said about these commentators' work.

Calvin's commentary on Hosea was published early in 1557 and was a transcript of lectures which he had given in the school in Geneva, in the *Auditoire* adjacent to the church of St. Pierre.[3] The exact dates of the thirty-eight lectures are unknown, but in view of what is known or can be deduced about Calvin's lecturing practice

---

[2] For a much more comprehensive study of the history of interpretation of Hosea 1–3 see S. Bitter, *Die Ehe des Propheten Hosea. Eine auslegungsgeschichtliche Untersuchung* (Göttingen, 1975).

[3] The Latin text appears in G. Baum et al. (ed.), *Ioannis Calvini Opera Quae Supersunt Omnia* (Corpus Reformatorum: Brunswick, 1863ff.), vol. 42, cols. 197–514, hereafter abbreviated as *OC* 42. For an English translation sponsored by the Calvin Translation Society see *Commentaries on the Twelve Minor Prophets by John Calvin* (tr. J. Owen), vol. 1 (Edinburgh, 1846), hereafter abbreviated as CTS Hos. On the general background see T.H.L. Parker, *Calvin's Old Testament Commentaries* (Edinburgh, 1986), pp. 13–29. I have made my own translations from the Latin in view of Parker's observations on the English translation (1986) pp. 2–3, but give page references to the latter for those who may wish to consult the context of the passages quoted. For the use of the *Auditoire* for the Hosea lectures see *OC* 42, cols. '183–84' (CTS Hos, p. xxii, mistranslates "in auditorio" as "of my hearers").

and the general relationship between his lectures and their publication it is likely that they were delivered in alternate weeks, three a week, over a period of about six months in 1556.[4] It so happens that the original Preface to the Hosea commentary, by Joannes Budaeus, and the Preface to the Minor Prophets as a whole (dated 1559), by Crispin, provide some of the most detailed information about the delivery of Calvin's lectures and the great care that was taken over their transcription. The lectures were extemporary, given without notes: Calvin brought with him only a Hebrew Bible,[5] from which he would read a verse and then translate it into Latin, with explanatory glosses as he went along. For example, he presents Hos. 9:9 as follows:

> They have deepened (so literally: others translate "they have multiplied", but this is wrong; others "they have thought cunningly", which I do not like either. But since the word which I have put ['profundaverunt'] is not Latin, and would be unclear, let us translate: "they are profoundly, or deeply, held fast, they have corrupted as in the days of Gibeah. He will remember their iniquity and punish their wrongdoings".[6]

Calvin's concern for a precise rendering of the Hebrew is evident here and often elsewhere.[7] He also frequently noted word-plays in the original (e.g. on Hos. 9:3, 6 and 15) and he shows himself to be alive to the grammatical structure of Hebrew (on 9:7) and even the significance of the Masoretic accentuation (ibid., in his translation of the verse). He knows something of Hebrew idiom: in Hos. 9:10 he translates באו as "went in" in a sexual sense, and in 10:5 he is able to give יגילו its regular sense of 'rejoice' by presuming that a relative pronoun is to be supplied before it, although it is not expressed (and need not be, especially in poetry) in the Hebrew. In

---

[4] The kind of evidence referred to by Parker, (1986) pp. 18–20, is only partially available for the lectures on Hosea 9 and 10: from this it is clear that lectures 25 and 26 and lectures 28 and 29 respectively were delivered on consecutive days.

[5] Cf. the Preface to the Commentary on Daniel, *OC* 40, pp. 23–24; CTS Dan 1, p. lxii.

[6] *OC* 42, col. 396; CTS Hos, p. 330.

[7] For recent reviews of Calvin's use of Hebrew (and rabbinic interpretation) see D.L. Puckett, *John Calvin's Exegesis of the Old Testament* (Columbia Series in Reformed Theology: Louisville, 1995), pp. 56–66 and M. Engammare, "*Joannes Calvinus trium linguarum peritus?* La question de l'hébreu", *Bibliothèque d'Humanisme et de la Renaissance* 58 (1996), pp. 35–60.

10:15 he knows that others render רעת רעתכם as equivalent to a superlative, "as is often the meaning of the genitive in Hebrew", but on this occasion he prefers a more straightforward interpretation of the phrase as a case of repetition for the sake of emphasis: "(because of) wickedness, your wickedness" (an interpretation which of course overlooks the fact that רעת is in the construct state). In the same verse he shows a rare interest in a variant reading, noting that some read כשחר, "like the dawn", in place of בשחר, "in (one) dawn", i.e. suddenly. But he retains the latter as both the better attested ("semper magis recepta") and the truer ("verior") reading – by the latter he seems to mean both truer to Hosea's teaching and more probable as an idiom.

How does Calvin understand the role of a prophet, and what contemporary application does he find for Hosea's words? T.H.L. Parker has given an invaluable account of Calvin's understanding of prophecy.[8] The prophets are seen by Calvin in the first place as interpreters of the Law (Institutes 4.8.6; Preface to Isaiah). They also focus on the union between God and Israel by virtue of election and the covenant, so that Israel's sin is fundamentally rebellion and treachery against her God. They proclaim the word of God, through the Spirit, and not just in the secondary sense of being interpreters of a God-given text. Calvin does not find predictions of Christ and the Church indiscriminately in the prophets and criticises other Christian interpreters for doing so.[9] On the whole he understands the prophets' statements about the future to refer to later Old Testament history, so as to avoid ridicule from the Jews. To this end he is interested to know when a prophet spoke and to whom, and he spends time elucidating the chronological information which the Old Testament provides.[10] The prophets' visions need special care and must be understood in the light of their teaching. On occasion a text which looks like an ordinary narrative is understood by Calvin to be a vision, or at least to have been presented to his contemporaries as such rather than as a factual account (as in the case of Hosea's 'marriage' to Gomer: Hosea could not, as a prophet, have married an immoral woman). Although he does not see the prophets as predicting the events of his own times, Calvin constantly applies what they say to

[8] Parker (1986) pp. 176–224.
[9] Cf. Puckett, (1995) pp. 53–56.
[10] Cf. Puckett, (1995) pp. 67–72.

his contemporaries, especially to the 'Papists' and their exaltation of tradition over scripture.

How far are these general features evident in Calvin's lectures on Hosea 9 and 10? Are there other important features there which should be noted? The basic perception of the prophets as interpreters of the Law is reaffirmed in Calvin's introduction to his Hosea commentary.[11] This perception seems, at first sight, to be the simple adoption of a very ancient Jewish approach.[12] But, perhaps to dispel any such suspicion, Calvin at once goes on to indicate that for him the Law embraces and indeed begins with a promise: "Now there are two parts to the Law, namely the promise of salvation and eternal life and then the rule of a devout and holy life". When he comes to summarise the prophets' teaching as interpreters of the Law, it is line with this dual character:

> So the prophets underscore the commandments of the Law about true and pure worship of God and about love, then they instruct the people in a devout and holy life, and finally they set forth the grace of God. And because there is no hope of reconciliation with God except through the Mediator, they constantly proclaim that Messiah whom the Lord had already promised before them.

Our chapters did not afford Calvin much opportunity to speak of the Messiah and in 10:12, at the one point where he might have introduced a Christological interpretation (as others, including Pusey, did), he takes the promise in a quite general way: "Finally, the Prophet here shows that, whenever God is sought from the heart and in sincerity by sinners, he comes to meet them and shows himself to be kind and merciful".[13] The one place in these chapters where Calvin does allow a clear reference to Christian belief is in 10:8, where he sees the final judgement of the world as an additional fulfilment of Hosea's words ("iterum tunc") in conjunction with their citation in Luke 23:30 and Revelation 6:15–16. There is some sign that Calvin tends to limit Christian interpretation of the Old Testament to passages which are actually cited in the New Testament.[14]

It is notable (though scarcely surprising in the light of the content of chapter 9 in particular) that Calvin's detailed exegesis has

---

[11] *OC* 42, col. 198; CTS Hos, p. 36.
[12] Cf. 2 Kings 17:13 and J. Barton, *Oracles of God: Perceptions of Ancient Prophecy in Israel after the Exile* (London, 1986), pp. 154–78.
[13] *OC* 42, col. 428; CTS Hos, pp. 380–81.
[14] Cf. Parker, (1986) pp. 202–205, on Christological interpretation of the Psalms.

much to say about true and false worship. For example, the reference to a "prostitute's hire" in Hos. 9:1 leads him first to a general
statement "Therefore, when we abandon the one God and fashion
for ourselves new gods to nourish us and provide us with food and
clothing, we are like prostitutes . . ." This is then specifically applied
to contemporary Roman practices (presumably of prayer to saints
and angels):

> Now the majority, despising God's blessing, flies off to another place
> and fashions false gods for itself, as we see happening within the realm
> of the Pope. For who are the nurses from whom they beg sustenance,
> if drought or any other time of trouble threatens barrenness and want?
> They have a crowd of gods without number, to whom they flee for
> refuge. So they are prostitutes.[15]

But as well as finding in the text warnings about false worship for
the Church of his own time, Calvin also drew attention to the positive value of the ordained practices of worship. In the following
verses he observes that the cessation of normal worship and pollution by unclean food is part of the threatened judgement of exile,
which presupposes that the ordinances in question are part of God's
blessings for his people. On this basis, when commenting on 9:5, he
commends the value of the outward ordinances of religion: they are
the "sign . . . by which the Lord gathers us to himself", "the exercises of devotion by which the Lord as it were holds us in his bosom",
and the Church should be in fear of any time "when, namely, the
Lord deprives us of our festival days, that is, he takes away all the
supports of our devotion, by which he holds us within his house and
shows that we are part of his Church".[16]

An indication of Calvin's concern, in his interpretation of prophecy,
with the wider practical teachings of the Law appears in connection
with his treatment of repentance in his comments on Hos. 10:12–13:

> The Prophet declaims only about the duties prescribed by the second
> table, as the Prophets when urging men to repentance often begin
> from the second table of the Law, because in that domain the wicked-
> ness of men is more gross and they can more easily be convinced.

One senses that Calvin found such concentration on social duties
somewhat surprising, perhaps in conflict with his own perception

---

[15] *OC* 42, col. 382; CTS Hos, p. 310.
[16] *OC* 42, col. 389; CTS Hos, pp. 319–20.

that the root of sin is rebellion against God himself (a perception that is in fact not foreign to Hosea), and had to explain why the prophet did not more directly call for a return to God himself. As will appear later, George Adam Smith was able to make a more constructive use of this passage.

An example has already been given of Calvin's application of Hosea's teaching to his Roman contemporaries, and his comments on Hosea 9 and 10 contain several more instances of this (see on 9:15, 17; 10:2, 8).[17] It is tempting to add to these explicit references a number of passages where 'hypocrites' are denounced (explicitly on 9:4, 16; 10:3, 11; and compare the elaborate description of hypocrisy in the comment on 10:4, where the word itself is not used). But on closer examination it turns out that in each of these cases Calvin is referring to Hosea's original hearers and it is not clear what (if any) particular contemporary application he may have had in mind. The fact that he refers to this fault so frequently (see the Index to the CTS translation of the Minor Prophets, for example, as well as that in the 1567 edition on which it is based) makes it worthy of further study, which might shed light on the reason for its prominence. It is possible, for example, that his own Genevan congregation is in view, as he did not spare them from stern exhortation, as in the comment on 9:10:

> Our situation today is similar. For God does not deem all worthy of this grace which has been offered to us, for he has shone upon us through his Gospel. Other peoples wander in darkness, the light of God dwells only among us: does not God show by this that we are his special delight? If we now remain in our natural state and reject him and turn our affections elsewhere, or rather desire snatches us away, is that not a detestable wickedness and perversion?

Another example of Calvin criticising fellow adherents of the Reformation appears in the comment on the reference in Hosea 9:3 to eating unclean food in exile in Assyria. He asks whether it can be right to adopt the rituals of idolaters when one lives in their midst, as it were "when in Rome to do as the Romans do". His answer is firmly and severely negative, but it was clearly not just a theoretical issue:

---

[17] This seems to have been a major reason why the commentaries appealed to the Calvin Translation Society in the mid nineteenth century: see CTS Hos, pp. vi, xi.

So also today, those who deviate from a sincere profession of their
faith and enter fellowship with the Papists renounce what is in them
of the grace of God and expose themselves to Satan's desires.

No doubt there were often situations in the Reformation period when
individuals or congregations were isolated within a region that was
predominantly Roman in its allegiance (one thinks indeed of England
under Mary at the very time when Calvin was giving these lectures)
and found the pressure to conform too great to resist. But in France
there had been the particular problem for the Reformers of "Nico-
demism", of people who professed loyalty to the principles of the
Reformation but continued to attend Roman services of worship,
and Calvin's words would have had especial relevance to them.[18]

The commentary on the Minor Prophets by E.B. Pusey, the Tractarian
leader who was Regius Professor of Hebrew at Oxford from 1828
to 1882, originally appeared in six quarto Parts between 1860 and
1877.[19] In fact three Parts appeared in quick succession in 1860 and
1861 (including of course the Hosea commentary in the first Part)
and the other three, after a gap, in 1871, 1875 and 1877. In the
'gap' came the publication of *Essays and Reviews* and the controversy
which followed it, to which Pusey's most substantial contribution was
the Oxford lectures which were published as *Daniel the Prophet* (1864;
2nd ed. 1868 with additions), and it would be an interesting subject
for future research to consider whether the later Parts were actually
written in the late 1860s and the 1870s or were substantially completed earlier, and in consequence to what extent they bear the marks
of Pusey's even more polemical stance following the publication of
Essays and Reviews.[20] The Hosea commentary at any rate clearly ante-

---

[18] This possibility was pointed out to me by A.N.S. Lane, Senior Lecturer in
Christian Doctrine at London Bible College, to whom I am also grateful for his
expert comments on other aspects of the section of this article which deals with
Calvin. See C.M.N. Eire, *War Against Idols: the Reformation of Worship from Erasmus to
Calvin* (Cambridge, 1986), pp. 234–75.

[19] *The Minor Prophets with a commentary, explanatory and practical, and introductions to the
several books* (Oxford, Cambridge and London, 1860–77). A new edition, in eight
octavo volumes, was produced in 1906 (London), with a commendatory Preface by
W. Lock, but it omitted the important (and hardly out of date) "Introductory
Statement" of Pusey on pp. vii–viii of the original edition (on which see below). I
give references throughout to the original edition.

[20] The answer is not evident from the standard *Life of Edward Bouverie Pusey* by
H.P. Liddon (4 vols.: London, 1893–97), which shows very little interest in the
actual writing of the commentary, but no doubt research in Pusey's voluminous

dates this particular controversy and the declared aims of the commentary in Pusey's "Introductory Statement on the principles and Object of the Commentary" are rather pastoral than polemical (so far as the two can be distinguished in Pusey's work).[21] The "object" is put very simply at the beginning as being "to evolve [i.e. to uncover] some portion of the meaning of the Word of God". Pusey declares that he will pass by "all shew of learning or embarrassing discussion, which belong to the dictionary or grammar rather than to a commentary on Holy Scripture". Likewise discussions of the renderings of the Ancient Versions and controversies with other modern commentators have no place, still less conjectural emendations or exercises in comparative Semitic philology. Pusey's aim is "to give the results rather than the process by which they were arrived at; to exhibit the building, not the scaffolding".

> My ideal has been ... to leave nothing unexplained as far as I could explain it; and if any verse should give occasion to enter upon any subject, historical, moral, doctrinal, or devotional, to explain this, as far as the place required or suggested. Then, if any thoughtful writers with whom I am acquainted, and to whom most English readers have little or no access, have expanded the meaning of any text in a way which I thought would be useful to an English reader, I have translated them, placing them mostly at the end of the comment on each verse, so that the mind might rest upon them, and yet not be sensible of a break or jar, in passing on to other thoughts in the following verse.[22]

The "thoughtful writers" turn out in practice to be the commentators of past centuries, Jewish sometimes as well as Christian, and Pusey picks out the compendious exposition of Hosea by his predecessor in the Oxford chair Edward Pococke for particular praise.[23]

---

surviving correspondence, as well as careful study of the later Parts of the commentary themselves, would provide the necessary information. An indication that at least Part 4 was close to completion is given by the reference in the first Advertisement to the intention of publishing the commentary in *quarterly* Parts.

[21] For the linkage of the pastoral and the polemical see e.g. Liddon (1893–1897) vol. 4 p. 19 note and the passage from an 1847 article cited below. Although the Hosea commentary lacks a strongly polemical note, this is not the case with the commentary on Jonah in the third Part (1861), where the historicity of the narrative is defended against "so-called Christians" with a vehemence which almost matches that of the lectures on Daniel. I am grateful to the Archdeacon of Huntingdon, the Venerable J.S. Beer, for drawing my attention to Pusey's interpretation of Jonah.

[22] Pusey (1860–1877) p. viii.

[23] E. Pococke, *A Commentary on the Prophecy of Hosea* (Oxford, 1685). It may be significant that Pusey's favoured predecessor belonged to the same seventeenth

The conception of the commentary was neither an isolated nor a new enterprise. In his "Introductory Statement" Pusey refers both to the "many years" during which the idea had been in his mind and to his hope that his *Minor Prophets* would form but a portion of a comprehensive commentary on the whole Bible based on the same principles. Although he states here that "the Commentary on St. Matthew is nearly ready for the press" and he wrote on 12 October 1862 that he anticipated a commentary on St. John's Gospel from John Keble,[24] no other volumes were ever published. But the origins of the plan went back to 1846, where it formed a frequent theme of Pusey's correspondence with Keble, as well as with others whom he tried, with little success, to persuade to take on a biblical book for the commentary.[25] Already at this point the character of the work was clearly defined. The exegesis of the Church Fathers was to be drawn on extensively and Christian application was explicitly required. But the exposition

> should be confined to one or two spiritual interpretations (where these are called for) relating to Christ and His Body the Church, or the soul of each individual member of Christ's mystical body, rather than give manifold spiritual meanings . . . In attempting this the writers would hope (following the Fathers) to take as their guides, leading interpretations in Holy Scripture itself.[26]

> They [sc. the contributors] are also convinced, that the great bulwark against modern scepticism lies in the reverent study and unfolding of the meaning of Holy Scripture itself; that Holy Scripture so studied does carry with it the conviction of its own Divinity; and that thereby alone (with corresponding life) can the Faith be maintained against the unbelief of "the last days".[27]

To one potential contributor to the series (T.E. Morris, whom he hoped to enlist for Genesis) Pusey wrote early in 1847:

> Our plan is to read all we can of the Fathers or old writers on it. On Genesis there is good store; our idea is to condense and rewrite, in short sentences if we can, giving the cream, or what seems most edi-

---

century to which it is often said that the Tractarians were seeking to return in their wider designs of church polity.

[24] See Liddon (1893–7) vol. 4, p. 19 note.

[25] Liddon (1893–7) vol. 3, pp. 149–58.

[26] Cited in Liddon (1893–7) vol. 3, p. 150, apparently from the *Guardian*, 26 May 1847, p. 336.

[27] *Guardian*, 26 May 1847, p. 336 (cited in Liddon (1893–7) vol. 3, p. 150).

fying, drawing it out of the text itself and then dwelling upon it, or expanding it, as seems best.[28]

Pusey offered to lend Morris some of the volumes that he would need.

What was Pusey's general conception of prophecy in the Bible, and how does it come to expression in his comments on Hosea 9 and 10? The "Introductory Statement" recognises that

> The prophets are partly teachers of righteousness and rebukers of unrighteousness; partly they declared things then to come, a nearer and a more distant future, God's judgments on unrighteousness, whether of his own sinful people or of the nations who unrighteously executed God's righteous judgments upon them, and the everlasting righteousness which He willed to bring in through the Coming of Christ . . . The fulfilments of these prophecies, as they come before us in the several prophets, it lies within the design of the present work, God giving us strength, to vindicate against the unbelief rife in the present day (p. viii).

Pusey believed that for modern readers the evident fulfilment of the prophecies of Christ and the Church could and should bolster belief in the accuracy which the prophets had shown in relation to their own times:

> To us . . . the then more distant future, the prophecies as to Christ, which are before us in the Gospels, or of the Church among all nations, whose fulfilment is around us, accredit the earlier. (*ibid.*)

The prominence of the themes of prediction and fulfilment, with the reference to contemporary unbelief, suggests that the ideas which came so loudly to expression in *Daniel the Prophet* were already taking shape here.

There is a noticeable contrast between Pusey's approach to prediction here and the one which he took in some lectures on "Types and Prophecy" which he delivered in Oxford in 1836.[29] These were never published and, as David Jasper has noted, they are virtually ignored in Liddon's *Life*.[30] In them Pusey sketched out (to judge from the studies of them which have been published) a view of prophecy which was at once more ancient (because he found it in the Fathers)

---

[28] Cited in Liddon (1893–7) vol. 3, p. 156.

[29] D.W.F. Forrester, *Young Doctor Pusey* (London, 1989), pp. 99–107. The manuscript of the Lectures is now in the archives of Pusey House, Oxford.

[30] D. Jasper, "Pusey's Lectures on Types and Prophecies of the Old Testament", in P. Butler (ed.), *Pusey Rediscovered* (London, 1983), pp. 51–70, esp. p. 51.

and more modern (almost Romantic in some ways) than the then standard 'orthodoxism' which relied on the accuracy of the prophets' specific predictions as an example of the miraculous which could be used to prove the truth of Christianity.

> Holy Scripture does not favour our mechanical views of prophecy, as containing so many items, as it were, as there are striking passages; as though prophecies admitted of being counted up, and the entire evidence of prophecy was to be weighed according to the number and contents and tangibleness of these several predictions. Rather the whole previous dispensation of the O.T., its people, its individual characters, its rites, its sayings, its history was one vast prophetic system, veiling, but full of the N.T.[31]

It is remarkable that by 1860, and still more when he wrote *Daniel the Prophet*, Pusey seems to have come to adhere to a view very like that which he had criticised in these early lectures. But it would be by no means the only instance of his abandoning a line of thinking opened up in his twenties and thirties.[32] However, as we shall see, it would be a great mistake to suppose that this was all that Pusey had to say about the prophets in 1860 and later: if it had been, his commentary would probably not have earned such widespread recognition and praise as it did.

How then does Pusey interpret chapters 9 and 10 of Hosea? First, he is true to his promise to use, and cite, the commentaries and spiritual writings of the past, especially the Church Fathers. There are nearly fifty attributed quotations in the commentary on these chapters alone, some of them quite lengthy, and there are nearly thirty more, mainly quite brief, which are set off by quotation marks without the author being explicitly named. Some of these latter at least could have been found in Pococke.[33] Among the explicit citations the largest number come from Rupert of Deutz (c. 1070–1129), closely followed by Gregory the Great and 'Osorius', who may be a sixteenth-century Spanish Catholic bishop of that name. Ambrose, Jerome, Bernard and Pococke are also cited several times. It is in

---

[31] Cited in Forrester (1989) p. 103.

[32] See on this the study of H.C.G. Matthew, "Edward Bouverie Pusey: From Scholar to Tractarian", *JTS* N.S. 32 (1981), pp. 101–124, and Forrester (1989) *passim*.

[33] Compare Pusey's unattributed citations on Hosea 9:10 (1860–77 p. 59) with Pococke, (1685) pp. 464 and 466. In these cases the words cited are not Pococke's own comments but parts of his summary of the views of others, specifically Abravanel, "Jerome and many others" and the Vulgate.

these citations that the lasting spiritual teaching of the prophet is particularly brought out, though it is not neglected in Pusey's own expository comments. A few illustrative examples must suffice. On the words *all their princes are revolters* in Hos. 9:15 Pusey comments:

> Their case, then, was utterly hopeless ... The political power which should protect goodness, became the fountain of corruption. "None is there, to rebuke them that offend, to recall those that err; no one who, by his own goodness and virtue, pacifying God, can turn away his wrath, as there was in the time of Moses". "Askest thou, why God cast them out of His house, why they were not received in the Church or the house of God? He saith to them, because they *are all revolters, departers*, i.e. because, before they were cast out visibly in the body, they departed in mind, were far away in heart, and therefore were cast out in the body also, and lost, what alone they loved, the temporal advantages of the house of God."[34]

Footnotes indicate that the citations are from Cyril (of Alexandria) and Rupert of Deutz. Pusey does not belabour the contemporary relevance, but it is evident. On *Israel is an empty vine* in 10:1 (which Pusey glosses as *a luxuriant vine*, but in the same negative sense) he remarks:

> For the more a fruit tree putteth out its strength in leaves and branches, the less and worse fruit it beareth. [Jerome is cited in support of this rendering.] The sap in the vine is an emblem of His Holy Spirit, through Whom alone we can bear fruit. *His grace which was in me*, says S. Paul, *was not in vain*. It is in vain to us, when we waste the stirrings of God's Spirit in feelings, aspirations, longings, transports, "which bloom their hour and fade" [from the Lyra Apostolica]. Like the leaves, these feelings aid in maturing fruit; when there are leaves only, the tree is barren and *nigh unto cursing, whose end is to be burned.*[35]

Again the contemporary application was too obvious to need explanation. In 10:12 Pusey (unlike Calvin) was confident that there was a prophecy of the coming of Christ:

> The Prophet, as is the way of the prophets, goes on to Christ, who was ever in the prophets' hearts and hopes. The words could only be understood improperly of God the Father. God does not *come*, Who is everywhere. He ever was among his people, nor did He will to be among them otherwise than heretofore ... The Prophet saith then, "Now is the time to seek the Lord, and prepare for the coming of

---

[34] Pusey (1860–1877) p. 61.
[35] Pusey (1860–1877) pp. 62–63.

Christ; for He, when He cometh, will teach you, yea will give you true righteousness, whereby ye shall be righteous before God, and heirs of His kingdom".[36]

The contemporary application was in this case underlined by a quotation from Pococke:

If Israel of old were so to order their ways in expectation of Him, and that they might be prepared for His coming; and if their neglecting to do this made them liable to such heavy judgments; how much severer judgments shall they be worthy of, who, after His Coming and raining upon them the plentiful showers of heavenly doctrine, and abundant measure of His grace and gifts of His Holy Spirit, do, for want of breaking up the fallow ground of their hearts, suffer His holy word to be lost on them. The fearful doom of such unfruitful Christians is set down by S. Paul.[37]

Pusey several times, usually with reference to Pococke, betrays his understanding of what the prophecy implies for the present situation of the Jews. Thus on Hos. 9:4 he writes:

Neither shall they be pleasing to the Lord; for they should no longer have the means prescribed for reconciliation with God. Such is the state of Israel now . . . In their half obedience, they remain under the ceremonial law which He gave them, although He called them, and still calls them, to exchange the shadow for the substance in Christ. But in that they cannot fulfil the requirements of the law, even in its outward form, the law, which they acknowledge, bears witness to them, that they are not living according to the mind of God.[38]

But Pusey is clear that this rejection applies only to the nation. Citing Pococke on 9:15, he says:

This was a national judgment, and so involved the whole of them, as to their outward condition, which they enjoyed as members of that nation, and making up one body politic. It did not respect the spiritual condition of single persons, and their relation, in this respect, to God.[39]

And what is said of the Jews again, according to Pococke, has an *a fortiori* application to any other nation:

---

[36] Pusey (1860–77) p. 68.
[37] Pusey (1860–77) p. 68.
[38] Pusey (1860–77) p. 56.
[39] *The Minor Prophets*, p. 61. The question of the implication of the prophets' teaching for contemporary Judaism is also raised in the Translator's Preface to Calvin's commentary on Joel, Amos and Obadiah, CTS Joel-Obad, pp. vi–ix.

If God so dealt with Israel on their disobedience and departing from His service, to whom he had so particularly engaged Himself to make good to them the firm possession of that land; how shall any presume on any right or title to any other, or think to preserve it to themselves by any force or strength of their own, if they revolt from Him, and cast off thankful obedience to Him? The Apostle cautioneth and teacheth us so to argue: *If God spared not the natural branches, take heed lest he also spare not thee*, and therefore warneth, *be not high-minded*, and presumptuous, *but fear*.[40]

Pusey's interpretation of Hosea therefore served at numerous points to reinforce his more general concern for a national revival of true religion. At least in the comments on these chapters there is no trace of specifically Tractarian themes, and this is perhaps why the commentary could receive such widespread acclaim.[41]

Two further characteristics of Pusey's commentary may be noted in conclusion. The first is his adeptness at finding a memorable phrase to sum up the teaching of the prophet. For example, he takes the plural *the high places of Aven* in Hos. 10:8 to imply a multiplicity of shrines: "Many such *idol-shrines* were formed around it, on its mount, until Bethel became a metropolis of idolatry."[42] Or again, to quote a more general remark from his Introduction to Hosea, which applies very well to chapters 9 and 10:

> The words of upbraiding, of judgment, of woe, burst out, as it were, one by one, slowly, heavily, condensed, abrupt, from the prophet's heavy and shrinking soul, as God commanded and constrained him, and put His words, like fire, in the prophet's mouth ... Each verse forms a whole for itself, like one heavy toll in a funeral knell.[43]

Secondly, alongside the practical and devotional aspects of the commentary a good deal of scholarship and learning is included. For example, there are a variety of notes on the Hebrew original, including the detection, possibly correct, of a word-play when in Hos. 10:8 it is said that thorns, not sacrifices, will "go up", עלה, on the altars.[44] In line with Pusey's declared intention there are relatively few such

---

[40] Pusey (1860–77) p. 62.
[41] The Scottish Presbyterian George Adam Smith is cited in the Preface to the 1906 edition of Pusey's *Minor Prophets*, p. xii, as having said: "Anyone who has worked at these prophets has found the Commentary [sc. of Pusey] indispensable: I always feel grateful to him when writing on the subject".
[42] Pusey (1860–77) p. 65.
[43] Pusey (1860–77) p. 6.
[44] Pusey (1860–77) p. 65.

notes in the Hosea commentary, but as he progressed through the Twelve he gave increasing space to them, commenting rather sourly in a note added to the 1877 edition that he found this necessary "as the use and abuse of Hebrew increased" (p. viii, note a).[45] Pusey also took note of the archaeological discoveries in Mesopotamia and drew on them at appropriate places, even in the Hosea commentary when the Assyrian texts had only recently been deciphered. For example, in a note on Hos. 9:17 he writes: "This appears both from the sculptures of Nineveh, in which multitudes of workmen, of countenance and form distinct from the Assyrians, are represented as working in chains, and from the inscriptions of the kings", and he quotes some examples.[46] He does not do this to prove the fulfilment of the prophecy or the accuracy of biblical history, as others were to do later; in fact the evidence is in some tension with the text under discussion, and he has to resolve this. The inclusion of such references bears witness to a wider educational aim which could exist alongside the earnest spiritual exhortations delivered elsewhere, without necessarily having to be subservient to them.

The balance between such historical knowledge and the commentator's religious purpose had clearly shifted by the time of George Adam Smith's commentary, which was first published in 1896.[47] Smith was at this time Professor of Hebrew and Old Testament Exegesis at the Free Church College in Glasgow: he was later (1910) to become Principal of the University of Aberdeen. In his Preface Smith had to defend himself against the accusation, levelled against his earlier commentary on Isaiah, of "prostituting prophecy" by applying it to "a problem of our own day". His reply is forthright:

> *The* prostitution of the prophets is their confinement to academic uses . . .
> The prophets spoke for a practical purpose; they aimed at the hearts
> of men; and everything that scholarship can do for their writings has
> surely for its final aim the illustration of their witness to the ways of

---

[45] On Pusey as a Hebraist, especially in his early career, see the learned study of A. Livesley, "Regius Professor of Hebrew", in Butler (1983) pp. 71–118.

[46] Pusey (1860–77) pp. 61–62, note 11.

[47] G. Adam Smith, *The Book of the Twelve Prophets* (London, 1896). It appeared as part of "The Expositor's Bible", a series of commentaries aimed at preachers. Quotations are from this edition, unless otherwise specified. The second edition, published in 1928 with numerous alterations, was one of a set which comprised only Smith's own commentaries on the prophetic books.

God with men, and its application to living questions and duties and hopes.[48]

But he had already made it plain on the preceding pages that he was firmly committed to the new developments in the textual and historical criticism of the Bible, even if at certain points he believed that they had been pressed to excess. In a later book, based on lectures given at Yale University in 1899, he was to spell out in detail how historical criticism was not only compatible with a belief in the lasting relevance of the Old Testament but could actually make that relevance clearer.[49]

Smith had by this time come to terms with the critical view of the religion of the Old Testament which saw in the prophets of the eighth century B.C. a huge step forward from belief in a purely national deity to what came to be called "ethical monotheism". This view had been spelt out in the writings of scholars such as Bernhard Duhm in Germany and William Robertson Smith in Smith's native Scotland, where many opposed it and Robertson Smith was deposed from his chair at Aberdeen after a lengthy heresy trial in 1881. George Adam Smith was chosen to take his place, as a young man of 25, but a revealing anecdote suggests that there was not much difference of substance between the two men's views.

> Professor Robertson Smith . . . was staying with his mother in Aberdeen. The newly-appointed substitute called upon him to seek his advice as to the conduct of the classes. The fiery little man seemed not too well pleased to see him, which was scarcely surprising. "What would you do", he demanded fiercely, "if I should refuse to obtemper the decision of the Assembly and insist on taking the class myself?" "Then", said George, "I would be proud to go and sit among your students".[50]

He was himself a noted authority on the geography of Palestine (his *The Historical Geography of the Holy Land* was first published in 1894) and he gave, in the Preface to his commentary on the Minor Prophets, a characteristic illustration of the difference which he perceived between the classical prophets and their predecessors. Speaking of

---

[48] Smith (1896) vol. 1, p. xi. Cf. the dedication of both editions to Henry Drummond, the renowned Scottish evangelist, who was a colleague and close friend of the Smiths in Glasgow: L. Adam Smith, *George Adam Smith* (London, 1943), p. 48.

[49] G. Adam Smith, *Modern Criticism and the Preaching of the Old Testament* (London, 1901).

[50] L. Adam Smith (1943) p. 19.

the Minor Prophets as a whole, which had been "haunted for centuries by a peddling and ambiguous title", he continued:

> Two of them, Amos and Hosea, were the first of all prophecy – rising
> cliff-like, with a sheer and magnificent originality, to a height and a
> mass sufficient to set after them the trend and slope of the whole
> prophetic range. The Twelve together cover the extent of that range,
> and illustrate the development of prophecy at almost every stage from
> the eighth century to the fourth.[51]

Smith's general approach to the prophets is also evident in the
overall plan of his first volume. It begins, after a brief account of
the Book of the Twelve as a whole, with a survey of early prophecy
in Israel, before Amos. The emphasis is very much on the deficiencies
of the prophets of this period. When he comes to the commentary
proper, the prophets are not arranged in their canonical order, but
in their (presumed) historical order: Amos, Hosea, Micah. Each has
a lengthy Introduction, with much detail on the historical background
and discussion of the authenticity of, for example, the passages referring to future hope and the need for repentance. The chapter on
Hosea's message is entitled "The Problem that Amos Left": it was
necessary for "the prophet of Law" or "the prophet of Conscience"
to be followed by "the prophet of Repentance", as Smith describes
Hosea, albeit in a context of divine love and grace. Referring to the
later prophets who took up Hosea's themes, Smith concludes: "These
others explored the kingdom of God: it was Hosea who took it by
storm".[52]

> From all this there clearly emerges the picture of prophecy as a devel-
> oping institution with which modern scholarship is familiar. Behind
> this there is also a clear belief in divine providence which ensures the
> continuing relevance of the book: in an age when the 'realism' of sci-
> ence and the workings of universal Law call in question the old
> ('Evangelical') ideas, Hosea's teaching on God's love for man and man's
> love for God and his fellows is needed all the more.[53]

Smith followed his textual commentary on Hosea with three
"Theological Essays", whose character is also redolent of a new
approach to the prophets which emphasises their overall religious
ideas more than the detailed wording of the text. The essays are

---

[51] Smith (1896) vol. 1, p. vii.
[52] Smith (1896) vol. 1, p. 230.
[53] Smith (1896) vol. 1, p. 231.

entitled "The Knowledge of God", "Repentance" and "The Sin against Love". A number of features can be recognised here which were to become prominent a generation later when many scholars turned their minds to "Biblical Theology" as a means of interpreting a historically conditioned Bible for the needs of their own day. There are word-studies (on 'knowledge' and 'return', for example), a focus on (salvation-) history as the chief means by which the people of God come to a knowledge of him, opposition to ancient Near Eastern religion and ritualism, and a more systematic approach to the prophet's words which almost overshadows the detailed exposition of the text. In the final essay, which is in some ways more like a sermon, the contribution of Hosea's subjective experience of marriage breakdown to his theology is emphasised (cf. the phrase "the most fundamental truth that *Hosea gave* to religion" [italics added] at the beginning of the first essay), but more traditional motifs appear in a rare reassertion of the prophecy-fulfilment pattern (with reference to Hos. 11:4) and the uncompromising, for all its new expression, picture of divine judgment: "Love abused is love lost, and love lost means Hell".[54]

What does Smith have to say about chapters 9 and 10 specifically? One's first answer might well be "Not much", especially after reading the many pages of Calvin and Pusey on the same chapters. Smith has eleven pages (pp. 279–289) on them, of which nearly four are occupied by his new translation of the text.[55] This cannot simply be put down to the limits on the space available in the commentary, but it does bear some relation to its format. The space devoted to introductory and concluding ('theological') essays might have been used for more detailed verse-by-verse commentary, and the choice of format is probably indicative of the same shifts in interpretation that we have already noted. History and theology are now more to the fore, when it comes to Christian interpretation of the Old Testament, than the text itself as an object of detailed exegetical study.

Smith saw chapters 9 and 10 as part of a major section of the book which he entitled "A People in Decay. II. Politically" (7:8–10:15),

---

[54] Smith (1896) vol. 1, p. 350. In the first edition the essay had a final paragraph (p. 354) which spoke of Hell not as a place of flames, but as "a dreary waste of ash and cinder, strewn with snow", but this was omitted in the second edition of 1928 (cf. p. 379).

[55] In the second edition there are fifteen pages, but the increase is mainly due to a more generous page layout, especially for the translation.

which followed a section headed "A People in Decay. I. Morally"
(4:1–7:7). It is somewhat surprising that there is no major section
headed "A People in Decay. Religiously". The theme of idolatry
does, it is true, appear in the sub-heading of chapter 10, but only
in second place to politics ("Puppet-kings and Puppet-gods"). There
is, at the least, a notable "foregrounding" of the significance of
national life in general for the prophet's message here. This shift is
also reflected in the detailed interpretation of the two chapters.

In 9:1–9 Smith focuses on "The Effects of Exile", which will break
up both the joy and the sacredness of the people's lives. But Israel's
doom is already being fulfilled by the corruption of her spiritual
leaders: Smith here follows the traditional interpretation of verses
7–9 as referring to false prophecy.[56] The following section (9:10–17)
is entitled "The Corruption that is through Lust". The introduction
of the sin of lust is at first surprising, but Smith refers back explicitly to the allusions to it in Hosea 4 and he probably had in mind
the fuller account of the episode at Baal-Peor (9:10) in Numbers 25,
although he does not actually cite that passage. Be that as it may,
most of the comment on this section is a lengthy diatribe against
the mores of Smith's own day, which include:

> ... the number of great statesmen falling by their passion, and in their
> fall frustrating the hopes of nations; the great families worn out by
> indulgence; the homes broken up by infidelities; the tainting of the
> blood of a new generation by the poisonous practices of the old, –
> have not all these things been in every age, and do they not still hap-
> pen near enough to ourselves to give us a great fear of the sin which
> causes them all? ... We have among us many who find their business
> in the theatre, or in some of the periodical literature of our time, in
> writing and speaking and exhibiting as closely as they dare to limits
> of public decency.[57]

The treatment of chapter 10 is especially brief (little more than a
page if the translation of the text and the critical notes on it are
excluded): "few notes are needed", Smith says. The comments are,
however, supplemented by the exposition of verses 11–12 at the end

---

[56] In the second edition (pp. 303–304) he adopted the now generally accepted
view that these verses refer to the rejection of Hosea's message by the people.
Another interesting change is from "the vision of the poet" as a description of
Hosea's gift (1st ed., p. 281) to "the vision of the prophet" (2nd ed., p. 305), which
suggests a withdrawal from a bold early literary evaluation in favour of a more traditional standpoint.
[57] Smith (1896) vol. 1, pp. 284–85.

of the essay on repentance, where Smith develops his favourite theme with a powerful elaboration of Hosea's imagery:

> Another familiar passage, the Parable of the Heifer, describes the same ambition to reach spiritual results without spiritual processes . . . Cattle, being unmuzzled by law at threshing time, loved this best of all their year's work. Yet to reach it they must first go through the harder and unrewarded trials of ploughing and harrowing. Like a heifer, then, which loved harvest only, Israel would spring at the rewards of penitence, the peaceable fruits of righteousness, without going through the discipline and chastisement which alone yield them. Repentance is no mere turning or even re-turning. It is a deep and an ethical process – the breaking up of fallow ground, the labour and long expectation of the sower, the seeking and waiting for Jehovah till Himself send the rain . . . A repentance so thorough as this cannot but result in the most clear and steadfast manner of life. Truly it is a returning not by oneself, but a *returning by God*, and it leads to the *keeping of leal love and justice, and waiting upon God continually* (xii.7).[58]

The three commentaries sampled here have in common a commitment to a contemporary Christian interpretation of the text which is not superficial but grounded in a serious grappling with the Hebrew original and the historical background as it was understood. All three writers use arguments from analogy (even the *a fortiori* in Pusey's case) to relate the text to their own times. Pusey sometimes achieves this by an allegorising or spiritualising interpretation, especially in his quotations from older sources, but in the cited case from his comments on Hos. 10:1 they are based on metaphorical language in the original, just like Smith's exposition of 10:11–12 quoted above. Smith too has a distinctive way of translating the prophet's message into contemporary terms, in the isolation of religious ideas with a permanent validity. There are some more striking differences. Both Calvin and Smith are notably restrained in speaking of a Christian fulfilment of prophecy, whereas Pusey freely claims such a connection. This traditional motif is certainly related to his high regard for the Church Fathers, where it is widespread, but one might have expected that its presence in the New Testament would have had as much influence on Calvin and Smith. It is Pusey too who considers most the relevance of the prophecy to the contemporary status of Judaism, a central topic for any Christian interpretation of the Old Testament. His conclusions are not entirely negative, but

---

[58] Smith (1896) vol. 1, pp. 344–45; cf. pp. 288–89.

they are more so than the text of both the prophets and the New Testament require. This is not the place to attempt a fresh account of how Hosea, and the prophets generally, may be understood in the context of Christian belief at the end of the twentieth century, but it may be hoped that the preceding analysis and reflections will place such an account on a firmer footing. Two new works of commentary promise to bring the interpretations of the Fathers into view in a way reminiscent of Pusey's plans;[59] but it is not only (and perhaps not in the first place) the commentaries of the distant past that deserve attention from those who must now take up the task of interpretation.

---

[59] The *Ancient Christian Commentary on Scripture* is due to begin with a volume on *Mark*, edited by T.C. Oden and C.A. Hall (InterVarsity Press, Downers Grove IL), in May 1998; and the one-volume *International Catholic Bible Commentary*, edited by W.R. Farmer (Liturgical Press, Collegeville MN), has been announced as forthcoming in September 1998.

WHOSE WORDS? QOHELETH, HOSEA AND ATTRIBUTION IN BIBLICAL LITERATURE[1]

BY

STUART WEEKS

Durham

The term 'Qoheleth' has puzzled readers for many centuries,[2] and perhaps since its very inception, but most commentators have taken it to be a real name or title by which the author of the book of Ecclesiastes wishes to be identified, so that the attribution is essentially the same as the attribution to an author on the fly-leaf of any modern book.[3] In this respect, the treatment of Qoheleth resembles the usual scholarly approach to authorial ascription in the Bible: when books are attributed to an individual, that individual is being identified, rightly or wrongly, as the writer or originator of the material within those books. Modern scholarship is not, of course, so naïve as to assume that all such attributions are reliable guides to actual authorship: few scholars would accept, for instance, that Solomon wrote Proverbs, any more than they would accept the authorial claims of many later apocalyptic books or testimonies. In

---

[1] I am grateful for the opportunity to thank Tony Gelston, not for the hard task of filling his shoes at Durham, but for a personal kindness long ago. The Society for Old Testament Study is noted for its warmth and collegiality, but for a young student at his first conference and still clinging to his supervisor's coat-tails, it proved a little intimidating. Tony, who didn't know me from Adam at that time, made a point of talking to me at meals and taking an interest in what I was doing, a kindness which I have since learned to be quite typical. Would that all fine scholars were such fine humans as well.

[2] The book of Ecclesiastes begins with a description of its content as "The words of Qoheleth, the son of David, king in Jerusalem", which is later given further specification by Qoheleth's claim to have ruled Israel from Jerusalem. What follows is a first-person speech by this Qoheleth, until in 12:9 a second voice describes Qoheleth and his writing in the third person. The word 'Qoheleth' does not seem to be a name, and is once used with the definite article (12:8; cf. LXX 7:27), suggesting that it may be a title; if so, there may be some connection with the root קהל, and thereby with 'summoning' or the 'assembly'. All this is very uncertain, though.

[3] G. Ogden, *Qoheleth* (Sheffield, 1987), p. 15, is fairly typical: "'Qoheleth' ... is the adopted name of the author of 1:2–12:8. He is an Israelite sage, who, according to the Editor's testimony in 12:9–10, stood firmly within the wisdom tradition".

such cases, though, the attributions are usually characterised as 'pseudonymous'; they are taken to have the same fly-leaf function as genuine attributions, but with the name of the real author replaced by that of another individual – usually someone famous from the past.

This approach seems to be informed more by the conventions of the modern and classical worlds than by ancient Near Eastern practice. The extant materials do not suggest that authorial attribution was expected for most non-documentary literature in the ancient world. Those texts, mostly Egyptian, which do bear attributions generally belong to particular literary genres in which monologues or dialogues play some central role, and the attribution is of the words to a speaker, not of the book to a writer.[4] Some examples may help to clarify the rationale behind this attribution of certain texts within literary cultures which generally preferred anonymity.

Two early instructions set the pattern: an Egyptian work attributed to Ptahhotep, and a Sumerian one attributed to Šuruppak.[5] Although both works are amongst the earliest poetic literature from their respective cultures, neither is as old as it claims to be. The *Instruction of Ptahhotep* presents itself as the advice given by a vizier of the Fifth Dynasty, who lived in the early 24th century B.C.E.; it is unlikely, however, to have been written any earlier than three or four centuries after this vizier lived. *Šuruppak* may actually have been composed earlier than the 24th century – the Abu Salabikh text is generally dated to the middle of the third millennium – but it presents itself as being antediluvian. Even were there any reason to take the figure of Šuruppak as historical, then, it seems clear that both texts have been substantially back-dated, and that neither attribution is to the real writer.

Rather than just write this off as 'pseudonymity', though, we might usefully ask why these works have been attributed to long-dead individuals. For *Ptahhotep* an answer is suggested by the material which

---

[4] In other cases, most notably literary letters, the attributions are clearly linked to the documentary form of the texts.

[5] We have each work in more than one version. The principal edition of *Ptahhotep* is Z. Žàba, *Les Maximes de Ptahhotep* (Prague, 1956). There is a valuable new introduction and translation in R.B. Parkinson, *The Tale of Sinuhe and Other Ancient Egyptian Poems 1940–1640 B.C.* (Oxford, 1997), pp. 246–72. For *Šuruppak* see especially B. Alster, *The Instructions of Šuruppak: a Sumerian Proverb Collection* (Copenhagen, 1974); there have been some subsequent textual discoveries. For fuller bibliography of these and other ancient instructions discussed below, see the appendix to my *Early Israelite Wisdom* (Oxford, 1994), pp. 162–89.

frames the basic advice. A prologue begins the work with a story *about* Ptahhotep, in which he approaches the king with a complaint about the infirmity of his old age, and asks permission to train up his successor. The king assents, and urges his vizier to teach "the speech of the past", making his student a model for all the sons of scribes to emulate. The advice which follows, then, is supposed in some way to be older even than Ptahhotep, and carries royal approval. The epilogue to the work then begins by stressing that the perfection of this advice will make it last for ever, and finishes with Ptahhotep's boast that he has prospered, and achieved the ideal 110 years of life. The value of the advice, then, is assured both by the status of Ptahhotep, who has achieved long life and high rank by following its principles, and by its own age: it has lasted so long because of its truthfulness and perfection. It is likely that similar ideas underpin *Šuruppak*. In this text the father is a more minor character, whose name is better-known as that of a city than as that of a legendary hero, but the son, Ziusudra, is the hero of the Sumerian flood story, who goes on to achieve immortality. This is in itself a commendation of the advice, but there may have been other implications apparent to the original audience.[6] In both works, then, the advice is set in a context and associated with individuals who lend weight to it.

Similar motives may have underlain the attribution of other early instructions, in which back-dating to some famous individual is common. Sometimes, however, more specific motives may be discerned. The *Instruction for Merikare*, for instance, is attributed to a king of the Heracleopolitan Dynasty in the First Intermediate Period, which enables it both to pursue the theme of kingship from a royal perspective, and to exploit the historical circumstances of the period to make its points; it may also emphasise, by implication, the more settled political conditions of the Middle Kingdom.[7] This approach is rather different from that of *Ptahhotep*. In that work, the status of the vizier was important, but had little direct relevance to the content of the advice: although supposedly intended for the training of a

---

[6] Lambert draws attention to a story in Berossus, which has the flood-hero bury writings for later recovery, and suggests that this text may have been associated with such ideas. See W.G. Lambert, *Babylonian Wisdom Literature* (Oxford, 1960), p. 93.

[7] For the text, see especially W. Helck, *Die Lehre für König Merikare* (Wiesbaden, 1977); there is a translation in Parkinson, (1997), pp. 212–34.

particular individual, for a particular post, Ptahhotep's words explicitly address the needs of individuals in a number of different situations. In *Merikare*, on the other hand, the royal status and past actions of the speaker are crucial to the content. This is an important clue to the nature of such attributions: they do not simply inflate the value of the book, but rather provide a story context, within which the words are to be understood.

So far as we can tell, the voice of Ptahhotep is only one of many which the author might have chosen: his requirement may have been no more than a famous individual who lived during the golden age of the Old Kingdom. Sometimes, though, the setting is very specific indeed; so, for instance, the *Instruction of Amenemhet* is presented as the words of the assassinated king Amenemhet I, founder of the Twelfth Dynasty, and is intended both to condemn the attempted coup which led to his death, and to legitimise his successor Senwosret.[8] The attribution and setting are not fixed, then, but designed to serve the particular needs of the work. This is also true of texts other than instructions. Another Twelfth Dynasty work, the so-called *Prophecy of Neferti*, again adopts the Old Kingdom setting beloved of Middle Kingdom writers, and presents the words of a lector-priest summoned to speak at the Fourth Dynasty court of King Snofru. These words describe, in conventional terms, a time of disorder which is brought to an end through the intervention of one 'Ameny': the text thus uses its past setting to make a political point for the time of its composition – Ameny is apparently Amenemhet I.[9] Other Egyptian works related to Neferti, notably the discourses attributed to Khakeperreseneb, Ipuwer, and Sasobek, set expressions of pessimism in the mouths of named individuals. The first of these, *Khakeperreseneb*, seems, interestingly, to begin with a rejection of ancient teaching; no narrative context is outlined, but the speaker's name is the prenomen of Senwosret II, and this may be intended to bear some significance. The beginning of *Ipuwer* is lost, but the speaker seems to be engaged in dialogue with a king; Sasobek is very fragmentary, but begins with an account of the speaker's wrongful imprisonment.[10]

---

[8] The fullest presentation of the text is in W. Helck, *Der text der "Lehre Amenemhets I, für seinen Sohn"* (Wiesbaden, 1969), but there have been several subsequent finds which have clarified the setting; for translation, see Parkinson (1997), pp. 203–11.

[9] W. Helck, *Die Prophezeiung des Nfr.tj* (Wiesbaden, 1970); Parkinson (1997), pp. 131–43.

[10] For *Khakheperreseneb* and *Ipuwer*, see A.H. Gardiner, *The Admonitions of an Egyptian*

Attributions are very much rarer in Sumerian material, and tend to be to legendary or divine figures.[11] Taken with the Egyptian evidence, though, they confirm the very strong impression that early attributions have little or nothing to do with the actual authorship of texts: the individuals to whom advice or lament is attributed are not authors but characters, often connected to a very specific narrative setting. They may be chosen as famous men of the past, but this is not necessarily so: the choice of protagonist is linked to the nature and purpose of each work.

When later texts use attributions to individuals who are otherwise unknown, we should not, therefore, take this as a sign that they have moved to some wholly different convention, in which the attributions are to the actual authors. The imposition of a setting seems to have imposed problems for some writers, and the use of famous characters may have been perceived as restrictive. It was all very well to place instruction on the lips of kings or viziers, but that was not the context in which most readers lived. One Middle Kingdom writer seems to have been driven by these considerations to anonymise his work, by entitling it simply *The Instruction by a Man for his Son*, and so to emphasise the universal applicability of its advice.[12] In the New Kingdom, works were regularly attributed to individuals of more ordinary rank – such as Any or Amenemope – whose experience would be more on a par with that of most scribes. There is no way to prove that these are not actually the names of the authors, but there are several indications that they are no less narrative characters than the protagonists of earlier works. The *Instruction of Any*, for example, is actually in the form of a dialogue, where the scribe's son responds to his father, politely but negatively; a similar clash is found in an Akkadian work.[13] Even granted the slim possibility that

---

Sage, from a Hieratic Papyrus in Leiden (Leipzig, 1909); Parkinson (1997), pp. 144–50, 166–99. The fragment of Sasobek (Pap. Ramesseum I A.17–19) is in J.W.B. Barns, *Five Ramesseum Papyri* (Oxford, 1956), pp. 1–10.

[11] As in, for example, the strange *Farmer's Instruction*, where the farmer is identified as Ninurta.

[12] An edition of this text is apparently being prepared by Fischer-Elfert; the best source at present is W. Helck, *Die Lehre des Djedefhor und die Lehre eines Vaters an seinen Sohn* (Wiesbaden, 1984), but this lacks many new texts.

[13] There is, notoriously, no reliable edition of *Any*: E. Suys, *La Sagesse d'Ani* (Rome, 1935) should be used with caution. The Akkadian work is known in copies from Ras Shamra, Emar, and Boghazköy, but the nature of its attribution is disputed. Nougayrol, in *Ugaritica v* (Paris, 1968), pp. 273–93, reads the names Šube'awilum

scribes might submit their heirs to the humiliation of public exposure – Any's son confesses his own inability to learn so much advice –
it is difficult to imagine that either the father or some third party
sat down to record such conversations for general consumption. At
most, the scribes are probably fictionalised versions of the authors,
comparable to, say, the third-person character of Kinky Friedman
in the detective novels written by Kinky Friedman. It is at least as
likely, though, that the characters are wholly fictional.

This supposition is given added force by the very late *Instruction
of ʿOnchsheshonqy*, which is once again set in the past, and begins with
an extensive, almost certainly fictional narrative.[14] Interestingly, this
work seems to have been influenced by the Aramaic *Ahiqar*, a work
which, in the earliest form we possess, is a similar mixture of tale
and teaching. The historical existence of Ahikar himself is often taken
for granted, on very late and tenuous evidence, but it is most unlikely
that any such figure was really responsible for writing the teaching
which bears his name.[15] Relevant Mesopotamian texts for this later
period are few and fragmentary; with the exception of the father-
son dialogue just mentioned, there are no published instructions with
their attributions intact. It is noteworthy, though, that on one of the
only occasions when we are almost definitely given the name of an
actual author, in the famous *Babylonian Theodicy*, the name is not presented explicitly as an attribution, but in the form of an acrostic.[16]

In short, then, ancient Near Eastern literature does not commonly,
if ever, use authorial attributions as a guide to the actual authorship of works. Rather, it is inclined to present certain sorts of material in the form of speeches, delivered by characters who may play
a role in a broader narrative. These characters can be drawn from

---

and Zurranku for the father and son, but Arnaud does not consider these to be
personal names in his *Recherches au Pays d'Astata. Emar vi, 4* (Paris, 1987), pp. 377–83.
  [14] S.R.K. Glanville, *Catalogue of Demotic Papyri in the British Museum, ii. The Instructions
of ʿOnchsheshonqy (British Museum Papyrus 10508)* (London, 1955). There is a translation and valuable study in M. Lichtheim, *Late Egyptian Wisdom Literature in the
International Context* OBO 2 (Freiburg and Göttingen, 1983).
  [15] For the text, see most conveniently, A. Cowley, *Aramaic Papyri of the Fifth Century
B.C.* (Oxford, 1923). J.M. Lindenberger's excellent *The Aramaic Proverbs of Ahiqar*
(Baltimore and London, 1983) does not include the narrative section. The only reference to a 'historical' Ahiqar is in a Seleucid Period text from Uruk, which has
probably been influenced by the literary tradition.
  [16] See Lambert (1960), pp. 63–89. Each line within each stanza begins with the
same syllable; taken together, these syllables spell out the Akkadian for "I, Sagil-
Kinam-ubbib, the incantation priest, am adorant of the god and king".

history or created from whole cloth; just possibly, they are some-times fictionalised versions of the actual writers. What we do not find, though, is any convention of ascribing literary works to their real authors, comparable to modern western convention. To under-stand the attributions which we find, it is perhaps easier to think in terms of the modern first-person novel. When Robert Graves wrote *I Claudius*, for example, he created a work with a double attribution, the real author of which presents his words as those of his leading character. Ancient attributions are rarely if ever comparable to the "Robert Graves" attribution, but are instead like the secondary attri-bution to Claudius. For this reason, the concepts of 'pen-names' or of pseudonymity are not entirely appropriate: the names which we are given do not stand in the place of author's names.

The likely response of the original readership is not easy to judge: although it is clear that the convention was recognised, ancient works were sometimes taken to have been composed by the individuals to whom they were attributed.[17] We might speculate that ancient read-ers were less concerned with the historical facts of the matter than we are. In any case, though, it seems unlikely that there was any intention to deceive readers.

Once we see a distinction between writer and speaker in ancient texts, an interesting question comes to the fore: how independent are these characters from their creators? Obviously, they are at one level simply ventriloquist puppets, speaking words placed in their mouths by the writers. It might be a mistake, though, to assume that they are no more than vehicles for the opinions of those writ-ers. In this respect, there is no reason to regard them as different from any other characters in ancient narrative. So it is, for instance, that Amenemhet and Merikare's father both speak as kings, although their words were almost certainly written by commoners, just as, conversely, the speeches of *The Eloquent Peasant* were probably com-posed by a scribe.[18] Furthermore, the presentation of ideas through speeches and narrative offers writers an opportunity to air views which are not their own. This is most obvious in dialogues, where the author may espouse radically different views through the words

---

[17] The most valuable evidence here is quite confusing: there is a eulogy to authors on Pap. Chester Beatty IV, but this itself seems to believe that *Amenemhet* was writ-ten by the famous scribe Khety.

[18] For the text, see R.B. Parkinson, *The Tale of the Eloquent Peasant* (Oxford, 1991).

of different characters – and none of these views need correspond to his own opinions. In the humorous Babylonian *Dialogue of Pessimism*, for example, a manservant finds justifications for all the absurd and contradictory proposals of his dithering master, and is probably the more sympathetic character; if the writer has a serious point, though, it concerns the human ability to reason in such contradictory ways, a point made by example: neither character actually presents the author's opinion, and both are the subject of his gentle mockery.[19] In the fine Middle Kingdom composition, *Dialogue between a Man Tired of Life and his Ba*, usually known more conveniently as the *Lebensmüde*, the arguments of each character for and against dying are both persuasive, and are voiced, indeed, by separate aspects of the same personality.[20] Here again, it seems that the writer is in full agreement with neither, but is interested in the dialogue between the two viewpoints. The point need hardly be laboured: characters may express ideas and opinions with which their authors do not necessarily agree.

In some works, indeed, there may be a deliberately satirical intention. This is a notoriously hard issue to judge; in the *Instruction of Any*, for example, the father's speech does seem to be deflated rather abruptly by the son's unexpected response, but it is not clear how far the reader is expected to sympathise with that response. A much later work, attributed to an unnamed "Scribe of the House of Life", on the other hand, is almost certainly a parody of older Egyptian instructions, with the scribe made to seem pompous and irrelevant.[21] In Israelite literature, of course, it has been suggested that the figure of Jonah is portrayed in a similarly satirical way, and we have already seen that the Babylonian *Dialogue of Pessimism* uses characters who are deliberately absurd. We should be very wary of presuming, then, that ancient writers expect us to take all of their characters seriously.

This brings me back to Qoheleth, and the assumption that the name or title used to describe the speaker in this work is actually a name or title adopted by the writer himself. In the light of evidence from elsewhere in the ancient world, it should be obvious that this assumption needs more justification than it usually receives. Setting

---

[19] Lambert (1960), pp. 139–49.
[20] Text in R.O. Faulkner, "The Man who was Tired of Life", *JEA* 42 (1956), pp. 21–40; translation: Parkinson (1997), pp. 151–65.
[21] R.J. Williams, "Some Fragmentary Demotic Wisdom Texts", in J.H. Johnson and E.F. Weite (eds.), *Studies in Honor of George R. Hughes* (Chicago, 1976), pp. 263–71, esp. pp. 270f.

consideration of the Hebrew prophetic corpus aside for the moment – and there is no good reason to associate Ecclesiastes with that literature – we have very few ancient examples of attribution to an actual author, and the balance of probability is strongly on the side of considering Qoheleth to be a creation of the real writer. Some commentators, indeed, have rightly taken this approach, and Michael Fox, most recently, refers to Qoheleth as a 'persona' of the author, who speaks in his own voice in the epilogue of chapter 12, but who is essentially in agreement with his creation.[22]

This seems a sensible conclusion, especially in the light of the actual attribution. Few scholars, if any, would accept that Solomon wrote this book, and yet this appears to be the claim made in the first two chapters, albeit rather coyly.[23] There seems no good reason at all to say that the author really was known as 'Qoheleth', but was lying about the Solomon bit, especially when, whatever else it may have been, 'Qoheleth' was almost certainly not the writer's name. I suspect, though, that Fox does not go far enough, that Qoheleth may be something quite different from a mere disguise, and that this book may be one in which the author and his character stand some way apart.

Perhaps the most obvious hint of this is in the epilogue to the book, which comments on Qoheleth and his work:

> Beyond the fact that he was a wise man, Qoheleth also taught knowledge to the people, and he measured, explored and arranged many sayings. Qoheleth sought to find words to take delight in, and uprightly wrote words of truth. The words of the wise are like goads, and like nails set (in them) are the sayings in the collections offered by each single shepherd. Beyond these things, my son, beware: the making of books is a constant process – there is no end (to it) – but constant study wears out flesh. (12:9–12)

I have taken a few slight liberties with the translation here; in particular, the making of books and the study in verse 12 are things done 'much' rather than 'constantly', but that is difficult to render in English. In any case, the sense seems clearer than some commentators suggest: after a complimentary start, albeit one that focuses on Qoheleth's style more than his content, the epilogue moves on

---

[22] M.V. Fox, *Qohelet and his Contradictions* (Sheffield, 1989).

[23] Apart from Rehoboam, not renowned for his wisdom, Solomon is the only "son of David" to have ruled Israel from Jerusalem in the biblical tradition (cf. 1:1,12).

to a rather strange simile. The "words of the wise" is a term used
to describe two of the collections of sayings in the Book of Proverbs,[24]
and here it seems similarly to indicate such written collections of
sayings, which are compared to the goads or prods used by shep-
herds. Continuing this simile, although perhaps a little clumsily, the
writer further suggests that each saying in each collection by each
wise man is like each nail in the goad used by each shepherd. The
point of the simile is reached in the final verse: such collections mul-
tiply endlessly, but to keep studying them is to wear out one's flesh
ever more from the lashings of these goads. It might just be possible to take "beyond these things", at the start of verse 12, to mean
that one should restrict oneself to the advice of Qoheleth (the expression has no exact parallel, and its meaning is not entirely certain);
that in itself, though, hardly excludes his advice from the general
assertion.

It is not easy to imagine many writers choosing this blurb for their
book: it could fill no reader, except, perhaps, the most morally
masochistic, with any strong desire to read works by "wise men"
like Qoheleth. Its praises of that author ring a little hollow, moreover. For all its many fine qualities, this work can have left few in
its audience with any conviction that they have been taught knowledge or received moral guidance in any conventional way. On a
more technical level, furthermore, the style of the work is not, overall, that of a sayings-collection: this is not a work created by someone anthologising and arranging separate sayings, as Qoheleth is
described doing in verse 9. If a separate epilogist added these remarks, it is almost hard to believe that he had read the book; if the
writer himself composed them, then there is a whiff of irony in the
air. In neither case is it easy to take this epilogue as a straightforward
recommendation.

Turning to the monologue itself, we find a Qoheleth whose character and inclinations are very much those of the wise man, but
whose explorations seemingly lead him into a contradiction of all
that such wisdom stands for.

The monologue begins, in 1:2, with the motto which sums up so
many of Qoheleth's later enquiries: everything is הבל. This term is
difficult, and seems to mean different things in different places; I
take its basic implication to be, though, that things are as fleeting

---

[24] See Prov. 22:17; 24:23.

and beyond one's grasp or influence as a breath of wind. The motto is followed by the central question which Qoheleth sets himself to answer: "what can humans accomplish?", and that question by a poem which seems to deny the possibility of any human influence: the world is fixed, and impervious to innovation. After this introductory material, Qoheleth plays the role of the wise king Solomon, who has seen "everything done under the sun", and who uses his wisdom in an attempt to understand the world, but who again sees no way to effect change in that world. In 1:18, he goes so far as to suggest that wisdom and knowledge actually increase frustration and despair.

These ideas are picked up and enlarged upon in much of what follows. The second chapter begins with Qoheleth's supposed memoir of his time as king, which is again a portrait of futility, as nothing he does has any lasting effect. It is not without its comic moments, though, as he assures the reader that he retained his wisdom while experimenting with drunkenness ("All in the cause of science . . ."), and it ends with his important conclusion that the profit may have been in the pleasure, not the consequence. This is followed by the assertion in chapter 3 that everything will happen in time, even though the eternal workings of God are concealed from humans. Because everything will happen, Qoheleth argues rather unconvincingly, there will be a divine judgement to sort the righteous from the wicked, but for the moment God has a reason to conceal this from humans: he is testing them by showing no differentiation. From this point on, the work shows much less coherence, although the voice is unmistakably still that of Qoheleth. After an initial complaint about oppression, and the lack of comforters for the oppressed, most of chapter 4 seems concerned with the theme of co-operation, and chapter 5 with, firstly, the need to avoid annoying God, and then the futility of wealth. This leads to a further discussion of the need to enjoy what one has, and to look no further, before chapter 6 climaxes with an extraordinarily radical set of statements:

> Whatever exists has already been called by its name, and it is known what the human is: he cannot play judge with what is stronger than himself.[25] As words multiply, they make more vanity, and what good is that for the human? For who knows what is best for that human

---

[25] The sense of לדין עם is uncertain, but I take the verb to mean something closer to its normal sense than 'strive' or 'contend'.

as he lives out the numbered days of his vain life and spends them like a shadow; who[26] can tell that human what will exist after him under the sun? (6:10–12)

These are strange things for a wise man to be saying. Wisdom is fundamentally concerned with teaching and acquiring the knowledge necessary to survive and prosper in life. If such knowledge is really unattainable, then wisdom is an impossible task. The book of Job voices similar concerns, perhaps, but Job does not pose as an expert wise man.

The next chapter seems to drive the point home, with a series of often mystifying statements. Some of these are conventional enough, but there is a bitter edge to the series, and perhaps a certain cynicism, not least when Qoheleth declares that "Wisdom is good with an inheritance" (7:11). He ends with a question that echoes the earlier 1:15, but now seems to ascribe the world's evils directly to divine action:

Consider the work of God: who can straighten out what he has made crooked? (7:13)

Although there are references to it at various points in chapters 7 and 8, the failure of wisdom is only first acknowledged explicitly at the end of chapter 8 and the beginning of chapter 9, when Qoheleth denies the validity of the wise man's claims to know "what is done under the sun", and asserts the inability of humans to discern what will or will not please God. This drives him once again to stress the importance of pleasure, in a world where nothing is certain, and skill is no guarantee of success. Chapter 10 launches into a series of sayings which is, if anything, even stranger than the previous series in chapter 7. The first saying suggests that wisdom can be overwhelmed by even a little folly, and the third saying undermines the second by taking its imagery quite literally. Verses 8–10 make the curious claims that, for example, "He who digs a pit will fall into it", or "He who quarries rocks will be injured by them", statements which are hardly universal truths. Conversely, towards the end of the series, the sayings seem to become quite absurdly obvious: even the babbling fool might work out, for instance, that "in the place where the tree falls, there it will lie". Once more, the sting of the series is in its tail, when Qoheleth observes that those

---

[26] The use of אשר here is difficult, but the general sense clear.

who busy themselves watching for the right weather will never finish their work, and should simply get on with it. This is apparently yet another attack on wisdom and its efficacy.

Although we have skipped rather rapidly through this difficult material, it should be apparent that there runs through this monologue a strong resistance to any claims that the world can be understood and changed, or that the best way to act can be known or taught. Qoheleth's conclusion, that one should enjoy what one can and accept one's lot is very far from the beliefs of most instructional and sentence literature, such as that found in Proverbs. It is very difficult indeed, more immediately, to reconcile such ideas with the portrayal of the character in the epilogue: just what is it that Qoheleth would have taught to the people, and how much of a painful goad is the advice to enjoy oneself? For all that he paints himself in traditional colours, Qoheleth is a long way from the conventional wise man of chapter 12.

I have described Qoheleth's message as though it were consistent, but it is not. The problem lies not so much in the direct contradictions or sudden expressions of piety, which have swallowed much scholarly ink over the years, but more in a general lack of cohesiveness. How do we explain, for instance, the sudden switches of form or theme, and the admixtures of conventional and deeply unconventional sayings? Why, when it comes down to it, does Qoheleth not simply say what he means to say? There are doubtless various factors at work here; these may vary from our inability to catch all the nuances through to some secondary additions. It seems very possible, though, that the characterisation of Qoheleth has had some part to play. So far we have looked at the message; let us turn briefly to the man.

First of all, there's that name. When the writer of this book created Qoheleth, he could have given him almost any name. Most obviously, he could simply have called him Solomon, since he has anyway to play the role of Solomon in the first two chapters. Instead he used a term which was apparently incomprehensible to readers within a relatively short time: our Septuagint version of the book, with its stab at a translation, is admittedly late, but nobody seems to have had any better ideas. If this term is a title, as the sporadic use of a definite article might suggest, then we might reasonably ask why such a title was used in place of a name. Whatever the reason, it is a strange attribution, made all the stranger by Qoheleth's identification with Solomon. However used ancient readers were to fictional attributions, there is no reason to think that they expected characters to change identity. Since Qoheleth is not apparently intended to be a name for Solomon, the author seems to be presenting us with a character who openly disguises himself as another character. Perhaps, more precisely, he shows us a wisdom writer, as described in the epilogue, adopting the conventional, fictional guise of Solomon. One consequence, of course, is that the reader knows Qoheleth's account of his kingship to be untrue: it is almost explicitly a device.

One important characteristic of Qoheleth's monologue is its rather autobiographical character. Even after the royal 'memoir', Qoheleth points constantly to his own experience as the basis for his message, claiming to have 'seen' something on more than 20 occasions.[27] This is a little curious. A few didactic compositions in the ancient world do rely heavily and explicitly on personal observation or experience: *Merikare* and *Amenemhet* are obvious examples. It is much more common, though, for such claims to remain implicit. For all that, say, *Amenemope* is supposed to sum up the life-experience of its protagonist, the advice is not directly presented as conclusion based on observation. Qoheleth talks about himself so much that his work overall, and not just in the first two chapters, almost takes on the flavour of a memoir. One writer has been led to compare it to the Akkadian genre of fictional autobiography.[28]

It is not only the royal aspect of this remembering which must seem a little suspicious to the reader: some of the claims are very extravagant indeed. Even if Qoheleth might conceivably mean, in 4:1, that he has seen every type of oppression in the world, rather than every incident of it, he clearly means in 4:15 that he saw every person alive, while he claims to have seen everything in, for instance, 1:14 and 7:15. Despite this wealth, perhaps glut, of experience, when Qoheleth cites actual incidents, he does so in the vaguest of terms, with short and often confusing stories, which carry little conviction as eye-witness evidence (e.g. 5:12ff.; 8:10; 9:13ff.). None of this resembles the detailed testimony of *Merikare*, or even the first-person para-

---

[27] See 1:14; 2:13,24; 3:10,16,22; 4:1,4,7,15; 5:12(ET 13), 17(ET 18); 6:1; 7:15, 8:9,10,17; 9:11,13; 10:5,7. In a few of these cases, Qoheleth is apparently expressing a conclusion rather than an observation.

[28] T. Longman, *Fictional Akkadian Autobiography: A Generic and Comparative Study.* (Winona Lake, 1991).

ble of Prov. 24:30–34. Qoheleth's ideas may be based upon his personal experience, but that experience lacks credibility throughout.

In the end, we seem to be dealing with a book where the author has created a wise man in whom the conventional characteristics of didactic writers are emphasised and exaggerated, perhaps almost to the point of satire; this character's speech is filled with the sort of poetic and verbal gymnastics in which ancient writers so often took great pride, but is more than a little rambling and inconsistent. The speaker's principal conclusions seem to be that one should avoid antagonising God, but accept that His world is impervious to human understanding; human activity is ineffectual, and sometimes futile, while wisdom offers no real insight, but merely a painful awareness of its own limitations. Ultimately, Qoheleth suggests that we should fear God, act in moderation, and enjoy what we do; though the very model of a wise man, he denounces wisdom and its claims to understanding. In 8:17, indeed, when he denies the wise man's claim to knowledge, Qoheleth condemns all that he stands for himself. We might say that the writer uses this character to embody his message: he creates a wise man to question the claims of wise men, both explicitly and through parody. On examination, then, the book of Ecclesiastes seems not so much an exception to ancient conventions, as a rather clever use of them. At the very least, the book gives us no good reason to believe that Qoheleth was its real author, and provides many grounds for supposing that he was not.

As a source for 'real' authorial attributions in Near Eastern literature, the corpus of Jewish prophetic literature seems, on the face of it, to offer strong possibilities. Most scholars accept, however, that there is a distinction between the actual composers of the prophetic books and the prophets to whom they are attributed. Although the traditional view envisages a process of collection and redaction by these composers, rather than wholly creative authorship, we may still describe, say, the book of Amos as a book about Amos by an unknown writer, rather than the product of the prophet himself. In such cases as Isaiah and Zechariah, indeed, we may reasonably wonder how much of 'their' books the original prophets would have recognised. This separation between book and prophet raises difficult questions, of course, about the historicity of the accounts, and the extent to which they are representative. With little or no information about their sources and motives, we cannot know how far the creators of the books selected and adapted the materials to suit their particular viewpoints. So, when a commentator claims that Amos was a prophet of doom, for instance, he is, technically, asserting more than the evidence warrants: we can speak only of the way in which the prophets are presented to us by the composers of the prophetic books.

From the perspective of ancient convention, prophetic literature must have posed a problem. Its long poetic speeches were, by accident or design, perfectly suited to long-established literary tradition, but representing the delivery of those speeches was more complicated. For the author of Ecclesiastes, say, or of Job, each speech could be attributed to a single appropriate character. In the prophetic literature, however, the speeches were the words of God, but spoken by the prophet, whose identity presumably assured the authenticity of his speech. The prophet could, moreover, speak in his own right, so that the same character was, in effect, two characters with two voices. This was potentially confusing, especially if the prophet was to be portrayed interacting with God. Some resolution of the problem was achieved by explicit attribution, making the words of God speeches within the framing speech of the prophet. So in Amos, for example, the book as a whole is described as the "words of Amos", and begins "And he said . . ." (1:1f.). The words of God are thereafter qualified using messenger formulae or other direct attributions. Where such devices are not used, matters can become more confusing, and the book of Hosea presents particular difficulties in this respect.

These difficulties are essentially confined to the first three chapters, after which the prophet speaks solely as a mouthpiece for God. The book itself is presented as "the word of YHWH which came to Hosea" (1:1), rather than as the words of Hosea, and describes God speaking 'with' or 'through' the prophet,[29] emphasising his role as spokesman and agent, rather than as speaker. The identities of prophet and God are strongly intertwined, though, in chapters 1 and 2. At God's command, the prophet takes a woman, and has three children by her. The nature of this woman has been discussed down

---

[29] A case can be made for understanding ב to mean 'to' here (cf., e.g., A.A. Macintosh, *Hosea* (Edinburgh, 1997), p. 7), as in, for instance, Num. 12:8 and Zech. 1:9, but it may equally have its common sense of agency. The sense is probably closer to "conversed with" than "spoke to", and אל is used in the same verse to imply direct address.

the years, but we can really say no more than that she and her children are apparently associated with promiscuity. Each of the children is given a symbolic name, at God's command, and the symbolism of the relationship and of the names is explained individually.

The relationship between Hosea and the woman is explicitly intended to symbolise or represent the relationship between God and Israel, who has forsaken him for promiscuity. This is probably to be understood as an 'instant' symbol: Hosea is tied to a promiscuous woman just as God is tied to a promiscuous people. If Gomer's promiscuity continued, there is no mention of it in the rest of the account, and, apart from her bearing of children, her subsequent actions go unremarked. The first of these children, incidentally, is explicitly Hosea's. The paternity of the others is unspecified, but there is no reason to believe that they had other fathers. The names of the children are similarly instant symbols, although they are qualified by the expectation of a later change to more acceptable names. The chapter does not portray a situation which develops symbolically, then, but a string of single, symbolic actions. In the initial relationship with Gomer, and in the naming of "Not my people", Hosea plays the role of God. In the divine speech which follows the account, though, God plays Hosea, apparently addressing the woman's children. Now the woman is actively promiscuous, and the children are to remonstrate with her lest she and they be punished. It is emphasised that God, not the prophet, is the speaker here: except for a single occurrence in 11:11, the book elsewhere refrains from the "says YHWH" expressions used in 2:15,18, and 23 (ET 13, 16, 21).

When we get to chapter 3, the perspective changes abruptly, to that of the prophet himself. The first chapter was presented by a narrator's voice, the second by God's, and now the prophet himself addresses the reader in the first person. The narrative of chapter 1 is picked up as Hosea describes how God again speaks to him. Now he is told to love an adulterous woman, just as God loves adulterous Israel. Interestingly, in the explanation for the action here, as in 1:2, God unusually speaks of himself in the third person. Along with the word עוֹד, 'again', this binds the two accounts together, and makes it improbable that either is a later insertion. More importantly, it militates against the view that chapter 3 is a separate reminiscence, preserved by the book's author. This opinion, common

among commentators,[30] seems to rest on little more than the idea
that first-person speech must be more authentic – a view which is
hard to sustain even within the biblical literature, let alone against
a long history of fictional autobiography in the ancient Near East.
If the composer of the book was prepared to adapt the wording to
link the passage with chapter 1, he was clearly not just anthologising or leaving the text as he found it: why, then, did he not just
put it in the third person, instead of leaving this sudden jump to
the first? This switch of perspective would seem to require another
explanation.

Hosea's behaviour in this account is rather different from that in
chapter 1. There, his only action was to obey the divine command
and take Gomer; now he goes and purchases a suitable woman.
That may not be the same as 'loving' one, but it is broadly in line
with what God required of him, and serves to create the symbol.
What he does next, though, goes beyond that requirement: he tells
the woman that she will remain faithful, promising to do the same
himself.[31] This establishes a new relationship and symbol, quite different from that initially commanded, and it is one which will function as a symbol through its durability. There is no suggestion that
Hosea is acting at God's command here, and his symbol, unlike
God's, is a symbol of fidelity and hope. When he speaks for himself in the first person, here, then, Hosea is also acting in his own
right, not as divine spokesman or agent.

It seems very possible that these switches of person are an attempt
to distinguish the different players and speakers in a potentially confusing context. In 1:2 and 3:1, God apparently speaks of himself in
the third person to keep the real and symbolic relationships distinct.
In chapter 3, correspondingly, Hosea's voice is not that of God, and
the change of person may be a device to point this up – a device
which was unnecessary in the first chapter, where Hosea never spoke
in his own right. If it seems a rather odd device, then we should
bear in mind, perhaps, that such luxuries as quotation marks were
unavailable to the writer. Instead, he uses a change of perspective,
which brings with it, however, a claim of authorship.

---

[30] See, for example, Macintosh (1997), p. 113: "3:1–4 . . . was written by Hosea
himself soon after the events described in it and preserved by him personally".

[31] Although a jussive implication is possible in 3:3, there is no explicit command,
as one might expect were Hosea giving a futile or optimistic order: the most natural reading of the sentence is as a prediction, not a command.

Later prophetic books show the influence of psalmody and of the apocalyptic testimonial style in their use of the first person, but it is interesting to observe that other early prophetic literature seems to use it in ways directly comparable to Hosea 3. The account in Isaiah 6–8 is probably the most obvious example, although any reading of that book is rendered difficult by its complicated redactional history. Amos furnishes a less problematic analogy. Although that prophet is never required to symbolise God's will in his personal life, the first person is used in the series of visions (7:1–9; 8:1–3; 9:1). These portray coming destruction, but also situations in which Amos confronts God as an independent actor. In the first two visions he actually dissuades God from carrying out the planned destruction of Israel, but in the next two is forced to pronounce judgement himself, through wordplay; in the last, he is merely a spectator. His actions and words here are his own, and he speaks in his own voice; when portrayed as a divine spokesman in 7:10–17, on the other hand, Amos is described in the third person.

Much caution is needed here, given our limited understanding of the way in which such books developed, but there do seem to be grounds for suggesting that prophets, in the early prophetic literature, are presented in the first person when required to describe situations in which they act or speak as individuals in their own right. Some such idea surely underpins the later characterisation of Jeremiah, also, although we may need to reckon with other influences there. If there is any truth in this suggestion, then the scenario envisaged in Hosea, and in Amos and Isaiah, for that matter, is clearly more strange and complicated than that of Ecclesiastes, the instructions, or most other ancient 'speech' literature. It is as though, in his role as prophet, we see Hosea speaking and acting side-on; and then in chapter 3, speaking as himself, he suddenly turns to face us. Whatever effect he was striving for here, though, the writer of the book has apparently chosen to use different perspectives, or attributions, to achieve it, and that brings us back to the point at which we started.

As modern readers, and trusting souls, we have a natural inclination to believe that, when an ancient text explicitly or implicitly attributes material to a particular individual, it genuinely expects us to accept that individual as the author of the material. This inclination can mislead us, though, into missing a very important point about ancient Near Eastern literature. For ancient readers and writers, the words on the page seem to have been not text so much as words, spoken by one or more characters, and to be understood in terms of those characters' own natures and perspectives. We might do better, indeed, to think more in terms of story and drama than in terms of essays. When we encounter different voices in a text, then, we need to be aware that there are different speakers. This may be obvious in texts like Job, but it is no less important a consideration in books as diverse as Ecclesiastes and Hosea.

THE SOCIAL BACKGROUND OF
THE BOOK OF MALACHI

BY

J.W. ROGERSON
Sheffield

Reconstructing social situations from literary texts is a hazardous business. However, in cases where the only evidence for the social background to a text is the text itself some attempt at reconstruction is necessary, unless the decision is taken to ignore any pointers in the text to extra-linguistic factors. In what follows, as a tribute to Tony Gelston's prolonged study and work on the Twelve Minor Prophets and as a token of friendship over many years, the attempt will be made to think around some of the pointers in Malachi to the possible social background(s) to the book's production.

Usual attempts to describe the social background to Malachi concentrate on the identity of the prophet, whatever his name might have been, and on the identity of possible redactors or editors of the book. Thus P.L. Redditt's recent article identifies the prophet as a reforming Levite, on the grounds of the book's down-playing of the distinction between Zadokites and non-Zadokites at the temple and its interest in collecting and supervising the tithe.[1] The identity of the redactor is harder to define. According to Redditt he may have been an active or disenfranchised Levite. If he was neither, he embraced the spirit of the reform of the prophet.

One of the problems of this kind of approach is that it is a hostage to varying theories of the history of composition of Malachi. Whereas Redditt can distinguish between a prophet and a redactor, E. Bosshard and R.G. Kratz distinguish three layers, and conclude that the book

---

[1] P.L. Redditt, "The Book of Malachi in its Social Setting", *CBQ* 56 (1994), pp. 240–55. Redditt ascribes two series of oracles to the prophet, the first (1:6–2:9; 2:13–16) directed against the priests, the second (2:17–3:1a + 5; 1:2–5 + 3:6–7; 2; 10–12; possibly 3:13–15) directed against the people. To a redactor is assigned the combining of the two series of oracles with the addition of 1:1, 3:1b–4, 3:13–21 and with 3:13–15 reapplied.

did not originate from a collection of oracles by an actual prophet
'Malachi'. Rather, the book is primarily a literary production which
has edited and enlarged what might have been isolated oracles of a
prophet or his circle.[2] In order to avoid the circularity of analysing
the book's literary structure as a basis for seeking its social setting,
a process in which social and historical-critical judgements inevitably
affect the decisions regarding literary structure and development, a
different approach will be followed here. It will be assumed that
even if the book of Malachi is a purely literary production and that
access to a prophet 'Malachi' is impossible to achieve, the book's
production will still have had a social background which will have
affected it in some way. Even if the book is an instance of *Schriftprophetie*[3] and even if it is the result of several stages of redaction, these
literary processes will not have happened in a social vacuum. The particular issues addressed will most likely have been provoked by social
situations. We are entitled to ask why the particular issues that surface in the texts have been dealt with and not other issues; and we
are entitled to think around the social issues that the texts deal with
and to draw tentative conclusions.

The first passage to be considered will be a well-known crux,
Malachi 2:10–16. The question of the unity of the passage will not
be considered, nor whether there are two separate oracles, 10–12
and 13–16. This is not because such questions are unimportant; neither is this meant to be an exercise in "final form" criticism. The
questions to be raised here do not ultimately depend on literary
decisions.

As is well known, much heated discussion had been generated by
verse 11, which can be translated literally as follows:

> Judah has been disloyal, and abomination has been committed in Israel
> and in Jerusalem. For Judah has defiled the sanctuary of the LORD,
> which he loves, and has married the daughter of a foreign god.

Two lines of interpretation have been advocated, both of which go
back to antiquity. The first, found in the Targum, traditional Jewish
exegesis and most modern commentators takes the reference to mar-
rying the daughter of a foreign god to mean that Jews had married

---

[2] E. Bosshard and R.G. Kratz, "Maleachi im Zwölfprophetenbuch", *BN* 52
(1990), pp. 27–46.
[3] H. Utzschneider, "Die Schriftprophetie und die Frage nach dem Ende der
Prophetie: Überlegungen anhand vom Mal. 1:6–2,16", *ZAW* 104 (1992), pp. 377–94.

foreign women who worshipped gods other than Yahweh. The second, found in the Septuagint and in a minority of modern interpreters, assumes that it is worship of a goddess within the Jerusalem cult that is being condemned. There is no need here to rehearse the arguments for and against both positions, seeing that they are well set out in the standard works.[4] Two observations may be made however. The strongest arguments in favour of the religious idolatry position are the claim that Judah, without qualification, has been disloyal, and that the offence is described as an abomination (Hebrew תועבה) a term almost always applied to *religious* actions repugnant to God.[5] If the passage is about mixed marriages, it is odd that the *whole* of Judah should be condemned for the offence. The word 'abomination' most naturally points to idolatry. The strongest argument in favour of the mixed marriage position is that, whatever the difficulties of translation and interpretation of verses 14–16 (assuming them to be connected with verse 11) they undoubtedly deal with divorce.

While, on the whole, I find the arguments in favour of the idolatry interpretation the more convincing, I shall argue that whatever view is taken the conclusion is inescapable from this verse, that there was either idolatry in the second temple when this section of Malachi was produced or rival sanctuaries where other gods could be worshipped. My starting-point is Glazier-McDonald's observation that both interpretations must be taken together in order to do full justice to the text. However, she does not work out the implications of this. Her own preference is for the intermarriage with foreign women theory, and she accuses proponents of the idolatry view of rarely discussing "how such illegitimate rites entered the Yahwism of the period".[6] Yet she provides the answer to the question by rightly pointing out that the problem with mixed marriages is that they may lure the Israelite spouse to worship other gods.

The practical question is this: if there were Israelites who were married to foreign women who worshipped other gods in the community addressed by Malachi 2:11, how did these women practise

---

[4] See R.L. Smith, *Micah – Malachi* (Waco, 1984), pp. 321–4: B. Glazier-McDonald, *Malachi: The Divine Messenger* SBLDS 98 (Atlanta, Georgia, 1987), pp. 113–20.

[5] See the evidence collected by Glazier-McDonald (1987), pp. 90–1. Her assumption that the term applies to intermarriage in Mal. 2:11 is not supported by any evidence independent of her interpretation of this verse, and the parallels that she adduces, Ezra 9:1,11,14 only prove the opposite of her position.

[6] Glazier-McDonald (1987), p. 119.

their religion? Even if we allow for a certain amount of private religion, if there was such a thing in ancient times, there must have been major festivals or other occasions on which the foreign women needed to take part in communal or institutionalised worship of their god. If such communal or institutionalised worship was not available, it is hard to see how an Israelite could be seduced to worship a god that did not have a cult. Unless one is going to maintain that Malachi 2:11 is a purely literary construction with no extra-textual referent, it seems to me that any other interpretation is bound to lead to the conclusion that provision was being made for the worship of another god or gods either in some part of the courtyard in the second temple or in a dedicated sanctuary apart from the temple. It is a nice point whether such a sanctuary, not being dedicated to Yahweh, would be regarded as breaking the deuteronomic law of the single sanctuary, for all that it would be seen as an abomination.

A second line of thought that will now be developed is dependent upon Rex Mason's *Preaching the Tradition*, without implying that Mason would want to endorse what is argued here.[7] The book is initially an examination of the addresses in Chronicles, a feature that marks them off particularly from the books of Kings. Mason suggests that these addresses reflect a tradition of preaching in the second temple, and later in the book he compares the themes and rhetorical patterns in Malachi with the addresses in Chronicles concluding that

> the manner and themes of his [Malachi's] message suggest that he stands firmly in the circles of the second temple 'rhetors', circles which have left their mark so clearly in the records of the preaching of the second temple period.[8]

From the point of view of the method adopted in this article I am concerned with the background to the book rather than the identity or placing of Malachi, if there was such a person, to whom material might be attached. I propose to consider two questions. First, why do the addresses in Chronicles concentrate so much upon

---

[7] R. Mason, *Preaching the Tradition: Homily and Hermeneutics after the Exile* (Cambridge, 1990).

[8] Mason (1990), p. 256. With regard to the respective dates of Chronicles and Malachi, I agree entirely with Mason's view on p. 237: "The usual practice is to set the book between the time of the ministries of Haggai and Zechariah and the coming of Nehemiah in 445 B.C.E. This may well be right, although none of the arguments advanced is conclusive".

cultic purity? Second, how does a possible answer to this question shed light on the background to Malachi?

That the addresses in Chronicles refer frequently to cultic purity can easily be indicated. Abijah, in his address to the army of Jeroboam and Israel prior to the battle in which the smaller army of Judah will defeat the much larger army of Israel, indicates the impossibility of an Israelite victory because of the impurity of the Israelite cult. They have with them the golden calves and unqualified priests. Judah has a qualified priesthood, worship acceptable to God, and priests present who will sound the battle trumpets (2 Chron. 13:4–12).

Azariah son of Oded encourages king Asa to remove idols from the land and to repair the altar in front of the temple vestibule. By reminding him that "for a long time Israel was without the true God, and without a teaching priest or without law" (2 Chron. 15:3), he assures Asa that if Asa seeks God, God will be found. The people enter into a covenant with God, part of which stipulates that anyone who does not seek God will be put to death. From the context, "seeking God" is a matter of faithfulness to the purified cult and priestly teaching (2 Chron. 15:2–15).

The letter of Elijah (2 Chron. 21:12–15) accuses Jehoram of forsaking the way of his fathers and of following the ways of Ahab. Although Ahab is mentioned several times in these chapters (2 Chron. 21:6,13, 22:3–6) his 'ways' are not explicitly detailed in Chronicles. It can be assumed, however, that the account of his reign as described in 1 Kgs. 16:29–33, with its catalogue of cultic aberrations, was part of the shared knowledge of the author and readers of Chronicles. Zechariah son of Jehoiada accuses the people of forsaking God and of transgressing his commandments, and informs them that they cannot possibly prosper because God has forsaken them. The occasion of the accusation is the worship of Asherim and idols on the part of the princes of Judah after the death of the priest Jehoiada (2 Chron. 24:17–22). The speeches of Hezekiah (2 Chron. 29:5–11, and cf. v. 7 "they have shut the doors of the vestibule" with Mal. 1:10) and Josiah (2 Chron. 35:3–6) also concern matters of cultic purity.

If it is asked why there is so much attention to cultic purity several answers can be given. The Chronicler is elaborating a theme that was found in his sources, whatever they were; or, matters of ritual purity would be of concern within the temple-based community within which Chronicles was produced. If, however, Mason's suggestion is followed up, that the addresses reflect the preaching of the second temple, the question can be asked why the addresses carry the emphases that they do. Although it is perhaps dangerous to extrapolate from modern Christian preaching to ancient Jewish preaching, it could be said that when preachers draw upon older traditions and apply them to the situations in which they preach, they emphasise those parts of the tradition that are most pertinent to the preaching situation. Applied to the addresses in Chronicles this would mean that the emphasis in the addresses on cultic purity would imply that the standards of what went on in the second temple left much to be desired. The intimate connection in the addresses between cultic purity, God being with his people, and the success that the divine presence assured, could indicate a situation or situations in which preachers feared that the state of affairs in the temple gave such cause for concern that unless there were radical reforms the divine favour would be withdrawn and the community would face disaster.

The book of Malachi seems to deal directly with problems that the addresses in Chronicles tackle by implication. The state of the sacrificial cult is explicitly criticised in 1:6–14, as are the standard and content of priestly or Levitical instruction in 2:1–9. There is probably, as argued above, a condemnation of some kind of foreign cult (2:10–12); there is a hope of reform of the levites at the temple in 3:1–4, and there is a complaint about non-payment of tithes in 3:6–12. All of these latter points, of course, are obvious from the content of Malachi. They appear in a different light, however, if they are seen in the context of a preaching tradition in Chronicles that was concerned with the consequences of a comprised cult.

A third passage for consideration is 1:6–14; again, I am not concerned with the literary problems of the passage but with social questions that it provokes. The complaint in this passage is that blind, lame, sick and blemished animals are offered to God in sacrifice and that this would not be done if the (presumably Persian) governor was the intended recipient. The law about sacrificial animals needing to be without blemish in Lev. 22:17–25 is usually cited at this point in the commentaries.

There are several reasons why worshippers might offer blemished animals in sacrifice, and why priests might be content to let them do so. The most cynical explanation, from a religious standpoint, would be that the worshippers performed their religious duties reluctantly, that they begrudged losing a potentially productive animal to the demands of sacrifice, and that they bribed the priests not to apply the law about sacrificial animals needing to be unblemished. It is also possible to consider the matter in a different way. Here, I can only raise some pertinent questions and leave it to others, or to myself at a later date, to do the necessary research.

If, as is sometimes suggested, the post-exilic community in Judah abandoned agriculture in favour of horticulture, from where did they get the animals to offer in sacrifice?[9] Presumably there was no longer a need for oxen to plough the fields, while the fact that olive trees did not need much attention until the olives were harvested and made into oil, (the cultivation of vines would, however, be more labour-intensive) meant that there was adequate labour for looking after sheep and goats. These could feed on natural vegetation, including that on and around areas that were devoted to growing olives and vines. However, what is not known is now horticulture and animal husbandry were organised, and on the basis of which social units.

The production of oil and wine involve investment in trees on which there is not an immediate return (they take several years to become productive) as well as investment in implements for converting the produce into oil and wine. There is a need for marketing and exchange to be organised, in which the temple probably played a leading role. These activities had to be organised alongside animal husbandry; but what would happen if the strategy of producing and marketing oil and wine and selling it in return for grain (compare Neh. 10:31) was so successful that animal husbandry became marginalised? Flocks might become too small to produce a pool of healthy animals. The reference to offering animals that were blind, lame or sick might then indicate a crisis in animal husbandry in

---

[9] See H. Kippenberg, *Religion und Klassenbildung in antiken Judäa* (2nd edition, Göttingen, 1982), p. 47. "Vielleicht darf man schließen, das die Getreideerträge des judäischen Berglandes nicht für die Ernährung der Bevölkerung ausgereicht haben. Würde diese Annahme zutreffen, dann wäre die judäische Bevölkerung dazu gezwungen gewesen, solche agrarischen oder handwerklichen Produkte zu erzeugen, die von den Gebieten mit den höheren Getreideüberschüssen benötigt worden und die als Tauschwerte mehr Getreide einbrachten, als der Boden je hervorbringen konnte. Olivenprodukte und Wein wären solche Produkte gewesen". Kippenberg notes, however, that there is insufficient evidence actually to prove this hypothesis. I. Finkelstein, "The Great Transformation: 'Conquest' of the Highlands, Frontiers and the Rise of Territorial States" in T.E. Levy (ed.), *The Archaeology of Society in the Holy Land* (Leicester, 1995), pp. 349–65 notes (353) that "cereal growing was a wrong economic strategy in these hilly parts of the highlands".

which animals were scarce and flocks too small. B. Rosen, while dealing with a much earlier period and foothills rather than the central highlands, estimates that a village of one hundred persons would require a herd of around 300 sheep to provide the 200 milking ewes that would produce the milk, cheese butter and (occasionally) meat to supplement the dietary needs not met by the growing of wheat.[10] Talal Asad, describing a modern group in the southern Sudan living in very different conditions from those of post-exilic Judah and dependent upon camel nomadism, nonetheless provides interesting information about the sizes of the flocks of sheep kept by the different households.[11] One household of seven possesses 120 sheep and 10 goats, another household of seven has 80 sheep and 7 goats.[12] Even making allowances for possible differences between types of sheep in the first millennium B.C.E. and modern breeds, these figures suggest that Rosen's figures may be on the low side.[13]

The figures given by Rosen and Asad do not answer any of the questions posed by the text of Malachi, but they do indicate that large numbers of sheep were and are needed to support populations in ancient or nomadic situations. In a society based more upon horticulture rather than agriculture, if this was the case in post-exilic Judah, those involved in animal husbandry would be dependent upon those who invested in, produced and marketed the oil and wine which were traded for cereals. Any disruption of this trade or unwise management of the relationship between various types of producers could force those who depended upon animals to consume them in order to survive. The stock would become depleted and in-breeding would produce sickly animals.

All this, of course, remains conjectural with regard to the background of Malachi 1:6–14, but the matter has been approached in this way in order to indicate questions that need to be considered regarding the complaint against the priests and people in this passage. They may hint at economic circumstances within the community in which

---

[10] B. Rosen, "Subsistence Economy in Iron Age I", in I. Finkelstein and N. Na'aman (eds.), *From Nomadism to Monarchy: Archaeological and Historical Aspects of Early Israel* (Jerusalem, 1994), pp. 339–351, and especially pp. 347–9.

[11] T. Asad, *The Kababish Arabs: Power, Authority and Consent in a Nomadic Tribe* (London, 1970).

[12] Asad (1970), pp. 48–9.

[13] On the types of sheep in the ancient Near East and their fertility, etc., see the article 'Ts'on' (Hebrew) in *Entsiqlopedia Hamiqrait*, vol. 6 (Jerusalem, 1971), pp. 645–9.

Malachi was produced, in which healthy animals were at a premium and bound up with the survival of the groups that depended upon them. The priests may have been acting as much on the basis of compassion or realism as lax standards, in accepting unfit animals for sacrifice.

If anything of what is hinted at in this article is correct, the community in which Malachi was produced is to be seen as a community in crisis. It is in crisis about its own identity; whether non-Israelites should be allowed to be married in to the community and whether provision should be made for the different religious needs of foreigners. It is facing an economic crisis in which animal husbandry cannot produce sufficient numbers of healthy animals for the sacrificial cult. In this situation the dialogue that is conducted or constructed in the book reflects the agonising that was taking place in the community. Were the priests and people being unfaithful to God in attempting to cope with the realities of the situation? Was the orthodox viewpoint of the book correct that reform of the cult would result in the kind of material plenty that would solve the social problems? It is inappropriate, in my view, to engage in holier-than-thou judgements directed against either the priests for laxity and compromise or the compilers of the book for insisting upon the letter of the law regardless of the disastrous social consequences that this might have. If religion is to play a part in people's lives as well as in their minds, problems such as those implied in Malachi are bound to arise and there will be disagreement about how they are to be handled. Part of the abiding fascination of the Old Testament is its candour in these matters, as well as its hope that, where human solutions fail, God will effect a cleansing leading to a state of affairs longed for by any right-minded person (Mal. 3:1–5).

APOCALYPTIC, REVELATION AND EARLY JEWISH WISDOM LITERATURE

BY

JAMES K. AITKEN

Cambridge

Included among the manuscript finds from Qumran are a number of Wisdom texts, which have enlarged our knowledge of that genre in the late Second Temple Period. Fragments of Job (4Q99–101), Proverbs (4Q102–103), Qohelet (4Q109–110), Ben Sira (2Q18, 11Q5 21:11–17; 22:1) and Ps. 154 (11QPs^a 18:1–16), previously only preserved in Syriac, have been known to us already, but attest to the presence of a wide range of Wisdom literature available in this period. Two manuscripts of Aramaic Targums to Job (4Q157, 11Q10) that differ from the previously extant Job Targum[1] also witness to a tradition of interpretation of the Wisdom texts. It is not surprising, therefore, to find evidence of a lively tradition of Wisdom writing in the late Second Temple period, and the previously unknown texts from Qumran amply supply this evidence.[2] There are traditional Wisdom formulations describing the righteous person (4Q420, 4Q421) or the actions of the wise (4Q413, 4Q424, 4Q425), a personification of the antonym of Wisdom (4Q184) and an historical review in the context of wisdom (4Q185; cf. Ben Sira 44–50). The many texts allow comparison with the Wisdom of Ben Sira, which until the Qumran discoveries seemed to have introduced a number of new

---

[1] See J.A. Fitzmyer, "The first century Targum of Job from Qumran Cave XI", *CBQ* 36 (1974), pp. 503–524, who shows that the language of the Qumran targum dates back at least as early as the first century B.C.E. There is a tradition that R. Gamaliel came across a written Targum of Job at around this period (*b.Shabbath* 115a), but the account reveals that this targum was officially disapproved of at the time.

[2] General surveys of the Qumran Wisdom literature can be found in L.H. Schiffman, *Reclaiming the Dead Sea Scrolls: Their true meaning for Judaism and Christianity* (New York, 1995), pp. 197–206; and J.J. Collins [1997a], *Jewish Wisdom in the Hellenistic Age* (Louisville, 1997), pp. 112–31. The texts have been translated with brief commentaries in D.J. Harrington [1996a], *Wisdom Texts from Qumran* (London, 1996), and volume 4.3 of the journal *Dead Sea Discoveries* (1997) is devoted to a discussion of them. Translations given here are my own.

features into Wisdom literature, but we can now see that these were part of a more widespread development in this genre. Collins has, therefore, spoken of a divorce of the form and world-view of this literature in the late Second Temple period, applying this particularly to the Qumran material.[3] The most important Qumran text in this regard is the extensive text known as *Sapiential Work A*,[4] which is extant in the manuscripts 1Q26, 4Q415–418 and 4Q423, although it is not impossible that some of the other Qumran sapiential fragments belong to this work.[5]

An obvious feature of the work is that it was at one time very large, although only small sections have survived in the fragments. In this respect it is similar to Ben Sira (*c.* 190 B.C.E.), the largest of the extant early Jewish Wisdom texts (amounting to 51 chapters), and it reflects an anthological approach comparable to the latter in its arrangement of groups of teaching on different themes without any obvious connection between the groups.[6] Both works also suggest an educational context for the Wisdom instructions, Ben Sira often addressing his words to "my son/pupil" (בני, e.g. 2:1, 3:17) and *Sapiential Work A* to "you understanding son/pupil" (בן מבין, e.g. 4Q417 2 i:18) or to "you who understand" (מבין, e.g. 4Q417 2 i:1, 13–14). *Sapiential Work A* is written in the Herodian script, placing the manuscripts in a period over a century later than Ben Sira, but

---

[3] J.J. Collins [1997b], "Wisdom reconsidered, in light of the Scrolls", *DSD* 4 (1997), pp. 265–281, esp. p. 280.

[4] Many scholars are beginning to prefer the title *Musar-le-Mevin* (derived from the addressees in the fragments) rather than *Sapiential Work A* for the set of fragments, since they contain much that is unfamiliar from other Wisdom texts. The title *Sapiential Work A* is kept here so that the reader may not be confused, since those works that use *Musar-le-Mevin* will usually indicate that this is also known as *Sapiential Work A*, whilst the reverse is not the case. Indeed, the argument offered here is that Wisdom is a broad concept and that the term 'Sapiential' when applied to Ben Sira is also misleading.

[5] 1Q26 has been published in D. Barthélemy and J.T. Milik, *Qumrân Cave 1*, DJD 1 (Oxford, 1955), pp. 100–102. For the cave 4 texts we must rely on preliminary editions. They have been reconstructed in B.Z. Wacholder and M.G. Abegg, *A Preliminary Edition of the Unpublished Dead Sea Scrolls: The Hebrew and Aramaic Texts from Cave Four*. Fascicle Two (Washington DC, 1994). 4Q416 and 418 have also been published in R. Eisenman and M. Wise, *The Dead Sea Scrolls Uncovered* (Shaftesbury-Rockport-Brisbane, 1992), pp. 241–255. Translations are available in F. García Martínez, *The Dead Sea Scrolls Translated* (Leiden, 1994), pp. 383–393, and Harrington (1996a), pp. 40–59.

[6] A comparison of the two works in some detail has been made by D.J. Harrington, "Two early Jewish approaches to Wisdom: Sirach and Qumran Sapiential Work A", *JSP* 16 (1997), pp. 25–28.

there is nothing in the content of the work to prevent one assuming that it may have been composed earlier. Nevertheless, the only witnesses are the manuscripts themselves and it is, therefore, perhaps a more cautious approach to maintain a date in the Herodian period for the composition of the work.[7] In the course of this article it will be suggested that the work reflects a development of the thinking of Ben Sira and hence in relative terms at least it should be placed later. As far as it is possible to reconstruct the outline of the work from the fragments,[8] it opens with traditional wisdom instructions that are concerned with topics to be found also in Ben Sira, namely financial transactions and business dealings, social relations, and relations with one's parents and wife (4Q416 2). A large margin, however, on the right-hand side of fragment 1 of 4Q416 may indicate that this was the very beginning of the work,[9] expounding God's cosmic acts and an eschatological promise for the righteous:

> In heaven He shall judge the work of wickedness, but all His children of faithfulness will be accepted with favour... And all iniquity shall come to an end until the period of destruction shall be finished. (4Q416 1:10, 13; preserved in part in 4Q418 2:2, 5)

This is where the divorce between the form (Wisdom) and worldview (formerly atemporal, now apocalyptic) takes place, and it is one of the most important contributions of the Qumran sapiential material to our understanding of the intellectual world in this period. The Wisdom instructions are placed in the context of God's ordering of the universe and they are to be undertaken in order that the righteous observer of the instructions may be vindicated at the time of judgement. Unfortunately fragment 1 is in a poor state of preservation so that little may be gleaned of its content and one may only guess at the identification of "the period of destruction". The threat of an impending judgement can also be discerned in the sapiential

---

[7] Harrington (1997), p. 25, suggests that since its emphasis on financial dealings and family matters implies an origin separate from the 'monastic' life of Qumran it is likely to have originated at a time roughly contemporaneous with Ben Sira. There is an illogicality espoused by some students of Qumran that if a text is non-sectarian it must be earlier than the community. It is, however, quite possible for a text to be written and be brought to Qumran during the lifetime of the community, or for a member to write a document that is not explicitly 'sectarian'.

[8] See T. Elgvin, "The Reconstruction of Sapiential Work A", *RQ* 16 (1995), pp. 559–580.

[9] Harrington (1996a), p. 41.

work 4Q185, and the apocalyptic notion of eternal fire for the wicked is introduced in 4Q184 (the so-called 'Wiles of the Wicked Woman').

This setting of the instructions in the context of an apocalyptic teaching concerning the vindication of the righteous may account for the emphasis on poverty throughout *Sapiential Work A*. The addressee is repeatedly reminded that he is poor (אביון אתה, e.g. 4Q416 2 iii:8, 12), borrowing is discouraged lest it increase his poverty (רושכה, 4Q416 2 iii:5–6), and he is told to honour his father "in [his] poverty" (ברושכה, 4Q416 2 iii:15). Although Harrington notes that it is hard to determine whether the prominence of the topic is an accident of preservation or an indication that it was a major theme, and whether the precise sense is economic or spiritual,[10] we can probably say of it that it seems to play an eschatological role. It is said that God has lifted up the addressee's head out of poverty and placed him in a glorious inheritance (4Q416 2 iii:9–12), and in the future judgement God will separate the good and the wicked, bringing vengeance on the "lords of iniquity" and vindication for the "poor" (4Q418 126:1–10). This continues the early biblical idea of the association of judgement with famine and salvation with plenty (Amos 4:7; 9:13–15), but a trend towards emphasizing the role of poverty in future speculation may be observed in the post-exilic period. In Hag. 1:6 the impoverished situation of the post-exilic community is described before the command to rebuild the Temple and the subsequent prosperity. "Those that earn wages," the prophet proclaims, "earn them to put into a bag with holes". The Targum to this verse translates צְרוֹר נָקוּב, "a bag with holes", by the Hebrew loanword מאירתא, "curse", which, although clarifying the meaning of the Hebrew, expresses more succinctly the impoverished state of the returnees. Not only is a cursed state associated with deprivation, but the semantic range of the Hebrew מארדה soon came to include poverty. The Vulgate and LXX of Deut. 28:20 (*fames*, ἔνδεια) and Prov. 28:27 (*egestas*, ἀπορία) and the Peshitta of Deut. 28:20 (*ḥwsrn'*) all understand מארדה to denote "want, poverty", as it came to mean in some instances in Rabbinic Hebrew (e.g. p.Sanh 28b, 29d, b.Ber 20b).[11]

---

[10] Harrington (1997), p. 29. Collins (1997a), pp. 118–19, opts for reading a physical poverty in the context of the guidance on financial matters and business dealings.

[11] There is already in the MT an association between curse and poverty at Prov. 28:27 where the curse connoted poverty, as also indicated by the LXX translation

The Targum to the Minor Prophets, which is certainly post-70 C.E. in its final composition but probably contains earlier traditions,[12] expresses an interest in the life that the righteous will enjoy in a new world (e.g. Targum to Hab. 3:2; Mic. 7:14) once the present order has been disbanded, and at Hag. 1:6 it may be attempting to underscore the former state from which the righteous will be delivered. In the book of Malachi a series of blessings and curses are uttered (3:6–12) before the writing down of those who fear the Lord (3:13–21) and before the prediction of the day of the Lord (3:22–24). God has already threatened to send a מארה upon the priests (Mal. 2:2), and then He declares in 3:9 that the whole nation is cursed with a מארה (Vulgate again translates as *penuria*) "because you are robbing me". There may be an irony implied in the prophet's words if God is going to deprive those who are depriving Him,[13] but certainly throughout this section there is an alternation between deprivation and reward. It is significant that the writer of *Sapiential Work A* alludes to Malachi in speaking of a "book of remembrance" (4Q417 2 i:15, 16) that is written in the presence of the Lord (cf. Mal. 3:16), and in the context of the Qumran text it seems to have apocalyptic overtones.[14] If the author of *Sapiential Work A* had been familiar with these texts and had he known of the semantic range of מארה, as the Versions would imply is possible, it may explain his apparent emphasis on poverty as a prelude to the Lord's deliverance. There may well have been increasing speculation in his time concerning the nature of poverty, as inferred from Malachi and possibly the Targum to Haggai. Indeed, in one second century B.C.E. text, the Epistle of Enoch (*1 Enoch* 92–105), the poverty of the addressees is implied and that too is in an apocalyptic context, promising restitution to the poor in the life to come.[15]

---

there. Ben Sira cautions his readers to avoid being cursed by the poor, to whose curse God will listen (4:5–6). It seems more likely that the Targum understands the lexeme as "poverty" than that it is treating נְקֻב as if it derived from נקב II (Lev. 24:11, 16). See K.J. Cathcart and R.P. Gordon, *The Targum of the Minor Prophets, translated with a critical introduction, appendix and notes*, The Aramaic Bible 14 (Edinburgh, 1989), p. 177.

[12] See Cathcart and Gordon (1989), pp. 16–18.

[13] On the irony of the curses as a reversal of the priestly blessing in Malachi, see M. Fishbane, *Biblical Interpretation in Ancient Israel* (Oxford, 1985), p. 333.

[14] A discussion of the book of remembrance and its context in *Sapiential Work A* can be found in A. Lange, *Weisheit und Prädestination: Weisheitliche Urordnung und Prädestination in den Textfunden von Qumran* (Leiden, 1995), pp. 66–90.

[15] Collins (1997a), p. 119, notes the comparison with the Qumran text, but does

The cosmology, ethics and apocalyptic of *Sapiential Work A* is rooted in an understanding that is expressed by the oblique term רז נהיה ("the mystery that is to be"),[16] which, according to Harrington,[17] occurs approximately thirty five times in the extant portions of the work. Honouring one's parents is encouraged, for example, since they uncovered one's ear to the רז נהיה (4Q416 2 iii:17), and the one who is poor is advised to study it (4Q416 2 iii:14). There is no definition given for the term, it being assumed that the reader would know to what it refers, whilst we are left to infer as much as we can from the context. The noun רז is a Persian loan-word, which is to be found, perhaps significantly, nine times in the Aramaic of Daniel and at Qumran many times in the *Community Rule* and 1QH. It is also to be found a few times in the *Book of Mysteries*, the closest in thought to *Sapiential Work A* and a text that contains the whole expression רז נהיה (also at 1QS 11:3–4).[18] The niphal participle נהיה occurs alone at 1QS 3:15 and CD 2:10. In *Sapiential Work A* the meaning of the expression can be discerned by its use in some instances with other phrases, which as Harrington has shown reveal that the mystery concerns creation, ethics, and eschatology, or, as Collins puts it, the mystery "seems to encompass the entire divine plan, from creation to eschatological judgment".[19] 4Q417 1 i:10–12 speaks of it in this manner: "Gaze on the רז נהיה and understand the birth-time of salvation, and know who is to inherit glory and evil". Whether the mystery is a book or body of teaching or more generally an understanding of the divine plan,[20] it is not clear, but the reference to the book of remembrance does suggest that there may be some specific teaching in mind.

---

not consider an eschatological connotation to the repeated references to poverty. In the Epistle of Enoch the emphasis rests on condemnation of the rich, including a series of pronouncements of woes against them.

[16] Eisenman and Wise (1992), pp. 241–255, translate the expression as "the mystery of existence", but its future rather than existential aspect is probably uppermost in view of its context in the work. Although it is not prefixed by a definite article, this is not unknown in Late Biblical Hebrew.

[17] D.J. Harrington [1996b], "The *raz nihyeh* in a Qumran Wisdom text (1Q26, 4Q415–418, 423)", *RQ* 17 (1996), p. 550.

[18] Published by L. Schiffman in T. Elgvin et al., *Qumran Cave 4. XV*, DJD 20 (Oxford, 1997), pp. 31–123.

[19] Harrington (1997), p. 35; (1996b), pp. 549–553; Collins (1997a), p. 122.

[20] Suggestions as to what the teaching or book are have been made by Harrington (1996b), pp. 552–553, and Collins (1997a), p. 123. Wacholder and Abegg (1994), p. xiii, also consider it to be a specific piece of writing, but there seems no reason to tie it to specific ideas or texts beyond the illusory book of remembrance.

The book of remembrance was given to man (אנוש) as an inheritance, but since the spirit of flesh does not distinguish between good
and evil, it is no longer bestowed to them, implying that only the
spiritual ones now receive it (4Q417 2 i:14–18).[21]·The addressee is
urged, following the report of this book, to "gaze on the mystery
that is to be and know the inheritance of all living", which relates
the inheritance of the book to the inheritance of all living, which
can be discerned by studying the רז נהיה. The book of remembrance
is mentioned alongside "the vision of meditation" (חזון ההגי), whose
meaning is not certain, but probably refers to the task of gazing
upon the mystery or the study of the book of remembrance. Later
on the addressee is told to "know . . . every vision" (4Q417 2 i:22,
כול חזון [ ] דע), and this is probably an indication of the acceptance
of a prophetic form, the vision, into the genre of Wisdom.[22] Although
visions may not have been an important feature of the revelation of
divine wisdom, it is one of many similarities to the language of the
Hebrew portions of the book of Daniel, and in that respect has asso-
ciations with apocalyptic.[23] Another similarity is the verb נלה "to uncover, reveal", which is used five times with the expression רז נהיה,
in the phrase "to uncover the ear (אוזן)" and has connotations of
revelation.[24]

Despite many similarities between Ben Sira and the Qumran Wisdom literature, they are normally contrasted when it comes to the
subject of apocalyptic speculation and divine revelation. Elgvin, for
example, observes how the apocalyptic motifs set *Sapiential Work A*
apart from Ben Sira,[25] and Harrington notes apocalyptic's "relative
absence in Sirach, and its impressive presence in Sapiential Work A
from Qumran".[26] Schiffman likewise concludes with reference to the
Book of Mysteries that, "This text, together with the related *Sapiential
Works*, encourages the reader to investigate these mysteries, as opposed

---

[21] The author seems to interpret Gen. 1–3 as recounting the creation of two
Adams corresponding to two types of humanity, a spiritual people and a "spirit of
flesh". Philo also derived a double creation of man from an exegesis of the biblical text (e.g. *de Opif.* 134–35). See Collins (1997a), pp. 124–125.

[22] So Collins (1997a), p. 125.

[23] T. Elgvin, "Early Essene Eschatology: Judgment and Salvation according to
Sapiential Work A", in D.W. Parry and S.D. Ricks (eds.), *Current Research and
Technological Developments on the Dead Sea Scrolls*, Studies on the Texts of the Desert
of Judah 20 (Leiden, 1996), pp. 131, 136.

[24] Harrington (1996b), p. 552.

[25] Elgvin (1996), p. 136, n. 23.

[26] Harrington (1997), p. 26.

to Ben Sira and the Rabbis, who discourage this speculation."[27] Whilst it is correct to draw a distinction between the thought of Ben Sira and, at least, *Sapiential Work A*, this distinction can often be over-simplified and ignore some of the possible similarities. A study of Ben Sira will assist in tracing the development of apocalyptic thought in Wisdom literature and will show how this author occupies a position between the biblical writings and the overtly apocalyptic Qumran texts.

The Wisdom of Ben Sira may appear to be an odd work to study for suggestions of apocalyptic thinking, since Boccaccini has shown how Ben Sira differs from two apocalyptic works (The Book of Watchers and the Book of Astronomy) in a number of respects.[28] There is a risk in Boccaccini's approach that apocalyptic is reduced merely to a series of features. Instead, in works that are not part of the literary genre itself, apocalyptic should be seen as a general interest in divine revelation, access to the divine will and in images associated with the eschaton. Nonetheless, Ben Sira himself appears to castigate research into such speculative matters (3:21–24):[29]

3:21   What is too sublime (פלאות) for you, seek not (תדרוש);
       into things beyond your strength, search not.[30]
3:22   What is committed to you, attend to;
       what is hidden (נסתרות) is not your concern (עסק).
3:23   With what is beyond you, meddle not;
       more than enough for you has been shown you (הראית).
3:24   Indeed, many are the speculations of human beings –
       evil and misleading fancies.

---

[27] Schiffman (1995), p. 210.

[28] G. Boccaccini, *Middle Judaism: Jewish Thought, 300 B.C.E. to 200 C.E.*, with a forward by J.H. Charlesworth (Minneapolis, 1991), p. 79. A simplistic definition of apocalyptic has enabled a distinction to be drawn between Ben Sira and apocalyptic writers by J. Cook, *The Septuagint of Proverbs – Jewish and/or Hellenistic Proverbs? Concerning the Hellenistic Colouring of LXX Proverbs* (Leiden-New York-Köln, 1997), pp. 332–333.

[29] The Hebrew of Ben Sira is from P.C. Beentjes, *The Book of Ben Sira in Hebrew: A Text Edition of All Extant Hebrew Manuscripts and a Synopsis of All Parallel Hebrew Ben Sira Texts* (Leiden-New York-Köln, 1997), the verse numbering is that of the Greek manuscripts, as given in J. Ziegler, *Sapientia Iesu Filii Sirach*, Septuaginta 12/2 (Göttingen, 1965), and the translations are those of P.W. Skehan and A.A. Di Lella, *The Wisdom of Ben Sira*, Anchor Bible 39 (New York, 1987).

[30] The translation for verse 21 is of Hebrew MS A. R.A. Argall, *1 Enoch and Sirach: A Comparative Literary and Conceptual Analysis of the Themes of Revelation, Creation and Judgment*, Early Judaism and its Literature 8 (Atlanta, 1995), p. 75, prefers the (slightly different) reading of MS C, whilst B.G. Wright, "'Fear the Lord and Honor the Priest'. Ben Sira as defender of the Jerusalem Priesthood", in P.C. Beentjes (ed.), *The Book of Ben Sira in Modern Research* BZAW 255 (Berlin-New York, 1997),

Despite the vagueness of the language in this passage it has been interpreted as a polemic against either Greek philosophical enquiry[31] or apocalyptic speculation (sometimes under the influence of b.Hag 13a and its corresponding mishnaic text).[32] The tendency with such suggestions is that the vocabulary in the passage is not considered in terms of the rest of the book. Therefore, the proposal of Prockter that Ben Sira would have been opposed to *merkabah* mysticism seems unlikely in view of the vision of the chariot (*merkabah*) being one of the very features that the scribe attributes to the prophet Ezekiel. In an extended analysis of possible polemical features in Ben Sira, Wright interprets this passage, with reference to other portions of Ben Sira, as a warning to his students not to investigate the secrets of the created order or the revelation of the future, topics studied by those responsible for portions of *1 Enoch*.[33] He is correct to observe that פלאות denotes the works of God (Ben Sira 11:4, 43:25) and that נסתרות are concerned with what the future holds (Ben Sira 42:19, 48:25). The problem is that Ben Sira is ambiguous in much of what he writes, often alluding without giving explicit assent to issues. Therefore, although 3:21–24 seems clear on the issue, in the very next chapter Ben Sira states that "I [Wisdom] will reveal (נליתי) to him [her follower] my secrets (מסתרי)" (4:18), choosing the same root as that of נסתרות. Of particular interest is that Ben Sira, in his review of history, devotes most space to Isaiah of all the prophets. This is probably because (trito-)Isaiah's vision of an ideal Jerusalem is fulfilled in the time of Ben Sira, who presents a glorious picture of his contemporary Simeon II celebrating in the Temple. Earlier in the book Ben Sira had prayed for the "vision" (חזון) to be renewed (36:(17)20), including the visitation of divine glory in the Temple (36:(16)19), and this is realized, he believes, in his day. Isaiah is spoken of as seeing

---

p. 208, n. 63, argues for a combination of A and C in the light of the Greek translation. The differences are not significant for our purposes.

[31] E.g. M. Hengel, *Judentum und Hellenismus: Studien zu ihrer Begegnung unter besonderer Berücksichtigung Palästinas bis zur Mitte des 2. Jhs v. Chr.*, WUNT 10 (Tübingen, 1969), p. 254; = *Judaism and Hellenism: Studies in their Encounter in the Early Hellenistic Period* (London, one volume edition, 1981), pp. 139–140; Skehan and Di Lella (1987), pp. 160–161.

[32] E.g. I. Gruenwald, *From Apocalypticism to Gnosticism: Studies in Apocalypticism, Merkavah Mysticism and Gnosticism*, BEAT 14 (Frankfurt, 1988), pp. 17–18; L.J. Prockter, "Torah as a Fence against Apocalyptic Speculation: Ben Sira 3. 17–24", in *Proceedings of the 10th World Congress of Jewish Studies (Jerusalem, August 16–24, 1989)*. Division A: The Bible and its World (Jerusalem, 1990), pp. 245–252.

[33] Wright (1997), pp. 208–212.

the future in a vision (חזה אחרית, 48:24), and in particular, "he foretold what should be (נהיות) till the end of time, hidden things (נסתרות)
that were yet to be fulfilled" (48:25). Here Ben Sira reveals his own
interest in the prophetic art of revealing in visions both what will
be (as in Qumran the niphal of "to be")[34] and the hidden things
that in 3:22 one should not investigate. Wright admits that Isaiah
has been shown these future realities, but that Ben Sira is distrust-
ful of them and feels he has already been shown enough, especially
since he does not anywhere make pretensions about knowing the
future.[35] Since, however, Ben Sira believes that he himself has
prophetic-like inspiration (e.g. 24:33) it would be surprising were he
to write about Isaiah in such terms without implying that his prophetic wisdom furnished him with similar faculties. As he presumably
saw himself as a true disciple of Wisdom, he would expect Wisdom
to reveal her "secrets" to him (cf. 4:18).

    The role of God as the purveyor of Wisdom is important in this
regard. He, as Wisdom, "makes known (מחוה) the past and the future
(נהיות), and reveals (מגלה) the deepest secrets (נסתרות)" (42:19), suggesting that it is God, perhaps through Wisdom, who reveals to
Isaiah the נהיות and נסתרות. Ben Sira uses the two terms in parallelism with each other (although they are not so found in the Hebrew
Bible), as he does when speaking of Isaiah's vision, and the verbs
collocated with them both connote revelatory activity (as in 4:18).
This statement on God's activity forms parts of Ben Sira's description of the created order, and in that respect implies that through
studying the creation one can come to know God's secrets. It is also
significant that this description of creation precedes the review of
Israel's history ("The Praise of the Fathers"), inviting the comparison to be drawn that as God and Wisdom can be seen in creation,
so also can they be seen in history. For Ben Sira, as for the author
of *Sapiential Work A*, creation and history are the sources for revelation and the understanding of God's plan.[36] Ben Sira differed,
however, in his more cautious statement of his position and in his
belief in the equation of Wisdom with Torah (24:23), which may

---

[34] The plural of נהיה is also found in CD 2:10, where it refers to predictions
about the future.

[35] Wright (1997), pp. 210–211.

[36] On Ben Sira's view of revelation, see also in brief M.N.A. Bockmuehl, *Revelation
and Mystery in Ancient Judaism and Pauline Christianity*, WUNT 2/36 (Tübingen, 1990),
pp. 66–67.

also indicate that for him revelation could be achieved through the study of the Torah.

Given Ben Sira's apparent interest in revelation and prediction of the future, it is informative to see what he has to say on the figure of Enoch, who played a prominent role in apocalyptic thought. At 44:16 he writes:

> Enoch walked with the Lord and was taken up,
> a sign for the knowledge (אות דעת) of future generations.

It is now probable from the omission of 44:16 in the Masada scroll, as well as from the Syriac version, that this first reference to Enoch is not in its original position. Yadin argues that the verse should be combined with a reference to Enoch at 49:14, assuming an early attempt to expunge part of Ben Sira's observations of Enoch in chapter 49 and to insert them in their chronological order before Noah.[37] A gap visible in the Masada fragment before Noah to indicate the start of a new section would have allowed an editor plenty of space to insert an additional verse.[38] Middendorp[39] and Mack, on the other hand, argue for no basis of originality for the reference in 44:16, Mack going as far as to suggest that the Greek and the Hebrew have nothing in common but the mention of Enoch, and that, therefore, one version is a later redaction in terms of the other.[40] The mention of Enoch walking with the Lord (44:16a) is a reference to Gen. 5:24, but what is more interesting is the appearance of the motifs of the transportation to heaven (49:14) and of the knowledge of Enoch (44:16b). Contradictory statements as to the implications of these motifs have been made. On the one hand, the knowledge of Enoch has been understood as referring to apocalyptic knowledge, which was later attributed to his communion with God after he had been transported alive to heaven.[41] On the other, Hayward suggests that Ben Sira's attitude to Enoch is "muted", possibly as a result of his suspicion of

---

[37] Y. Yadin, *The Ben Sira Scroll from Masada* (Jerusalem, 1965), p. 38.

[38] See the facsimile in *ibid.*, plate 8.

[39] T. Middendorp, *Die Stellung Jesu Ben Siras zwischen Judentum und Hellenismus* (Leiden, 1973), pp. 53–54.

[40] B.L. Mack, *Wisdom and the Hebrew Epic: Ben Sira's Hymn in Praise of the Fathers*, Chicago Studies in the History of Judaism (Chicago, 1985), pp. 199–200. The Greek text says that Enoch was a "sign of repentance" (ὑπόδειγμα μετανοίας).

[41] J.T. Milik, with the collaboration of M. Black, *The Books of Enoch: Aramaic Fragments of Qumrân Cave 4* (Oxford, 1976), p. 11.

"Apocalyptic".[42] In similar fashion, Wright sees it as "little more than a tipping of the hat to Enoch, a somewhat veiled acknowledgment of these traditions".[43] This second opinion may be based upon an unfair comparison with the more developed legends of Enoch, and the fact that Ben Sira alludes to something, if only briefly, should be taken seriously. He is highly selective both in the choice of people he mentions and in what he says of them.

The meaning of דעת has become clearer with the discovery at Qumran of Aramaic fragments of *1 Enoch*, which have enabled us to date more accurately the various sections of the book. The oldest MS, 4QEnastr^a, has been dated to the mid-third or early second century B.C.E., i.e. to the same period as Ben Sira. As this section of *1 Enoch* is the 'Astronomical Book', we may say that in Ben Sira's time Enoch's knowledge would at least have signified astronomical, especially calendrical, knowledge. Milik suggests that Ben Sira had the 'Book of Watchers' also in mind and hence the דעת also signifies apocalyptic knowledge. דעת is the normal designation for ethical knowledge in the Wisdom literature;[44] Ben Sira appears to combine the Wisdom of the sage with calendrical knowledge, a combination that he reveals in his own writing when describing the created order. One may also compare *Jubilees* 4:17,[45] where Enoch, who was the first among men to learn writing and *knowledge*, was set in Eden "as a *sign* that he should recount all the deeds of the generations until the day of condemnation". In the *Genesis Apocryphon* Methuselah is said to have gone to his father Enoch "to learn from him all in truth" (column ii, l. 22).[46] Unfortunately for our purposes the meeting between the two is missing from the extant manuscript, and we may have learnt more from that event. Nevertheless, it does demonstrate that there was an early tradition of Enoch's prophetic knowledge, and Ben Sira's allusion to the knowledge of Enoch may

[42] C.T.R. Hayward, "The New Jerusalem in the Wisdom of Jesus Ben Sira", *SJOT* 6 (1992), p. 131, n. 18.

[43] Wright (1997), p. 216.

[44] So C. Taylor and J.H.A. Hart, "Two Notes on Enoch in Sir. xliv 16", *JTS* 4 (1902–1903), p. 591.

[45] E.g. P. Grelot, "La Légende d'Hénoch dans les Apocryphes et dans la Bible: Origine et Signification", *RSR* 46 (1958), pp. 181–182; J.C. VanderKam, *Enoch and the Growth of an Apocalyptic Tradition*, CBQ monograph series 16 (Washington, 1984), p. 88, n. 40.

[46] N. Avigad and Y. Yadin (eds.), *A Genesis Apocryphon: A Scroll from the Wilderness of Judaea* (Jerusalem, 1956), pp. 16–17.

well have included this. He does not express any disapproval of this knowledge, and hence was reflecting the current trend towards granting to Enoch a mythical status.

In comparing Ben Sira and *Sapiential Work A* it can be seen that the Wisdom text is explicit where Ben Sira is implicit. *Sapiential Work A* has a clearly defined understanding of the divine plan in its expectation for the wise, its belief in the obscure רז נהיה and its awareness of the book of remembrance. It also betrays a belief in angels, and its appeal to special revelation is contrary to the spirit of traditional Wisdom literature.[47] Ben Sira may have implied that the sage had special insight, but that insight was available to all who were willing to devote themselves to Wisdom. Ben Sira shares with Qumran the vocabulary of revelation, visions, and "what is to be", as well as with other Qumran texts of "hidden things", and the prevalence of such terms in many Qumran texts suggests that perhaps by the time of Ben Sira these terms had apocalyptic connotations. Ben Sira's reserve in his thinking, counselling against (improper?) investigation into such matters, may place him in a time earlier than the authors of the Qumran sapiential texts. If Ben Sira is taken as the first traces of apocalyptic thinking in Wisdom literature, it has arisen as the result of the special learning that a follower of Wisdom acquires and from meditation on the acts of God in creation and history. It is significant in this regard that *Sapiential Work A* opens with references to the cosmos and that the Wisdom of Solomon combines its historical portrayal with apocalyptic overtones concerning the judgement of the dead.[48] It was the preserve of a wise man to consider the world and to derive a religious understanding from it. Both Ben Sira and the author of *Sapiential Work A* are united in trying to do this, and where they differ is the extent to which they wish to develop their apocalyptic leanings. It is a pleasure to offer this article to a scholar who has always been meticulous in his research and observant in his belief, and, like the Wisdom writers, has delighted in encouraging his students to seek after understanding.

---

[47] Collins (1997a), p. 128.
[48] See J.J. Collins, "Cosmos and Salvation: Jewish Wisdom and Apocalyptic in the Hellenistic Age", *HR* 17 (1977), pp. 121–142.

JUDITH, TOBIT, AHIQAR AND HISTORY[1]

ALAN MILLARD

Liverpool

"In the twelfth year of the reign of Nebuchadnezzar, who ruled the Assyrians from his great city of Nineveh, Arphaxad was ruling the Medes from Ecbatana" (Judith 1:1, *REB*). In these terms the book of Judith claims a chronological setting with the correlation and location of two emperors. Subsequent verses tell of a war between the two kings, which Nebuchadnezzar won in his seventeenth year, killing Arphaxad. Failure by people of the Levant to send troops in support of Nebuchadnezzar resulted in his charging his general, Holofernes, to subdue the region in the next, his eighteenth, year. The Israelites living in Judaea were terrified at the news of his approach, "They had just returned from captivity, and only recently had all the people been reunited in Judaea, and the sacred vessels, the altar, and the temple been sanctified after their desecration" (4:3, *REB*). Joakim the High Priest rallied them to resist. There is no need to relate the rest of the story. This summary is sufficient to demonstrate the author's historical confusion; we shall not consider the equally eccentric geography of the book.[2]

1. Nebuchadnezzar did not rule from Nineveh and it was certainly not his capital (its description "the great city" is identical with Jon. 1:2; 3:2 LXX), nor was he deemed king of Assyria, as Judith consistently portrays him (cf. the Assyrian army, 2:14; 5:1, etc.; an Assyrian outpost, 14:2,3; Assyrians 14:12 and Assyria 15:6). It is just possible that the name 'Assyria' lived on into the Persian period as a general term for an empire based in Mesopotamia, as in Ezra 6:22,[3]

---

[1] This is an expanded version of a paper entitled "Facts Fade as Time Passes" read at The XVI Congress of the International Organisation for the Study of the Old Testament held in Oslo, 2–7 August, 1998.

[2] On Judith and on Tobit see the extensive discussions by C.A. Moore in the *Anchor Bible Commentary, Judith* and *Tobit* (New York, 1985 and 1996).

[3] I am grateful to Peter Williams for drawing my attention to this point; see H.G.M. Williamson, *Ezra, Nehemiah* (Waco, 1985) *ad loc.*

just as the Greeks referred to the Persians as Medes long after Median power had disappeared, but it is not clear it was still current in this way when Judith was written.

2. There was no king of Media named Arphaxad. Nebuchadnezzar's contemporaries were Cyaxares (in cuneiform Umakištar) and Astyages (Ištumegu),[4] and there is nothing in the meagre surviving sources to hint that Nebuchadnezzar conquered a Median king or looted Ecbatana.

3. The general Holofernes bears a name of Old Persian type and so does his steward Bagoas, but all the known names of Nebuchadnezzar's officials are Babylonian, both those known from Babylonian sources, such as Nabu-zer-ibni, Atkal-ana-Mar-Esagila, Bel-eresh,[5] and those known from biblical texts, Nergal-sharezer (Jer. 39:3, 13), who eventually ruled Babylon 559–553 B.C.E. and is known through Greek authors as Neriglissar, Nebushazban (Jer. 39:13), Nebuzaradan (Jer. 39:13; 40:1,5; 41:10; 43:6; 52:12,15,26 = 2 Kgs. 25:8,11,20).

4. Nebuchadnezzar's twelfth year was 593–92 B.C., his seventeenth 588–87. Far from Israelites recently returning to Jerusalem and rebuilding the Temple, their earlier deportations to Babylon had not long taken place in 593; in 587–86, Nebuchadnezzar's eighteenth year, the final attack on Jerusalem was under way, bringing the destruction of the city and the Temple and another deportation.

Reasons for these divergences from known history have been sought in the supposition of several stages in the story's growth or in the use of code-names. Apart from Nebuchadnezzar and Assyria, there are other indications of a Persian context, hence some have found an Achaemenid ruler behind Nebuchadnezzar, usually Artaxerxes III Ochus (358–338 B.C.E.). He had a general Holofernes with a servant Bagoas and Nehemiah mentions a post-exilic Joiakim (12:26). Yet even if the author was disguising the tyrant of his own time, he left the villain, Holofernes, marked with a Persian name. Alternatively, it is suggested, a second century author might have wished to conceal references to Seleucid kings, choosing pseudonyms which would be transparent to his Jewish readers. Neither supposition explains or excuses the chronological muddle. Either the author purposely con-

---

[4] See A.K. Grayson, *Assyrian and Babylonian Chronicles* (Locust Valley, NY, 1975), pp. 212, 214.
[5] Many are listed on a prism from Babylon, E. Unger, *Babylon, die heilige Stadt* (Berlin, 1931), pp. 282–94; cf. A.L. Oppenheim in *ANET*, pp. 307–08.

structed a setting, with the Babylonian king victorious far away to the east at the time when Jewish historians told of his attack on Jerusalem, which he expected his audience, aware of their national history, would understand to be artificial, or he had little knowledge and did not anticipate others to be better educated.

The other book of Hellenistic date to be discussed, which relates a story in an earlier historical setting, is Tobit. Again, the narrator's opening is significant: "This is the story of Tobit . . . of the tribe of Naphtali. In the time of King Shalmaneser of Assyria he was taken captive from Thisbe which is south of Kedesh-naphtali in Upper Galilee above Hazor" (1:1–3). Tobit himself continues, "After the deportation to Assyria in which I was taken captive and came to Nineveh. . . . the Most High endowed me with a presence which won me the favour of Shalmaneser, and I became his buyer of supplies . . . Shalmaneser died and was succeeded by his son Sennacherib . . . the king was murdered by two of his sons, and . . . his son Esarhaddon succeeded to the throne" (1:10,13,15,21). Recently C.A. Moore has followed earlier commentators in affirming that the book displays "errors" which "argue against the story's being essentially historical".[6] Examples given are:

1. the exile of the tribe of Naphtali by Shalmaneser [V], not by Tiglath-pileser III, as in 2 Kgs. 15:29;

2. Sennacherib being the 'son' of Shalmaneser when, in fact, he was the son of Shalmaneser's successor, Sargon II, who does not appear in Tobit, and who was possibly another son of Tiglath-pileser III;[7]

3. Tobit was taken to Nineveh and there gained Shalmaneser's favour, although that city was not the royal seat at the time, Shalmaneser having most likely resided at Kalah (Nimrud) where his father had built a palace and where the only known inscriptions of Shalmaneser V were found, a series of bronze weights bearing his name and titles in cuneiform, with their values also in Aramaic.[8]

---

[6] Moore (1996), p. 9.

[7] F. Thomas, "Sargon II., der Sohn Tiglat-pilesers III.," in M. Dietrich and O. Loretz, (eds.), *Mesopotamica – Ugaritica-Biblica: Festschrift Kurt Bergerhof* AOAT 232 (Neukirchen-Vluyn, 1985), pp. 465–70.

[8] T.C. Mitchell, "The Bronze Lion Weights from Nimrud," *Res Orientales* 2 (1990), pp. 124–38; F.M. Fales, "Assyro-Aramaica: The Assyrian Lion Weights," in K. van Lerberghe and A. Schoors (eds.), *Immigration and Emigration within the Ancient Near East: Festschrift E. Lipiński*, Orientalia Lovaniensia Analecta 65 (Leuven, 1995), pp. 33–55.

These matters are not all serious, and some may only appear to be erroneous. The biblical report of Tiglath-pileser deporting the Naphtalites does not imply a single action complete in one year (733–32 B.C.E.): the process may have been extended. More likely, Shalmaneser may have repeated the policy as he came to reduce the rebel Hoshea in Samaria in 725 B.C.E. After Shalmaneser's death rebellion broke out in several Levantine cities and Sargon claimed the capture of Samaria and deportation of its citizens after he had crushed that revolt. Making Sennacherib the son of Shalmaneser is a common form of 'telescoping' and 'son' need not be taken literally, as many cases show. Tobit is mistaken in its last verse, naming the Median king who captured Nineveh in alliance with the Babylonians as Assuerus. Assuerus is an alternative to Xerxes as a Greek rendering of Ahasuerus (cf. Ezra 4:6). That name is given in Daniel 9:1 for the father of Darius the Mede and the gentilic may have suggested that name to the author of Tobit. The ruler in question was Cyaxares (c. 623–584 B.C.E.). Whether these ameliorations are acceptable or not, Tobit does display a good level of historical accuracy and has the Assyrian kings in their correct sequence: Shalmaneser V, [Sargon,] Sennacherib, Esarhaddon. That can be explained if the greater part of the framework of the story is drawn from the biblical text of Kings and from the Aramaic narrative of Ahiqar which, likewise, have the Assyrian kings correctly, Ahiqar representing the Assyrian court well and supplying Tobit with the details of Ahiqar's court position (1:21). Only the final verse of Tobit fails, choosing to give to the Median conqueror of Nineveh a wrong name, applied to a Mede in another context.

In contrast, the book of Judith has no evident sources. While the personal names are found elsewhere or are plausible, the historical setting is wrong, derived distantly from biblical texts. In this respect Judith displays a sort of historical confusion exhibited by other Hellenistic texts which purport to tell of ancient near eastern history. Much of the blame for their misrepresentations has to be laid upon Ctesias of Cnidos, the doctor who worked at the Persian court of Artaxerxes II (405–359 B.C.E.) and wrote a notoriously garbled and erroneous account of history and customs, the *Persica*.[9] Later Greek authors drew on that rather than the more accurate reports

---

[9] F.W. König, *Die Persika des Ktesias von Knidos* AfO Beiheft 18 (Graz, 1972); see R. Drews, *The Greek Accounts of Eastern History* (Cambridge, MA, 1973), pp. 113–17.

of Berossus, the Babylonian priest who wrote his *Babyloniaca* about a century later.[10] The ignorance which existed is exemplified by the Jewish historian Eupolemus, working in the first century B.C.E. He followed Ctesias in naming Nebuchadnezzar's Median contemporary Astibares (Fragment 4), and may have indulged in invention in calling the Pharaoh of Solomon's day Vaphres (Fragment 2.30–32), using the name of Hophra (589–570 B.C.E.) known from Jeremiah's prophecy (Jer. 44:30; LXX 51:30, Ουαφρη),[11] rather as the author of Tobit used Assuerus. Josephus, too, suffered from inadequate information: at one point "there are grounds for believing that Josephus 'reduced' the Persian period by at least as much as two generations" in identifying Artaxerxes II with Artaxerxes III, perhaps Darius II with Darius III and Sanballat, governor of Samaria in Nehemiah's time with his namesake Sanballat of the mid-fourth century.[12]

Patently, the availability of sources affected the accuracy of these Hellenistic writings. Some authors, like Ctesias, wanted to parade their knowledge and either created information to fill gaps or put together whatever they could learn, hoping it would be satisfactory to their audiences. Others built up a picture which they thought adequate on the basis of the information available to them, as the author of Judith did for the background to the story and as Eupolemus and Josephus did, lacking better sources, or not knowing they existed. For all of these authors it is fair to suppose that there were problems of access to sources and barriers of language – and educated Greeks apparently had an aversion to reading foreign languages. Although it is wrong to suggest books were rare, they were not in everyone's hands, and a writer might find it difficult to gain access to the most relevant or most reputable works, even if he knew they existed. (Josephus under the imperial aegis in Rome was in a privileged position to command the works he needed, yet he was still restricted.) Although Aramaic had spread throughout the Persian empire as an administrative tool, imperial decrees were issued in it and Darius' 'Behistun' text was available in Aramaic in fifth century

---

[10] See S.M. Burstein, *The Babyloniaca of Berossus: Sources from the Ancient Near East* 1.5 (Malibu, CA, 1978).

[11] B.Z. Wacholder, *Eupolemus: A Study of Judaeo-Greek Literature* (Cincinnati, 1974), pp. 230–36, 135–36; F. Fallon, 'Eupolemus' in J.H. Charlesworth (ed.), *The Old Testament Pseudepigrapha* 2 (London, 1985), pp. 861–72.

[12] H.G.M. Williamson, "The Historical Value of Josephus' *Jewish Antiquities* XI. 297–301", *JTS* 28 (1977), pp. 49–66, see p. 64.

B.C.E. Elephantine,[13] hardly any literature survives in contemporary form. The Words of Ahiqar remain the only extensive example, although the Bar Punesh fragment[14] and the historical romance on the walls of the Sheikh Fadl tomb in Egypt[15] imply that there was much more. (The oldest extant text of Ahiqar is Achaemenid: the composition itself may be earlier, even from the time of Esarhaddon according to the late Jonas Greenfield.)[16] That there were straightforward historical narratives and chronicles about that time has to remain conjectural (the book of Esther's story about a record of notable events kept and read to Xerxes, is suggestive, Est. 2:23; 6:1, 2). There is no indication that the cuneiform tablets or monuments of the Assyrians and Babylonians were commonly translated into Aramaic. The remnant of the cuneiform writing scribes in Babylonia who maintained their skills at least as late as the first century C.E. could transfer texts from Akkadian into Aramaic and from Akkadian into Greek, but there is little evidence of Greek authors seeking such lore. The priest Berossus is the only Babylonian who is known to have written an account of his nation's past for a Greek audience, drawing upon native sources such as the Babylonian King Lists and Chronicles. His work is only accessible through quotations made by Josephus and later authors from the extracts and summaries Alexander Polyhistor prepared in the first century C.E. Nevertheless, what is preserved is reliable in its sequence of events and rulers for the first millennium B.C.E., although there are some puzzling details. Equally close to Babylonian sources for the sequence of kings is the Canon of Ptolemy, where we note especially how the years when Sennacherib ruled Babylon are labelled 'kingless', in exactly the same way as the Babylonian Chronicle treated them.[17] Without the cuneiform texts, it is true, many of the Assyrian and Babylonian royal names in these two Greek books would be hard to comprehend, such major ones as Merodach-baladan, Sennacherib and Nebuchadnezzar perhaps

---

[13] B. Porten, A. Yardeni, *Textbook of Aramaic Documents from Ancient Egypt. 3. Literature, Accounts, Lists* (Jerusalem, 1993), pp. 59–71.

[14] Porten and Yardeni (1993), pp. 54–57.

[15] A. Lemaire, "Les inscriptions araméennes de Cheikh-Fadl (Égypte)," in M. Geller, J.C. Greenfield and M.P. Weitzman, (eds.), *Studia Aramaica*, Journal of Semitic Studies Supplement 4 (Oxford, 1995), pp. 77–132.

[16] J.C. Greenfield, "The Wisdom of Ahiqar," in J. Day, R.P. Gordon and H.G.M. Williamson, (eds.), *Wisdom in Ancient Israel: Festschrift for John Emerton* (Cambridge, 1995), pp. 43–52.

[17] Grayson (1975), p. 81, iii 28.

owing their better preservation to scribes acquainted with them from biblical texts.

At this point we turn to ways of writing the Assyrian names in Tobit. The Greek texts give the name Shalmaneser as ενεμεσσαρος, with several variants, whereas the Old Latin has *salmanassar*, followed by the Vulgate, and Syriac has *šlmnʿsr* (1:2,13,16). Sennacherib appears as σενναχηρειμ, with variants, in the Old Latin as *sennacherib* and in Syriac as *snḥyryb* (1:18,22) and Esarhaddon as σαχερδονος, with variants (1:21,22; 2:1). The Syriac mixes the last with Nebuchadnezzar to produce *srwḥdwnṣwr*, which is echoed by the Old Latin *archedonosor, sarcedonosor*. (The agreement between the Syriac and the Old Latin against the Greek over these names is notable, the Vulgate's forms possibly supporting Jerome's report that he worked from an Aramaic version beside the Old Latin.) Nebuchadnezzar takes the standard LXX form, Ναβουχοδονοσορ (14:15). Some of these spellings in the versions can now be compared with Aramaic writings in the fragments of Tobit among the Dead Sea Scrolls.[18] There Esarhaddon is acceptably *ʾsrḥdwn* (lines 8, 9 = 1:22), but Sennacherib's name has been mixed with his son's by scribal error to yield *ʾsrḥryb* (line 8). The other names are not preserved. The Dead Sea Scroll forms may further be compared with the way the names of the same kings are represented in the Ahiqar papyrus of the fifth century B.C.E. There Esarhaddon is *ʾsrḥʾdn*, Sennacherib *slśnḥʾryb*. As in Tobit, an erroneous mixture of the two names is found once, *ʾsrḥʾryb* for Sennacherib, in the earlier copy on the verso of the roll, whereas the main text of the same passage has the correct form (line 64).[19] That instance apart, the Aramaic Ahiqar reflects accurately the phonetic shapes of the royal names current in the days of those Assyrian kings. In this it is comparable with the Hebrew biblical texts which present those and other Assyrian royal names with equal accuracy.[20] While Semitic authors may be expected to give renderings of Assyrian names closer to the originals than Greek or other Indo-European translators, the fact that these names are preserved as they were spoken in the contemporary Assyrian dialect, not with Babylonian forms, as would surely have been the case if

[18] J.A. Fitzmyer, 'Tobit' in M. Broshi, et al., *Qumran Cave 4. XIV, Parabiblical Texts Part 2* (Oxford, 1995), pp. 1–76.

[19] Porten & Yardeni (1993), pp. 24, 25 col. 3. 19, cf. pp. 34, 35.

[20] A.R. Millard, "Assyrian Royal Names in Biblical Hebrew", *JSS* 21 (1976), pp. 1–14.

they figured in works created after the fall of Nineveh, or based upon later sources, needs re-emphasis.

What is in question here is, again, the sources. The example of Tobit is significant. Where Tobit could use Ahiqar, the order of the Assyrian kings is correct (the Syriac and Arabic versions of Ahiqar reverse Sennacherib and Esarhaddon). The omission of Sargon is in keeping with 2 Kings, which does not name him, and the notice of Sennacherib's assassination (1:21) follows 2 Kgs. 19:37 closely. Where some faults may be found is in the opening and closing passages of the book, dealing with details for which there was no direct source. The problems of those have been discussed already. As the initial verses rest on the narrative of the end of Israel in 2 Kgs. 17, with the assumption of exile in Nineveh, so in the final verse correct recollection of the Median role brought a need to name the Median king and Daniel's reference seemed to fit. In contrast, the book of Judith has no obvious sources and the historical setting is wrong, although the personal names are known or plausible.

The books of Judith and Tobit each exemplify different opportunities for ancient writers about past times. Those in the first category had received or learnt a little which they altered and supplemented to suit their purposes, or else they deliberately selected from more extensive information the names and events they thought most appropriate, regardless of precision. Beside Judith, Ctesias and Eupolemus fall into this category. Josephus' apparent compression of the fifth and fourth centuries can be attributed to lack of clear sources. He may be put in the second category, classed with those authors who were able to refer to fuller records and tried to incorporate them into their compositions without altering their tenor. Berossus is the prime example, with the author of Tobit standing nearby, his Median Assuerus being the best he could do to supply a missing name.

The date of composition for Tobit has been placed as early as the fourth century[21] and as late as 170 B.C., with most commentators preferring a later rather than an earlier date. Judith is agreed to belong to the second century, either to the time of the Maccabees or the Hasmonaeans. Both books show some familiarity with vari-

---

[21] J.C. Greenfield supported the late Persian date, see "Ahiqar in the Book of Tobit," in M. Carrez, J. Doré and P. Grelot, (eds.), *De la Tôrah au Messie: études d'éxègese et d'herméneutique bibliques offertes à Henri Cazelles pour ses 25 années d'enseignement à l'Institut catholique de Paris* (Paris, 1981), pp. 329–36, "as a working hypothesis" (329), cf. Greenfield (1995), p. 46, n. 16.

ous parts of the Hebrew Bible, including the historical writings. If the final composition of the books of Kings were to be placed in the Hellenistic period, as some currently maintain, then it occurred in very favourable circumstances where old and reliable documents were to hand. Wherever statements in Kings can be checked against cuneiform sources they show a high degree of accuracy, even to the spelling of royal names. Facts fade as time passes, so the story of Judith could find acceptance in the second century, despite its historical absurdity. In contrast, at the same time, Tobit was circulating, with its largely correct reports, and the books of Kings, or their sources, which prove to be even more trustworthy. Whatever fantasies were spun to stimulate or edify the faithful, sober facts about Israel's history under her kings also existed to teach their lessons.

The care and accuracy which characterised the best ancient authors and scribes were already evident when Tony Gelston was a fellow-student and have marked his career ever since, coupled with the deep faith which underlies his work and the quiet humour which flavours his conversation. It is a pleasure to offer a small token of regard to a long-standing friend.

"DEATH IS SWALLOWED UP IN VICTORY" (1 CORINTHIANS 15:54): CANAANITE MOT IN PROPHECY AND APOCALYPSE

BY

J.F. HEALEY

Manchester

Since R. Bultmann introduced the term 'demythologization' into the discourse of biblical scholarship to refer to the theological/kerygmatic project of stripping the New Testament of the cultural baggage of a mythopoeic world-view, it has come to be used also in the study of the way that biblical texts sometimes adopt 'mythic' themes while stripping them of the polytheistic implications of the pagan source from which they were borrowed. This approach to 'mythic' themes is, in my view, too simplistic and it implies far too radical a distinction between the pagan culture of the biblical world (polytheistic, myth-ridden, dominated by often immoral ritual, magic and demons) and the uniform monotheistic culture of ancient Israel and the New Testament (only one divine power, free of myth, sanitised and spiritualized ritual). The acceptance of this simplistic contrast is a consequence of the uncritical acceptance of the official version of ancient Israelite religion presented in the Hebrew canon and of the orthodox church understanding of the New Testament texts. In fact the (non-biblical) archaeological and epigraphic evidence suggests that the religious reality was not so simple. Temple orthodoxy may have frowned, but the average Israelite entertained a variety of gods and magical practices. In the early church, until orthodoxy asserted itself, the newly converted pagans continued, perhaps less enthusiastically, their devotion to other deities and certainly to magical practices derived from paganism.

It is thus arguable that we should speak of 'transmythologization', a term used by D.E. Nineham,[1] when discussing the phenomenon of

---

[1] D.E. Nineham, "Demythologization", in R.J. Coggins and J.L. Holden (eds.), *A Dictionary of Biblical Interpretation* (London, 1990), pp. 171–74.

the adaptation of "mythic" ideas and traditions to a new religious context. For it can hardly be denied that ancient Israelite religion and Christianity had their own myths (in the technical sense of the word, not 'myth' = 'untruth'), stories about divine intervention in the world and man's salvation. And both incorporate adapted motifs taken from other mythic traditions.[2]

The mythic theme of the Death of Death, at first sight thoroughly Biblical and thoroughly Judaeo-Christian, has its roots in the 'Canaanite' mythology represented in the Ugaritic texts and continued in Phoenician tradition. It runs through the Old and New Testaments and into the popular religion of the early church, represented both in Greek and Syriac sources.

1. *The Canaanite Death of Death*[3]

Our main evidence for Canaanite mythology comes from the Ugaritic mythological texts.[4] Mot is there found as one of the enemies of Baal (alongside Yam, the sea-god). Baal represents principally the life-giving fertility associated with essential autumnal rainfall, while Mot represents the death-dealing sterility associated with the summer heat and drought. Mot, called "the Warrior" (*ǵzr*, e.g. *KTU* 1.4 vii 46–7), overcomes Baal and the latter has to descend into Mot's underworld domain. Baal is reported dead (*KTU* 1.5 v–vi), but the goddess Anat goes looking for him and attacks Mot (*KTU* 1.6 ii 30–5, cf. also v 11ff.):

> She seized divine Mot,
> With a sword she split him,

---

[2] The rich tapestry of Christian mythology is illustrated by G. Every, *Christian Mythology* (London, 1970).

[3] Much of the basic Ugaritic data presented here is discussed more fully in J.F. Healey, "Mot", in K. van der Toorn, B. Becking and P.W. van der Horst (eds.), *Dictionary of Deities and Demons* (Leiden, 1995), cols. 1122–32. See also N.J. Tromp, *Primitive Conceptions of Death and the Nether World in the Old Testament* (Rome, 1969); P.L. Watson, "The Death of 'Death' in the Ugaritic Texts," *JAOS* 92 (1972), pp. 60–4; J.C.L. Gibson, "The Last Enemy", *Scottish Journal of Theology* 32 (1979), pp. 151–69; J.F. Healey, "Burning the Corn: new light on the killing of Motu", *Or* 53 (1984), pp. 245–54. Translations of Ugaritic texts are mostly my own, though similar to those found in standard versions.

[4] I can here merely mention the difficulty of knowing how far the Ugaritic texts are representative of Canaan: the evidence of Philo of Byblos certainly suggests continuity with later Phoenicia.

> With a sieve she winnowed him,
> With fire she burned him,
> With mill-stones she ground him,
> In the field she scattered him.[5]

Mot is vanquished, Baal revives and the two protagonists fight (*KTU* 1.6 vi 16ff.). Eventually Mot is forced to concede, at least temporarily.

The main characteristic of Mot is that he is a voracious consumer of gods and men. He has an enormous mouth and appetite. At one point he defends himself against Anat by saying: "My appetite lacked humans, my appetite lacked the multitudes of the earth" (*KTU* 1.6 ii 17–19). *KTU* 1.5 ii 2–4 pictures his mouth:

> A lip to the earth, a lip to the heavens,
> . . . a tongue to the stars!
> Baal must enter his stomach,
> Go down into his mouth.

It is dangerous to get too near to him,

> lest he make you like a lamb in his mouth,
> and like a kid you be crushed in the crushing of his jaws
> (*KTU* 1.4 viii 17–20).

In this voraciousness Mot is closely associated with the underworld, a place of decay and destruction, where he dwells. This is most explicit in *KTU* 1.4 viii 1ff., in which Baal despatches messengers to Mot in his subterranean realm, a city which is reached through an entrance at the base of the mountains and of which Mot is king (see *KTU* 1.6 vi 27–9). Descent into the gullet of Mot is the equivalent of descent into the underworld.

There are other texts where Mot is a demon to be held in check.[6] *KTU* 1.23 describes among other things the birth of the divinities Šahar and Šalim and the ritual destruction of Mot in sympathetic magic plays a part in this. Under the double epithet *mt wšr*, perhaps "Death and Dissolution," and described as carrying "the sceptre of

---

[5] There is uncertainty as to whether Mot should be seen in a specifically agricultural role: see Healey (1984), pp. 245–54. Mot cannot be interpreted as grain as a positive product of agriculture. The imagery is based on the *destructive* treatment of grain. Note the similar treatment of the Golden Calf in Exod. 32:20.

[6] Mot's demonic nature may be suggested by his absence from the Ugaritic cult and personal names.

bereavement" and "the sceptre of widowhood", he is pruned like a vine, i.e. attacked, in an apotropaic ritual to protect the deities who are to be born.

Here we focus on three major elements in the Mot mythology:

(a) The underworld deity embodying death and destruction;
(b) Death as a devourer;
(c) The mythological battle with Death.

2. The Continuing Tradition

Before proceeding to a discussion of the Biblical material it may be worth noting that Mot, the Death-god, appears in the slight evidence we have of the Phoenician religion of the first millennium B.C.E., again in a mythical context, in the account of Phoenician mythology presented in Philo of Byblos, where Μώτ/Μούθ plays a small role. Μούθ was regarded as a son of Kronos and the text states that "the Phoenicians call him Death and Pluto" (*Praeparatio Evangelica* 1.10.34).[7]

It may be noted also that while there is plenty of evidence of underworld deities and demons in ancient Mesopotamia, there is only limited evidence of the personification or mythologization of Death.[8] So far as mythology is concerned, ^{d}mu-tu appears as a Death deity in a seventh century B.C.E. Assyrian text describing an underworld vision.[9] The general absence of any Death deity in Mesopotamian mythology is remarkable and M. Smith has tentatively suggested that the Mesopotamian theme of the hero who descends to the underworld, is sought and lamented by a spouse and returns to the earth has been replaced in West Semitic tradition by a conflict between the hero-figure and personified death. The new form of the narrative may have been formed on the pattern of the Baal-Yam conflict.[10]

---

[7] H.W. Attridge and R.A. Oden, *Philo of Byblos: The Phoenician History: Introduction, Critical Text, Translation, Notes*, CBQ Monograph 9 (Washington, 1981), pp. 56–7.

[8] M. Civil, I.J. Gelb, A.L. Oppenheim and E. Reiner, *The Assyrian Dictionary of the Oriental Institute of the University of Chicago* (Chicago, 1977), M/II, pp. 317–8.

[9] W. von Soden, "Die Unterweltsvision eines assyrischen Kronprinzen", *ZA* 43 (1936), pp. 1–31 (Akkadian p. 16:43; German p. 22:43).

[10] M.S. Smith, *The Early History of God* (San Francisco, 1990), p. 72.

3. *The Old Testament*

Many Old Testament passages allude to personified Death. It is not always possible to be certain whether a mythological element is involved. There are, however, at least some passages where a mythological overtone may plausibly be seen. In accordance with what has been stated earlier I believe J.C. de Moor was wrong to make a radical distinction between the Canaanite perception of Death and that of the Israelites.[11]

In Isa. 25:8, within the Isaiah Apocalypse, Yahweh is expected to swallow up (*blʿ*) Death for ever, taking on the swallower at his own game. This is a clear parallel to the Canaanite mythology: normally it was Mot who did the swallowing, but in this case Yahweh makes nonsense of Canaanite myth by himself swallowing the swallower. This seems to imply awareness of the Mot myth. There may be a similar play on tradition in Hos. 13:1, perhaps to be translated "he incurred guilt with regard to Baal and died (= came under Mot)."

In another important passage Death appears in a personified guise in Hos. 13:14:

> Shall I ransom them (Ephraim) from the power of Sheol?
> Shall I redeem them from Death?
> Death, where are your plagues?
> Sheol, where is your destruction? (RSV)

Here the personification is very clear, and mythological overtones may be present. Tromp regarded Death/Sheol here as a person, plague(s) and destruction (*dbr*/*qṭb*) as his servants.[12] In the following verse the scourge of the east wind is threatened and Smith would associate this with Mot.[13]

In other texts there is mention of specific characteristics of Death which have some sort of parallel in the picture of Mot painted by the Ugaritic texts. Thus in Hab. 2:5 the insatiability of personified

---

[11] J.C. de Moor, "O Death, where is thy sting", in L. Eslinger and G. Taylor (eds.), *Ascribe to the Lord. Biblical and other studies in memory of P.C. Craigie*, JSOTSS 67 (Sheffield, 1988), pp. 99–107.

[12] Tromp (1969), pp. 163–4.

[13] Smith (1990), p. 53.

Death is mentioned ("whose greed is as wide as Sheol, and like Death he is never satisfied"). The same idea, though applied to a personified Sheol, is found in Isa. 5:14 ("Therefore Sheol has enlarged its appetite, and opened its mouth beyond measure" (RSV): and cf. Prov. 1:12; 27:20; 30:15–16; Ps. 141:7). It is, however, difficult to be sure whether these texts reflect awareness of the Baal-Mot conflict, since the voracity of Death may have been an idea which existed independently of the myth.

The voraciousness of Death is found also in Ps. 49:15, which says of the over-confident:

> Like sheep they are appointed for Sheol;
> Death shall be their shepherd; straight to the grave
>   they descend. (RSV)

Here we have Death leading people into Sheol and this reflects the way the Ugaritic texts convey the idea that it is necessary to beware of Mot, since he can entrap the innocent and is specifically mentioned as consuming sheep (*KTU* 1.4 viii 17–20).[14]

Another example of the theme of the battle with Mot may be found in Hab. 3:13, though it involves emendation. Albright read *mwt* for MT *mbyt* (after LXX θάνατον), a reading which gives the meaning: "You struck the head of wicked Mot."[15] This, if correct, would give very explicit evidence of a battle-like conflict between Yahweh and Mot, but the emendation has not been accepted by all scholars.[16]

---

[14] A doubtful case of an echo of Canaanite myth is found in Jer. 9:20, which alludes to Death entering by means of windows. Some scholars have made comparison with the Ugaritic episode of Baal's reluctance to have windows incorporated into his palace because of fear of attack (*KTU* 1.4 vi–vii). It has been noted, however, by M.S. Smith, "Death in Jeremiah, ix, 20", *UF* 19 (1987), pp. 289–93, that the attack on Baal was to come from Yam (*KTU* 1.4 vi 12), not Mot. In Jer. 9:20 (ET 9:21) Death is an attacking demon, as in *KTU* 1.127:29. S.M. Paul, "Cuneiform Light on Jer. 9, 20", *Bib* 49 (1968), pp. 373–6, makes a comparison with the Mesopotamian *lamaštu* demon.

[15] W.F. Albright, "The Psalm of Habakkuk", in H.H. Rowley (ed.), *Studies in Old Testament Prophecy* (Edinburgh, 1950), pp. 1–18, specifically pp. 11–13, 17.

[16] In Hab. 1:12 Tromp (1969), p. 203, emended *l' nmwt* to *l'n mwt*, supposedly "the Victor over Death". Note also Ps. 55:16, emended by some to give "Let Death come upon them". A text which is usually emended, Ps. 48:15, can in fact be read as referring to Yahweh's leading his people "against Mot". In fact this phrase, *'almūt*, is usually corrected to *'ōlāmōt* and often read as the title of Ps. 49. All four of these "Yahweh v. Mot" passages are, therefore, problematic.

4. The New Testament[17]

It is an essential element of Christian soteriology and mythology that Christ conquered death. One might expect that Canaanite Death, already 'demythologised' to some extent, though not completely, in the Old Testament, would be completely forgotten, but even in the New Testament traces can be found of the Death-god. This is not really surprising, since it is arguable that the Gospels are more concerned with the defeat of demons and power over Satan than with abstract, let alone Trinitarian notions of salvation.

Paul explicitly describes the Christian salvation in terms of the mythological conflict between the saviour-god and the voracious death-god in the climax to his discourse on resurrection: "Death is swallowed up in victory. O Death, where is they victory? O Death, where is thy sting?" (RSV) (1 Cor. 15:54–5, alluding to Isa. 25:8 and Hos. 13:14). This is one of the most explicit New Testament passages referring to this conflict, but there are others.

The apocalyptic theme is taken up, as one might expect, in Revelation, which often alludes to earlier mythology. In Rev. 20:12–14, "the dead were judged by what was written in the books, by what they had done. And the sea gave up the dead in it, Death and Hades gave up the dead in them, and all were judged by what they had done. Then Death and Hades were thrown into the lake of fire" (RSV). Rev. 12, in another echo of ancient mythological tradition, depicts the battle in heaven between the great red dragon with seven heads (the Devil and Satan) (see the many-headed dragon in Ugaritic [*KTU* 1.5 i 1ff.] and *Odes of Solomon* 42 [below]).

Is it plausible to read such descriptions of the defeat of voracious Death in a totally 'demythologized' way? It seems to me that it would only be possible to do so on the basis of determining that

---

[17] I am conscious of the fact that I am here skipping, for want of time and space, the intertestamental literature. Much useful evidence is assembled by R. Bauckham (though in the context of the Harrowing of Hell theme) in "Descent into the Underworld", in D.N. Freedman (ed.), *Anchor Bible Dictionary* (New York, 1992) II, pp. 145–59, and there is no doubt that it has much to add by way of further illustration of continuity. See also J. Kroll, *Gott und Hölle: Der Mythos vom Descensuskampfe* (Leipzig/Berlin, 1932).

author and audience and the earliest Church would have found the 'mythological' understanding of the text ridiculous or blasphemous. Did they all make a mental note to the effect that: "This is a purely metaphorical way of speaking. Christ, as the son of God, had no real battle with a separate Power of Death. The scriptures speak in this way because of our difficulty in understanding divine realities"? Surely not. After all, the old mythology of the Ancient Near East and Greece was not dead in the first century C.E. The victory of Bel and Nabu over Tiamat was still celebrated at Palmyra[18], and at least some of the Jews of Palestine made use of old mythological ideas, as is clear from Jewish apocryphal works and some of the Dead Sea documents (e.g. the War Scroll with its eschatological battle).

5. *The Early Church*

In addition it is clear that the earliest Christians did not all abandon such 'pagan' notions, since there are Christian apocrypha, works popular in the new community, which celebrated the victory over death in a very vivid way. Most notable is the so-called Descent into Hell section attached to the *Acts of Pilate* (*Gospel of Nicodemus*),[19] though this is but one example of the genre.[20]

Here the setting is the underworld after the crucifixion. Death/Hades is described as a devourer, like the Ugaritic Mot. Abraham, Isaiah, John the Baptist, Adam and Seth are there and rejoice at the com-

---

[18] See most recently L. Dirven, "The exaltation of Nabû. A revision of the relief depicting the battle against Tiamat from the temple of Bel in Palmyra", *Welt des Orients* 28 (1997), pp. 96–116.

[19] Quotations are from F. Scheidweiler in W. Schneemelcher (ed.), E. Hennecke, *Neutestamentliche Apokryphen in deutscher Übersetzung 1 Evangelien* (Tübingen, 3rd edition, 1959), pp. 330–358 = *New Testament Apocrypha I Gospels and Related Writings* (London, 1963), pp. 444–481 (Greek text: C. Tischendorf, *Evangelia Apocrypha* (Leipzig, 1876²), pp. 322–32). The date of the traditions is far from certain, but consensus assigns the final work at the earliest to the 5th century: F.L. Cross and E.A. Livingstone (eds.), *Oxford Dictionary of the Christian Church* (Oxford, 1997³), p. 1287.

[20] The linking of the defeat of Death and the consequent liberation of his captives is later associated with Matt. 27:52f., recounting the resurrections which occurred at the time of Christ's death, which tradition links with the allusion in 1 Peter 3:18–20 to Christ's preaching to "the spirits in prison". This led to the doctrine of the Descent into Hell which appears in the Apostles' Creed and the Athanasian Creed. On the whole history of this theme see Kroll (1932).

ing of the great light which is the sign of their forthcoming liberation. Christ is about to arrive and Satan prepares to take hold of
him. Satan addresses Hades as "O insatiable devourer of all", "O
all-devouring and insatiable Hades". Hades complains: "I a short
while ago swallowed up a certain dead man called Lazarus, and
soon afterwards one of the living snatched him up forcibly from my
entrails with only a word". He guesses that Jesus must be the cause
of his problem and is full of fear: "I see that all those whom I have
swallowed up from the beginning of the world are disquieted. I have
a pain in my stomach". They will all be disgorged: "None of the
dead will be left for me". The outcome is the binding of Satan and
his utter defeat by Christ. This passage from the *Acts of Pilate* quotes
Isa. 26:19 and takes 1 Cor. 15:55 to refer to Isa. 25:8.

R. Bauckham, surveying this and related material,[21] expresses the
view that the Ugaritic myth is too remote to have influenced the
early Christian literature, finding instead influence from Jewish apocalyptic literature. While there is obviously no question of direct
Ugaritic influence, it is clear that the image of Death the Devourer
was maintained in popular culture through the intervening centuries,
surfacing from time to time in poetic and less rigorously orthodox
works. We have seen the allusions in the Old Testament above.

In the early Syriac literature too this theme of the conflict with and
defeat of Death finds a place. In the *Odes of Solomon*, for example:[22]

> Sheol saw me and was shattered,
> and Death ejected me and many with me . . .
> . . . and I went down with it as far as its depth . . .
> . . . And I made a congregation of the living among his dead . . .
> (*Ode* 42:11–14).

Again

> Death has been destroyed before my face,
> And Sheol has been vanquished by my word (*Ode* 15:9),

---

[21] Baukham (1992) II, pp. 145–59, specifically 157.
[22] English translations from J.H. Charlesworth in J.H. Charlesworth (ed.), *The Old
Testament Pseudepigrapha* 2 (London, 1985), pp. 725–71; Syriac text ed. and trans.
J.H. Charlesworth, *The Odes of Solomon* (Missoula, 1977).

and

> He who caused me to descend from on high,
> and to ascend from the regions below;
> And he who gathers what is in the middle,
> and throws them to me;
> He who scattered my enemies,
> and my adversaries;
> He who gave me authority over chains,
> so that I might loosen them;
> He who overthrew by my hands the dragon with seven heads,
> and placed me at his roots that I might destroy his seed... (*Ode* 22:1–5).

Allusions to the battle with Death are also found in the apocryphal *Acts of Thomas* 1:10:[23]

> Christ, Son of the Living God, the undaunted power which overthrew the enemy, the voice that was heard by the archons, which shook all their powers, ambassador sent from the height who didst descend even to Hell, who having opened the doors didst bring up thence those who for many ages had been shut up in the treasury of darkness.

To cite a final example, Ephrem the Syrian too is fond of this theme.[24] Death is defeated by Christ:

> Happy are you, living wood of the Cross,
> for you proved to be a hidden sword to Death;
> for with that sword which smote Him
> the Son slew Death, when He Himself was struck by it.
> (*Hymn on the Crucifixion* 9:2),[25]

and disgorges him:

> with its branches [the olive] depicted the symbol of his dying, with its leaf it depicted the symbol of the resurrection: the flood disgorging it, as Death disgorged Christ (*Hymn on Virginity* 7:13–14).[26]

---

[23] Translation from G. Bornkamm in W. Schneemelcher (ed.), E. Hennecke, *Neutestamentliche Apokryphen in deutscher Übersetzung 2 Apostolisches Apokalypsen und Verwandtes* (Tübingen, 3rd edition, 1964), pp. 297–372 = *New Testament Apocrypha 2 Writings Relating to the Apostles Apocalypses and Related Subjects* (London, 1965), pp. 425–531.

[24] The dialogue of Satan and Death, analogous to the dialogue of Satan and Hades in the *Acts of Pilate*, is the main theme of *Hymn on Nisibis* 52: E. Beck, *Des heiligen Ephraem des Syrers Carmina Nisibena* II (*CSCO* 240–1) (Louvain, 1963), pp. 73–5 (Syriac); pp. 63–4 (German).

[25] Translation from S.P. Brock, *The Luminous Eye: The Spiritual World Vision of Saint Ephrem the Syrian* (Kalamazoo, 1992²), p. 81.

[26] Brock (1992), p. 59. For the specific theme of the descent, see R. Murray,

The impact of the mythology of the Death of Death continued into later Christian tradition, being reflected in the liturgy especially at Eastertide. On the day I wrote some of the above I found myself singing in church a version of the hymn *Ad regias Agni dapes*, the middle portion of which runs as follows:

O Thou from whom hell's monarch flies,
O true, O heavenly sacrifice:
Death's captives all are now set free,
And endless life receive from Thee.
For Christ, arising from the dead,
From conquered hell victorious sped:
He thrusts the tyrant down to chains
And Paradise for man regains.[27]

In this short essay, my argument is that the assertion of the transcending of death by the divine was not, at the time of the texts in question, reducible to an abstract theoretical statement. The peoples of the ancient Near East and of Late Antiquity had a vivid awareness of the demonic and destructive powers of the underworld and the assertion of divine supremacy over them was inevitably mythological, drawing on an age-old tradition. If there is a moment in the history of ideas which marks the end of the mythic way of thinking about death, it is not reached until much later (perhaps the Renaissance or the Enlightenment). Centuries of Christian theology and religiosity passed during which the mythic imagination was still fully operative and indeed still creative, as is clear from the way that the Harrowing of Hell became such a popular theme in medieval Christian mythology.

Symbols of Church and Kingdom: A Study in Early Syriac Tradition (Cambridge, 1975), pp. 228–36; Brock (1992), pp. 29–30; J. Teixidor, "Le Thème de la Descente aux enfers chez S. Ephrem", *L'Orient Syrien* 6 (1961), pp. 25–40.

[27] Translation from *The Daily Missal and Liturgical Manual* (1961), p. 667. There are several variant English versions of the hymn, all beginning "At the Lamb's high feast we sing".

ENTHRONEMENT AND APOTHEOSIS:
THE VISION IN REVELATION 4–5

BY

MARGARET BARKER

Borrowash

The Book of Revelation is an anthology of visionary and prophetic material compiled according to the traditional pattern. It is clear from the vision of the Man among the seven lamps that the first three chapters are set in the *hekhal* where the *menorah* stood. The seer hears a voice summoning him to a higher place to learn "what must take place after this". The vision then moves into the holy of holies and the seer stands before the throne, to see the mystery of what is to be, the *rāz nihyeh* of the Qumran texts (4Q 300; 416.2; 417.2).

The seer, for the moment we will call him John, saw first a Man in the *hekhal* and wrote letters at his dictation. He was commissioned to carry the Man's messages from heaven to earth as were Isaiah (Isa. 6:8) and Enoch (1 Enoch 15–16) before him. Like Enoch he was then summoned to enter a house within the house where he saw the heavenly throne. In other words, John (and Enoch) entered the holy of holies. The vision described in chapters 4–5 takes place in the holy of holies; the Lamb approaches the throne and takes the scroll with seven seals. As the Lamb opens the seals, the riders move out from the holy of holies and eventually in chapter 7 'John' sees the temple courts and all the people assembled there.

Only the high priests were permitted enter the holy of holies, which suggests that these sanctuary visions were connected with their office. The *Testament of Levi* describes a similar experience; the angel who ascended with Levi through the heavens said: "You shall stand near the Lord. You shall be his priest and you shall tell forth his mysteries to men" (T.Levi 2:10). Levi ascended and eventually: . . . "the angel opened for me the gates of heaven and I saw the Holy Most High sitting on the throne" (T.Levi 5:1).[1] There is

---

[1] J.H. Charlesworth (ed.), *The Old Testament Pseudepigrapha 1 Apocalyptic Literature and Testaments* (London, 1983), pp. 788 and 789.

no agreement as to the date and origin of the *Testaments* but Psalm 73, dating probably from the first temple period, describes exactly the experience of 'John'. Confronted with the triumph of evil doers, the psalmist went into the sanctuary of God – he must have been one of those allowed to enter – and perceived their end (Ps. 73.17), literally *what is after*. In a time of persecution for the young church, John on Patmos was summoned into the holy of holies to see what must take place *after this*. He, like Levi in his vision, was to learn the mysteries of God (Rev. 10:7) and the end of evil.

Revelation 4–5 stands in a priestly tradition and can only be understood as a temple text, a *merkavah* text which describes the enthronement of a Lamb. Similar texts describe the enthronement of a Man (Dan. 7:14), of the Chosen One (1 Enoch 51:3; 61:8), of the exalted Enoch after he has been transformed into Metatron, the angel whose name means *the throne sharer* (3 Enoch 10).[2]

There is nothing, apart from its position in the New Testament, to suggest that this vision is a Christian text. The pattern is: a throne from which come thunder and voices and lightnings, someone seated on the throne who holds a sealed scroll, seven torches burning before the throne, twenty four elders in white garments enthroned around it and four living creatures full of eyes. The creatures and the elders worship the one on the throne and praise his work in creation. A Lamb with seven eyes and seven horns, who bears the marks of death, appears and takes the scroll. Immediately he becomes the object of worship. The heavenly host sing a new song because the blood of the Lamb has 'ransomed' people from every nation and made them priests to reign on earth. All creation then joins in the worship of the Lamb.

The sanctuary setting of Revelation 4–5 suggests looking in the Old Testament for rituals associated with the holy of holies which could explain what is happening in the vision. There is very little evidence for what happened in the holy of holies, but what there is illuminates Revelation 4–5 in a remarkable way. When Solomon was

---

[2] W.F. Ferrar (ed.), Eusebius, *The Proof of the Gospel Being the Demonstratio Evangelica of Eusebius of Caesarea*, (London, 1920), 4:15 pp. 202–203 discusses this name and links it to Ps. 45.8. "The Anointer, being the Supreme God, is far above the Anointed, He being God in a different sense. And this would be clear to anyone who knew Hebrew . . . Therefore in these words you have it clearly stated that God was anointed and became the Christ . . . And this is He Who was the Beloved of the Father, and his Offspring, and the eternal Priest, and the Being called the Sharer of the Father's throne".

made king, he sat *on the throne of the LORD as king*, (1 Chron. 29:23), and the assembly blessed the LORD and bowed their heads *and worshipped the LORD and the king*, (1 Chron. 29:20). In other words, the Chronicler tells us that when Solomon sat on the throne in the holy of holies, he became divine and was worshipped, an exact parallel to the scene in Revelation 5. The language employs the same idiom: they worshipped the LORD and the king, compare "To him who sits upon the throne and to the Lamb be blessing" (Rev. 5:13, RSV). This suggests a Semitic original underlying the Greek. There were not two persons on the throne but one; the human had become the LORD. This was the apotheosis of the throne-sharer. Hence the better reading at Revelation 6:16–17: "Hide us from the face of him who is seated on the throne and from the wrath of the Lamb, for the great day of *his* (singular) wrath has come".[3]

A second sanctuary ritual was when the high priest entered once a year on the Day of Atonement, carrying a bowl of blood which he sprinkled on the mercy seat. There is no account of this ritual in texts which are agreed to be pre-exilic, but the anthology of royal material preserved in the *Similitudes of Enoch* shows that the blood of the king, the Righteous One, was offered before the throne (1 Enoch 47). Once the blood had been brought, the judgement could begin. There is a strong resemblance to Isaiah 53.[4] Whatever the Day of Atonement ritual had become during the second temple period, the writer to the Hebrews, and presumably the recipients of the letter too, knew that the Day of Atonement offering in their time was a substitute for the blood of the anointed high priest (Heb. 9:11–12). In the *Similitudes*, we glimpse the original: the blood of the Anointed One taken before the throne so that the judgement can begin. The cries of the martyr souls under the altar in Rev. 6:10 are those of the righteous in 1 Enoch 47:2: "That the prayer of the righteous may not be in vain before the Lord of Spirits, that judgement may be done unto them, and that they may not have to suffer for ever".[5] The writer of the *Similitudes* and the writer of Revelation 6 were describing the same scene.

---

[3] A singular where one might have expected a plural is found in 7:11; 11:15; 20:6; 22:1–3.

[4] M. Black, *The Book of Enoch or 1 Enoch* (Leiden, 1985), p. 209.

[5] R.H. Charles, *The Apocrypha and Pseudepigrapha of the Old Testament in English with Introductions and Critical and Explanatory Notes to the Several Books* (Oxford, 1913), volume 2, p. 215.

These two parallels, the enthronement of Solomon and the blood rite of the Day of Atonement, are the setting for the vision in Revelation 4–5. There is no agreement about what happened when a king was enthroned in the first temple period, but it is thought to have occurred in the autumn, in other words, at the same time of year as the later Day of Atonement. It is not impossible that the two were originally related and that the writer of Revelation 4–5 has preserved the original sequence: the sacrificed Lamb enthroned so that the judgement can begin.

I have argued elsewhere that the Lamb in Revelation is the Servant.[6] No other *merkavah* vision describes the ascent of an animal and even on the level of wordplay alone,[7] the Servant is the obvious choice for the one who ascended. Here, in the vision, the Servant/Lamb enacts what Isaiah described in the fourth Servant Song. He was the one who poured out his life (Isa. 53:12), saw the light, (LXX and 1Q Is^a 53:11) and then triumphed (Isa. 53:12).[8] It is only the variant reading in 1 QIs^a 52.14, מׁשׁחתי, anointed, instead of מׁשׁחת marred, which shows that the Servant was an anointed figure, and enables us to identify, at last, the verse referred to in Luke 24.26: "Was it not necessary that the Anointed One should suffer these things and enter into his glory?" Luke attributes this saying to Jesus, suggesting that he saw himself as the Servant. John the Baptist identified him as the Lamb i.e. the Servant, who would take away the sin of the world (John 1:29).[9] The earliest Christology was a Servant Christology (Phil. 2:6–11; Acts 3:13; 4:30), and this highlights the importance of the Lamb vision for understanding Christian origins. The sequence in Philippians 2 is exactly that of Revelation 5: death, exaltation, receiving the great Name and then being worshipped by everything in heaven, on earth and under the earth.

The vision of the Lamb being enthroned in the holy of holies is a vision of "what must take place after this", a glimpse behind the veil which screened the sanctuary. In temple tradition, the area beyond the veil was beyond both time and the material world. It was the place of the invisible and eternal part of the creation.

---

[6] M. Barker, *The Risen Lord* (Edinburgh, 1996), pp. 111–138.

[7] *ṭly'* meaning lamb or servant in Aramaic.

[8] In Isaiah's original, the sharing of booty referred to the spoils of war after the Assyrian retreat, the Fourth Servant Song being a reflection on the illness of Hezekiah and his subsequent recovery, in the light of the existing royal ideology of the Servant.

[9] That 'Lamb' here indicated the Servant was first suggested by C.J. Ball, "Had the Fourth Gospel an Aramaic Archetype?", *ET* 21 (1909–10), pp. 91–3.

The temple/tabernacle was a microcosm of the creation; and the building of the tabernacle corresponded to the days of creation. The veil which screened the holy of holies corresponded to the creation of the firmament on the second day, and so everything beyond the veil represented the works of Day One. Most sources are reticent about these, and reading about the works of Day One was forbidden as was reading about the chariot throne (m Ḥag. 2:1). In other words, the lore of the sanctuary was not revealed to ordinary people. How then did the early Christian seer know about it? The great work of Day One was the creation of light which the Fourth Gospel (John 1:4) and the Targum (T. Neofiti Exod. 12:42) identified as the Word. This was not the light of the sun and moon, created on the fourth day, but the cosmic light. In the Fourth Gospel, the Messiah originates in this light of Day One.[10] John attributes to Jesus the confidence that he will return to the light of Day One, that is, to the heavenly sanctuary: "Glorify thou me in thy own presence with the glory which I had with thee before the world was made" (John 17:5, RSV). In Revelation 5:6 the seven horns represent this light of the first day. Just as Moses' face had light beams[11] when he had been with the Lord (Exod. 34:30), so the Lamb has seven horns i.e. sevenfold beams, suggesting here too a Semitic original. The sevenfold light was the light of Day One. Thus the Lamb in the vision had what Jesus was confident he would regain: the Glory which he had had in God's presence at the beginning, i.e. in the sanctuary.[12]

The sanctuary was the source of creation and so the hymns of the sanctuary extol as Creator the one seated on the throne. The twenty four elders sing: "Thou didst create all things, and by thy will they existed and were created" (Rev. 4:11, RSV), and the four living creatures use a form of the Name which may also indicate God's role as Creator. "Holy Holy Holy is the Lord God Almighty", the song of the sanctuary in Isa. 6:3 and 1 Enoch 39:12, is followed by "Who was and is and is to come" in Rev. 4:8. This form of the Name is most closely paralleled in the Targums to Exod. 3:14 which not only separate the Name into past and future aspects, but also imply creative activity rather than simply being. Thus T. Neofiti

---

[10] The Fourth Gospel does not begin with the Christmas stories.
[11] Hebrew קרן usually means a horn.
[12] See W.F. Smelik, "On Mystical Transformation of the Righteous into Light in Judaism", *JSJ* 26 (1995), pp. 122–144.

interprets the Name revealed to Moses as "He who said and the world was there from the beginning and is to say to it: Be there, and it will be there". The Fragment Targum has "He who said to the world from the beginning: Be there and it was there; and is to say to it: Be there and it will be there." This coincides with suggestions that the original Name should be read as a hiph'il form: *he who causes to be, he who creates.*[13] This is clearly the best way to understand the Name in 1QS 3:15 which seems to be taking *God of Knowledge* from 1 Sam. 2:3 and then rendering the *yhwh* that follows by *making all that is and shall be.* The Song of the four living creatures in Revelation 4:8 also extols the Creator and should perhaps be understood: *Who created and does create and will create.* This would make the song of the creatures the same as the song of the elders.

When the creatures and the elders sing for the newly enthroned Lamb, their song is of atonement: "Thou wast slain and by thy blood didst ransom men for God" (RSV) (Rev. 5:9). The Day of Atonement ritual renewed the cosmic covenant, and thus recreated the world by the sprinkling of the blood of the one who emerged from the sanctuary, from heaven.[14] The hymns to the One Enthroned and the hymn to the Lamb are hymns of praise to the Creator.

Philippians describes the Servant as one who died and was exalted. He was then given the Name and worshipped by the whole creation. In Revelation 5, the Lamb is worshipped after he has taken the scroll, suggesting that taking the scroll and receiving the Name were comparable events. Taking the scroll was the moment when the Lamb became divine. Now texts which describe the exaltation of human figures also describe how they are given knowledge, which may explain the scroll. The Servant in Isa. 52:13–14 was exalted and became wise, יַשְׂכִּיל (LXX συνήσει, shall have understanding); Enoch was anointed, which transformed him into an angel, and then he was shown the books of the secrets of the creation (2 Enoch 22); Enoch/Metatron was shown the mysteries of the world after he had been enthroned (3 Enoch 11:1). The link between knowledge and divinity, however, was rooted in the more ancient religion of Jerusalem which was all but obliterated by the seventh century reformers. It was the reformers who wrote the Eden story in Genesis 2–3, who

---

[13] Summary in W.H. Brownlee, "The Ineffable Name of God", *BASOR* 226 (1977), pp. 39–46.

[14] M. Barker, "Atonement. The Rite of Healing", *SJT* 49 (1996), pp. 1–20.

taught that it was a sin to want the knowledge which made humans divine, *like gods* (Gen. 3:5). The reformers also warned against any interest in this secret knowledge: *the secret things belong to the Lord our God* (Deut. 29:29). The knowledge was acquired by people who went up to heaven (Deut. 30:12) and learned the secrets of the creation (Prov. 30:3–4). This secret knowledge is the key to Deutero-Isaiah's argument against the gods of the nations. In the heavenly court, they are challenged to prove their power by demonstrating their knowledge of the future (Isa. 41:21–4): "Tell us what is to come hereafter that we may know that you are gods" (Isa. 41:23, RSV). Only the LORD has this knowledge and so he is the only God: "Who has announced from of old the things to come? Let them tell us what is yet to be" (Isa. 44:7, RSV). Knowledge of the future was proof of divinity. The Book of Revelation describes this knowledge of the future which Jesus had been given in his visions: **The revelation of Jesus Christ which God gave to him to show to his servants what must soon take place** (Rev. 1:1). Early Christian writers remembered that Jesus had revealed knowledge of the past, the present and the future, because he was the high priest who had passed thorough the curtain.[15]

The Scrolls have several references to this knowledge: the Hymns tell of one who has learned marvellous mysteries and become their interpreter (1QH I.21; II.13–14; XII.10–15). There were seven mysteries of knowledge (4Q 403), which may account for the seven seals on the scroll, and one of the Day of Atonement prayers mentions the hidden and revealed things (4Q 508). The Teacher of Righteousness was the one whom God chose to stand before him (4Q 171.3), to whom he made known the mysteries of the words of the prophets (1Qp Hab. 7).

The scroll which the Lamb opens reveals the immediate future of Jerusalem: the natural disasters of the first four seals, the persecution of the faithful with the fifth seal, and the supernatural signs of the Day of the Lord with the sixth seal, (Rev. 6:17).[16] These signs

---

[15] Ignatius, *Philadelphians* 9 in K. Lake (ed.), *The Apostolic Fathers* (Cambridge, Massachusetts, 1952), p. 249: "and only to him (Jesus) have the secret things of God been entrusted"; compare Clement *Miscellanies* 6.7 and 7.17. Origen *Celsus* 3.37 in A. Roberts and J. Donaldson (eds.), *The Ante-Nicene Fathers: Translations of the Fathers down to A.D. 325* 4 (Edinburgh, 1885, reprinted 1994), p. 479: "Jesus . . . beheld these weighty secrets, and made them known to a few".

[16] The sequence of the seals corresponds to the predictions attributed to Jesus in

of the future are summarised in the Synoptic Apocalypses and cast as the last sayings of Jesus about the fate of Jerusalem and the temple. In other words, the gospel writers believed that Jesus knew and revealed the contents of the scroll which made the Lamb divine. The Jesus whom John portrays claims this heavenly knowledge (e.g. John 3:31–32) and John his servant was the seer **who bore witness to the word of God and to the testimony of Jesus Christ, to all that he (i.e. Jesus) saw** (Rev. 1:2).

The Lamb took his place among the twenty four elders and the four living creatures. The Songs of the Sabbath Sacrifice describe the heavenly worship of *chariots with cherubim and gods* (4Q 403.1). Gods and chariots (i.e. *thrones*, plural) in the heavenly sanctuary is a remarkable piece of evidence that the enthroned elders of Revelation 4 would have been familiar to those who sang those Songs of the Sabbath Sacrifice. Since the worship of the temple was a counterpart of the worship in heaven, with the priests as angels and the high priest as the LORD, the twenty four elders of the vision were probably the angel counterparts of the heads of the twenty four priestly courses (1 Chron. 24:1–6). In the first century C.E. these leading priests were known as *the elders of the priesthood* (m Yoma 1.5) and all were present at the great festivals of Passover, Pentecost and Tabernacles (m Sukkah 5.7). In the vision they wear the white vestments of the sanctuary, the dress of angels. As priests they offer incense and prayers before the throne (Rev. 5:8) and they are privy to the secrets of heaven (Rev. 5:5; 7:14) These elders appear throughout Revelation, but always worshipping (Rev. 4–5 *passim*; also 7:11; 11:16; 14:3; 19:4).

The ultimate origin of the elders, however, lies in the heavenly council. On the Day of the LORD, according to the Isaiah Apocalypse, the host of heaven would be punished in heaven together with the kings on earth who were their counterparts (Isa. 24:21). There would

---

the Synoptic Apocalypses (Mark 13 and parallels). The first seal brings the rider on a white horse, the false Messiah with his crown cf. Mark 13:6: "Many will come in my name saying I am he". The second seal brings the rider on the red horse to take peace from the earth cf. Mark 13:7: "war and rumours of war" The third seal brings the rider on the black horse, famine; in Matthew 24 this is the third devastation, in Mark 13 and Luke 21 it is the fourth. The fourth rider brings death, whom Luke describes as pestilence. The fifth seal reveals the blood of the martyrs under the altar, the persecution predicted in Mark 13:9–13. The sixth seal brings the supernatural catastrophes of the Day of the Lord; the stars fall and the skies vanish: cf. Mark 13:24–25.

be signs in the sun and moon "For the LORD of Hosts will reign on Mount Zion and in Jerusalem and before his elders (but Syriac: Holy Ones, i.e. angels) he will manifest his glory" (Isa. 24:23, RSV). Psalm 82.1 is similar: "God takes his place in the assembly and holds judgement in the midst of the gods". **The scene in Revelation 5 describes the Lamb taking his place in the midst of this heavenly council so that the judgement can begin.**

The scene in Revelation 5 corresponds to the enthronement ritual underlying Psalm 2 and Psalm 110. Both give important information for establishing a wider context for this vision. In Psalm 2:7 the king reports words he has heard from the LORD: "You are my son. Today I have begotten you. Ask of me and I will make the nations your heritage" (RSV). The earliest account of Jesus's baptism (Mark 1:9–11), describes what must have been a personal experience: he saw the heavens open, he heard a voice from heaven. Jesus himself must have spoken of this experience, and of the voice addressing him as "My beloved Son". What is thought to be the earlier version of Luke 3:22 makes the link to Psalm 2 quite explicit. The heavenly voice says: "You are my son. Today I have begotten you". The baptism was the moment when Jesus experienced enthronement,[17] but he had known the traditions of the temple mystics after his initial contact with them as a boy. This is the significance of his meeting with the teachers in the temple (Luke 2:46–50).

This experience of ascent and enthronement was not unique but seems rather to have been cultivated by the temple mystics. An enigmatic Qumran text (4Q 491) is the words of someone who claims to have a *throne of strength in the assembly of the gods*. "I have taken my seat in ... heaven, I am numbered among the gods and established in the holy congregation". The language is that of Deutero-Isaiah's challenge to the other gods: "Who will attack what I say ... who will call me into judgement ... I am reckoned with the gods ..." There is no indication who this person might have been, but comparable material elsewhere suggests that he was the heir to the royal traditions. In Ezekiel the Tragedian's play about the life of Moses,[18] Moses describes his dream experience of being enthroned on Mount Sinai and looking down on the stars far below him. Philo attributed

---

[17] Origen *Homily 1 On Ezekiel* compares Jesus's experience at baptism with Ezekiel's by the river Chebar, i.e. both saw the chariot throne. See Barker (1996), pp. 41–55.
[18] Eusebius *Preparation of the Gospel* 9.29.

a similar experience to Moses on Sinai, but described it as entering the darkness of the presence of God rather than as ascending a mountain.

> For he (Moses) was named God and King of the whole nation, and entered, we are told, into the darkness where God was, that is, into the unseen, invisible, incorporeal and archetypal essence of existing things. Thus he beheld what is hidden from the sight of mortal nature (Life of Moses 1.158).[19]

Philo's description of the unseen and invisible world is a description of the holy of holies, the place beyond the temporal and material world, literally a place of complete darkness but representing the light of the presence of God. In other words, he attributes to Moses the mystical experience of the ancient kings in the holy of holies; they entered the presence of God and became God and King. Hence Ps. 68:25: the processions of "my God, my King . . ." and the vision of Isaiah in the temple: "I have seen the King, the Lord of Hosts" (Isa. 6:5).

Psalm 110 reveals more of the ancient kingmaking. A reconstruction based on the LXX,[20] suggests that the opaque Hebrew of v. 3 conceals a description of the 'birth' of the king in the holy of holies:

> . . . in the court of the holy ones,
> from the womb of the Dawn like the dew I begot you.

This would give a context for the enigmatic oracle in Isa. 9:6–7 and also explain who were meant by the *Sons of the Dawn*, addressed in 4Q 298. These were initiates for whom the kingmaking was not just a memory of ancient times but a living tradition. The one born as the divine Son was the Melchizedek priest.

The Qumran Melchizedek text reveals what was believed about him: he was the one spoken of in Ps. 82:1 as Elohim standing in the assembly of El, giving judgement in the heavenly council. The Melchizedek of 11QMelch also makes atonement for the children of light and brings vengeance on the hordes of Belial, rescuing his own from their power. He fulfils Isa. 52:7 bringing the good news of salvation and proclaiming the kingdom of God. All these prophecies are to be fulfilled at the appointed time, the Day of Atonement at

---

[19] *Philo: English Translation by F.H. Colson in Ten Volumes*, Loeb Classical Library 6 (London, 1929–62), p. 359.

[20] N. Wyatt, "Les mythes des Dioscuroi et l'idéologie royale dans les littératures d'Ougarit et d'Israël", *RB* (1996), pp. 481–516.

the end of the tenth jubilee. The text is damaged, but Melchizedek seems also to be the messenger who proclaims the good news and is the Anointed One prophesied in Dan. 9:25. The briefest glimpse at Mark 1 will show that **what was expected of Melchizedek shaped this evangelist's presentation of Jesus**: "the time is fulfilled and the Kingdom of God is at hand", followed by an exorcism to rescue a man from the power of unclean spirits.

What is most interesting is Mark's description of Jesus' experience in the desert, something which Jesus must himself have described to his disciples as he was alone during that time. **He was with the wild beasts and the angels served him**. Beasts and angels is a significant combination. Although it is possible to distinguish in Greek between the wild animals of the desert and the living creatures of the heavenly throne, the Hebrew word חיה could have been used for both (Ezek. 1:5, throne creatures, Ezek. 14:15 wild animals). In combination with serving angels, it is more likely that Jesus described the throne creatures which he experienced in a desert vision, when he, like the unnamed person in 4Q491, was enthroned. He believed that he had become Melchizedek, the royal high priest who was to make the atonement sacrifice of the tenth jubilee The supplementary material in the Q accounts of the desert experience (Matt. 4:1–11; Luke 4:1–13) suggests Psalm 2 as a context. Jesus was tempted to doubt his sonship: he was set on a high place in Zion and he was offered another way to gain power over all the kingdoms of the world which he saw from a high place in a single moment of time (Luke 4:5). He was tempted away from the role of Melchizedek, which was to offer himself as the atonement sacrifice of the tenth jubilee.[21] Thus when Peter suggests that he should not suffer, Jesus hears this as the voice of Satan, again (Mark 8:31–33).

What Jesus experienced in the desert was the vision we now read as Revelation 4–5. He saw the sacrificed Servant approaching the throne and taking his place as Melchizedek in the midst of the heavenly assembly, to begin the judgement. As his death approached, he revealed to his disciples what would be inaugurated by that event; the enthronement of the sacrificed Servant and the onset of the judgement.

It is with great pleasure that I offer this to Anthony Gelston, a small gift for a gentle and learned friend.

---

[21] See Barker (1996).

OF WARS AND RUMOURS OF PEACE:
APOCALYPTIC MATERIAL IN
APHRAHAT AND ŠUBḤALMARAN

BY

D.J. LANE
Mickley

1. *Introduction*

Forty years ago Dr. Gelston and I first met at Professor Driver's
Hebrew Text classes, and it is a pleasure to offer this token of appreciation to a friend and colleague of such long standing, whose encouragement and scholarly advice has been as much welcomed as his
scrupulous researches and writings have been admired. The present
essay touches upon Syriac Christianity and its methods of biblical
interpretation, with both of which Dr. Gelston has engaged, and does
still engage. This study of two Syriac writers' approach to "the worst
of times" commemorates our association as "the best of times".

Aphrahat and Šubḥalmaran, living some two hundred and fifty
years apart, share an oriental Christianity, yet the works attributed to
them show marked divergences both in the use of biblical material
as a matrix to interpret the disasters of the times and in their culture. Their writings present difficulties which face students of Syriac
history and literature: reliance on tradition led scribes and historians,
concerned for the prestige of their own, to err in ascription of material
and in description of authors' lives and persons.

2. *The Authors' Homeland*

Our two authors lived in a shadowland between east and west where
there developed a Christianity of a genre different from that of the
familiar Mediterranean world, whether Roman or Byzantine. It lies
within the empire of the Sasanians, who, between the time of Ardashir I at the end of the first quarter of the third century A.D. and of
Yazdagird III in the mid seventh, looked behind the periods of the

Parthians and (more especially) of Alexander the Great, attempting to recreate and to hold the older Persian empire of the Achaemenids.[1] Not surprisingly, the new empire had the same inherent geographical and historical weaknesses as the one which was its ideal and exemplar. In the first place its extent stretched from the southern province of Persia adjoining the Indus to the debatable land of the Roman provinces of Mesopotamia and Osrhoene in the north; and from the western boundary of the Euphrates to the eastern frontier city of Merv near the Oxus river, on the silk road to China. In the second place there were two necessities to be grasped by any successful claimant to the title of King of Kings of Iran and non-Iran. The first was an internal one: that of holding in check the threats of the Zoroastrian priesthood, family rivals, and cliques of nobles. The second was an external one: the defence of northern and eastern frontiers from aggressive and rapacious marauding tribes of Huns as well as the provision of a buffer against Rome in the prosperous trading centres of Mesopotamia.[2] Thus there were exact replays of such earlier events as the triumphs of Cyrus, the hard-won glories of Darius, and the succumbing of their successors to the victories of Alexander.

Aphrahat's mid fourth century presented a threat in the northwest: Šubḥalmaran's late sixth/early seventh century revealed the entire range of problems for inhabitants of a failing Persian empire. Nevertheless, in each case Persian initiative on the Persian/Byzantine frontier precipitated cataclysms which merit the title of "the last time". Both writers lived in periods when an apparently strong Sasanian Empire came into conjunction with a doubtfully strong Roman Empire; rivalry for possession of such cities as Nisibis, Amida and even Antioch led to marching and countermarching in the area between the upper reaches of the Tigris and the Euphrates.[3] This

---

[1] R.N. Frye, "The Sasanians," *The History of Ancient Iran* (Handbuch der Altert. Abt. 3; Teil 7, München, 1983), pp. 287–339 provides a brief history of the Sasanians with summary of authorities.

[2] On the nature and prosperity of the area see M.M. Mango, "The Continuity of the Classical Tradition in the Art and Architecture of Northern Mesopotamia", in N. Garsoïan, T.F. Mathews and R.W. Thomson (eds.), *East of Byzantium: Syria and Armenia in the Formative Period, Dumbarton Oaks Symposium 1980* (Dumbarton Oaks, 1982), p. 116.

[3] "Warfare in the Sasanian period with which we are concerned was not a matter of static operations but of fluid raid and counter raid which carried the Persian armies to Antioch, Jerusalem, and the suburbs of Constantinople, and Byzantine

area has been well described as a bridge, a buffer-zone and a battle-ground,[4] all three terms exemplified by the location in it of Haran of the Patriarchs, otherwise Carrhae of the First Triumvirate. In the mid fourth century, against the expectation of many, the Sasanians triumphed; in the early seventh-century a previously overwhelming Sasanian strength, for the reasons suggested above, became fatally flawed. In consequence, Islam became a national as well as a religious entity, permanently changing the international pattern. No longer was the Middle East dominated by the relationship between Sasanian East and Roman West,[5] whether a formal one of professed peace or declared hostilities, or an informal one of cultural exchange.

This essay[6] compares and contrasts these writers' scriptural interpretations of contemporary events. It was suggested above that the momentum for cataclysm came from problems on the Byzantine frontier. Now there is a clear correlation between Roman-Sasanian hostility and Sasanian persecution of Christians, as J. Duschene-Guillemin comments

> It was during Shapur's reign that Constantine officially recognised Christianity. From then on, waging war against Rome and persecuting the Christians were to Iran two facets of one struggle, and persecution took place especially in the north-west provinces and the regions bordering on the Roman empire.[7]

It might seem, then, that the writings of our two authors fit into a simple and shared pattern, that is to explain the persecution of Christian Persians by such scriptural passages as Mark 13:9–13 and its parallels. Neither writer takes such a simple and obvious step. The former relies chiefly on verses from Daniel interpreted by passages notably from Genesis, Kings, Isaiah and Ezekiel; the latter on passages from Matthew 24 and 1 and 2 Thessalonians. Further, both enlarge

---

retaliations to the vicinity of the Sasanian capital of Ctesiphon", N. Garsoïan, "Byzantium and the Sasanians", in E. Yarshater (ed.), *The Cambridge History of Iran* 3 Part 1: *The Seleucid, Parthian and Sasanian Periods* (Cambridge, 1983), pp. 568–592, p. 569.

[4] Mango (1982), p. 116.

[5] For a critical assessment of hostility and interaction between the two empires see Garsoïan (1983), pp. 568–592.

[6] D.J. Lane, "The Last Things: Šubḥalmaran and His Times," *The Harp* VIII,IX (July 1995–1996), pp. 138–149, referred briefly to Aphrahat. This study takes up that remark in a more considered way.

[7] J. Duchesne-Guillemin, "Zoroastrian Religion", in Yarshater (1983), Part 2, pp. 866–908, p. 886.

the discussion to embrace the entirety of God's governance of the universe and the moral qualities necessary as its human counterpart.

Our writers' methods differ because of dissimilarities of circumstance, of presupposition, and of method. Circumstances differ, in that Aphrahat deals with a single occasion and the precipitate act of an individual; Šubḥalmaran deals with the massive interactive range of complex social, political and religious interactions which token the end of an empire. Presuppositions differ, in that Aphrahat engages in a debate on faith, namely an apologia against Judaism; Šubḥalmaran is influenced rather by Zoroastrian culture, where there is an expectation that declining standards and confusion of ways are precursors of deliverance. Methods differ, too, namely their choice and handling of scripture. But consideration of the authors must come before these are discussed: there are problems of ascription and historicity.

3. *Aphrahat*

This name is familiar to those who know something of the history of the oriental, or pre-Chalcedonian, churches; but in fact all that is known about that name's owner is that a collection of 23 discourses, or Demonstrations,[8] is ascribed to him. Gwynn's comment

> Aphrahat's literary lot was the singular one, that his work survived in an alien tongue for alien readers when the original had well-nigh perished out of the memory of his own people[9]

suggests that he achieved what Rudyard Kipling desired: that there be no studies of his person, only of his works.[10] Attempts to give him a personal name (Jacob), and to give him a personal history (that he was a monk of the monastery of Mar Matta, in the mountain area near the present Mosul, and that he had the rank of bishop) are the result of late chronicling by which the Jacobite party claimed both author and monastery as their own.

---

[8] The *editio princeps* is that of W. Wright, *The Homilies of Aphraates, the Persian Sage, edited from syriac manuscripts of the fifth and sixth century in the British Museum*, (London, 1869). The edition used here is that of J. Parisot, *Patrologia Syriaca* I,1 (Paris, 1894), I,2 pp. 1–489 (Paris, 1907).

[9] J. Gwynn, *A Select Library of Nicene and Post-Nicene Fathers*, 2nd series, 13 (London, 1898), p. 119.

[10] See also R. Kipling, *Something of Myself*, R. Hampson (ed.) with an Introduction by Robert Holmes (London, 1987), p. 16.

Admittedly his work is clearly dated, in the body of the material, to two periods of activity. XXII, 25 dates the first ten Demonstrations to the equivalent of A.D. 337, and the next twelve to the equivalent of A.D. 344. Demonstration XXIII is dated to the following year. In the course of an important study of Demonstration V against the background of the activities of Constantine and Eusebius' chronicling of them T.D. Barnes concludes[11] that the date of Demonstration V should be July 337 so that

> The war whose coming Aphrahat heralds was not an ordinary frontier campaign initiated by the Persian king, and Aphrahat was not writing in the knowledge that Constantine was already dead. He wrote about a war in which he expected Constantine to invade Persia and to conquer the area in which he lived.[12]

Other information is less certain: it is by way of being editorial additions to manuscripts, reflecting assessments of the contents, or uncritical tradition. About a century and a half after the writer's death he is described by Gennadius, continuator of Jerome's work on illustrious men, as "Jacobus cognomento Sapiens Nizebenae nobilis Persarum modo civitatis episcopus" – a confusion with a near contemporary, not a Persian, who was bishop of Nisibis and died in 338. The oldest relevant manuscript,[13] dated 474, designates the author as "The Persian Sage", as does a sixth century one.[14] Another sixth century one, bound up with and under the same number as the first, dated 512, designates him "Mar Jacob the Persian sage" a cautious enough term, yet suggesting episcopal status, even though the term may signify no more than honour for a monk.[15] The thirteenth-century Gregory Barhebraeus gives the name 'pharad' – a title 'chief' rather than a personal name, to "The Persian Sage". A fourteenth century manuscript provides the developed title of "The sage Aphrahat, who is Jacob Bishop of Mar Matta".[16]

What has happened is this. The contents of the Demonstrations in general have been taken as referring to an ascetic life described

---

[11] T.D. Barnes, "Constantine and the Christians of Persia", *Journal of Classical Studies* 75 (1985), pp. 126–136. The discussion of dating is on pp. 128–130.

[12] Barnes (1985), p. 130.

[13] British Library, Additional Manuscript 17182.

[14] British Library, Additional Manuscript 14619.

[15] Joseph Simonius Assemanus, *Bibliotheca Orientalis. . . .* 3 vols. (Rome 1719–1728), 3.1, p. 189.

[16] British Library, Oriental Manuscript 1017. For a discussion of evidence, see Gwynn (1898), pp. 154–158.

in such a way that it could have been done only by someone within it. The ascetic pattern has been taken to be a formal monastic one, on the pattern of a later time.[17] Again, Demonstration XIV is taken to be a letter, drafted by a senior bishop, from an assembly to a council. This takes the piece to have an origin in a specific occasion, and to have specific persons as targets. But the Demonstration opens with a paragraph which builds phrases from Phil. 1:1; Acts 15:22–23; and 1 Cor. 1:2 to make an appeal from an entire church in various unnamed places to an entire church in Seleucia, Ctesiphion and elsewhere. It is a literary construction based upon the pattern of Philippians which stresses the necessity for unity and harmony. As a measured reproach to Christians of fourth-century Iran, it fits well as an integral part of the second group of 12 Demonstrations whose initial letters correspond with successive letters of the alphabet and whose contents are linked by an association of ideas.[18] Finally, J.M. Fiey comments that to undertake a history of the monasteries of which Mar Matta is one is to approach a veritable Penelope's web. In brief, our writer lived before the foundation of the monastery, and even its eponymous martyr – let alone the ecclesiastical structure that would make its abbot second bishop of a province. In short, the title given in the last mentioned manuscript recreates Aphrahat in an image familiar to itself in order to add lustre to its environment where there is then a more developed monasticism[19] and ecclesiastical structure. Our writer is among those whose name has perished but whose children stand to the covenant.[20] When he wrote his contemporaries were faced with Judaism or Christianity as the fulfilment of promise and Covenant, and with the need to set current events within phases of the divine plan.

---

[17] The formal structure of Syriac monasticism comes with the sixth-century Abraham of Kashkar, Abraham of Nathpar, and Babai the Great. See J.M. Fiey, "Les Communités Syriaques en Iran des Premiers Siècles à 1552", reprinted in Variorum Reprints (London, 1979), pp. I, 279–297, p. 285. On Babai, see below, in the discussion of Šubḥalmaran.

[18] This argument follows that of G. Nedungatt in OCP XLVI (1980), pp. 62–88, except for the comment that the pattern of 1 Thess. suggests a literary rather than historical basis. Nedungatt rightly takes the Demonstration as a general one suitable for the year 344 rather than as a specific attack in an earlier year on Papa.

[19] On the history of Mar Matta, person and monastery, see J.M. Fiey, *Assyrie Chrétienne: Contribution à l'étude de l'Histoire et de la Géographie Ecclésiastiques et Monastiques de Nord de L'Iraq*, vol. II (Beyrouth, no date), pp. 759–770. Pp. 756–784 discuss the whole region and its later chroniclers.

[20] See Sirach 44:9, 12.

4. Šubḥalmaran

Faith is the dominant virtue for Aphrahat, to give him his familiar designation; for Šubḥalmaran it is love. His contemporaries faced the traditional alternation of war and peace between Sasanian and Byzantine empires and the increasing destabilisation of both in the half-century or so before Islam expanded northwards.[21] They had to face, too, the feuding and disharmony within an amalgam Persian Christianity trying to find imperial support and to maintain a theological and ecclesiastical credibility when the distinction between Persian and Byzantine empires found a corresponding conflict between native Persian theology and one under Byzantine influence.

The difficulty of finding accurate information about the writer of the Persian Sage's Demonstrations is matched by confusion about the authorship of folios 1r to 73r of British Library Oriental Manuscript 6714.[22] Throughout, the author is stated to be Šubḥalmaran, bishop and metropolitan of Beth Selok – now Kirkuk, to the South West of Mosul. Abdisho's catalogue[23] refers to him and his writings, and he is fairly taken to be, as J.M. Fiey suggests,[24] the last known bishop of that see in the Sasanian period. He is described as a man renowned for quality of monastic life, and as a contemporary of the martyr monk George, of the royal favourite and financier Yazdin, of the meretricious immoral and scheming court physician Gabriel of Singar, and of the theologian and monastic reformer Babai the Great.[25]

---

[21] "The empire which Khusrau ruled was in its glory, but already showing signs of decay in a spirit of pessimism and decadence prevalent among many of its citizens". R.N. Frye, "The Political History of Iran under the Sasanians" in Yarshater volume 1 (1983), pp. 116–180, p. 160.

[22] See D.J. Lane, "Mar Shubhalmaran's "Book of Gifts", An Example of a Syriac Literary Genre" OCA 229 (Rome, 1987), pp. 411–417 for a description of the manuscript and a discussion of faulty earlier cataloguing.

[23] Assemanus (1719–1728), p. 189.

[24] J.M. Fiey, *Assyrie Chrétienne*, vol. III, *Bét Garmaï bét Aramaye et Maisan Nestoriens* (Beyrouth, 1968), p. 29.

[25] See: A. Scher (ed.), "Chronique de Seert," II, pp. 201–209 = *Patrologia Orientalis* XIII, (1919), pp. 521–530; E.W. Brooks (ed.), I.-E. Chabot tr. *Chronica Minora* 22 (20) = COSCO ser III 4; *Liber Turris* = H. Gismondi (ed. and tr.), *Amri, Maris et Slibae de Patriarchis Ecclesiae Orientalis commentaria*, (Rome, 1896/97), vol. 1, pp. 49–54; vol. 2, pp. 29–32; P. Bedjan, *Histoire de Mar Jabalaha, de Trois Autres patriarches, d'Un Prêtre et des Deux Laïques Nestoriens* (Paris, Leipzig, 1895), pp. 520–21. Babai's works are listed in Geevarghese Chediath, *The Christology of Mar Babai the Great*, (Kottayam, 1982), pp. 17–41.

However things are not entirely straightforward. A seventh or eighth century Syriac manuscript, no. 1034 of the St. Catherine's Monastery in Sinai,[26] contains 75 pages entitled "Commentary on Holy Scripture by Babai the Great", followed by 60 headed "Sermons of Šubḥalmaran, metropolitan bishop of Karka and Beth Selok". The latter includes a sermon on the last things, which sounds like the material discussed later in this article. However, some of Mère Philotea's summaries of Babai's work look remarkably like summaries of material ascribed to Šubḥalmaran: for example "The mysteries of all the religions . . ." like matter on fol. 62v; "The manifestation of the one who is lost . . ." like some on fol. 62v or 64v; "The sufferings which the impious make the faithful endure . . ." like some on fol. 63r; "How to listen to the voice . . ." like some on fol. 68r. Babai the Great was invited to join Šubḥalmaran and others in theological discussions with Chosroes II's advisers: he declined, protesting ill health, but undertook to send written material.[27] The association of these two churchmen may have led collectors and transcribers of manuscripts to make faulty ascriptions; or there may have been genuine confusion about the respective literary remains of two close contemporaries associated with the Mt. Izla monastery. Here the London manuscript's attribution is followed.

5. *Aphrahat's Fourth Century*

Aphrahat responds to a specific question, "concerning our faith; how it is and what its foundation is, and on what structure it rises, on what it rests, and how it has a completion and crowning, and the actions which are its requisites".[28] In Demonstration V Aphrahat turns to the drawn-out contest between the Romans and Persians for control of the cities on the route between the upper Euphrates and Tigris, arguing this falls within God's governance of the universe, encapsulated in the phrase

---

[26] M. Philotea du Sinaï, "Les nouveaux manuscrits syriaques du Mont Sinaï", *OCA* 221 (Rome, 1983), pp. 333–339. There is, alas, no further information available yet, either in catalogue or reproduction of the manuscripts.

[27] The matter will receive further attention in the writer's nearly completed edition.

[28] Inquirer's letter, 2.

It is inevitable that good will come to be, and happy is he through whom it comes; it is inevitable that evil will come, and alas for the one through whom it comes.[29]

This is an expanded form of Matt. 18:7, found also, as Parisot notes, in the Pseudo-Clementine Homilies XII:29 and Epitome 96. This form of the dominical saying interprets by added contrast,[30] fitting in well with Aphrahat's expressive methods of handling his main text of reference, Daniel. He moves on to another dominical saying,

Everyone who exalts himself will be brought low, and he who makes himself low will be raised up,[31]

which fits precisely into a set of circumstances. Barnes[32] emphasises the importance of getting the historical circumstances exactly right, and does so in such a way as to make plain the full inwardness of the discourse. He concludes first, that the text should be understood to have been written "in the fifth year after the great massacre of martyrs in the eastern region;"[33] second, that Constantine was planning a deliberate religion-driven campaign to free those Christians who were in Persian territory; third, that Shapur launched a pre-emptive strike in the expectation that Constantine's activity on the Danube would give him a certain hope of success.[34] Aphrahat handles passages from Daniel to demonstrate that Constantine's looked-for victory fulfils the prophecy that the defeat of a wicked empire by a righteous one is a prelude to the time of fulfilment. The only comment needed on such clear arguments is that much of the evidence about Constantine comes from Eusebius whose emphases need to be taken into account; and that Constantine's actions would find justification if it were only to recover or deliver Romans who had been deported and re-settled by Ardashir and Shapur I.

---

[29] V, 1.

[30] P.S. Alexander, "Jewish Aramaic Translations of the Hebrew Scriptures", in M.J. Mulder (ed.), *Mikra: Text, Translation, Reading and Interpretation of the Hebrew Bible in Ancient Judaism* (Assen/Maastricht/Philadelphia, 1988), pp. 217–253.

[31] Luke 14:11.

[32] Barnes (1985), p. 130.

[33] This takes the relevant passage "in the fifth year *the year* when there was the great massacre" to contain a doublet – "the year", here italicised: Barnes (1985), p. 129.

[34] Barnes (1985), p. 132.

6. *Šubḥalmaran's Late Sixth and Early Seventh Centuries*

The background to which our second author writes is more complex.[35] The late sixth century had seen a further two and a half centuries of struggle for possession of the present northern Iraq, with a settlement in 363 which saw a boundary agreement placing Edessa, Tella, Dara and Amid in the Roman sphere of influence, and Nisibis in the Persian; and which split the monastic Tur Abdin area. The territorial and political division was reflected in theological and ecclesiastical affairs, so forming what J.M. Fiey referred to as *L'Église Syrienne Orientale* and *L'Église Syrienne Occidentale*.[36] Each jurisdiction appealed to Chosroes II for support, but he wished to recognise neither, leaving the Catholicate in suspension after the death of Gregory I. His courtiers, and tradition says his wives, between them supported both sides; factions had succeeded in intruding Gregory I as Catholicos: a candidate without royal approval, which had been given to another of the same name. The theological school at Nisibis was split, a large faction under Ḥenana coming out against the Persian tradition of exegesis associated with Theodore of Mopsuestia. Rival political factions had hindered Chosroes II's assumption of the throne, so that he achieved it by the aid of the Emperor Maurice: the latter's murder impelled the Persian ruler to punitive measures. In Beth Selok there had been 40 years of persecution from 540; the surrounding province had suffered ten years of plague from 570. In effect, every element of life had been subject to dissent, faction and tragic disturbance. Our writer himself was exiled for life, and a Persian, George of Izla, martyred, as a consequence of their rebuke of the royal favourite, the court physician Gabriel of Singar. He had married twice and attempted to expropriate monastic property. Such events generated despair, a quality that underlay Zoroastrian thought, and which also called to mind the eschatological discourses of the Gospels and the comments of St. Paul in Thessalonians.[37]

---

[35] A summary with further illustration is found in Lane (1995–6).

[36] Fiey (1979), p. 279.

[37] See the literature mentioned at note 25 above. Summaries may be found especially in A. Christensen, *L'Iran sous les Sassanides* (Copenhagen, 1936, revised edition 1944: the revisions are in fact minimal), and in J. Labourt, *Le Christianisme dans L'Empire Perse* (Paris, 1904). More recently, J.M. Fiey, *Jalons pour un Histoire de L'Église en Iraq* (Louvain, 1970) or, less critically, W.G. Young, *Patriarch, Shah and Caliph*, (Rawalpindi, 1974).

7. Aphrahat's Method

Aphrahat takes passages from 2 Kings, Isaiah and Ezekiel to tease out elements from Daniel. The evidence in Demonstration V (On Wars) supports the conclusions reached by R.J. Owens: that is, Aphrahat quotes generally *memoriter* rather than by transcription from a Peshitta text. Further, his mind is furnished by scripture so as to provide allusion as well as identifiable reference; and of course "he writes not a bible commentary, but theological essays".[38] His mind is formed by Jewish interpretative method[39] and so can here follow the pattern indicated by Neusner:

> He copiously cites the Hebrew Scriptures, rarely the New Testament . . . His exegeses of Scriptures are reasonable and rational, for the most part. . . . (based) on the plain sense of Scripture as he thinks everyone must understand it. More often than not, he quotes without exegesis at all, thinking that the meaning is obvious, the implication clear. It is frequently alleged that his arguments are exegetical, but this seems to me far from the case. The arguments are fundamentally historical. Exegesis of Scriptures actually plays a small part. What dominates is *citation* of Scriptures as one would cite a historical document, for facts available to anyone, not for interpretations acceptable only to the initiated.[40]

Aphrahat's argument is a simple one, with a single point of reference, so that it is easy enough to enter the working of his mind. He says that a thought has struck his mind about the approaching turbulence and large force assembled for slaughter.[41] He demonstrates that the cause of this impending tumult is the coming campaign of Shapur II, which will end in the Romans' dominance of Persia. For him this falls within God's governance of the universe: Shapur, the arrogant initiator of the campaign, will be brought low, and the Christian church (for a short while under the protection of a Christian

---

[38] R.J. Owens, *The Genesis-Exodus Citations of Aphrahat the Persian Sage* (Leiden, 1983), p. 242. See also pp. 20–27 for a summary of Aphrahat's method.

[39] "The Targum on the Prophets was in use in Babylonia in the early fourth century, since R. Joseph bar Ḥiyya, head of the academy of Pumbeditha, quotes from it several times", E. Schürer, *History of the Jewish People in the Age of Jesus Christ*, revised and edited by G. Vermes and F. Millar, 3 vols. in 4 parts (Edinburgh, 1973–87), vol. 1, p. 102.

[40] J. Neusner, *Aphrahat and Judaism: The Christian Jewish Argument in Fourth-Century Iran*, Studia Post-Biblica 19 (Leiden, 1971), p. 5.

[41] Dem V, 1.

Rome) will, in place of the Jews who have forfeited their claim, be exalted at the coming of the Christ.

His argument is supported by a reading of Daniel, expanded and interpreted with references to prophetic and historical scripture. This has the irony that its ostensible background is the court of the last Assyrian, while underlying the whole exegetical enterprise is an unexpressed assumption, a commonplace among Jews of the Babylonian diaspora: namely, that the Roman empire would triumph.

> For exegetical reasons the rabbis supposed that the Romans were the stronger of the two empires, but that did not indicate that they hoped for a Roman victory.[42]

Neusner cites here R. Papa who was told by Rava that King Shapur was to be eclipsed by Caesar, as was proved by Dan. 7:23 "It (the fourth beast) shall devour the whole earth and trample it down . . ." The same point is made by Neusner elsewhere,[43] where he discusses Jewish responses to the rise of Sasanian power and of the Magi and quotes a comment by R. Yohanan that Roman power was irresistible.

Aphrahat is not, therefore, examining the text of Daniel to give an objective interpretation of this expressive book: his approach is topical, and scriptural material is taken to demonstrate that the victorious power is that of Rome. His choice of Daniel is an obvious one enough, for it had been produced and was subsequently used as interpretation of current events. It is not surprising that versions of Daniel are found in Qumran material, for example 4Q246.[44] The Peshitta version of Daniel, which is both translation and interpretation, includes glosses which expand and explicate the text. Richard A. Taylor identifies these, and in commenting on those in ch. 8 states

> Their purpose is to unfold for the reader the historical significance of certain cryptic passages in the Book of Daniel. Like those in chapter seven, these glosses are significant because of their relatively early date, being found in the oldest Syriac manuscripts, and because of the insights which they provide for the history of biblical exegesis in the Syriac speaking milieu.[45]

---

[42] J. Neusner, *A History of the Jews in Babylonia*, volume IV, *The Age of Shapur*, Studia Post Biblica 14 (Leiden, 1969), p. 48.

[43] J. Neusner, *A History of the Jews in Babylonia*, volume II, *The Early Sasanian Period*, Studia Post Biblica 11 (Leiden, 1966), pp. 52–57.

[44] See F.M. Cross, *The Ancient Library at Qumran* (Sheffield, 3rd edition, 1995), pp. 189–190.

[45] R.A. Taylor, *The Peshitta of Daniel* (Leiden, 1994), p. 219.

Much of the work of explicit identification of the beasts of Daniel has been done already by the Peshiṭta translator(s): all Aphrahat has to do is to exercise ingenuity in making a close correlation between Roman history and the Daniel text. There are three stages in this. The first is to redistribute the empires among the beasts: his four kingdoms are Babylon; Media/Persia; Alexander; Romans. The second is to follow a traditional identification of "the sons of Edom" with Rome. The third is to state that the third and fourth are the same, that is of the same order. Hence the interplay between Jacob (standing for the Jews) and Esau (standing for the Romans) prepares the way for the ultimate triumph of those within the Covenant. An ingenious adjustment of Roman rulers to fit the text of Daniel makes possible the roles envisaged for Constantine and Shapur; and a redefinition of the Saints of the Most High makes Christians rather than Jews the beneficiaries of a Christian Roman rule before the coming of Christ to whom the kingdom belongs.[46]

The identification of the beasts is based on a juxtaposition of Daniel with Gen. 6:10 (the sons of Noah) and Gen. 10 (the table of the nations), so that the three sons of Noah, Shem, Ham and Japheth, are types of the later kingdoms. The sons of Ham are the seed of Nimrod, and so stand for Babylon; Japheth, understood as the younger, is the originator of both Persians and Medes as the Greeks are brothers of the Medes; the sons of Shem are taken as the sons of Esau. Japheth the younger gives way to Shem the elder,[47] signalling the displacement of the Greeks by the Romans.

In the second phase of the argument the fourth beast is identified with Rome, since the rule of Octavian displaced that of Alexander, with the defeat of Antony. The Roman emperors are thus the continuators of Alexander's domination, as illustrated by the unbroken use of the term "the year x of the Greeks" as a designator of time. The concluding stage of this part of his argument is that the Roman dominion will continue only "until such time as there comes the one to whom the kingdom belongs".[48] This is an expanded quotation

---

[46] Barnes (1985), pp. 133–134 admirably demonstrates Aphrahat's re-shaping of imperial history to suit his use of Daniel: "Beneath the confusions of this bizarre computation, there seems to hover an assumption that the central fact of Roman imperial history is the conversion of the empire to Christianity".

[47] Targum Ps J at Gen. 10:21 takes Japheth to be the elder. Aphrahat interprets the text to suit his argument of Roman strength.

[48] This links Dan. 2:44 with Dan. 7:13,14.

from Gen. 49:10, not as found in the early Peshiṭta tradition, though
it is to be found in a ninth-century lectionary margin, in two eleventh
century lectionaries, and in a group of manuscripts after the twelfth
century.[49] The hermeneutic pattern may indeed be bizarre, but it is
consistent with the statement of Neusner:

> Judaism's response to historical events of a cataclysmic character nor-
> mally takes two forms, first, renewed messianic speculation, and sec-
> ond, a search in Scripture for relevant ideas, attitudes, and historical
> paradigms.[50]

There is an element of the Targumic about it, for biblical material
is updated, other and complementary passages are woven with it to
provide interpretation, and circumstance dictates interpretation.

8. Šubḥalmaran's Method

Šubḥalmaran's approach is entirely different. His presupposition is
not grounded in the Jewish influence which shaped Aphrahat, rather
in that of Christian eschatology and Zoroastrian pessimism.[51]

> It is really the knowledge of the directly imminent beginning of the
> last epoch of the world, in which Good and Evil would be separated
> from one another, which he (i.e. Zoroaster) gave to mankind. It is the
> knowledge that it lies in every individual's hand to participate in the
> extirpation of falsehood and in the establishing of the kingdom of God,
> before whom all men devoted to the pastoral life are equal, and so
> to re-establish the milk-flowing paradise on earth.[52]

The writer uses three ways of addressing the last days. The first,
and shortest, is by quotation of Matt. 24 (fols. 61v–62r). This passage reads:

> (3) The disciples *therefore* went *on one occasion to our Lord and said* to him:
> "Our Lord, when *does your kingdom, for which we long*, come; and what
> sign is there of *its* coming, and of the consummation of the world?"
> (4) *He however* said *"When the time of its coming approaches, there will be* (6)

---

[49] 9l5mg; 11l4,5; 12b2 etc.
[50] Neusner (1966), p. 52.
[51] For a discussion of other passages as evidence of his use of Scripture see D.J.
Lane, "The Well of Life: Šubḥalmaran's Use of Scripture", *OCA* 256 (1998),
pp. 49–59.
[52] Quoted by R.N. Frye, *The Heritage of Persia*, (London, 1962), p. 33. He takes
it from H. Humbach, *Die Gathas des Zarathustra* 1 (Heidelberg, 1959), p. 74.

wars *and plagues and* (7b) earthquakes in different places; (7a) and nation will arise against nation and kingdom against kingdom, *and every people will be divided against itself, for the sake of destruction and not for the sake of victory*, and there will be great (21) *turbulence in all the world, and oppression which terrorises and terrifies everyone. And then they will see* (11, 24a) deceiving messiahs and prophets who prophesy lies; and they will give signs in the heaven and mighty deeds *upon earth, and cast fear and trembling in every soul*, (24b) and will lead astray, if possible, even those chosen. (12) And because of the greatness of the wickedness the love of many will fail. *So then indignation and offence will rule all, and they will hate each other and betray each other. See that you are not disturbed and made to go astray after them.* (26) If people say to you, See *here* is the messiah, and See, *there* he is, do not believe. (27) Just as the lightning flashes from the east and is seen as far as the west and *it gives light to everything that is under the heaven*, so *also will my last* coming *be from heaven:* (30) glorious, *splendid, and swift. And there is no need for anyone to say Where is the messiah? Because in my* (30) glory *and in the splendour of the* (31) angels *I am revealed to lead you*".

A comparison with the Syriac text,[53] whose verse numbers are inserted, reveals differences, indicated by italics. The basic structure is from Matt. 24, but with elements of 1 Thess. 4:16, Jn. 6:39 and 1 Cor. 15:51 to present a schematised portrayal. This method of handling scripture resembles Aphrahat's, though here the basic material is New Testament: part quotation, part comment, part synthesis, part re-ordering and part imaginative creation. There is also allusion to events: here may be discerned Jewish messianic movements of the mid sixth century, the plagues of Bet Selok, the earthquakes which devastated Antioch, the persecutions of Chosroes II, the theological and personal recriminations between Jacobites and Diophysites, and the wars which took Persian armies to Constantinople and Roman ones to Seleucia. It also shows how difficult it is to reconstruct scriptural text on the basis of patristic quotations.[54]

The second method used by our writer is the pastiche, or speaking likeness – an anatomy, in the old sense of the word. Šubḥalmaran begins with a passage which follows the one just quoted and which takes its references from 2 Thess. 2:3,6,7.

---

[53] *The New Testament in Syriac*, British and Foreign Bible Society, (London, 1905–20). G.A. Kiraz, *Comparative Edition of the Syriac Gospels*, (Leiden, 1996) does not show any correlations between our text and any Gospel version.

[54] On this problem, see M.J. Suggs, "The Use of Patristic evidence in the Search for a Primitive New Testament Text", *New Testament Studies* 4 (1957–1958), pp. 139–147.

So Blessed Paul hinted at the end and his coming, when he bared his
heart. The mystery of wickedness begins to have effect only if there
is removed that which restrains it until the determined last time of
which only our Lord is knowledgeable: that is, the providence and
governance and restraining power of the divine mercy. Then there will
be revealed dereliction and wickedness, the man of sin and son of
perdition in which it dwells, and there is revealed the one who was a
murderer from the beginning.

Then he presents the first portrait: a mirror image of Christ, namely
one born of a mother habituated to fornication and of Jewish descent,
who undertakes her son's abominable deeds until such time as he is
large enough to do them on his own behalf rather than through her
agency. She has the capacity to assume such forms as the wisest of
men or a fortress for demons, and is proportionate to her wickedness
as our Lord is to his goodness. There seem here to be allusions to
unspecified apocalyptic material "the so-called revelations written in
the honoured name of the apostles – if they are true" (fol. 62v).

The second portrait is that of the one who goes astray, dethroned
by pride, and whose real nature is revealed at the end of the age.
His was the authority over the crucifiers, and his is the authority
which corrupts and intermingles contradictory religions so that they
focus worship on him. His authority holds demons in loyalty to him,
and he promises earthly satisfactions as the means of entry to resurrection and guarantees of restoration to former companions. His
function is to reveal the true character of goodness as well as the
nature of evil (fol. 63r). Further portraits follow to the same effect;
possibly the best comment is found on this same folio:

> Praise to the patience of your goodness, O God of Righteousness, our
> kind creator, who allows the evil to accomplish their evil desires accord-
> ing to their will. . . . in the death of your beloved you gave satisfac-
> tion to both sides. By his murder the wicked had respite from the mad
> passion and grudging envy that they had against you, and the good
> lived by his death and are made perfect by his rising.

9. *Conclusion*

The essay has demonstrated the ways in which our two writers approach the matter of the last things. Aphrahat has done it within
a Jewish context of material and thought; Šubḥalmaran within that
of more obviously Christian material. Their resemblances reflect their

shared Persian Christianity; their differences, changed circumstances and presuppositions. The exegetical disposition of the one is shaped by a handling of material which, broadly speaking, may be called Targumic; that of the other by a familiarity with Zoroastrian pessimism and determinism which finds expression in a Christian faith. Both merit the dominical approval, suited for the sage of the kingdom who brings forth from his treasures things both old and new, currency matching circumstance.

THE "DEMONSTRATION ON LOVE" BY APHRAHAT THE SAGE: A TRANSLATION WITH INTRODUCTION

BY

L. STUCKENBRUCK

Durham

1. *Introduction*

The following article offers a brief discussion and translation of a "Demonstration on Love" composed in Syriac by Aphrahat "the Persian sage" ca. 336 C.E. This treatise is the second of twenty-three such works[1] by Aphrahat, and herewith is published in English for the first time. It has thus far not attracted much attention among scholars, perhaps because the views expressed by Aphrahat here are so characteristic of the other treatises as, for instance, his largely negative attitude towards Judaism. At the same time, however, the "Demonstration on Love" contains ideas not preserved in the other works; this is especially apparent in the way Aphrahat drew upon and interpreted the Jewish scriptures, as he addressed the character of God's love by drawing attention to references to time and duration in the story of Israel. While Aphrahat's thought has been noted primarily for its 'anti-Judaism', his reliance on the Jewish scriptures indicates how indispensable they were for his understanding of Christian faith. Below, after considering the circumstances in which the collection of twenty-three treatises were produced, I shall offer brief comments on Aphrahat's thought regarding Judaism and time in the "Demonstration on Love". It is a privilege to offer this article in honour of Dr. Anthony Gelston, whose own work in Syriac studies over the years has been nothing less than exemplary.

---

[1] Also often referred to as 'demonstrations' based on the Latin translation of I. Parisot (see n. 7 below).

2. Aphrahat's 'Demonstrations': Their Significance and socio-political Context

The extent to which Aphrahat's twenty-three treatises became influential from the fourth century through to the medieval period may at first seem to have been rather limited. John Gwynn, who in 1898 offered an English translation for eight of the demonstrations, gave such an impression in his introduction to the translation. Noting the relative paucity of manuscripts of the demonstrations and the long obscurity of their author's identity, he reached the following conclusion:

> In an excited age of controversy, these quiet hortatory discourses, . . . dealing with no burning question of the time, nor with any disputes more recent than those of the two previous centuries, or those between Jew and Christian, would hardly attain to more than a local circulation.[2]

Two main reasons allow one to cast doubt on Gwynn's assessment. First, it is misleading on the basis of scanty manuscript evidence to suppose that Aphrahat's compositions were only used in geographically proximate areas.[3] It is known that within the first hundred years following their composition, the treatises were used by Isaac of Antioch,[4] were at least identified and listed by Gennadius in the West,[5] and

---

[2] See J. Gwynn, "Selections Translated into English from the Hymns and Homilies of Ephraim the Syrian, and from the Demonstrations of Aphrahat the Persian Sage", in *The Nicene and Post-Nicene Fathers*, Second Series, vol. 13 (Grand Rapids, Michigan, 1979), pp. 113–412, citation from p. 159.

[3] This point is even admitted by Gwynn himself; see *ibid.*, pp. 153–55.

[4] A leader of the Armenian church whose literary activity (in Syriac and Armenian) flourished during the early fifth century, Isaac quoted extensively from Aphrahat's treatises on fasting (no. III). In addition, he seems to have known the "Demonstration on Faith" (no. I). On this, see the early discussion of J. Forget, *De Vita et Scriptis Aphraatis* (Louvain: Excudebant Vanlinthout Fratres, 1882), pp. 138–48.

[5] In the late firth century, Gennadius' expansions of Jerome's *De scriptoribus ecclesiasticis* drew on works by later authors, including some from the East who had not been included by Jerome; see chapter 1 in J.P. Migne (ed.), *Patrologia Latina*, vol. 58, cols. 1060–61, reproduced by G. Bert, *Aphrahat's des persischen Weisen Homilien. Aus dem Syrischen übersetzt und erläutert* Texte und Untersuchungen 3–4 (Leipzig, 1888), pp. xxv–xxvi. An English translation of Gennadius was first published in 1892 by E.C. Richardson, "Jerome and Gennadius", in *The Nicene and Post-Nicene Fathers*, Second Series, vol. 3 (Grand Rapids, Michigan, repr. 1979), pp. 348–568 (see p. 386). Though Gennadius claimed to know twenty-six treatises, the ones he actually listed number twenty-three (not '24', as in Bert (1888), p. xxvi). Gennadius, however, attributed the Demonstrations to Jacob the bishop of Nisibis, and not Aphrahat, as was also done by the fifth century Armenian version (see n. 8 below). The reason may perhaps lie in the designations applied to the author among his traditions: "the Persian sage" or even "Jacob the Persian sage", designations that date in the Syriac manuscripts to the fifth and sixth centuries. This mistake continued to be

were discussed by Georgius, a bishop among the Arabs.[6] In addition to the Syriac manuscripts (not discovered until the nineteenth century),[7] we know that some or all of the treatises were translated into Armenian,[8] Arabic,[9] and Ethiopic.[10] Secondly, while Gwynn's characterisation of the period during which Aphrahat wrote may be accurate, his description of the general tone of the treatises may lead one to infer that Aphrahat's thought was at best only a 'soft' response to events and controversies of his own time. From considerations adduced below, however, it may be shown that the opposite is more likely to be true.

---

made well into the nineteenth century; cf. e.g., B.H. Cowper, *Syriac Miscellanies; or Extracts relating to the First and Second General Councils, and Various other Quotations, Theological, Historical & Classical* (London, 1861), p. 108 n. 61. A composition in Nisibis is to be excluded from consideration (and therefore its bishop), as the city did not belong to the Persian empire until later in the fourth century (364 C.E.); cf. Bert (1888), p. xx n. 2. An authorship by Aphrahat is confirmed in the margin of one of the Syriac manuscripts, as reported by W. Wright in his *Catalogue of Syriac Manuscripts in the British Museum, Acquired Since the year 1838*, vol. 2 (London: British Museum, 1871), p. 401 col. 2: "Aphrahat the Wise is Jacob the bishop of the monastery Mar Mattai".

[6] During the eighth century, he discussed at length the content and author of the demonstrations in a Syriac letter address to a friend in Mesopotamia. For the text, see W. Wright (ed.), *Homilies of Aphraates v. 1: The Syriac Text* (London, 1869), pp. 19–37; for translations into English and German respectively, see Cowper (1861), pp. 61–75 and Bert (1888), pp. xxxvii–li.

[7] The oldest, ms. 'B' (see this n. below), was copied in Edessa; cf. Wright (1869), pp. 19–37. Largely eclectic and reasonably accurate editions of the Syriac manuscripts were offered by both Wright (1896), and I. Parisot, "Aphraatis sapientia persea, Demonstrationes", in R. Graffin (ed.), *Patrologia syriaca*, vols. 1–2 (Paris, 1894 and 1907). Whereas Wright transcribed the text using the original *Estrangela* script, Parisot presented it in *Serto* and translated the whole into Latin based on his pointing. For a brief assessment of these editions, see R.J. Owens, *The Genesis and Exodus Citations of Aphrahat the Persian Sage*, Monographs of the Peshitta Institute Leiden (Leiden, 1983), pp. 9–16, esp. p. 16: "though generally accurate, [they] are not entirely free of errors". In this article, I adopt the designations proposed by Wright for the manuscripts (A, B, <u>B</u>, C) in (1871), pp. 401–405. Manuscripts A (sixth century) and B (fifth century) combine to comprise almost the entire text.

[8] This version was published with Latin translation by N. Antonelli in 1756, based on a manuscript preserved at the Armenian monastery in Venice. Despite its early date (fifth century), only the first nine treatises are included (nos. I–IX) and these are arranged in an order which departs from that in the Syriac manuscripts. See the bibliography in Owens (1983), p. 251 n. 15.

[9] See B. Yousif and K. Samir, "Le version arabe de la troisième démonstration d'Aphrahat (sur le jeûne)", in K. Samir (ed.), *Actes du deuxième Congrès International d'Études Arabes Chrétiennes* (Rome, 1986), pp. 31–66.

[10] See Gwynn's report (1979), p. 154, concerning an existing Ethiopic translation of the "Demonstration on Wars" (no. V). Furthermore, T. Baarda, in "Another Treatise of Aphrahat the Persian Sage in Ethiopic Translation", *NTS* 27 (1981),

The Demonstrations of Aphrahat were originally written as a collection and, on the basis of internal evidence alone, may be dated
rather precisely. The first twenty-two each open with a successive
letter of the alphabet, an acrostic that the author himself mentions
at the end of treatises X, XXII, and XXIII. In the latter, he writes:

> I have written to you this letter . . . after I wrote those previous twelve
> treatises which one after the other are ordered according to their
> letters.[11]

As for dating, one learns from demonstrations V, XIV, XXII, and
XXIII that, respectively, they were written in the years 336/7 (V,
year 648 of Seleucid reckoning), 344/5 (XIV, XXII, year 35 of
Shapur II's reign and Seleucid era year 655), and 345 C.E. (XXIII,
Seleucid era year 656). The first ten, constituting the earlier part of
the collection, were thus composed some eight years before the next
twelve, while the final treatise was produced a year later.

The significance of this precise dating for determining the socio-
historical context of Aphrahat's treatises cannot be overestimated.
It is clear that the first demonstrations are primarily concerned
with beliefs, issues, and practices of concern to the Christian
community: faith (I), love (II), fasting (III), prayer (IV), wars (V),
monks (VI), repentance (VII), resurrection (VIII), humility (IX), and
pastors (X). Among the remaining ones, however, Aphrahat's attention focuses more explicitly on problems posed by Judaism: circum-
cision (XI), passover (XII), sabbath (XIII), eating of meats (XV),
Gentiles as God's people (XVI), Jesus as the Messiah (XVII), vir-
ginity (XVIII, subtitled "Against the Jews"), scattering of Israel (XIX,
also entitled "Against the Jews"), alms (XX), and persecution (XXI;
see below). Admittedly, though the second group is not exclusively
devoted to a repudiation of Judaism,[12] neither do the writings in the
first group ignore the question of conflict between Christianity and
Judaism.[13] Nevertheless, the shift of concern among the demonstra-

---

pp. 632–40, offers evidence for an Ethiopic translation of treatise VIII "Concerning
the Resurrection of the Dead".

[11] The Syriac text: *ktbt lk 'grt' ḥd' . . . btr dktbt hlyn 'sryn wtryn rš' qdmy' dsymyn 'l
'twt' ḥd btr ḥd.*

[12] E.g., Demonstrations XIV ('Exhortations'), XXII ("Death and the Last Times"),
and XXIII ("The Grape"). Actually, XIV assumes the form of a letter written by
Aphrahat on behalf of a synod, addressing the people and Christian leaders in
Seleucia and Ctesiphon because of a schism.

[13] A good example is found in the "Demonstration on Love" translated below.

tions is unmistakable, and one is made to ask whether there are any known circumstances from fourth century Persia which may provide an explanation.

To this end, both internal and external evidence suggest a plausible scenario that is commonly accepted among scholars.[14] The final treatise was authored in the thirty-sixth year of Shapur the king who, according to Aphrahat, "carried out the persecution" and which was written "in the fifth year after he [Shapur] uprooted the congregations, in the year of the great destruction of confessors in the land of the East".[15] If this information holds true – and there is no reason to think otherwise – a persecution under the Sassanid empire was instigated against the Christian community between the writing of the first and second groups of demonstrations. In addition, between XXII and XXIII, the persecution had apparently led to a number of deaths. One need not look very far among the treatises to find Aphrahat's explanation for these tumultuous events. In his discussion on wars (V), he is disparaging of the Persian state which he metaphorically labels "the children of Jacob", while his sympathies are placed with the rival Roman empire which is termed "the children of Esau".[16] Before treatise XXIII Aphrahat does not offer political reasons for the persecution; but when he broaches the subject in demonstration XXI, his discussion is not directed against the heathen of the Persian state, but rather against a certain Jewish 'sage', a dialogue partner who has charged that the Christians' current plight indicates their religious illegitimacy:

---

[14] Cf. e.g. Bert (1888), pp. xxxii–xxxiii; S. Funk, *Die haggadischen Elemente in den Homilien des Aphrahates, des persischen Weisen* (Vienna, 1891), pp. 10–14; E.J. Duncan, *Baptism in the Demonstrations of Aphraates the Persian Sage* (Washington, D.C., 1945), pp. 21–23; J. Neusner, *Aphrahat and Judaism. The Christian-Jewish Argument in Fourth-Century Iran* Studia Post-Biblica 19 (Leiden, 1971), p. 4; J.L. Kautt, "Aphrahat in der Auseinandersetzung mit den Juden: Ein Vergleich seiner Argumentation in den antijüdischen Demonstrationen mit der Justins im Dialog mit Trypho" (Masters Thesis, Eberhard-Karls University of Tübingen, 1995). The most thoroughgoing treatment is that of F. Gavin, *Aphraates and the Jews. A Study of the Controversial Homilies of the Persian Sage and their Relation to Jewish Thought* Contributions to Oriental History and Philology 9 (Toronto: Journal of the Society of Oriental Research, 1923), esp. pp. 7–31.

[15] See the text in Parisot (1894, 1907), vol. 2, p. 150, lines 5–11.

[16] It is possible, though not clear, that Aphrahat's nomenclature suggest that he regarded the Jews as sided with Shapur against the Christian community. For the passage, see Wright (1869), p. 507*; see the translations in Gwynn (1979), p. 361 par. 24 and Bert (1888), pp. 69–70 n. 1.

Thus is there not any wise person among all your people whose prayer is heard and who asks God to free you from your persecution?[17]

This rhetorical taunt at least suggests that the political oppression under Shapur had agitated Jewish-Christian tensions.

This picture is consistent with an account extant in two late fifth century recensions recounting the martyrdom of St. Simeon bar Sabba'e, the bishop of Seleucia-Ctesiphon (ca. 344).[18] These records, one of which purports to contain an account written before the year 407, report from a Christian perspective that the Jews were calumniating Simeon by associating him with Caesar. The second recension (late fifth century) even more explicitly attributes to Jews the charge that Christians were clandestine supporters of Rome, Shapur's arch-enemy.[19] Furthermore, a more favourable status of Jews than Christians in the Sassanid empire is indicated by the close relationship that apparently existed between some Jewish citizens and Shapur's mother.[20] The Christian bias of these accounts, which attempted to draw parallels between the role played by Jews in the deaths of Jesus and Simeon, should caution one from assuming their historical veracity in every detail.[21] It remains difficult, however, to escape the conclusion of Edward Duncan:

> ... since the persecution of Shapur II against the Christians had begun in 340, we might expect to find in this circumstance some reason for the intensification of Aphraates' opposition to Judaism, the more so because of the not unfavourable position of the Jews under the Sassanids.[22]

It would be too simplistic to explain the nature and severity of the Persian persecution on the basis of the Jewish influence in the royal court. As the first ten Demonstrations written before 340 show, there were sharp religious and ideological tensions between the Christian and Jewish communities, and these could easily have set

---

[17] Cf. the text in Wright (1869), p. 364*.

[18] Cf. M. Kmoskó (ed.), "S. Simeon Bar Sabba'e", in *Patrologia Syriaca*, vol. 2 (Paris, 1907).

[19] *Ibid.*, cols. 737 and 740.

[20] *Ibid.*, cols. 693–94.

[21] For a thorough discussion of such tendencies in the accounts of Simeon's death, see G. Wiessner, *Untersuchungen zur Syrischen Literaturgeschichte v. 1: Zur Martyrerüberlieferung aus der Christenverfolgung Schapurs II* Abhandlungen der Akademie der Wissenschaften in Göttingen Philologisch-Historische Klasse 67 (Göttingen, 1967), pp. 46–79.

[22] Duncan (1945), p. 22.

the stage for the ensuing crisis. Against this background, the anti-Jewish tone of Aphrahat's earlier treatises acquires a significance that merits attention. Among them was, of course, the "Demonstration on Love" (II), to which the present discussion now turns.

3. *"Demonstration on Love": Aphrahat's Attitude Towards Judaism and Interpretation of Time in the Jewish Scriptures*

Aphrahat's treatise "on Love" is, in the first instance, concerned with the two commandments from which Jesus derived the law and the prophets: the love of God and of neighbour (Matt. 22:37). Why, given their derivatory nature, did it become 'necessary' for the law and prophets to have been written at all? Aphrahat attempts to answer this question in the first part of the Demonstration (sections 1–9), while in the second part (10–17) he recounts instances from the Jewish scriptures and the New Testament in which the love commandments were fulfilled.

In the first part Aphrahat's argument requires him to justify the existence of the law and prophets and, in turn, to explain the salvation-historical discontinuity between them and "our Giver of Life" (Christ). Having underlined the importance of the old covenant, Aphrahat finds himself able in the second part to state ways in which the two commandments singled out by Jesus were already being observed "in former times".

Citing 1 Timothy 1:9, the sage argues that the law was only given because of 'evildoers' (par. 2). Thus the law and its commandments function much less as exhortation than as a warning. At the same time, Aphrahat asserts that the law has a positive function: to demonstrate "The power [i.e., love] of God". This use of the law, however, is limited; the law is predicated on the existence of sin and the death which resulted (cf. Rom. 5:12,20). In ways reminiscent of some early Jewish traditions (e.g., *Jubilees*), Aphrahat describes the patriarchal era as a time when figures like Abraham, Isaac, Jacob, and Joseph could observe "the law" long before it was actually given through Moses (par. 2). Therefore, and reminiscent of Paul's argument in Romans 2, Aphrahat maintains that the law's observance does not depend on its existence (cf. Rom. 2:14,26–27). From this, it is not much of a logical step for Aphrahat to conclude that the law was superfluous, that is, a 'necessary' evil.

The superfluity of the law and, by contrast, the perennial quality of Jesus' commandments to love are each underscored by Aphrahat through an appeal to how time is handled in scripture. Whereas, for example, God's original promise to Abraham was that his progeny would be enslaved for 400 years (Gen. 15:13; par.'s 4,8), the time which actually elapsed was 430 years (par.'s 3–4,8). For the author, this difference in time span does not reflect an inconsistency; instead, the extra 30 years of enslavement in Egypt are explained, on the one hand, as (a) the punishment of Israel for rejecting Moses (Exod. 2:14) and, on the other hand, as (b) an example of God's patience in ensuring Israel's victory over the Amorites whose sins *by that time* merited punishment. Instead of repenting from their rejection of Moses during the 30 additional years given to them, the people of Israel "scorned the patience of God" (9). The implication of Aphrahat's argument is that despite God's love for Israel, Israel did not love God and, therefore, did not live according to the first of the two 'love' commandments.

If for Aphrahat the extension of a period of time illustrates divine forbearance in relation to Israel, the shortening of time in scripture marks the severity of human accountability before God. Thus Aphrahat reads the ante-diluvian account to mean that the 120 years to remain before the great flood (Gen. 6:3), due to unbridled sin on the earth, actually ended up amounting to only 100 years (cf. Gen. 5:32; 7:6), while Isaiah's prophecy of the fall of Ephraim in 65 years (Isa. 7:8) is calculated to have been fulfilled in only 20 years (par. 8). For Aphrahat, these discrepancies are due neither to arbitrariness nor to divine ignorance, but rather reflect the 'skill' of God who knew ahead of time that his people would not take seriously the time measured to them for repentance (par. 9). Aphrahat does not indicate whether the adjustment of time in scripture has any implications for eschatology. He adopts from "our great sages" a 6,000-year periodization of world history followed by a 'sabbath'[23] and makes no effort

---

[23] It is not clear who the 'sages' referred to are. While the 1st person plural possessive suffix may imply that Aphrahat derives the scheme from Christian predecessors, his explanation for it could simply be Jewish. However, the chronology itself is only attested in the Zoroastrian *Oracle of Hystaspes* composed near the turn of the common era; on the document, which is only partly extant through citations and references in Justin Martyr (*Apology* I.20), Aristokritos (*Theosophy*), and Lactantius (*Divine Institutions* VII.14–17), see J.R. Hinnells, "The Zoroastrian Doctrine of Salvation in the Roman World. A Study of the Oracle of Hystaspes", in E.J. Sharpe and J.R. Hinnells (eds.), *Man and His Salvation: Studies in Memory of S.G.F. Brandon* (Manchester,

to place his own time within that scheme (par. 13). Given Aphrahat's interpretation of time and divine prerogative in scripture, his lack of attempt to co-ordinate events within the framework of this ideal chronology may be deliberate. An irreversible divine plan of judgement (par.'s 13,16) and, conversely, of redemption from death (par.'s 2,13,17) does exist, but humankind lives under the shadow of a God who skilfully casts and recasts time in a way that discourages a principled reliance on an indefinitely extended duration of divine patience. Just as a lack of faithfulness in the Jewish scriptures resulted in the readjustment of time allotted for repentance, so there is an implicit warning that Christians should be relentless in demonstrating a life of love to God and neighbour. For all Aphrahat's apparent interest throughout the "Demonstration on Love" in the reckoning of time, Christian redemption depends more on fulfilling the two most important commandments than on calculations whose precise manner of fulfilment remain at God's disposal.

Aphrahat's polemic against the Jews in the present treatise presupposes the notion that Jews were somehow responsible for Jesus' death. Before he brings up Israel's rejection of Moses, he emphasises that the Jews have rejected Jesus, and it is on this account that the law – that is, its precepts and sacrificial cult – has been abolished (par. 6). Since the Jewish religion has been replaced by a better sacrificial system, the blood of Christ, any cultic practices they endeavour to undertake are now obsolete and, by definition, are to be regarded as 'evil'! Since the Jews did not embrace "his [Christ's] kingdom", the kingdom with which they had been entrusted was wrested from them. As his Christian predecessors often reasoned, Aphrahat finds divine punishment for the Jewish rejection of Christ in the destruction of the temple cult (par. 6). In paragraph 12 he states more explicitly that "because they poured out innocent blood, there was no further atonement for Jerusalem; instead, he [God] delivered her into the hand of her enemies and uprooted her". Since the rejection of Christ is so closely bound up with the commandment to love God, it constitutes proof for Aphrahat that the Jews do not love God.

1973), pp. 125–48 (esp. p. 128) and H. Kippenberg, "Die Geschichte der Mittelpersischen Apokalyptischen Traditionen", *Studia Iranica* 7 (1978), pp. 49–80 (esp. p. 71). The Hellenistic-Persian provenance of this periodization of history in the *Oracle of Hystaspes* fits well with the Sassanid context of Aphrahat's own activity.

The treatment of Christ by Jews is, of course, not the lone reason why their sacrificial system has been destroyed. Aphrahat considered the Jews' treatment of Jesus as a characteristic pattern of behaviour that had always been in effect. He attempts to illustrate this point by appealing to passages in the Psalms, Isaiah, Jeremiah, and Amos. What in the Hebrew scriptures operates as an inner-religious critique concerned with abuse of a system is interpreted by Aphrahat in a manner that contrasts outsiders from insiders: God was not only displeased with Jewish rejection of the true sacrifice, Jesus, but also *never* was pleased by their sacrifices to begin with.

Regarding the command to love one's neighbour, Aphrahat's comments are primarily concerned with the Christian community. This injunction is radicalised in the light of Jesus' exhortation to love and forgive one's enemies (par. 16; cf. Luke 6:35). This view might lead one to expect Aphrahat to have admonished his Christian community to love those "on the outside". The force of his argument, however, is *maiores ad minores*; he reverts to the notion of loving one's neighbour, that is, fellow members in the church. After providing several examples of loving enemies from scripture (David, Elisha, and Jeremiah), Aphrahat says that if Christians are going to be held accountable to this command to love one's enemy, it is no less the case if they hate one of their own (that is, the body of the Messiah), since it is equivalent to hating the Messiah himself. Though Jews are not actually referred to in this passage (par. 16), Aphrahat may be suggesting that such in-fighting among Christians is especially reprehensible because it follows along the lines of the Jews' ill-treatment of Jesus. Just as the Jews lost a 'kingdom' by "pouring out innocent blood", so the show of hate towards a 'brother' results in being "separated from the children of God".

4. *Translation*

In the translation below, the following methods and guidelines have been followed. At some points comparisons are made between the editions of William Wright and Ioannis Parisot (see n. 7 above), including a few emendations and textual variants. In addition, some of the more significant departures from the translations of Parisot (Latin) and G. Bert (German; see n. 5 above) are noted. The numbering of the paragraphs adopted here corresponds to the divisions introduced by Wright; the further paragraphing is my own. In the text, scripture citations are presented in *italics*; supplied words which are either implicit or which make for a smooth reading, are placed in parentheses. Because of the significance of numerology for Aphrahat's argumentation, such numbers are not written out but given as Arabic numerals. Finally, a few extraneous explanatory words, such as biblical references, are supplied in square brackets.

DEMONSTRATION ON LOVE

1. Assuredly,[24] my beloved, all of the law and prophets hang on two commandments, as our Saviour has said. For the one who does not (want) to be persuaded, the law and prophets are (only) a little help for persuasion. For our Savour said, *On these two commandments hang the law and the prophets: when one loves the Lord his God with all his soul and all his strength and all his possessions; and further when one loves his neighbour as himself* [Matt. 22:37–39].

2. And since you are commencing an investigation of these two commandments on which the whole strength of the law and prophets depends,[25] if these two commandments on which the whole strength of the law and prophets depends had been fixed in the heart and mind of humanity, then it would not have been necessary for the law and prophets to be written. So it is written: *The law is not given for the righteous, but for the evildoers* [1 Tim. 1:9]. Thus on account of evildoers the law was given. And if righteousness had persisted among humanity, the law would not have been necessary. Moreover, had the law not been given, the power of God would have been known among all generations and through all the wonders which he manifested.

And through the transgression of the commandment by the house of Adam, death was decreed over the world; and the power of God will appear when all humanity rises in the last time, so that the power of death will come to an end. And because of evildoers in

---

[24] The meaning of the opening expression is not fully clear. See the discussions on *bpys'* in Parisot (1894, 1907), vol. 1, cols. 47–48 n. 1 and Bert (1888), p. 20 n. 1. A literal rendering would be "in persuasion".

[25] Both Parisot (1894 and 1907) vol. 1, col. 47 and Bert (1888), p. 21 supply a phrase equivalent to "then may you know that . . ." in order to avoid two consecutive protases.

the days of Noah, the power of God appeared in the waters of the flood. And because Abraham observed the righteousness which was in the law though the law had not been given, the power of God was made manifest in him by means of righteousness; for he overcame the captivity of Sodom by the power of God and did not stretch out his hand for the booty. And after that day the Lord said to him, *Your reward will be very great because of your righteousness* [Gen. 15:1]. And because the law was not (yet) given, he showed him the works of the law; but the law was not necessary for (attaining) his righteousness. Thus there was also no need for his sons Isaac and Jacob to be given the law for their righteousness, because Abraham had commanded them to practice righteousness and justice, as it is written that the Lord said concerning Abraham, *I know him who commands his children after him*[26] *to keep all my commandments* [Gen. 18:19]. And Joseph also practised the righteousness in the law in that he was not obedient to his mistress. For he said, *How can I do this great evil and sin against God* [Gen. 39:9]? Now even Moses observed the righteousness in the law when he refused to be called the son of Pharaoh's daughter. On account of this the Lord made him worthy, so that through him he could give the law to his people. Now all of these (men) demonstrated the works of the law; yet the law had not been given for their righteousness. They were a law unto themselves.

3. When the time of the law arrived, it was added because of transgression. And with regard to it he showed that the law was an addition. Why, then, was there this addition, if not because of the calling of the nations who of old had already been promised the law?[27] And the law was a guardian and an instructor until the seed by whom the nations have been blessed had come. For the word of the oath, which was promised to Abraham and is the promised covenant, was that which God spoke to him: *Through your seed all the nations will be blessed* [Gen. 18:18; 22:18; 26:4]. Now this is the word which was the covenant 430 years before the law was given; it was promised to Abraham by whose seed, the Messiah, the nations would be blessed.

And the law came after these 430 years. For when Abraham

---

[26] Ms. A adds "and the children of his house", which assimilates to the passage in Gen. 18:19. Compare the discussion in Owens (1983), p. 143.

[27] This theme is elaborated by Aphrahat in Demonstration XVI (on the Gentiles as God's people).

received this promise, he was 85 years old.[28] And from that time until Jacob went to Egypt were 205 years; and from the time Jacob entered Egypt until the people went out by the hand of Moses were 225 years.

4. And the matter concerning their habitation has been recorded, that the children of Israel dwelt in the land of Egypt 430 years. And why, my beloved, if they dwelt there 225 years, was 430 years written for them? (Why), if not because of the moment when he said to Abraham, *You shall surely know that your seed will be a sojourner in a land which is not theirs, (that) they will serve among them and be subjected for four hundred years* [Gen. 15:13]. For in that time when this word, *You will have a child through faith* [Gen. 15:4], was spoken to Abraham, it was formed in Abraham's heart, as it is written, *Abraham believed in God, and it was reckoned to him as righteousness* [Gen. 15:6]. And even the word concerning the servitude to which his children were subjected in Egypt was conceived in Abraham's heart. And he began to be anxious as to how his seed would come into slavery; thus his heart was in subjection in Egypt.

So Isaac and Jacob were also thinking of the slavery, and their thinking was in subjection in the midst of Egypt. And the slavery was promised with respect to the seed[29] of Abraham until they were born. For the word came 15 years before the birth of Isaac, and the promise concerning slavery came 205 years before their entry into Egypt. And the promise that all the nations would be blessed through Abraham's seed came 430 years before the law. And the law was not able to nullify the promise. Therefore, the law was an addition beyond the word of promise until its time came.

5. And this word was preserved 1,794 years from the time when it was promised to Abraham until it came (into effect). For 1,364 years after the law had been given, this (word) was in safe-keeping. Thus this word came 430 years before the law. And when it came (into effect), it abolished the observances of the law. The law and prophets were consummated in these two commandments concerning which our Lord spoke. For the word is written, *All the law and the prophets prophesied until John the Baptizer* [Matt. 11:13]. And our Lord said, *I did not come to abolish the law and the prophets, but to fulfil them* [Matt. 5:17]. Again it is written, *The truth of the law came through Jesus* [John 1:17].

---

[28] Not '89', as in Bert (1888), p. 22.
[29] Correct 'Namen' (a misprint) in Bert (1888), p. 23, to 'Samen'.

6. Now what were the law and prophets lacking and requiring for fulfilment, if not the covenant, that is, the word of promise which was hidden in them? For this covenant was not concluded[30] (at the time) when it was given to Moses until another covenant came which was earlier, which was promised earlier and written down later.

And the bringer of the covenant died, confirmed both covenants *and made them both into one and abolished the law of precepts by his command-ments* [Eph. 2:14,15]. For the uses of the law were annulled at the coming of our Giver of Life. He offered himself in place of the offer-ings (written) in the law, was led as a lamb to the slaughter in place of the lambs of atonement, and was killed for us as a fat bull, so that we do not need to offer cattle. He came and ascended upon the cross in order that no offerings and sacrifices would be required from us. He gave his blood in place of all humanity in order that the blood of animals would not be needed by us. And he entered the house of the sanctuary not made with hands and became priest and minister of the sanctuary. For from the time he came, he abolished the observances in the law; and from the time they bound him, the feasts were bound in chains. And because they wanted to judge the innocent one, he removed (the force of their) judgement[31] from them. And because they rejected his kingdom, he took from them a king-dom; for *he came, whose was the kingdom* [Gen. 49:10], ascended as a living sacrifice in our place, and abolished their sacrifices. And the children of Israel have lived without sacrifices, without an altar, and without an ephod or the giving of incense. He abolished from them the seers and prophets, because they did not listen to the great prophet. And the first covenant was fulfilled by the last one. And the works in the law were obsolete and old and became evil. For from the time the new was given, he abolished the old.

But it was not on account of the time of our Saviour's coming alone (that) sacrifices were rejected, but also (because) their sacrifices did not please him earlier, as it is written, *I do not consume the flesh of calves, and the blood of goats I do not drink, but offer God thanksgiving and make your vows to the Highest* [Ps. 50:13,14]. And again he said, *A bro-ken heart God will not reject* [Ps. 51:17]. And further he said, *I do not desire sacrifices, nor do I accept whole burnt offerings* [Jer. 6:20]. *The sacrifice*

---

[30] Literally 'sealed'.
[31] Cf. Parisot (1894, 1907), vol. 1, cols. 59–60 (*dayyane'* = 'iudices'); it is also pos-sible to point the word to read *dyna'* ('judgment').

of God is a humble spirit [Ps. 51:17]. And Isaiah the prophet also said, *I do not need the abundance of your sacrifices, says the Lord* [Isa. 1:11]. And again he said to them, *I have hated and despised your feasts, nor will I smell your religious assemblies* [Amos 5:21; cf. Isa. 1:14].

7. Now this word which our Saviour has spoken and on which the law and prophets depend is beautiful, good, and honourable; for thus spoke our Lord: *Not one letter 'yud' will pass away from the law and prophets until everything comes to pass* [Matt. 5:18]. For he took the law and prophets, hung them upon the two commandments, and did not abolish any of them.

And if you pay close attention to this word, it is truly so: The observance in the law and everything which is written in it come under this word, *Love the Lord your God with all your soul and all your strength and all your heart* [Deut. 6:5; Matt. 22:37]. And everything which has been done through the law has happened in order that they might draw near to the love of the Lord their God and (that) one love his neighbour as himself. These two commandments are over the whole law.

And if you consider and give heed to the law, at the beginning of the whole law it is written thus: *I am the Lord your God who has brought you up from the land of Egypt. You shall not make for yourself any image or likeness* [Ex. 20:2,4]. And if anyone does not make for himself another god, he comes under the word upon which the law and prophets depend. My beloved, you remember that I have written to you that the law was not given for righteousness, because whoever observes righteousness is above the commandment, law, and prophets. And the word which our Lord has spoken is true: *Not a letter 'yud' will pass away from the law and prophets* [Matt. 5:18]; for he has consummated and hung them on two commandments.

8. Now, my beloved, hear the explanation of this word. If anyone says "Why is this word written concerning their habitation, (that is) that the children of Israel dwelt in the land of Egypt 430 years, if when it was promised, it was said to Abraham that there would be 400 years? Did they receive 30 (years) in addition?"

Now I will show you, my beloved, how (this) could have been. For when the time of fulfilment arrived – the 400 years – Moses was sent to deliver them. When he killed the Egyptian and they rejected their deliverer, Moses fled to Midian. And wrath came over them, so that they remained in Egypt 30 years (more). For they were saying to Moses, *Who has raised you as a ruler and judge over us* [Exod.

2:14]? And when they rejected their deliverer, the wrath of God held them back in Egypt 30 years. And Moses was in Midian 30 years: then, when the distress upon them was great, he brought them out from Egypt. God demonstrated his patience; first, so that they would be chastened for rejecting Moses and, second, so that the sins of the Amorites would be full. More than when he made the promise to Abraham, he added 30 years for the people. And for the Amorites he was patient 70 years: 30 in Egypt and 40 in the wilderness. And when the 430 and 40[32] years completed the fullness of the sins of the Amorites, he brought them into the land of promise.

Now you know, my beloved, that God is without the law.[33] For in a given period he can expand or shorten (the time) and in another he can add (to it) because it is (too) little. For in the days of Noah he promised that the days of humanity would be 120 years on account of iniquity. And he blotted them out in the 600th year of Noah's life. For he said, *There will be one hundred and twenty years upon the earth* [Gen. 6:3] and in the 600th year of Noah's life, they were blotted out. Now he shortened (the time) by 20 years.

And again it is written that because the evil of the sinful kingdom of the house of Ephraim was great, when Jeroboam the son of Nebat ruled over them – for he had sinned and had caused Israel to sin – and they sinned, he made a promise concerning them through the prophecy of Isaiah the prophet, who said to them, *After sixty-five years Ephraim[34] will fall off from the people* [Isa. 7:8; cf. 17:3]. And in the first year of Ahaz this word came to pass. And in the fourth year of Hezekiah, Shalmanassar the king of Assyria came up against them, and after him Tiglathpilassar, and he exiled them from their land. For Ahaz ruled over them 16 years. And in the fourth year of Hezekiah, they were under the dominion of the kings of Assyria. There were only 20 years until Ephraim fell (off) from the people of Israel; thus he took away 45 years from them. And this is what he predicted: he indicated the time period, but it was not fulfilled just as he had determined.

9. Not because he was ignorant did he make a promise concerning them that the years would be thus, and then they were shortened or added. Rather, (he made the promise in this way) because he

---

[32] Mss. A and B have '4', which Parisot (1894, 1907), col. 65, line 12 and n. 2 and Bert (1888), p. 26 n. 4 have correctly emended to '40'.

[33] Cf. Parisot (1894, 1907), vol. 1, col. 66: "Deum nulla lege obligari".

[34] *Contra* Bert's paraphasing in (1888), p. 27: "wird Israel aufhören ein Volk zu sein".

was skilful: for he knew that to a certain degree they would come. And because he loved them he gave a time for repentance, so that humanity would be without excuse; but humanity scorned the patience of God. And when they heard that there was more time before the promised wrath would come, they dared to sin before him, saying, *What the prophets say, he has prophesied for a distant time* [Ezek. 12:27], he [God] said to Ezekiel, *As I live, says the Lord of lords, there will be no more postponement of my words; for the word which I speak I do quickly* [Ezek. 12:28]. And the time which he had (already) determined beforehand he gave for repentance to humanity, that perhaps they might repent; but they scorned the patience of God and did not repent. Thus he even falsified, set up, and determined the time for them. But he did not do it as one (who is) ignorant, but just as it is written: *Woe to the one who plunders! You shall not rob, and let no deceiver falsify among you. For when you want to plunder, you will be plundered, and when you want to deceive, there will be deception among you* [Isa. 33:1]. It is further written in Jeremiah, *If I should say concerning the people and the kingdom (that I intend to uproot, ruin, defeat, and destroy them), and the people repent from their evil, then I will also falsify my word and turn away from them what I have spoken against them* [Jer. 18:7,8]. And again Jeremiah said, *If I say concerning the people and the kingdom (that I intend) to build and plant (them), and the people do evil before me, then I will also falsify my word and turn away from them the good which I have spoken (I would) do for them* [Jer. 18:9,10].

10. Now I have written all these things to you, my beloved, because earlier in the first treatise, which is concerning the history of faith, I showed you that through faith the foundation of this covenant in which we stand can be laid. And in this second treatise I write and remind you that all the law and the prophets depend on two commandments; they are those concerning which our Saviour spoke, and in these two commandments are contained all the law and prophets. And in the law is contained faith, and through faith true love is established. It is that which is from these two commandments, so that after a person has loved the Lord his God, he also loves his neighbour as himself.

11. Therefore, my beloved, hear (me) about the love which is from these two commandments. When our Giver of Life came, he demonstrated the perseverance of (true) love. For he said to his disciples, *This is my commandment, that you love one another* [John 15:12]. And again he said to them, *I give you a new commandment, that you love*

one another [John 13:34]. and further, while he was teaching about love, he admonished them thus: *Love your enemies; bless the one who curses you; pray for those who harm and persecute you* [Matt. 5:44; Luke 6:27,28]. And again he said this to them: *If you love the one who loves you, what is your reward? for if you love the one who loves you, so also do the godless behave; they love the one who loves them* [Luke 6:32; Matt. 5:46]. Again our Giver of Life has said, *If you do what is good to one who does what is pleasant for you, what is your reward? For behold, so also do tax-collectors and sinners behave. But because you have been called children of God who is in heaven, you are like the one who loves even those who deny (his) mercy* [Luke 6:32–33]. Our Saviour said further, *Forgive, and it will be forgiven you; let loose, and it will be loosened; and give, and it will be given to you* [Luke 6:37,38]. Again he spoke and put us in awe: *Unless you forgive others the sins which they commit among you, the Father will not forgive you* [Matt. 6:15]. For thus he admonished, saying, *If your brother sins against you, forgive him; and if he sins against you seven times in one day, forgive him* [Luke 17:3,4].

12. When Simon Cephas heard this word, he said to our Lord, *If my brother sins against me, how many times should I forgive him? Seven times? Our Lord said to him, Not only seven, but up to seventy-times seven*[35] [Matt. 18:21,22]. For if (someone) should sin against you 490 times, forgive him on one day, and he will become like his good Father who multiplies his forgiveness over Jerusalem: When he delivered the children of Israel captive to Babel, he instructed them there for 70 years; and when he revealed his mercy, he gathered them into their land through Ezra the scribe and multiplied forgiveness to them during a half of his day, 70 weeks of years, that is, 490 years. And because they poured out innocent blood, there was no further atonement for Jerusalem; instead, he delivered her into the hand of her enemies and uprooted her; and no stone remained upon another, nor (did) any foundations (remain) for the Lord. And he did not say to the children of Edom that they would be avenged because they did not call to Jerusalem, *Uncover (her), uncover (her) to her foundations* [Ps. 137:7; cf. Ezek. 25:12–14]. But during a half of his day, that is 490 years, God forgave and bore their sins. Then he uprooted her, even Jerusalem, and destroyed her through the hand of foreigners. Thus our Giver of Life commanded them that on one day one should forgive his brother 490 times.

---

[35] The mss. read *šb ʿyn zbnyn šbʿ šbʿ*.

13. My beloved, do not find the word which I write you difficult, that during the half of his day God forgave Jerusalem. For thus it is written, in the ninetieth psalm of David: *A thousand years in the eyes of the Lord are as a day which, when completed, has passed by* [Ps. 90:4]. And also our great sages speak thus: as in 6 days the world was made by God, so at the end of 6,000 years the world will be destroyed by him. And the sabbath of God is like the sabbath after the 6 days, just as our Saviour clarified and showed us concerning the sabbath. For so he said, *Pray that your flight will not be during the winter or on a sabbath* [Matt. 24:20]. And the apostle also said, *The sabbath of God still remains* [Heb. 4:9]. *Let us again become worthy to enter his rest* [Heb. 4:11].

14. Furthermore, when our Lord taught prayer to his disciples, he said to them, *You should pray thus: forgive us our debts and we also will forgive our debtors* [Matt. 6:12]. And again he said, *When you want to present an offering and remember that you are seized by some wrath against your brother, leave your offering before the altar, go and be reconciled with your brother, and then come (and) present your offering* [Matt. 5:23,24]. (This is) that when someone prays, *Forgive us our debts and we will forgive our debtors* [Matt. 6:12], he will not be ensnared by his mouth and it will be spoken to him by the one who receives prayers, "(If) you do not forgive your debtor, how can we forgive you?" And your prayer will remain upon the earth.

And again our Lord showed us an example of the man who began to take account from his servants. When his servant who owed him many talents approached him when his lord pressed him to give him whatever he owed, and when he could not pay back the debt to his lord, his lord gave the command, freed him, and cancelled all that he owed him. Now this servant did not remember the forgiveness of his lord – how much he had multiplied forgiveness – because of his evil. *And when he went out, he found one of his companions who owed him one hundred denarii, seized him, tormented him, saying to him, Give me what you owe me* [Matt. 18:28]. And he did not accept the plea of his companion who begged from him, but went and had him shut up in prison. And because, though forgiven much, he did not forgive his companion the little, he was delivered up to guards who would restrain him until he paid whatever he owed, and he said to them, *Thus may my Father in heaven do to you, if you do not forgive your brother* [Matt. 18:35].

15. See again, my beloved, how the blessed apostle praises love

when he says, *If you are zealous for great gifts, I will show you what is the most beneficial gift* [1 Cor. 12:31]. And he said, *If I have prophecy and know all mysteries, (and have) all knowledge and all faith so as to move a mountain, but have not love, I gain nothing. And if I feed the poor (with) all that I have and surrender my body to be burned, but have not love, I again do not gain anything* [1 Cor. 13:2,3]. For he said thus: *Love is patient and kind; it does not envy; it does not boast and is not puffed up; it does not seek anything which is pleasure for itself alone, but what is good for many. Love hopes all, bears all; love never fails* [1 Cor. 13:4–7]. And the apostle has shown and clarified that after faith love is the most beneficial, and on it the true building is erected.

And he showed that prophecy is based on love, (that) knowledge is made completed through it, and that faith is found to be true through love. And whoever has in him faith to move a mountain, but has no love, has no gain. And if everything which belongs to himself he gives to the poor and the alms are not given through love, he has no inheritance. And even if on account of the name of his Lord he has his body burned in fire, he is not helped (in) any way. And he further showed that patience and endurance and kindness[36] and humility and that one not contending against his brother – these things are found as the fulfilment of love. And even endurance and humility and sociability subsist in love. For faith is laid in the rock of the building, and love in the beams of the building through which the walls of the house are supported. And if any deceit is found in the beams of the house, the whole structure will collapse. So also when in love there is found doubt, the whole faith falls. And faith is not able to remove jealousy and strife until the love which can has come. In like manner, a building cannot rise properly until the walls are supported by beams.

16. Again I will show you, my beloved, that love is more beneficial than anything else. By it the first righteous ones were made perfect. For he teaches concerning Moses that he gave himself for the children of his people and wished to be blotted out from the book of life (so that) the people alone would not be blotted out. And even when they rose up to stone him, he brought a petition before God on their behalf so that they would live. And also David showed an example of love while he was being persecuted by Saul. Whenever

---

[36] With Parisot (1894, 1907), l. 1, col. 83 – 'mansuetudinem') *contra* Bert (1888), p. 33: "der Glaube".

his life was being hunted in order that he be killed, David practised compassion with great love toward Saul, his enemy who sought his life. He was delivered twice into the hands of David, but did not kill him and repaid (him) with good instead of evil. On account of this, God did not depart from his house, and he who forgave was forgiven. But (as for) Saul, who repaid with evil instead of good, evil did not depart from his house. He cried out to God, but he did not answer him; and he fell by the sword of the Philistines. And David cried over him bitterly and fulfilled beforehand the commandment of our Saviour, who said, *Love your enemies and forgive, and it will be forgiven you* [Luke 6:35]. So David loved and he was loved; and he forgave and it was forgiven him.

And also Elisha demonstrated concerning this love when his enemies came upon him to seize him in order to do him evil. He did good to them, placed bread and water before them, and let them go from his presence in peace. And he fulfilled the word which is written: *If your enemy hungers, feed him; and if he thirsts, give him to drink* [Prov. 25:21]; and also Jeremiah the prophet prayed before God for those who made him captive in the pit and (who) tortured him.

Our Saviour taught this example from former times, that we should love our enemies and pray for those who hate us. And if he commanded us to love our enemies and to pray for those who hate us, what excuse will there be on the day of judgement? For behold, we hate our brothers and our members. For we are of the body of the Messiah, and our members are his members. Indeed, whoever hates one of the members of the Messiah will be cut off from the whole body; and whoever hates his brother will be separated from the children of God.

17. That which our Saviour taught us has shown the diligence of love. For at first he perfected it in his life. Then he taught his hearers. He reconciled our enmity with his Father because he loved us; and he surrendered his purity on behalf of the debtors; the good one suffered dishonour on behalf of the evil ones; the rich one was for our sake made poor; the living one died in place of the dead, and through his death he has made our death alive. The Son of the Lord of all took on the likeness of a servant for our sake; and he, to whom all is subjected, subjected himself in order to free us from the bondage of sin. With great love he gave a blessing to the poor in spirit [Matt. 5:3]. He promised peacemakers that they will be his brothers and be called children of God; he promised the

humble that they will inherit the land of life;[37] he promised the mourners that they will make supplication; and he promised the hungry satisfaction in his kingdom. And he has gladdened those who weep by his promise. He promised the compassionate that they will receive mercy; and to those who are pure in their heart he said that they will see God. And he promised further to those who are persecuted on account of righteousness that they will enter the kingdom of heaven; and to those who are persecuted because of his name he promised a blessing and rest in his kingdom. And he has changed our nature of dust and has made us (into) true salt; and he has delivered us from the kingdom of the snake. He has called us the light of the world, so that he might save us from the power of death; and he has made us good instead of evil and honourable instead of hated. He has given us love instead of hate. He has made us partake of the good man who brings out good things from his treasure; and he has saved us from him who brings out evil things out of the overflowing abundance of his heart.

And because of his abounding love, he healed the wounds of the sick. For he cured the son of the centurion on account of his faith. He has silenced from us the storms of the sea with his power and has driven out from us demons by the legion because of his goodness. And through his compassion he brought the daughter of the head of the synagogue back to life and purified the woman from unclean blood. He opened the eyes of two blind men who approached him and also gave his twelve the power and authority over every disease[38] and infirmity, and even us through their hands. And he has prevented us from (going on) the way of the heathen and Samaritans and has given us power through his compassion, so that we might not be afraid when we go before the rulers of the world. He has placed division on the earth for the sake of his great peace. And he forgave the many sins of the sinful woman because of his mercy, and he has made us worthy, on account of his goodness, to build a fortress at his expense. And he has driven out from us unclean spirits and has made for us a dwelling for his divinity. He sowed among us a good seed, so that he might produce fruit: the one into a hundred and sixty and thirty. And he was placed in the world in the likeness of the treasure which is placed in a field. He showed

---

[37] Ms. A omits 'life'.
[38] Correct Wright (1869), p. 42, line 7 *b'b* to *k'b*.

his great power when he was hurled from height to depth and was not harmed. And he satisfied the weary hungry with five loaves of bread and two fishes, five thousand men beyond children and women. He showed the greatness of his splendour. And because of his great love, he heard the Canaanite woman and raised her daughter from her infirmity. By the authority of the one who sent him, he made the tongue to speak of the dumb man whose ear was dear. And blind men have seen his light and praise through him the one who sent him. When he ascended the mountain to pray, the radiance of the sun was overcome by his light. And he made known his surpassing power in the boy whom a spirit was seizing, and the demoniac he changed by his word. He has given us an example and model to be like children and enter the kingdom of heaven. And he spoke and demonstrated concerning the little ones that no one should look down on them, *because their angels are always seen by the Father in heaven* [Matt. 18:10]. Again he showed his full healing power in the man who for thirty-eight (years) had been sick, and he multiplied his grace to him and healed him. Furthermore, he has given us the commandment to forsake the world and turn to him. And he has revealed to us that whoever loves the world cannot please God (as) in the case of the rich man who relied upon his possessions and in the case of the man who took delight in his goods, whose end is in Sheol; and he [the latter] asked for water on the tip of his little finger, and no one gave him (any). And he has hired us as workers to labour in the vineyard of him who is the true vine.

All these things our Giver of Life has done for us on account of his great love. And also we, my beloved, are participants in the love of the Messiah when we love one another and perfect these two commandments on which all the law and prophets depend.

The demonstration concerning love is complete.

THE THREE JEWISH CHILDREN AT BERLIN: COTTON MATHER'S OBSESSION

BY

LINDA MUNK

Toronto

> Yea, who knowes what Use the Lord may make of such an Essay?
> Cotton Mather, *The Faith of the Fathers*

In February 1704, Samuel Sewall, minister of the Second Church of Boston and an avid eschatologist, recorded in his diary Cotton Mather's "unsuccessful attempt to convert to Christianity a Boston Jewish merchant, one of the Frazon brothers – evidently by some jugglery with holy texts." According to Sewall: "'The forgery was so plainly detected that Mr. C.M. confest it, after which Mr. Frasier [Frazon] would never be persuaded to hear any more of Xianity.'"[1] The historian Lee M. Friedman remarks: "The ambition to be the means of converting a Jew to Christianity was so near an obsession on the part of Cotton Mather that it is easily possible to understand how he overstepped the bounds of propriety when one realizes his Puritan viewpoint." From Mather's millennial point of view, "to be the means of converting a Jew was not merely a matter of personal glory, but another step accelerating the establishment on earth of the Kingdom of God."[2]

Born on February 12, 1663, Cotton Mather was the first of nine children of Increase Mather and Maria, daughter of the great John Cotton. It seems that "young Cotton had begun to pray as soon as he could speak. His father began to suspect that this gifted child was one of the happy few (a tiny fraction of the elected saints) who are

---

[1] L. Hühner, "The Jews of New England (Other than Rhode Island) Prior to 1800," *Publications of the American Jewish Historical Society* II (1903), p. 79, n. 3.

[2] L.M. Friedman, "Cotton Mather's Ambition," in *Jewish Pioneers and Patriots* (Philadelphia: Jewish Publication Society of America, 1942), p. 98. This chapter of Friedman's monograph is a revision of an essay that appeared in 1918: "Cotton Mather and the Jews," *Publications of the American Jewish Historical Society* 26 (1918), pp. 201–211. Hühner (1903), p. 79 n.

given a saving faith and a virtuous character in their very infancy."[3]
By the time Cotton was twelve, "his proficiency in Latin was so good
that while listening to the Sabbath sermon, which was delivered in
English, he could take notes on it in Latin." He also "read Greek capa-
bly." By the age of fourteen, he could write in Hebrew. At fifteen
the prodigy and visible saint graduated from Harvard College, "having consumed enormous numbers of books in most of the arts and
sciences known to seventeenth-century scholars."[4] Some of those books
were out of date; his Harvard thesis of 1678 pleads a lost cause: "An
Puncta Hebraica sunt Originis Divinae. Affirmat Respondens Cot-
tonus Matherus."[5] At eighteen he "preached so effectively in Grandfather
Cotton's First Church in Boston that some auditors declared themselves hardly able to forbear crying out aloud during the sermon."[6]

He died on February 13, 1728, a day after his sixty-fifth birthday.
"In every church [we read in Perry Miller's *The New England Mind*]
there were discourses on Cotton Mather, three of which were printed."
Benjamin Colman described him as "'the first Minister in the Town,
the first in Age, Gifts and in Grace.' From the beginning of the country to this very day, no leader of these churches amassed so great a treasure of learning 'and made so much use of it, to a variety of pious
Intentions, as this our Rev. Brother and Father, Dr. Cotton Mather.'"[7]
The focus of this essay is Mather's conversionism – his pious intention,
or obsession, to convert Jews.

Christ's return to earth was imminent, Mather believed; the true
Church, true Israel, must prepare itself for the bridegroom, the thief
who comes in the night, and Mather intended to expedite his coming. Unregenerate children among the Puritan elect must be saved;
otherwise, like Papists, Turks, and other heretics, they would perish
in the "tremendous Conflagration, which is to precede the New
Heavens and the New Earth."[8] As for the "infidel" Jews, at Christ's

---

[3] D. Levin, *Cotton Mather: The Young Life of the Lord's Remembrancer, 1663–1703*
(Cambridge Mass., 1978), p. 10.
[4] R. Middlekauff, *The Mathers: Three Generations of Puritan Intellectuals, 1596–1728*
(New York, 1971), pp. 194–95.
[5] D. de Sola Pool, "Hebrew Learning among the Puritans of New England Prior
to 1700," *Publications of the American Jewish Historical Society* XX (1911), pp. 66, 80.
[6] Levin, (1978), p. 62.
[7] P. Miller, *The New England Mind: From Colony to Province* (Cambridge Mass., 1954),
p. 482.
[8] Cotton Mather, letter to Gordon Saltonstall, August 3, 1724, *Diary*, II, p. 804.
First published in 1911–1912 in 2 Volumes by the Massachusetts Historical Society,

return, they would be reclaimed from apostasy; all Israel would be saved. Their gracious conversion to Christianity would "inaugurate the last days," envisioned by Mather (and his father, Increase) in premillennial terms: "Christ will physically appear, the earth will be refined but not consumed by fire, and for a thousand years paradise will reign. Satan with all his power and party (i.e., Rome) will be 'Chased off the Face of the Earth.'"[9]

Before looking at conversionist tracts written or reprinted by Cotton Mather, I shall place them in a twentieth-century context. At the Southern Baptist conclave held in June 1996, a resolution was passed by "14,000 'messengers' . . . calling for Baptists to direct their 'energies and resources toward the proclamation of the Gospel to the Jewish people.'"[10] With about sixteen million members, the Southern Baptist Convention is the second-largest religious body in the United States, after the Catholic Church. Missions to the Jews are not new; but since the extermination of six million Jews by the Nazis, many Christians have reformulated their relationship to Judaism. At Vatican II, Catholics "were told that the Jewish people continue to be God's chosen people, that their religion remains for them a source of divine grace, and that it is the task of Christians to engage in conversation and cooperation with them."[11] The Rabbis taught that all the righteous have a portion in the world to come.

James Sibley is unimpressed by doctrines of universal grace. Appointed by the Home Mission Board of the Southern Baptist Convention as its missionary to the Jews, he denies the element of graciousness in Judaism:

the *Diary of Cotton Mather* was subsequently reprinted. I am using a mismatched set: *Diary of Cotton Mather* [Volume I] *1681–1708* (Boston: Massachusetts Historical Society, 1911); *Diary of Cotton Mather: Volume II, 1709–1724* (New York: Frederick Unger, no date). References to Mather's *Diary* are cited in the body of the present essay.

[9] Miller (1954), pp. 187–88

[10] J. Goldberg, "Some of Their Best Friends Are Jews," *The New York Times Magazine*, March 16, 1997, p. 42. In response to the passage cited above, one reader of *The New York Times*, a survivor of Bergen Belsen, wrote to the editor: "As I read this, I shuddered and recalled Claude Lanzman's epic documentary 'Shoah,' in which he interviewed Poles who were willing participants in or passive witnessses to the slaughter of our people. They justified their bloody deeds by saying that this was the fate of those who rejected Jesus. It was one thing to hear those words from the seasoned anti-Semites of Hitler's Europe but something else to hear them echoed by the leader of the second-largest religious body in the United States." Rebbetzin Esther Jungreis, "Letters," *The New York Times Magazine*, April 13, 1997, p. 12.

[11] G. Baum, "Catholic Dogma After Auschwitz," in A. Davies (ed.), *Antisemitism and the Foundations of Christianity* (New York, 1979), p. 137.

Following the Holocaust, a lot of Christian denominations began to back off of evangelism toward the Jews ... There was a feeling that they shouldn't continue to bother the Jewish people anymore, that they had suffered enough. But this was an overreaction on the part of Christians – sort of a guilty conscience – because as terrible as the Holocaust was, it will fade into insignificance in comparison to God's future judgment. There will be a Holocaust of all people who don't accept Jesus. The Nazi Holocaust shouldn't be a reason for us to stop bringing the Good News.[12]

Compare Cotton Mather, an eminent forefather of the Southern Baptist Convention, writing in 1713 about the "Jewish Infidelity" and addressing his warning text to imaginary Jews. Like James Sibley, Mather urges Jews to convert before they are destroyed in the Conflagration:

I must like Paul to his Gaoler, cry out with a loud Voice unto you; Do thy self no Harm. Self-destroying Sinners; 'Tis to your own Confusion, that you Provoke Him that can Destroy you, for what you do. Oh! come to your selves and say, Destruction from God is a Terror to me! . . .

It will be so, when the Lord JESUS, will be revealed from Heaven, with His mighty Angels, in flaming Fire, to take Vengeance on them that know not God, and obey not His Gospel. . . . The great Day of the Lord is near, it is near, and it hasteneth greatly upon us! . . . So, O unthinking Children of Disobedience, How will you be able to Stand, when the Lord of Heaven and Earth, shall come with Power and in great Glory, and shall say, I AM HE, whom you have so often wronged by your Ungodliness. I AM HE, who am now to Judge you for the Wrongs done to me in your Ungodly Disobedience!

Consider these Things, ye that Wrong the Lord; Lest He tear you to Pieces. . . .[13]

Apart from his rhetoric of doom, what links Cotton Mather to a large, influential group of Southern Baptists is premillennial dispensationalism. The conversion (or "calling") of the Jews will be the most significant event to occur before the Second Coming; until the mid-1720s, when he renounced conversionism, Mather took the "glorious deliverance of the Jewish nation" to be "the first sign of a new

---

[12] Goldberg (1997), p. 42.
[13] Cotton Mather, *Things To Be More Thought Upon: A Brief Treatise on the Injuries Offered unto the Glorious and Only Saviour of the World: In many Instances, wherein the Guilty are seldome Aware of their being so Injurious to the Eternal Son of God. With a more Particular Conviction of the Jewish and Arian Infidelity* (Boston, 1713), pp. 104–105.

order."[14] In some versions of the cosmic drama, the calling of the Jews, or a saving remnant of Jews, will immediately precede the Conflagration ("a Holocaust of all people who don't accept Jesus," in Sibley's terms) and usher in the earthly millennium. Infused with saving grace, Jews "would be converted to the faith of Christ [i.e. Puritanism]; and the Antichrist – the Bishop of Rome – would be pulled from his throne and destroyed."[15] In April of 1692, Mather "obtained of God, that Hee would make use of mee, as of a John, to bee an herald of the Lord's Kingdome now approaching, and the Voice crying in the Wilderness, for Preparation thereunto" (*Diary*, I, p. 147). The 'Preparation' that concerns us is Mather's attempt to prepare Jews for "salvation" and thus for "the Lord's Kingdome," where the Elect will rest under their vines and fig trees.

We begin with Mather's *Diary*, which, as David Levin has observed, is "not a diary at all. Mather himself called these manuscripts his "Reserved Memorials", and the text, beginning in 1681, demonstrates on page after page that the narrative and reflections, though dated precisely, had been copied and revised retrospectively from originals which Mather destroyed."[16] A cross between autobiography and a Saint's Life, the *Diary* records Mather's proud acts of Christian abasement: prostrations in the dust, secret vigils, secret supplications, secret alms, fasts, and devotional confessions of sins that made him "unfit for the Kingdome of God" (I, p. 225). "Prostrate in the Dust, I loathed and judged myself before the Lord, for my Miscarriages. . . . Especially my Impurities, and my Hatred and Malice toward other Men. . . . I received the pardoning Mercy of God" (II, pp. 234–35). "I set myself, to wrestle with the Lord, prostrate in the Dust before Him, on behalf of whole Nations" (I, p. 223). On July 18, 1696, Mather confessed his desire to convert the Jews, or one Jew, at least:

> This Day, from the Dust, where I lay prostrate, before the Lord, I lifted up my Cries;
> For the coming of the Kingdome of my Lord Jesus Christ; and my Acquaintance with the Characters and Approches of it.

---

[14] M. Scult, *Millennial Expectations and Jewish Liberties: A Study of the Efforts to Convert the Jews in Britain, up to the Mid Nineteenth Century* (Leiden, 1978), p. 49. Scult is citing Cotton Mather's unpublished essay of 1703, *Problema Theologicum*, which is subtitled, "An Essay Concerning the Happy State to be Expected for the Church Upon the Earth."

[15] Middlekauff (1971), p. 28.

[16] Levin (1978), p. 63.

For the Conversion of the Jewish Nation, and for my own having
the Happiness, at some Time or other, to baptise a Jew, that should
by my Ministry, bee brought home unto the Lord. (I, 200)[17]

An editor's footnote to the passage above states that in 1702, "Mr.
Bradstreet, of Charlestown [Massachusetts], baptised Simon, a Jew,
for whose conversion he was instrumental."[18] Thus one infers that
Mather himself was "instrumental" in the conversion of 1702, but
he was not; the pronoun "he" refers to Mr. Bradstreet. Samuel Sewall
reports the conversion in his diary for September 1702: "Mr. Bradstreet
baptiseth Simon the Jew at Charlestown, a young man whom he
was instrumental to convert."[19] One Jew may have been "brought
home" by Mather: "This Day," we read in his *Diary* for September
1699, "I understand by Letters from Carolina, a thing that exceedingly refreshes mee; a Jew there embracing the Christian Faith, and
my little Book, *The Faith of the Fathers*, therein a special Instrument
of good unto him" (I, p. 315). *The Faith of the Fathers* was published
in April 1699.

This Week [Mather writes in his *Diary*], I attempted a further service
to the Name of my Lord Jesus Christ. I considered, that when the
Evangelical Elias, was to prepare the Jewish Nation, for the coming
of the Messiah, he was to do it, by, bringing down the Heart of the
Fathers upon the Children. And I considered, that it would not only
confirm us Christians in our Faith exceedingly to see every Article of
it, asserted in the express Words of the Old Testament, but that it
would mightily convince, and confound the Jewish Nation. Yea, who
knowes what Use the Lord may make of such an Essay? Wherefore,
with much Contrivance, I drew up a Catechism of the whole Christian
Religion, and contrived the Questions to fitt the Answers, whereof I
brought every one out of the Old Testament. I prefaced the Catechism,
with an Address unto the Jewish Nation, telling them in some lively
Terms, That if they would but return to the faith of the Old Testament,
and beleeve with their own ancient and blessed Patriarchs, this is all
that we desired of them or for them. I gave this Book to the Printer,

---

[17] The list of inhabitants in Boston for 1695 includes the names of two Jews,
Raephaell Abandana and Samuel (sometimes Samuell) the Jew. See L.M. Friedman,
Early American Jews (Cambridge Mass., 1934), p. 5.

[18] The editor's source is Samuel Sewall's *Diary*.

[19] Cited in Hühner (1903), p. 79 n., who gives his source: *Diary of Samuel Sewall*,
reprinted in *Collections of the Massachusetts Historical Society*, Volume 6, 5th series (Boston,
1879), p. 65. "1702, Baptized Sept. Mr. Simon (quondam Judeus Barns)," Records
of the First Church in Charleston, Mass.," cited in Hühner (1903), pp. 79–80 n.
See also Friedman (1934), p. 154. n. 16.

and it was immediately published. Its Title is, THE FAITH OF THE
FATHERS. (I, pp. 298–99)

Like other conversionists, Mather "contrived the Questions to fitt
the Answers"; not that there was much contriving to do, since his
catena of proof-texts is standard. The title sets out his thesis: "The
Faith of the Fathers. Or The Articles of the True Religion, All of
them Exhibited In the Express Words of the Old Testament. Partly,
To Confirm those who do profess that Religion of God, and His
Messiah. But Chiefly, To Engage the Jewish Nation, unto the Religion
of their Patriarchs." Christianity is the true Judaism, Mather claims,
and Jews are not really Jews.

> Here is now put into your Hands, an Irresistible and Irrefragable
> Demonstration, That tho' you say, You are Jews, you are not so. . . .
> Be amazed, O ye Rebellious & Rejected People of our Great Lord
> Messiah; We Christians have by the Wonderful Work of God, been
> brought unto the Faith of the Fathers; but you are fallen from that
> Faith, & under Strong Delusions, you are Pining away in your Iniquities.
> Return, O backsliding Israel! All that we Christians desire of you, or
> for you, (and we all desire it!) is, That you would Return to the Faith
> of the Old Testament.[20]

According to Mather, the conversion of Jews to Christianity is a
returning to Judaism – the "Faith of the Old Testament." James Sibley
of the Southern Baptist Convention expresses himself in chiasmus
or antimetabole, so that the order of words in successive phrases is
reversed – put back to front: "'What I want is for the world to follow the Jewish Messiah. I don't want a world without Jews. I want
a Jewish world.'"[21] Christianity is not an offshoot of Judaism; Judaism
is a heretical offshoot of Christianity.

In part, Mather's *The Faith of the Fathers* reads like a parody of
Justin's *Dialogue with Trypho*. Expounding the doctrine of the Trinity,
for example, Mather alludes to the Shema:

> Q. Can there be One God in Three Persons?
> A. Yes. It is written, Deut. 6.4. Hear O Israel; The Lord, our God,
> the Lord, is One.
> Q. Hath not God a Son? Or, Is not that Word of God, which is the
> second Person in God, the Son of God?

---

[20] Cotton Mather, *The Faith of the Fathers* (Boston, 1699). There is no point giving page references to this 24-page pamphlet.
[21] Goldberg (1997), p. 44.

A. Yes. It is written, Prov. 30.4. Who hath Established all the Ends of the Earth? What is His Name, and what is His Sons Name?

And so on, turning the Hebrew Bible into nothing but a collection of proof-texts for Christianity – an apologist's rag-bag. The Messiah was to be born while the Second Temple was standing (see Haggai 2); the Messiah was to be born shortly after the last books of the Old Testament were written (see Malachi 3); the Messiah was to be born four hundred and ninety years after the proclamation to rebuilt Jerusalem (see Daniel 9); the conception of the Messiah was to be in Nazareth (see Jeremiah 31); his birth must be at Bethlehem (see Micah 5); there must be two comings of the Messiah (see Zechariah 9). And onward, through the Virgin Birth (see Isaiah 7), Christ's entry into Jerusalem (see Zechariah 9), the events leading to the Crucifixion (see Psalm 69), the Resurrection (see Psalm 16), the Judgment, and the Resurrection of the Dead. The "Hailed Saints" shall "Eternally Live & Shine with the Lord Messiah, while Others are Damned unto Eternal Confusion" (see Daniel 12). Compare Southern Baptist rhetoric: "'The Bible says the Messiah would be born of the line of King David. Jesus is a descendant of David. The Bible says the Messiah would be born in Bethlehem. . . . The Jewish people just have to turn away from their blindness.'"[22]

Near the end of his twenty-four page conversion tract, Mather shifts gears: it is time for threats and the gnashing of teeth.

Q. Must the Israelitish Nation for their contempt of the Messiah, be made a Contemptible and a Miserable Nation?
A. Yes. It is written, Psal. 69.23,24,25,27. Let their Eyes be Darkned that they see not, and make their loins continually to shake. . . . Add Iniquity to Iniquity. . . .

Q. Must the utter Loss of their Genealogies, be one Special & Signal Article, in the Destruction, that comes on the Unbelieving Jews?
A. Yes. It is written, Psal. 69.28. Let them be Blotted out of the Book of the Living.

Now come the Fall of Rome and its sequel – the restoration of power and glory to those Jews who have been "brought in to the Belief of the Messiah." The passage below is typical of writings by seventeenth-century millenarians such as Joseph Mede, Thomas Bright-

---

[22] Goldberg (1997), p. 44.

man, and Increase Mather. Here is Cotton Mather, making the ascendency of the Nation of Israel contingent upon the end of the despised Papacy:

> Q. Must there arise among the Gentiles, &c. even in that Wicked Kingdom of the Romans a Little Bishop, who shall with a Sharp sighted Craft, not only extend his Temporal Jurisdiction, over Three of the Ten Kingdoms, & his more Spiritual Jurisdiction over near a Third Part of the old Roman Empire; but also, blasphemously Assume to himself the Power of a God, & cruelly persecute the People of God, for twelve hundred & fifty years together?
> A. Yes. It is written [see Daniel 7].

The Faith of the Fathers is mentioned several times in Mather's *Diary*, along with a mysterious "infidel Jew." It seems that Mather has

> for diverse Years, employ'd much Prayer for, and some Discourse with, an infidel Jew in this Town; thro' a Desire to glorify my Lord Jesus Christ in the Conversion of that Infidel, if Hee be pleased to accept me in that Service. I this day renew'd my Request unto Heaven for it. And writing a short Letter to the Jew, wherein I enclosed my, *Faith of the Fathers*, and *La Fe del Christiano*, I sent it to him. (I, p. 300)

The unidentified Jew appears again in a *Diary* entry for February 12, 1710, Mather's forty-ninth birthday. Petitions are made: one concerns the publication of Mather's huge "Biblia Americana," six folio volumes that are still unpublished; the other concerns the "poor Jew" – "And that the Lord may be glorified in the Conversion of that poor Jew, for whom I was concerned now sixteen or seventeen Years ago; and towards whom the Dispensations of Heaven have been singular and wonderful" (II, p. 41). Again, in July 1713, having kept a "Vigil . . . prostrate in the Dust before the Lord," and bemoaning the "abominable Impurities, which [his] life had been filled withal," Mather cries aloud "unto the Lord, for His Grace to be given unto my Children; particularly my son Increase"; then he prays "For the Conversion of the poor Jew, who is this Day returned once more unto New England, and who has now for nineteen years together been the Subject of our Cares, and Hopes, and Prayers. My Mind seemed singularly satisfied in the success of my supplication on that one Article; the Recovery of the Young Man I am so concerned for" (II, pp. 218–219). The "poor Jew" is probably Samuel Frazon (Frazier, Frasier), whom Mather had tried to convert "by some jugglery with holy texts." ("'The forgery was so plainly detected that Mr. C.M. confest it, after which Mr. Frasier would never be persuaded to hear any more of Xianity,'" according to Samuel Sewall.) His brother, Joseph Frazon, died in 1704.[23]

Mather appears to be confounding Frazon ("the Young Man I am so concerned for") with his own unregenerate son, Increase (1699–1724). A *Diary* entry for 1713 records prayers for "a Blessing on my Family, especially in the Disposal of my Son Increase; and for the Conversion of the Jew, for whom I have been so long and so much concerned" (II, p. 233). About four years later, the Jew appears in the *Diary* for the last time: "I am this week entertained, with surprising Advice, concerning the Jew, with and for whom we were so much concerned, three and twenty years ago. A matter for some revived and renewed Supplication" (II, p. 500). In spite of those prayers and supplications, the Jew who had been the "object of the years of prayers on the part of the Mathers" died in Jamaica "a hardened wretch," we read in an editor's note to the *Diary*.[24]

Mather claims he is "Catechizing . . . among the Jews" (II, p. 234); most likely his tracts served as homiletic devices and warning tales for Puritans. In 1700, having received a "charming" story about the "Conversion made by a Jew, one Shalome Ben Shalomoh at his joining lately to a Congregational Church in London," Mather made it "an Appendix to the Book of the Greek Churches" (I, p. 370).[25] Thus in 1701, *An Appendix. Containing A Relation of the Conversion of a Jew, Named, Shalome Ben Shalomoh, As himself uttered it, unto a CHURCH of the Lord Jesus Christ, Assembled in Rose Mary Lane, London. Sept. 29. 1699* was published in Boston. As transcribed, or contrived, by the Congregationalist minister Thomas Humfrey, the "Narrative of the Conversion of Shalome Ben Shalomoh, the JEW" includes a testimony: "I Shalome Ben Shalomoh, was born of Jewish Parents . . . was circumcised the eighth Day in Pusnonny in Poland, where I lived till I was twelve years of Age, at which time it pleased God (who works all things for the good of his Elect) that all our Family (my self alone excepted) died in a great Plague." Inclined to travel and see the world, the orphan meets up with a pious Christian employed by the Duke of Brandenburg. Shortly thereafter, the hero's eyes are fully opened:

---

[23] Friedman (1934), p. 6.

[24] Note to Cotton Mather, *Diary* II, 741. On Samuel Frazon see Friedman (1934), p. 153, n. 13.

[25] Cotton Mather, *American Tears upon the Ruines of the Greek Churches. A Compendious, but Entertaining History of the Darkness come upon the Greek Churches, in Europe and Asia* (Boston, 1701).

I thought I saw Jesus Christ, yea the very God head shining round about me through the Man hood of Jesus, for in him dwells the Fulness of the Godhead bodily. And now I am perswaded whether I direct my Prayer to God the first Person in the Trinity, or to Jesus Christ the Second, it is the same, they being the same in Essence, equal in Power & Glory.

In his "Preface" to the bildungsroman of Shalome Ben Shalomoh, Mather contends that Christianity is "The Religion of the Old Testament, from whence the modern Jews are fallen" (just as Puritanism is the true Christianity, from whence Rome is fallen):

We Believe & Expect a Day, when the Jews will be remarkably Saved, from the Blindness, in and for which they are now Rejected of God. . . . Now, the general and Obstinate Unbelief, of the Jews, during all the Time of the Antichristian Apostasy [i.e., Roman Catholicism], may be improved by us, as an Argument for our Faith, of the Prophecies concerning their Turning to the Lord, upon the Removal of the Vail now upon their minds. . . . But that our Faith mayn't be left wholly without some support . . . We are also now and then revived with Examples of a few particular Jews, that have the Light of the Evangelical Truth, by the Irresistible Spirit of our Lord Jesus Christ Shot into them; and that have clearly discerned the infallible Demonstrations, of our JESUS being the CHRIST.[26]

Cotton Mather published over three hundred titles; some are short pamphlets; others, like the tale of Shalome Ben Shalomoh, are reprinted at second or third hand. Mather's *Things To Be More Thought Upon* (1713), a "Confutation of Judaism" (II, p. 492), is directed to Jews "in reach of this Expostulation"; the tract outlines the "Indignities which our Blessed JESUS continues to suffer from you."[27] Yes, Mather says benevolently to no one in particular, "I know you do it Ignorantly in Unbelief"; yet the more Jesus is reproached by Jews, the more Mather's faith in prophecy is confirmed. The prophets wrote that the Messiah would be despised and rejected; that he would be given gall and vinegar; that the Jews' table would become their snare; that their eyes would be darkened; that they would be blotted out of the book of the living; that their genealogies would not be preserved; that the Messiah would come five hundred years after their return from captivity; that Jerusalem would be besieged; that

---

[26] Mather (1702), pp. 57–58.
[27] Cotton Mather (1713); for the complete title, see note 13 above. I see no reason to supply page references in these notes.

they would receive false prophets. When the time is ripe, Mather promises, their dispersion will come to an end.

"But now and then," he adds, getting to the point of *Things To Be More Thought Upon*, "there comes in One of your Nation, whom God Enlightens with the Knowledge of the Redeemer; and makes part of those First-Fruits, which will e're long be followed with a mighty Harvest, when the Redeemer shall come unto Zion, and shall turn His whole favoured and preserved name from Ungodliness." Mather appeals to reason and Isaiah 53: Jews are "Reasonable Souls"; if they are scandalized at "the Cross of our JESUS," the scandal was foretold by Isaiah. And "indeed, it is to be wondred at, how any of you can shut your Eyes against the Light of so bright a Chapter!" Like other exponents of conversionalism, Mather leans on the motif of a suffering Messiah: "I beseech you, Syrs, to Read it [Isaiah 53] over again. It is most certain that if the MESSIAH be not already come, yet whenever He does come, he must appear in just such, I say, just such Circumstances of Humiliation, as those for which your most lovely JESUS, is now disliked among you."

Apparently, "Hundreds of Jews, have in our Days, been brought over to Christianity, by the Blessing of God." If for Jews the Trinity is a stumbling block, consider the proleptic figures of threeness in the Hebrew Bible: "the Repetition of that name JEHOVAH three times in the Benediction prescribed in the Book of Numbers" signifies "Three Powers" and "Three Substances." Jews may recognize a mystery in the "Treble Benediction"; however, "We Christians do now see further into this Mystery." Mather's tone swings: "Strokes of the Divine Wrath will touch you and vex you." The "Self-destroying Sinners" are warned that the day of the Lord is terribly near: "'tis very certain, That there will one Day be an Appearing of the Great God, and our Saviour Jesus Christ, unto the Confusion of those that are His Adversaries."

The title of the present essay – "The Three Jewish Children at Berlin" – alludes to one of Mather's conversionist tracts: *Faith Encouraged. A Brief Relation of a Strange Impression from Heaven, on the Minds of some Jewish Children At the City of Berlin* (Boston, 1718). Once upon a time (according to a text received by Mather, reprinted verbatim in *Faith Encouraged*, and promoted to school children in Boston), three Jewish sisters under the age of twelve, Sprinz, Guttel, and Esther, were graciously converted.[28] Fleeing from their parents' home in Berlin, the children sought refuge and instruction in the house of a Lutheran minister named Kahman. Examined one at a time by commissioners and clergymen (who "began to think they had, perhaps, met with some severe Usage at Home"), the children declared with one voice: "They would not return to their Parents again, but would be made Christians and Children of Eternal Salvation." Indeed, the sisters "were fully resolv'd rather to dye, than to leave their Jesus." In order to "try their Sincerity," some persons exaggerated the "uneasy and troublesome" life of a true Christian:

> they would be despised and forsaken, even among the Christians themselves, and be forced to work hard for their Livelihood: They replied that they would work till the very Blood spurted out from their Nails, provided they might be made Children of Eternal Salvation; and, that, though they should not be happy in this World, they hoped to be so in the next. And when it was represented to them, on the other Side, how easily and comfortably they might live among the Jews; and that their Father had made fine Cloaths for them, &c. they reply'd, They did not value that at all; the Cloaths must remain in the World; they would be Children of Salvation, and not return to their Parents again.

Of course the parents (Isaac Veits and Sophie Moses) tried to win back their children with "many fine Presents," as such parents will; they "kiss'd their very Hands and Feet, and melted away into Tears," but to no avail. The pious children declared that if the "Parents would but become Christians too, they should be their Parents still"; otherwise, Sprinz, Guttel, and Esther "would not return to their Parents again." The youngest child (eight years old, "or as the Mother pretends, but Six") spoke these heartfelt words to the weeping throng gathered in the minister's house: "If you will give me nothing, let me die of Hunger, or cut off my very Head; for I had rather lose

---

[28] C. Roth, in his *Magna Bibliotheca Anglo-Judaica*, lists a version of the story: *Remarkable Account of the Conversion of Three Jewish Children in Berlin in 1715 — From a Letter of Dr. Jablonski, a Lutheran Minister.* I have not compared that text with Mather's reprint; the "Reverend Dr. Jablonski" is one of the commissioners named in Mather's text. On efforts to promote the story of the three Jewish children in Boston, see *Diary* II, pp. 491–92, 494, 503, 524. "Encourage some Schole-Masters, to have the Story of the Jewish Children at Berlin, read in their Schools, with Application" (II, p. 524). "I would send my Account of the Jewish Children at Berlin unto the Master of our Grammar-Schole, with my Desire than it be read publicly unto the

my Life, than be separated from my dearest Jesus, who dy'd for me; and if you refuse to take me, he is always ready to receive me in his Arms." An account of the miracle was sent to his Majesty, the King of Prussia, "whose answer is daily expected."

Ever on the lookout for the Second Coming, Mather reads the children's conversions as "signs of encouragement" and "tokens for good": they foretell "the Conversion of the Israelitish Nation."[29] Along with the exemplary story of Sprinz, Guttel, and Esther (and of the severe usage met by their Jewish parents), he reprints his *Things To Be More Thought Upon* (1713): the Jews' "Infidelity" confirms Mather's faith; the Jews will be "blotted out of the Book of the Living"; their "Genealigies" [sic] will no longer be preserved; and so on and on.

"I hear of a Jew in this place," Mather writes in 1717. "I would seek some Conversation with him" (II, p. 468). Later that day he recalls his "design of Conversing with a Jew, in this Place." The matter is dropped. By about 1724, having failed utterly in his mission "to baptise a Jew, that should by my Ministry, bee brought home unto the Lord," Mather notes in his *Diary* that "the Man of Sins M.CC.LX years are up" (II, p. 805); the signs had all been given. "My God has convinced me, that the second coming of my SAVIOUR is to be at and for the Perdition of the Man of Sin; and that the tremendous Conflagration which is to precede the new Heavens and the new Earth, is then to carry all before it; and that there is nothing that we know of remaining to be done, before this astonishing Revolution; so that it may with reason be daily looked for" (II, p. 740). Therefore, he concluded, "there appears to be no

---

Children in the Schoole, and that he make suitable Remarks thereupon unto them" (II, p. 492).

[29] See also Mather's lecture *Tokens for Good*, whose title page is hard to decipher: *Menachem: A very brief Essay on Tokens for Good: wherein, Together with the Good Signs which all Good Men have to Comfort them, there are Exhibited also some Good Things of Late Occurrence, and of a Great Importance, which have a Comforting Aspect on the Protestant Religion in General [ ] particularly on a Country of Distinguished Protestants. A Sermon* (Boston, 1716). "There is at this Time in the City of Berlin, a strange Motion from GOD, among the Children of the JEWS, who Live thereabouts. These Children, under Twelve Years of Age, make unaccountable Flights unto the Protestant Ministers, to be Initiated in the Christian Religion. They Embrace Christianity, with a mighty Zeal; and they cannot see the Name of our JESUS, in a Book, but they discover a Transport of Affection to it, and fall into a Flood of Tears. They are so firm in their Adherence unto HIM, that all the Endeavours of their Parents to reclaim them, have only this Reply from them, We never shall Return to you; 'Tis time for you to come over to us" (pp. 39–40).

cause, why further fulfillment should in this world be looked for."[30] The conversion of the Jews would not accelerate the establishment on earth of the Kingdom of God.

More than a year after Cotton Mather's death in 1728, Samuel Sewall wrote to the young Samuel Mather: "'I have one unhappiness befallen me, viz., Dr. Cotton Mather's vehemently insisting on the Conflagration, so that he seems to think there is no general Calling or conversion of the Jews, Or that it is already past and gone.'"[31] Two years before he died, Mather understood that the salvation of "all Israel" promised in Romans 11 had taken place just after 70 C.E., when the second Temple was destroyed. Echoing Richard Baxter's preterist stand "Against the Bold Asserters of a Future Calling and Reign of the Jews" (1691), Mather renounced conversionism: "Alas, I was a very Young Man; I understood not the true Israel; I Recant; I Revoke; and I now make my most public Retraction."[32] At his second advent, Christ would return "with His mighty Angels, in flaming Fire"; and those flames would set off the Conflagration. If the "cursed remnant" of Jews were meant to be saved at the Second Coming, they must be converted amidst the fiery flames of "the tremendous Conflagration" (or in the words of James Sibley, "a Holocaust of all the people who don't accept Jesus"). For Mather, the notion was manifestly absurd.

As far as I know, the story of Shadrach, Meshach, and Abed-nego, the three Jews cast into the "burning fiery furnace," is not part of the Southern Baptists' conversionist repertoire, nor have I come across it in Mather. "Then Nebuchadnezzar came near to the mouth of the burning fiery furnace, and spake, and said Shadrach, Meshach, and Abed-nego, ye servants of the most high God, come forth and come hither." And the three men "came forth of the midst of the fire" (see Daniel 3).

---

[30] Scult (1978), p. 49, citing Cotton Mather's "Paradisus" manuscript (American Antiquarian Society).

[31] R. Smolinski, Introduction to *The Threefold Paradise of Cotton Mather*, an edition of "Triparadisus," R. Smolinski (ed.) (Athens and London, 1995), p. 36.

[32] Smolinski (1995), pp. 314–15.

GEORGE STANLEY FABER:
NO POPERY AND PROPHECY

BY

S.W. GILLEY
Durham

"Defoe says, that there were a hundred thousand stout country-fellows in his time ready to fight to the death against popery, without knowing whether popery was a man or a horse".[1] Such anti-Catholicism has been a central strand in English culture since the Reformation, a prejudice "into which we English are born, as into the fall of Adam",[2] as part of a nationalist assertion of the virtues of Protestant Britannia against its Popish enemies, France and Spain, and as the very heart of an English epic of liberation from Rome in the sixteenth century. The story needed a villain, as Jack needed a giant; and what better villain than Giant Pope? The fires of Smithfield were burnt into the popular mind by George Foxe's *Acts and Mouments*, commonly called his *Book of Martyrs*, the most widely read of all works after the Bible, and the British epic identified Romanism with continental despotism and tyranny, with poverty and wooden shoes, so that the Reformation became the mother of English enlightenment and liberty.[3]

Anti-Catholicism had a continuous history from 1520, and in the eighteenth century was an essential part in the definition of British nationhood.[4] Its passions among the quality, however, abated some-

---

[1] W. Hazlitt, *Sketches and Essays and Winterslow* (London, 1912), p. 71.
[2] Henry Edward Cardinal Manning, cited in J. Pereiro, *Cardinal Manning: an Intellectual Biography* (Oxford, 1998), p. 174.
[3] For a survey, see P.B. Nockles, "'The Difficulties of Protestantism': Bishop Milner, John Fletcher and Catholic Apologetic against the Church of England in the Era from the First Relief Act to Emancipation, 1788–1830", *Recusant History*, vol. 24 (October, 1998), pp. 193–236. Some of the principal recent works in this area are C. Haydon, *Anti-Catholicism in eighteenth-century England: a political and social study* (Manchester, 1993) and D.G. Paz, *Popular Anti-Catholicism in Mid-Victorian England* (Stanford, 1992).
[4] L. Colley, *Britons: Forging the Nation 1707–1837* (New Haven and London, 1992), pp. 11–54.

what in the second half of the century. The Catholic Relief acts of 1778 and 1791 were the work of a respectable opinion which treated Romanism with indifference. English Catholics were accepted as a small but decent element in English society, living quietly among their friends and neighbours. The Gordon Riots of 1780 seemed to show that their chief foe was the mob, which was feared by elite society as well, and "the years between 1780 and 1800 saw a hiatus in the history of anti-Catholicism",[5] even if it only went underground. Even more feared after 1790 was the French Revolution, the work, it was believed, of atheists, Deists and scoffers at all religion, and the French émigré clergy, exiles from the Revolution, were welcomed in England as the persecuted priesthood of a sister Establishment, and were supported by the State and private charity. The mobs in the early 1790s turned on Unitarians and other radical Dissenters suspected of revolutionary sympathies, while the British government funded the new Irish seminary at Maynooth and the Scottish Catholic clergy, in a tacit return for the Church's opposition to revolution on the continent and in Ireland. These developments suggested the emergence of a new and closer relationship between British society and the Roman Catholic Church, in a common contribution to the cause of counter-revolution, the heightening of Catholic participation in British life and the reversal of the enmities of centuries.

But other changes pointed in a different direction. England was undergoing an industrial revolution, the first nation in the world to do so, with an attendant population explosion in the towns of the manufacturing north, and in these towns after 1790, there was a great growth in the Protestant Dissenting Churches, especially the various branches of Methodism, which were close to the anti-Catholic tradition. The quickening pace of emigration from Protestant and Catholic Ireland into these towns was to mean a new heat in relations between the Churches; while the rebellion in Ireland in 1798 inaugurated a new Catholic nationalism which has only abated in our own day. Anti-Catholicism was reinforced by anti-Irishness, hostility to the continental Catholic enemy without being echoed in suspicion of the Irish Catholic enemy within.

Moreover the expansion of Catholicism and Dissent posed a challenge to the position of the Established Church, which made no

---

[5] J. Wolffe, *The Protestant Crusade in Great Britain 1829–1860* (Oxford, 1981), p. 2.

proper provision for the new industrial towns, and was attacked by political radicals for her internal corruptions and the inefficiencies and inequalities of her pastoral provision and her clerical incomes. The scandalous sloth and wealth of some of the higher Anglican clergy and the increasing inadequacies of the Anglican parochial system were especially notable in the diocese of Durham, with its substantial English Catholic minority. Both in Durham and Northumberland, Catholics found champions in their Whig and liberal neighbours, noblemen and gentlemen like the Marquess of Cleveland and Earl Grey, against the Tory interest championed by the Bishop and his clergy. English Catholics were not as radical as Irish ones, but they had no love for Anglican Tories or the Church Establishment, and they joined happily in the radical attack, so that the Durham diocese saw many a skirmish in the new round of war between the Church of England and the Church of Rome.

The Bishop of Durham from 1791 was a cleric of a recently ennobled family, Shute Barrington, the sixth and youngest son of the theological writer the first Viscount Barrington; "his brothers included an admiral, a general, a judge and a Chancellor of the Exchequer".[6] As Bishop of Llandaff he had been best known for his bill "for the more effectual discouragement of the crime of adultery". In Durham, he urged charity to Roman Catholics as individuals and gave an annual offering to the Poor Clares who took refuge in his own diocese, and was in favour of "*every degree of toleration, short of political power and establishment*".[7] This meant, however, that he was strongly opposed to Catholic representation in parliament or government, arguing that Rome bred revolution, and in a Fast Day sermon before the House of Lords in 1799, he urged, in the words of his biographer, "that the principal cause of the French Revolution was the total indifference to, and contempt of, the Christian religion, arising from the corruptions of Popery, and the identification of those corruptions with Christianity itself".[8] "To Popery, to the errors and defects of Popery", he wrote in his Charge of 1801, "we cannot but impute, in a great degree, the origin of that revolutionary spirit, which has gone so far

---

[6] L. Gooch, "Lingard v. Barrington, et al.: Ecclesiastical Politics in Durham 1805–29", *Durham University Journal*, vol. 85 (January, 1993), p. 11.

[7] G. Townsend (ed.), *The Theological Works of the First Viscount Barrington . . . with a brief Memoir of his son, Shute Barrington, the Late Bishop of Durham*, 3 vols (London, 1828), vol. I, p. XLIX.

[8] Townsend (1828), p. XLVIII.

towards the subversion of the ancient establishments of religion and civil government".[9] The French Revolution had been caused by infidelity, but infidelity was the consequence of the popish corruption of Christianity which brought religion into contempt by making it absurd. The corollary was that Protestantism alone could preserve the nation from infidelity and so from political revolution. On this understanding there was an obvious contradiction in any counter-revolutionary alliance between England and Rome, whose combination of despotism and superstition merely produced by reaction revolution and unbelief. By their own superstitious principles, Catholics were incapable of understanding free British institutions, and full political rights could therefore be denied them.

Yet Barrington considered radicals and Dissenters to be equally beyond the pale, indeed as little better than infidels, with whom they posed a threat to the establishment, and discerned in Popery, Infidelity and Nonconformity a threefold challenge to Church and State. It was this view which sustained a nation embattled with Napoleonic France, as the authorities clamped down on internal unrest, and as mainstream opinion rallied to the Church of England. During the fifteen-year rule of the Prime Minister Lord Liverpool from 1812 to 1827, political and religious reform was postponed *sine die,* and had to wait until 1828–29. In his strong attachment to the status quo, Barrington was representative of the conservative Anglican mind of his era. He died in 1826 in his ninety-second year, and the nineteenth-century revival of No Popery can be traced in part to the influence of his High Tory mentality upon the Church of England.

Barrington, however, had a particular domestic problem, that the Roman challenge was nearer home than Rome. The French Revolution exiled to Durham a branch of the first Catholic seminary abroad at Douai, to County Durham, to Crook Hall in 1794 and then in 1808 to Ushaw.[10] The Bishop's charge of 1806 against Popery, subsequently reprinted in 1807 as a tract against the national proponents of Catholic Emancipation in the 1807 election,[11] and later extended with an attack on Transubstantiation,[12] was answered by a

---

[9] S. Barrington, *A Charge Delivered to the Clergy of the Diocese of Durham, at the Ordinary Visitation of that Diocese, in July 1801* (reprinted London, 1811), p. 288.

[10] D. Milburn, *A History of Ushaw College* (Durham, 1964).

[11] S. Barrington, *The Grounds on which the Church of England separated from the Church of Rome, stated in a Charge delivered to the Clergy of the Diocese of Durham* (London, 1807).

[12] S. Barrington, *The Grounds on which the Church of England separated from the Church*

member of the Catholic seminary staff John Lingard, the rising historian of English Catholicism.[13] Lingard had his polemical work cut out for him, and during the subsequent decades he replied to attacks by numerous local clerics and to the Bishops of Gloucester, Lincoln, St David's and Peterborough.[14] There was a response to his reply to Barrington from the redoubtable Henry Phillpotts, who became one of Barrington's chaplains in 1806, received the valuable living of Gateshead in 1808 and a succession of prebendal stalls from 1809, and in 1820, the golden rectory of Stanhope, one of the richest livings in England. Phillpotts owed this rise, which took him to the see of Exeter in 1830, after an about-face on the issue of Catholic Emancipation, to his doughty controversial championship of Anglican Toryism, especially against Roman Catholics, and he was to die like Barrington in his ninety- second year.[15]

Barrington astutely used his extensive patronage of valuable livings to promote other clergymen who devoted their talents to the anti-Roman cause. The Bishop encouraged the Rev. George Townsend to reply to the Catholic Charles Butler's *Book of the Roman Catholic Church* and preferred him to a canonry.[16] Townsend subsequently edited George Foxe's *Book of Martyrs*, and still lives on as the hero of Ronald Knox's delightful essay, "The man who tried to convert the pope", on a visit to Rome in 1850.[17] William Gilly attracted Barrington through his work of 1824 describing his visit to the Waldensians or Vaudois of the valleys of Piedmont in northern Italy, whose survival he held to prove the continuity of the true Church of Christ through the centuries of popish corruption.[18] Another anti-Catholic polemicist who benefited by Barrington's patronage and who crossed swords with Lingard was George Stanley Faber. Faber

---

of Rome reconsidered, in a view of the Romish Doctrine of the Eucharist; with an Explanation of the antepenultimate answer in the Church Catechism (London, 1809).

[13] J. Lingard, *Remarks on a Charge delivered to the Clergy of the Diocese of Durham, by Shute Barrington, Bishop of Durham at the Ordinary Visitation of that Diocese, in the Year 1806* (London, 1807).

[14] Gooch (1993). See also M. Haile and E. Bonney, *Life and Letters of John Lingard* (London, 1911), pp. 383–6.

[15] G.C.B. Davies, *Henry Phillpotts, Bishop of Exeter 1778–1869* (London, 1954).

[16] See my "Nationality and liberty, protestant and catholic: Robert Southey's *Book of the Church*", in Stuart Mews (ed.), *Religion and National Identity: Studies in Church History*, vol. 18 (Oxford, 1982), pp. 409–32.

[17] R.A. Knox, *Literary Distractions* (London and New York, 1958), pp. 114–33.

[18] W. Gilly, *Narrative of an Excursion to the Mountains of Piedmont, and Researches among the Vaudois or Waldenses* (London, 1824).

argued like Gilly that the Vaudois, with the Albigensians, proved the visible continuity of the true Christian Church,[19] and it was Faber whom Lingard ridiculed, in a grand panjandrum pamphlet against his critics, for opposing Rome from the viewpoint of Protestant prophecy.[20]

I first met Faber in a work of 738 pages which had belonged to Cardinal Manning, entitled *Faberism Exposed and Refuted: and the Apostolicity of Catholic Doctrine Vindicated: against the second edition, "revised and remoulded", of Faber's "Difficulties of Romanism".*[21] The author was Frederick Charles Husenbeth, the biographer of the redoubtable "English Athanasius",[22] John Milner, Bishop of Castabala and Vicar Apostolic of the Midland District, a writer, fighter and biter of English Protestants and of Anglo-Gallican or "Cisalpine Catholics" whom he thought to be less than loyal to Rome. The unexposable and irrefutable Faber turned out to be the uncle of the most popular of Victorian Catholic spiritual writers, Frederick William Faber of the Brompton Oratory, the author of the battle hymn of English and Irish Catholicism, "Faith of our Fathers". Fr. Faber combined a flamboyant prose-style with an encyclopaedic knowledge of the wider and sometimes wilder realms of Roman Catholic mysticism and hagiography, and his taste for odd and unusual subjects was one that he shared with his uncle.

Yet their common background was ordinary enough. George Stanley Faber was the son and grandson of Anglican clergymen, a middle class family with gentry connections. The one touch of the exotic was his descent on his grandmother's side from a French Protestant Huguenot refugee, Henri de Dibon, who according to the account in his Bible, inherited by the Fabers, had his legs burnt with wreaths of straw by soldiers enforcing the outlawry of French Protestantism in 1685. Fr. Faber's biographer Ronald Chapman sug-

---

[19] G.S. Faber, *An Inquiry into the History and Theology of the Ancient Vallenses and Albigenses: as exhibiting, agreeably to the promises, the perpetuity of the sincere Church of Christ* (London, 1838).

[20] J. Lingard, *A General Vindication of the Remarks on the Charge of the Bishop of Durham, containing: A Reply to a Letter from a Protestant Clergyman of the Diocese of Durham: A Reply to the Observations of the Rev. Thos. Le Mesurier, Rector of Newnton Longville; A Reply to the Strictures of the Rev. G.S. Faber, Vicar of Stockton upon Tees; and Some Observations On the more fashionable Methods of interpreting the Apocalypse* (fourth edition, Dublin, 1811).

[21] (Norwich, 1836). See G.S. Faber, *The Difficulties of Romanism* (London, 1826); and its second edition, *"revised and remoulded"* of 1830. For further on the controversy, see below, notes 49 and 50.

[22] The title is said to have been conferred on him by Newman. See Wilfrid Ward, *The Life of John Henry Cardinal Newman*, 2 vols. (London, 1913), vol. I, p. 119.

gests that "Faith of our Fathers" may owe something to his family's tradition of persecution by Catholics,[23] and the inherently persecuting character of Roman Catholicism was an article of faith to Fr. Faber's uncle.

George Stanley Faber's external career was also conventionally Anglican.[24] He passed from a fellowship and tutorship at Lincoln College, Oxford, and marriage to a daughter of the sometime M.P. for Stockbridge, to serve as a curate to his father in Yorkshire. In 1805, Barrington appointed him Vicar of Stockton-on-Tees in County Durham, where he displayed his dedication as a pastor. His subsequent parishes were at Redmarshall and Long Newton, also in County Durham, and he showed his devotion to his people by refusing an offer from the ultra-conservative Lord Eldon, made at Barrington's suggestion, of an adjoining living to be held in plurality with his own, a common practice of the time. The historian Robert Surtees is said to have heard of this late at night, and ordered his horse to be saddled so that, *mirabile dictu*, he could look upon a minister who had refused a second living. Faber remained a close friend of Barrington and his successor William Van Mildert, who appointed George Stanley Faber's layman brother to be his secretary; the secretary's son, the future Fr. Faber, therefore grew up at Auckland Palace. Bishop Burgess made George Stanley Faber a Prebendary of Salisbury in 1831, and Van Mildert appointed him Master of Sherburn Hospital in County Durham in 1832. Here he pulled down the old Master's residence, and rebuilt it for his greater comfort. There is no doubting his industry, founded on his habit of rising by six in summer and winter for writing and study. Nor was this at the expense of his pastoral care. He was an assiduous visitor to the poor, but was also convivial, "with a rich store of racy anecdotes" and stories in the dialect of his native Yorkshire.[25] He died aged eighty in 1854, having written more than forty works, mostly controversial, beginning with his first published doublet of sermons, preached before the University of Oxford in

---

[23] Ronald Chapman, *Father Faber* (London, 1961), p. 2.

[24] There is very little in print about Faber, apart from the entry in the *Dictionary of National Biography* and the 'Memoir' by Francis A. Faber prefixed to the second edition of *The Many Mansions in the House of the Father* (London, 1854). There is also an essay in Henry Heavisides, *The Annals of Stockton-on-Tees; with Biographical Notices* (Stockton-on-Tees, 1865), pp. 101–5; an obituary in *The Durham Advertiser*, 3 February 1854 (I am grateful for these references to Roger Norris); and a notice in *The Gentleman's Magazine*, vol. XLI (May 1854), pp. 537–9.

[25] Heavisides (1865), p. 103.

1799, *An attempt to explain by recent events, five of the seven vials mentioned in the Revelation, and an Inquiry into the Scriptural signification of the word Bara*. One of his last books, which appeared in 1851, *The Many Mansions of the House of the Father*,[26] dedicated to his old friend John Bird Sumner, Archbishop of Canterbury, set out to discover from Scripture the precise locality of the future Heaven of the Blessed, which he argued consisted in a literally renewed and renovated earth. Its second edition contains his memoir.

No modern scholar has seen fit to study Faber's theology, presumably on the grounds that his viewpoint was 'pre-critical', except for Peter Toon in his monograph on the Evangelical response to the Oxford Movement.[27] Indeed Faber's topics sound more than a little eccentric, – his early taste was "for singular and recondite subjects"[28] but this was not the case in their day. His learning was immense, and it was in all innocence that he asked whether he should sit his ordination examination in Latin or English. His leading idea, expressed with consistency and detail through a series of multivolume works, was a systematic theological explanation of the history of the world, using the Scriptures as its basis: an idea rooted in turn in the ordinary classical western assumption that all the religions of the world had a common origin. One particular preoccupation denotes his frame of mind. He was fascinated by the earliest era of human history, which he argued against Bishop Warburton belonged to a first, universal, patriarchal, dispensation or divine revelation to mankind, before the Levitical dispensations to the Jews, and the New Testament to the Christians.[29] In the first age of the world, after the exile from Paradise, Jehovah was manifest between the cherubim at the gates of Eden, as He would be manifest in Christ's return at the Last Day. The worship of the first age had been the offering of animal sacrifice to God, an offering prophetic of the atonement of Christ's sacrifice on Calvary. Cain's infidel offering of vegetables had been refused, because it was a rejection of the atonement before the event, with the outcome of the first murder, and "*the entire discarding of bloody*

---

[26] For the germ of this work, see G.S. Faber, *A Treatise on the Genius and Object of the Patriarchal, the Levitical, and the Christian Dispensations*, 2 vols. (London, 1823), vol. I, p. 23.

[27] P. Toon, *Evangelical Theology 1833–1856: A Response to Tractarianism* (London, 1979).

[28] Faber (1854), p. xiii.

[29] Faber (1823), vol. I, p. 23.

piacular sacrifices and the systematic adoption of vegetable eucharistic offerings" – shades of Romanism – in an apostasy from divine revelation. This had in "its practical effects closely resembled the fruits, which a not dissimilar infidel philosophy has produced in the course of the antichristian French Revolution".[30] The great flood was a punishment of Adam's descendants for their rejection of their duty of sacrifice, which no doubt included an attack on the gates of Eden, a theory which Faber buttressed with references to Hesiod and Ovid, and compared with the infidel attacks on the Christian Church in his own day.

The antediluvian apostasy was followed by a postdiluvian one, as Faber, like George Eliot's Mr. Casaubon, sought the key to all the mythologies. The orgies in which the Flood was remembered became the basis of the pagan mysteries, while in the imagination of those born after the Deluge, Adam and his three sons at creation prefigured Noah and his three sons, Shem, Japeth and Ham, thereby giving rise to the theory of metempsychosis. As the earth had risen from the waters of chaos, so the ark had risen above the water of the Deluge, and the renascent earth above the Flood, and earth and ark had become the crescent symbol of the earth goddesses and moon goddesses of primitive paganism. Ham may have been the propagator of this idolatry, for "he was not only ignorant of the sanctifying influence of pure religion", but "was a stranger to the laws even of common decency".[31] Noah became a sun-god, as he and his sons were deified by Ham's grandson the apostate Nimrod, the builder of the tower of Babel, with the consequent disintegration of mankind's original primitive language into a multitude of tongues, and of the mystic Babylon, mother of harlots, which foreshadowed both pagan and papal Rome. This takes the reader straight into No Popery. "The analogy", concluded Faber, "is obvious: as the pure worship of the patriarchs was first authoritatively corrupted at Babel, so was the divine religion of Christ at Rome".[32]

Unlike other Christian writers, like Faber's great theological mentor Bishop Samuel Horsley, who saw reflections in paganism of the

---

[30] Faber (1823), vol. I, p. 11.

[31] G.S. Faber, *A Dissertation on the Mysteries of the Cabiri; or the Great Gods of Phenicia, Samothrace, Egypt, Troas, Greece, Italy, and Crete; being an Attempt to deduce the Several Orgies of Isis, Ceres, Mithras, Bacchus, Rhea, Adonis, and Hecate, from an Union of the Rites commemorative of the Deluge with the Adoration of the Host of Heaven*, 2 vols. (London and Oxford, 1803), vol. II, p. 11.

[32] Faber (1803), vol. II, p. 14.

doctrine of the Trinity, Faber derived every triad of Gods, from China to Peru, from Nimrod's deification of the three sons of Noah, and lavished a mass of erudition on his 'helio-arkite' theory, which is perfectly sensible on the basis of his initial premise, that Genesis contains in skeletal outline the literal history of the human race, which had once worshipped the one true God, and could only have fallen into paganism by the wilful misunderstanding of patriarchal religion. This did not seem absurd to Barrington, to whom Faber dedicated his principal opus upon this theme, *The Origin of Pagan Idolatry Ascertained from Historical Testimony and Circumstantial Evidence*, of 1816. Its intellectual respectability was also severally guaranteed by Viscount Barrington, the learned Bishop of St David's and the Chancellor of the Exchequer, to whom Faber dedicated the three frontispieces of his work; and by the Archbishops of Canterbury and York and the numerous other bishops and peers who subscribed to it. Indeed the view that paganism was the ruin of a primitive revelation to Adam and Noah remained common for another generation, and was to be maintained by Gladstone against those who argued for a naturalistic origin for religion.[33]

Faber was, however, prepared to reinterpret the six days of creation as six eras of great length, on the basis of the just emerging fossil record, and of a learned disquisition of the meanings of the word 'day',[34] and one should not underestimate the excitement of the seemingly scientific character of his fusion of rationalism and Biblical literalism, offering precision on every point, with a romantic vision of superhuman figures half lost in the mist of high antiquity. Faber loved the poems of Sir Walter Scott and Robert Southey, especially those on mythological subjects; he devoured Gothic romances and mastered Arabic and Hindu mythology. "He had a taste for oriental lore and tales of enchantment, and this made him particularly prefer the TEMPEST and the MID-SUMMER NIGHT'S DREAM amongst Shakespeare's plays".[35] His was a frame of mind which might seem to do little harm, but his theory of the primaeval apostasies from antediluvian and postdiluvian orthodox religion as prefiguring and paralleling the popish apostasy, sustained his view

---

[33] D. Bebbington, "Gladstone and Grote", in P.J. Jagger (ed.), *Gladstone* (London, 1998), p. 173.
[34] *Dispensations*, vol. I, pp. 111–66.
[35] Heavisides (1865), p. 103.

of Roman Catholicism, which also drew upon the same combination of imaginative romance and literal biblical history.

Here Faber stood in a tradition of learned interpretation of the two most famous prophetic books of Scripture, Daniel and Revelation, believed by a long line of Christian scholars to hold the key to human history.[36] The Book of Daniel was, on the face of it, written about Daniel the Prophet in the sixth century before Christ. According to modern scholars, it was primarily composed in the second century B.C.E. to encourage the Maccabean Jews in their resistance to the Greek Seleucid king, Antiochus IV Epiphanes, who had set up an "abomination of desolation", a statue of Zeus, in the temple in Jerusalem.[37] Nebuchadnezzar's dream in Chapter 2 was of a statue of gold, silver, brass and iron, with proverbially celebrated feet of iron and clay, and Daniel's vision in Chapter 7 was of four beasts, the fourth with iron teeth, brass claws and ten horns. The statue and beasts originally represented the four great kingdoms of the world, of Babylon, Media, Persia and the Hellenistic empire of Alexander the Great and Seleucia, and the eleventh Little Horn of the fourth beast was Antiochus IV. The four beasts of Daniel, however, reappear in the monster of Chapter 13 of the Book of Revelation, with ten horns, seven heads, bear's feet and a lion's mouth, which the Fathers of the Church took to be the Roman Empire. Puritan exegesis made the ten horns its successor barbarian kingdoms, and the survival of the empire in one form or another, under Byzantium in the East and Charlemagne's heirs in the west, was another fruitful theme for prophecy. In Chapter 17, a woman in purple and scarlet rides the beast and is the mystic Babylon, the city of Rome, with her name, "MYSTERY, BABYLON THE GREAT, THE MOTHER OF HARLOTS AND ABOMINATIONS OF THE EARTH", emblazoned on her forehead, after the custom of the prostitutes of Rome.

While reordering Daniel's empires to make the last the Roman, the Protestant Reformers extended these images to papal Rome, so that in Protestant mythology, the Little Horn of Daniel's fourth beast and the Scarlet Woman in Revelation were the Roman Church and

---

[36] The subject is covered from an Adventist perspective in an exhaustive and not very accurate manner in Le Roy Edwin Froom, *The Prophetic Faith of our Fathers: The Historical Development of Prophetic Interpretation*, 4 vols. (Washington D.C., 1946–54).

[37] L.F. Hartman and A.A. Di Lella, *The Book of Daniel* (New York, 1978); A. Lacocque, *Le Livre de Daniel* (Paris, 1976) = *The Book of Daniel* (London, 1979).

Pope, who was also denounced as the Man of Sin in the second Epistle to the Thessalonians and the Antichrist of the Johannine Epistles. The second beast in Revelation Chapter 13, with lamb's horns, became the ecclesiastical and papal analogue of pagan Rome. It was, then, this body of dark, bloody, apocalyptic images which lay at the heart of the Protestant rejection of Rome, the images of the Roman Church as beast, horn and whore, the very embodiment of this-worldly evil, within an interpretation of the four great empires spanning recorded human history.

This view of prophecy went with a chronology. The seventeenth-century Puritan Joseph Mede found in Daniel the period of the Little Horn as a time, times and half a time, three and a half times or years, or forty two months or 1,260 days. This was the period for which it was predicted that the abomination of desolation would stand within the Temple, and recurs in Chapter 12 of the Book of Revelation as the duration of the exile and captivity of the Christian Church. Mede translated these 1,260 prophetic days as years, on the principle that a prophetic day is a year, during which the papal Antichrist would persecute the saints of God. In the century after Mede, this 'historicist' interpretation of the 1,260-year domination of Antichrist was accepted both by Sir Isaac Newton and his episcopal namesake Thomas, whose *Dissertations on the Prophecies* made the theory wholly respectable. But when the French Revolution turned upon the Roman Church in 1792, it seemed to some that the 1,260 years was now accomplished, and the Scottish interpreter William Cunninghame dated the beginning of Antichrist's reign, by subtraction of 1,260, to A.D. 533, when the pope's universal jurisdiction was allegedly recognized by the Emperor Justinian. The other periods in Daniel, of 1,290 and 1,355 days, 30 and 75 days or prophetic years beyond 1792, gave the world another 75 years of life to 1867, in a time of toil and trial and tribulation which the new political and industrial revolutions were inflicting on the earth.

The complexities of this vast new prophetic literature are not easily summarised.[38] The historicist Antichrist could be harmonised with a futurist vision of the Antichrist who, whether a power or a

---

[38] S.C. Orchard, *English Evangelical Eschatology 1790–1850* (University of Cambridge Ph.D., 1969); W.H. Oliver, *Prophets and Millennialists: The Uses of Biblical Prophecy in England from the 1790s to the 1840s* (Auckland, New Zealand, 1978). For Faber, see Froom (1946–1954), especially vol. III, pp. 338–46.

person, was still to come, and who would reign for a literal three and half years. A parallel controversy concerned the meanings of the 2,200, or 2,300, or 2,400 days or years of Daniel Chapter 8, which varied with versions of the text, and the seventy weeks of years, or 490 years, of Chapter 9. Cunninghame's was only one of a number of prophetic systems, and was developed in answer to Faber's. Yet these systems had a common inspiration and origin. The French Revolution and social and political unrest reawakened the Protestant apocalyptic mentality, with a new attention to the letter of the Scriptural text which proved that the last days had come. To those witnessing the profoundest political and social change in modern history, there was the reassurance that the key to these events was in the Bible, so that Christianity could make sense of them.[39]

Some manifestations of this concern were simply eccentric, like Richard Brothers, who foreshadowed the British Israelite theory that the British were the lost tribes of Israel, or even more famous in her day, Joanna Southcott, of the notorious black box, who as the woman clothed with the sun in Revelation, Chapter 12, claimed to be pregnant with the new Messiah.[40] Yet the prophetical tradition was a learned one, and inspired both radical politicians and conservatives fearing revolution, both abroad and at home. The ablest bishop in the Church of England, Samuel Horsley, welcomed the French Catholic refugees to England as exiles from revolution, and saw the true figure of the coming Antichrist not in Roman Catholicism but in French revolutionary infidelity. Horsley's establishmentarian prophetic writing had both a conservative thrust against internal radical sedition in Britain, and a patriotic message for the fight against the Gallican continental colossus with which Britain was at war.

Faber worshipped Bishop Horsley as his "Master in Israel",[41] and like Horsley, denied that the Pope was Antichrist, who must rather be an unbeliever. "The donation of the name of *Antichrist* to the Pope is purely gratuitous. It rests upon no certain warrant of Scripture: and, indeed, it may rather be said to contradict it. The predicted Antichrist is an infidel and an atheist".[42] In this respect, Faber's

---

[39] J.F.C. Harrison, *The Second Coming: Popular Millenarianism 1780–1850* (London, 1979), pp. 57–134.
[40] R. Matthews, *English Messiahs: Studies of Six English Religious Pretenders 1656–1927* (London, 1936), pp. 43–126.
[41] Faber (1854), p. xiii.
[42] G.S. Faber, *The Sacred Calendar of Prophecy: or a Dissertation on the Prophecies, which*

hostility to the demonic atheism of the French Revolution resembled the kind of ultra-conservative and apocalyptic anti-revolutionary Roman Catholicism to which he was opposed. But while acknowledging with Horsley that the Pope was not the Antichrist to come, Faber did not abandon the historicist scheme of a 1,260 year-old papal apostasy, and his plan, worked out in its finest form in his *Sacred Calendar of Prophecy*, dedicated to Barrington's successor at Durham, William Van Mildert, is a masterpiece of ingenuity in which the whole of human history is shown to be explained by the various images in the Book of Revelation of seals, trumpets, woes and vials.[43]

Faber dated the beginning of the two Little Horns, the Roman and the Mahometan, from the simultaneous recognition of the papal power by the Byzantine usurper Phocas and the rise of Islam in the early seventh century. This neat parallelism meant for Faber that the Little Horns would last the predicted 1,260 years until 1864. But for Faber neither Little Horn was the Antichrist of the last days, who was foreshadowed in the seventh head of the imperial beast of Revelation Chapter 13, the revived Roman Empire in the form of the Napoleonic Empire, which Faber thought must arise again after its fall in 1815. He had the melancholy satisfaction of living to see his prophecy fulfilled in 1852, in the Second Empire of Louis Napoleon, declaring in his all but final work that "I told you so".[44] "When he had once ventured upon an elucidation of prophecy according to his fixed canons", declared *The Gentleman's Magazine*, "he was never swayed towards a varied interpretation under the immediate presence of events apparently irreconcilable with his first deliberate impression".[45] Antichrist, therefore, was to be not a person but a French-inspired revolutionary infidel power, in union with papal Rome. Like Barrington, Faber saw Popery as the mother of infidelity, and argued that Antichrist would be "the ostensible ally of his ancient colleague the false prophet or the ecclesiastical two-horned wild-beast".[46] This alliance was given point in British politics by the radical politics of

---

Treat of the Grand Period of Seven Times, and Especially of its Second Moiety or the Latter Three Times and a Half, 3 vols. (London, 1828), vol. II, p. 209.

[43] *Ibid.*, vol. III, pp. 487–95 for a chronological summary.

[44] G.S. Faber, *The Revival of the French Emperorship anticipated from the necessity of prophecy* (London, 1853).

[45] *The Gentleman's Magazine*, p. 539.

[46] Faber (1828), vol. II, p. 259.

English and Irish Catholics, and it was this highly conservative conception, that Popery and French and English democratic infidelity were allies, prefiguring the return of Antichrist, which lay behind Faber's counteroffensive against the Roman Catholic revival in England.

Yet Faber was a learned man, who unlike strict Protestant Evangelicals, was not satisfied with refuting Roman Catholicism on the basis of the Bible alone. His erudition extended to the early centuries of the Christian era, and he was enough of a High Churchman to defend, like other High Churchmen, his convictions from the witness of the Fathers as well as from the Scriptures. He dismissed the usual Protestant understanding of private judgement as "every man his own pope". Indeed he declared that Scripture uninterpreted can decide nothing, on the rather sophisticated position that any text requires a reliable interpreter. Thus "we must, for the interpretation of this our Sole Rule, Scripture, resort, not to the wantonness of our own arbitrary dogmatism, but to the ascertained Concurrence of the Primitive Church from the beginning".[47] He sought the primitive doctrine, which was both scriptural and patristic. There was, therefore, an objective external standard for finding Biblical truth in the meaning held by the Early Church, at least during its first three centuries of life, on the basis of the Vincentian Canon that the Catholic Faith is that which is held by Catholics at all times everywhere. Thus in defending the doctrine of the Trinity against the Unitarians, Faber urged that Transubstantiation was only condemned because both Scripture and the Fathers had denied it.[48] *The Difficulties of Romanism* of 1826, his attack on a Roman Catholic anti-Protestant apologetic work, amusingly entitled a *Discussion amicale*, by J.F.M. Le Pappe de Trévern, the Bishop of Strasbourg,[49] is a massive appeal to the testimony of the early Fathers. It was this which brought him into dispute with both Trévern and Trévern's translator Husenbeth, a dispute which turned on the rival merits of their translations of

---

[47] Toon (1979), p. 132.

[48] G.S. Faber, *The Apostolicity of Trinitarianism: or, the Testimony of History, to the Positive Antiquity, and to the Apostolic Inculcation, of the Doctrine of the Holy Trinity*, 2 vols. (London, 1832), vol. I, pp. xxxviii–ix.

[49] G.S. Faber, *The Difficulties of Romanism in Respect to Evidence: or the Peculiarities of the Latin Church Evinced to be Untenable on the Principles of Legitimate Historical Testimony* (second edition, London, 1830). The history of Faber's controversy with Trévern and Husenbeth is given in the Preface.

patristic Greek and Latin texts, which all three of them argued through nearly a round dozen volumes.[50]

Faber's enthusiasm for patristic evidence gave him a unique position among Protestant divines as an opponent of the new Oxford High Churchmen of the 1830s. It was on patristic as well as Scriptural grounds that he opposed their teaching that infants are automatically regenerate at baptism, and his responses to Alexander Knox and John Henry Newman on the theme of justification by faith were arguably the most learned that they received.[51] Yet Faber's appeal to the Fathers was denounced as a betrayal of Scripture by those Protestants who saw no difference in point of principle between him and Dr. Pusey. Both made the Church the effective judge of the meaning of the Biblical text. Indeed though indulgent to Calvinists, Faber rejected on patristic grounds the Calvinist, Arminian and Lockean doctrines of election and predestination. He found one element of the Arminian theory in Clement of Alexandria, but claimed that the Calvinist doctrine had been invented by Augustine. The witness of the Scriptures and the Fathers together was not to the election of individuals to heaven or hell, but to membership of the communion of the saved, the Christian Church, from which they might still fall away. It was election to the Church that was preached by St Paul, and that was the doctrine of most of the Fathers after him.[52]

Faber was prepared to be called an "Evangelical High Churchman"; though this extended, he thought, no further than his belief in "the aboriginal appointment of Episcopal Ecclesiastical Polity", the apostolic origins of the episcopate, without unchurching or 'samarianising', as he put it, "every Reformed Church which from its local infelicity was organised unepiscopally": which was so unlucky as to

---

[50] Thus Husenbeth translated the Bishop's reply to Faber (1828). Faber replied to the Bishop with *The Testimony of Primitive Antiquity against the Peculiarities of the Latin Church: being a Supplement to the Difficulties of Romanism* (London, 1828). Husenbeth wrote *A Reply* to this *Supplement* (Norwich, 1829). Faber replied with *Some Account of Mr Husenbeth's Attempt to Assist the Bishop of Strasbourg* (London, 1829). Husenbeth replied with *The Difficulties of Faberism* (Norwich, 1829). Faber replied with the expanded second edition of *The Difficulties of Romanism* (London, 1830). Husenbeth replied with *Faberism Exposed and Refuted*... (Norwich, 1836). Faber replied with *An Account of Mr. Husenbeth's professed Refutation of the Argument of the Difficulties of Romanism* (London, 1836); and Husenbeth wrote *A Further Exposure*... *of Faberism* (Norwich, 1836).

[51] See Toon (1979), pp. 141–6.

[52] G.S. Faber, *The Primitive Doctrine of Election* (London, 1834).

have lost its bishops.[53] He was "far from denying to any individual in communion with the Church of Rome the appellation of CATHO-LIC: for I believe his particular limited Church to be a branch, though a very corrupt branch, of the Catholic Church of Christ".[54] But the Romish bishops in England and Ireland were schismatical emissaries, unlawfully intruded by an Italian prelate, the Pope. As the Church of Rome was a Church, Faber recognized the existence of saints like Fénelon and Pascal within her, and admitted that as the Anglican Richard Hooker had said, thousands within her had found mercy with the Lord. There was a prophetical Old Testament analogy: ancient Israel had lapsed into the idolatry of subordinately worshipping dead men and women, but still had seven thousand within her who had not bowed the knee to Baal; so in the similarly fallen and blighted Church of Rome, the Lord would have a living people, though theoretically labouring under the strong hereditary delusion of the Man of Sin. Yet Faber felt assured that most of the incorrigible Papists would be accessories to the union with Antichrist, and would only seek to exploit it as Catholics had done in joining forces with unbelieving radicals, both in Durham and in Ireland. It was for England to make reparation for granting political conces-sions to papists, who would strengthen unbelief and reinforce the last confederacy of Antichrist in its war upon the saints of God.

Faber predicted that this antichristian confederacy would rise and then fall to its doom in 1864, and so he did not expect to witness it himself. His last years were darkened by his nephew's apostasy to Rome, a desertion to the forces of the apocalyptic foe from the hosts of light. His view of the world, so sanely rooted in the Protestant tra-dition and in the soil of County Durham, might strike the modern reader as a wasteland of the human spirit, or like a kind of wild poetry, a confirmation of Chesterton's view that "though St. John the Evangelist saw many strange monsters in his vision, he saw no creature so wild as one of his own commentators".[55] But taken lit-erally, and made logical, the poetry looks like mania. As Chesterton puts it, "The poet only asks to get his head into the heavens. It is the logician who seeks to get the heavens into his head. And it is his head that splits".[56] Yet Faber lived the most prosaic of lives. He

---

[53] Toon (1979), p. 42.
[54] 'Preface' to Faber (1836, second edition), p. xxv.
[55] G.K. Chesterton, *Orthodoxy* (London, 1909), p. 27.
[56] Chesterton (1909), p. 27.

was writing history, not fantasy; it is our changed viewpoint which considers his millennialism manic. The foundation of his apocalyptic Protestant historicism was thoroughly undermined by S.R. Maitland, in his attack upon the year-day rule, before being abandoned altogether.[57] There are, of course, still millions of Protestants who see Rome as he did, but they are not numerous in these islands outside Ulster, and they no longer have the high patronage of the bishops of the Church of England. Faber's type of prophetic study, with its insistence upon the literal truth of the text of Scripture, gave rise to Biblical fundamentalism in this century;[58] and that still flourishes, though without the learning which created the mind of Faber. Indeed his framework of reference, a set of Scriptural prophecies applied literally to history, has been destroyed by the liberalism which he foresaw as the ultimate anti-Christian enemy. On other points, the strongest antagonists of the modern Church of Rome are no longer Paisleyite Protestants but liberals who dislike Rome for its continuing attachment to the wider Christian orthodoxy which it shares with George Stanley Faber. No Popery is now more common among those hostile to mere Christianity, and it is in Rome that Infidelity finds its ultimate enemy. Faberism is dead, rather than "exposed and refuted"; but Faber's anti-Romanism lives on, which simply shows that when people lose one set of reasons for hating a thing, they are sure to find another.

[57] S.R. Maitland, *An Enquiry into the grounds on which the Prophetic Period of Daniel and St. John has been supposed to consist of 1260 years* (London, 1826); *A Second Enquiry into the Grounds on which the Prophetic Period of Daniel and St. John, has been supposed to consist of 1260 Years* (London, 1829); *An Attempt to Elucidate the Prophecies concerning Antichrist* (London, 1830); *The twelve hundred and sixty days, in Reply to a Review in the Morning Watch* (London 1830); *The twelve hundred and sixty days: in reply to the strictures of W. Cunninghame* (London, 1834).

[58] E.R. Sandeen, *The Roots of Fundamentalism British and American Millenarianism 1800–1830* (Chicago, 1970); David N. Hempton, "Evangelicalism and Eschatology", *The Journal of Ecclesiastical History* 31 (April, 1980), pp. 179–94.

APPRECIATION OF THE
REVEREND DR. A. GELSTON

It is an honour to be asked to write a brief appreciation for this collection of essays. Tony Gelston and I for many years had rooms on the same landing, and happily exchanged undergraduate pupils for supervisions in areas in which each was a specialist. And as I joined the department full-time when Tony had been one of its distinguished members for several years, I had the advantage of being able to learn much from him about the importance of pastoral as well as academic care of students. Indeed, if one were to forget that Tony is an ordained priest in the Church of England, one would be on the way to misunderstanding his whole identity. If we need to think of a representative of the "learned clergy", Tony would be one of those whose name would quickly come to mind. It is entirely in character that one of his projects in the happy years since he resigned from full-time teaching should be a book on prayer. And his life as a preacher and pastor in the Church continues, as it always has, in the service of the Diocese of Durham and beyond. Nor should it be forgotten that much of his ministry has been in the Methodist Churches of the North East. Methodists as well as Anglicans owe much to his enrichment of their living and thinking, as well they know. And both Roman Catholic and Anglican ordinands who read Theology in Durham acknowledge how much they imbibed from him, least of all when he was conscious of what he represented to them in all his integrity of life and scholarship.

Tony's contribution to the life of Durham University extends beyond its Theology department. He is warmly remembered by those who taught in the School of Oriental Studies and who shared with him the teaching of Syriac and Aramaic. His colleagues in the Theology department also know him as a man intent on the highest possible academic standards both in his own work and in the demands he made on students. The same standards he applied to his administrative tasks, and he set for the rest of us benchmarks of meticulous attention to detail and the completion of chores on time which few of us want to emulate! He was an admirable Dean in the days when we had a Faculty of Divinity, and his clarity and efficiency were always infused with the kindliness and gentleness so characteristic of him as a person. His period as President of the Society for Old Testament Studies brought much distinction to the department of Theology.

Tony's students remain enthusiastic about the way in which he inspired them with love for the Hebrew language and for texts in Hebrew, as well as for his magisterial exposition of the Old Testament and its theology. And he taught an extraordinary range of material, with Liturgy kept alive as an academic discipline in Durham entirely as a result of his own willingness to extend himself by teaching it and supervising graduate students. Even those who did not take Liturgy as an option with him were made aware of its importance by him by the biennial visit to a synagogue in Gateshead, and by his delight in the organ music which he now has more time to enjoy!

His friends are deeply and warmly appreciative of lasting friendship with him – no easy matter to sustain as careers diverge and as time passes. Here Tony's utter reliability becomes much-prized fidelity and courtesy to those to whom he is committed. His generosity to others, and his clarity of mind are much valued by those who have the privilege of knowing him. We are delighted that now he is free to continue his pursuit of long-term and quite fundamental scholarly projects he will flourish as he should. And I think he would want us to acknowledge the importance to him of Anne's life shared with him, and of all that she has made possible in the years of their happy marriage together. To Tony then we offer our affection and admiration, and warmest good wishes.

Ann Loades
Durham

PUBLICATIONS OF ANTHONY GELSTON

(a) Books

Vetus Testamentum Syriace III, 4, Leiden, 1980.
(Dr Gelston was responsible for pages VII–XXV (top), XXXI and 1–100 (except for readings of lectionary manuscripts noted in the second apparatus), and he edited the biblical manuscripts of the Twelve Prophets and wrote the corresponding part of the Introduction).

The Peshitta of the Twelve Prophets, O.U.P., 1987.

The Eucharistic Prayer of Addai and Mari, O.U.P., 1992.

(b) Articles

"The Royal Priesthood", *Evangelical Quarterly* 31 (1959), pp. 152–163.
"The Wars of Israel", *Scottish Journal of Theology* 17 (1964), pp. 325–331.
"The Missionary Message of Second Isaiah", *Scottish Journal of Theology* 18 (1965), pp. 308–318.
"The Foundations of the Second Temple", *Vetus Testamentum* 16 (1966), pp. 232–235.
"A Note on יהוה מלך", *Vetus Testamentum* 16 (1966), pp. 507–12.
"A Sidelight on the Son of Man", *Scottish Journal of Theology* 22 (1969), pp. 189–196.
"Some Notes on Second Isaiah", *Vetus Testamentum* 21 (1971), pp. 517–527.
"A Note on II Samuel 7¹⁰", *Zeitschrift für die Alttestamentliche Wissenschaft* 84 (1972), pp. 92–94.
"Kingship in the Book of Hosea", *Oudtestamentische Studiën* 19 (1974), pp. 71–85.
"A Note on the Text of Psalm xxviii 7b", *Vetus Testamentum* 25 (1975), pp. 214–216.
"The Future of Mattins and Evensong", *The Churchman* 89 (1975), pp. 58–65.
"The Psalms at the Daily Services", *The Churchman* 89 (1975), pp. 267–275.

"The Lessons at the Daily Services", *The Churchman* 90 (1976), pp. 24–33.

"The Church of England Calendar and Lectionary", *Scripture Bulletin* 8, 1 (1977), pp. 6–9.

"Di euchês logou", *Journal of Theological Studies* NS 33 (1982), pp. 172–175.

"A Note on Psalm lxxiv 8", *Vetus Testamentum* 34 (1984), pp. 82–87.

"The Future of Advent", *Scripture Bulletin* 18, 1 (1987), pp. 15–19.

"A Note on the Text of the *Apostolic Tradition* of Hippolytus, *Journal of Theological Studies* NS 39 (1988), pp. 112–117.

"Some Readings in the Peshitta of the Dodekapropheton" in P.B. Dirksen and M.J. Mulder (eds.), *The Peshitta: its Early Text and History*, Monographs of the Peshitta Institute, Leiden, 4 (Leiden, 1988), pp. 81–98. (He also contributed two items to the Appendix to this volume:

9d2 – Dodekapropheton (III, 4) on pp. 267–269, and

11d2 – Dodekapropheton (III, 4) on pp. 290–292).

"Cranmer and the Daily Services" in M. Johnson (ed.), *Thomas Cranmer: Essays in Commemoration of the 500th Anniversary of his Birth* (Durham, 1990), pp. 51–81.

"Isaiah 52:13–53:12: An Eclectic Text and a Supplementary note on the Hebrew Manuscript Kennicott 96", *Journal of Semitic Studies* 35 (1990), pp. 187–211.

"Sacrifice in the Early East Syrian Eucharistic Tradition" in S.W. Sykes (ed.), *Sacrifice and Redemption: Durham Essays in Theology* (Cambridge, 1991), pp. 118–125.

"Universalism in Second Isaiah", *Journal of Theological Studies* NS 43 (1992), pp. 377–398.

"Knowledge, Humiliation or Suffering: A Lexical, Textual and Exegetical Problem in Isaiah 53" in H.A. McKay and D.J.A. Clines (eds.), *Of Prophets' Visions and the Wisdom of Sages* (Essays in honour of R. Norman Whybray on his Seventieth Birthday) *JSOT* Supplement Series 162 (Sheffield, 1993), pp. 126–141.

"Behold the speaker": a note on Isaiah xli 27", *Vetus Testamentum* 43 (1993), pp. 405–408.

"Theodore of Mopsuestia: the Anaphora and Mystagogical Catechesis 16", *Studia Patristica* 26 (1993), pp. 21–34.

"The Relationship of the Anaphoras of Theodore and Nestorius to that of Addai and Mari" in G. Karukaparampil (ed.), *Tûvaik:*

Studies in honour of Revd Jacob Vellian, Syrian Churches Series XVI (Kottayam, 1995), pp. 20–26.

"The End of Chronicles", *Scandinavian Journal of the Old Testament* 10, 1 (1996), pp. 53–60.

"The origin of the anaphora of Nestorius: Greek or Syriac?", *Bulletin of the John Rylands University Library of Manchester* 78 (3) (1996), pp. 73–86.

"The Lessons in the Daily Offices", *Tufton Review* 1 i (1997), pp. 1–13.

"The Intercessions in the East Syrian Anaphoras of Theodore and Nestorius", *Studia Patristica* 30 (1997), pp. 306–313.

"Was the Peshitta of Isaiah of Christian origin?" in *Writing and Reading the Scroll of Isaiah: Studies of an Interpretive Tradition*, edited by Craig C. Broyles and Craig A. Evans, Supplements to Vetus Testamentum LXX,2 (Leiden, 1997), 563–582.

"The Twelve Prophets: Peshitta and Targum" in *Targum and Peshitta*, edited by Paul V.M. Flesher, Targum Studies, 2 (Scholar Press, Atlanta, Georgia, 1998), 119–139.

"Notes on a Citation of Chrysostom by Severus", *Journal of Theological Studies*, NS 50 (1999), 162–163.

INDEX OF SOURCES

ARAMAIC TARGUMS OF THE PENTATEUCH

TARGUM OF THE PROPHETS

TARGUM OF THE WRITINGS

QUMRAN SCROLLS

APOCRYPHA

PSEUDEPIGRAPHA

JEWISH WRITINGS IN GREEK

RABBINIC SOURCES

CHURCH FATHERS

INDEX OF MODERN AUTHORS